Useful Equations for HP 35s or HP 33s Calculator for the Civil PE Exam

First Edition

Allan G. Abubakar, P.E.

ERRATA

The author diligently reviewed and tested the programs in this book. However, if you find an error, please notify the author via email at usefulequations@gmail.com or visit the website at www.usefulequations.com. The author will appreciate every error found for the improvement of this book.

Notice

The equations, keystrokes, figures, suggested procedures, notes, and sample problems are for general information and educational purposes only. While the author made his every effort to insure the accuracy, these programs should not be used or relied upon for any specific purpose or project without competent engineering judgment, examination, and verification.

Neither the Hewlett-Packard Company nor the author guarantee the completeness and accuracy of information presented herein and are not responsible for any damages including but not limited to direct and indirect damages as a result of use of this material. Anyone who uses this material does so at his/her own risk and accepts any and all liability resulting from such use.

Printed in the United States of America

ISBN-13: 978-1483951508

ISBN-10: 1483951502

First Printing: May 11, 2013

Updated: January 4, 2014

TABLE OF CONTENTS

About The Author

Allan G. Abubakar, PE is a registered professional engineer in the state of Florida. He works as a project engineer at Universal Engineering Sciences, Inc. (UES), a consulting engineering firm in Florida and Atlanta, Georgia specializing in geotechnical engineering, hydrologic/geophysical, environmental sciences, construction materials testing, and threshold inspection. He has over nine years of experience in geotechnical engineering and is a member of the American Society of Civil Engineers (ASCE). Allan received his bachelor's degree in civil engineering from Notre Dame University in Cotabato City, Philippines in 1992.

He immigrated with his wife to the United States in 1995. He took the Fundamentals of Engineering (FE) exam also known as Engineer-In-Training (EIT) exam in April of 2002 and passed. Allan landed an engineering job at UES in July of 2003 as a staff engineer. He classifies soil samples, writes geotechnical reports, provides recommendations for shallow and deep foundations, ground improvements, pavement design, and retaining wall parameters, performs settlement and L-pile analyses, prepares boring logs using gINT, and assists civil engineers for their projects. He started studying for the Principles and Practice of Engineering (PE) examination in civil engineering with geotechnical "depth" in 2008. He passed the PE exam in April of 2009 and promoted to project engineer. Since then, he started signing and sealing proctors and density reports.

On weekends and evenings, Allan typed the text, created the programs of each equation, and tested each equation using reference books. During his spare time, he likes to sing karaoke, work out, dee-jay with his iPad, and sometimes solves the Rubik's Cube puzzle. He also cheers for his favorite NBA team the Miami Heat. Go Heat!!!

Preface

In order to pass the Principles and Practice (PE) exam in civil engineering, one must have speed and accuracy. The primary purpose of this book is to aid students, engineers, and civil PE examinees who would like to store useful equations in their HP 35s or HP 33s scientific calculator(s). The equations in this book are essential to solve problems (where applicable) that you may encounter in the civil PE exam. People who use this book will learn how to solve common civil engineering problems using HP 35s or HP 33s calculator for rapid calculation and accurate result.

For instance, in geotechnical, you might want to find the void ratio of a soil with given moist (wet) density, specific gravity, and moisture content. With the right equations, you can solve this in just 20 seconds. The first step is to use Equation No. 9 to find the dry density followed by Equation No. 8 using the SOLVE function.

To find the total active force per linear length of a wall with water table between top and bottom of wall, use Equation No. 52. If equivalent fluid pressures are given, use Equation No. 46.

For problems involving open channels such as the case of a circular pipe flowing partially full, use Equation No. 118 to calculate the flow rate by entering the constant, Manning roughness coefficient, depth of water, diameter of pipe, and slope of energy line. If you need to find the slope of energy line for a pipe flowing full with given flow rate, diameter of pipe, and Manning roughness coefficient, use Equation No. 113 using the SOLVE function.

There is limitation, however, that the equations in this book can not solve problems having two unknowns. For example, a dry soil sample has a unit weight of 100 pcf; when completely saturated, its unit weight is 115 pcf. Determine its porosity. The two unknowns in this problem are specific gravity and void ratio. This type of problem can only be addressed using hand calculations. The solution for this problem is

$$\gamma_d = \frac{G\gamma_w}{1+e}$$

$$100\frac{lb}{ft^3} = \frac{G}{1+e}\left(62.4\frac{lb}{ft^3}\right)$$

$$100\frac{lb}{ft^3} = \frac{62.4\frac{lb}{ft^3}G}{1+e}$$

$$100\frac{lb}{ft^3}(1+e) = 62.4\frac{lb}{ft^3}G$$

$$100+100e = 62.4G$$

$$G = 1.602+1.602e \quad \text{(eq. 1)}$$

$$\gamma_{sat} = \frac{(G+e)\gamma_w}{1+e}$$

$$115\frac{lb}{ft^3} = \frac{62.4\frac{lb}{ft^3}G+62.4\frac{lb}{ft^3}e}{1+e}$$

$$115\frac{lb}{ft^3}(1+e) = 62.4\frac{lb}{ft^3}G+62.4\frac{lb}{ft^3}e$$

$$115+115e = 62.4G+62.4e$$

$$52.6e = 62.4G-115$$

$$G = 1.843+0.843e \quad \text{(eq. 2)}$$

Equate 1 and 2

$$1.602+1.602e = 1.843+0.843e$$

$$0.759e = 0.241$$

$$e = 0.318$$

Calculate the porosity

$$n = \frac{e}{1+e}$$

$$n = \frac{0.318}{1+0.318}$$

$$n = 0.241$$

To scroll equations in HP 35s, use the [⌃] or [⌄] key by holding it down or pressing it one at a time. If your current equation is somewhere in the middle of the equation list, and you want to access the top line of the equation list, press [↱] followed by [⌃]. To access the last line of the equation list, press [↱] followed by [⌄]. Doing this saves time when the equation you want to use is near the top line or near the last line of the equation list.

To scroll equations in HP 33s, use the up or down large silver keys located just on top of [y^x] key by holding it down or pressing it one at a time. If you want to access the top line of the equation list, press [↰] followed by [⤒] and if you want to access the last line of the equation list, press [↰] followed by [⤓]. I used 2 HP 33s calculators and placed the Interpolation Equation on each calculator at the top line of the equation list for quick access.

Keystrokes are included with checksum so that you can store the equations correctly. Typical sample problems are also included with step-by-step, straightforward, and comprehensible solution to manifest the engineering principles involved and which equation(s) to use to solve the problems.

It is hoped that this book will prove beneficial as you prepare for the PE exam in civil engineering.

Good Luck!

Acknowledgments

I would like to express my profound gratitude to my wife, Marisol, who provided me with love and support and to my lovely daughters, Lauren and Lourdes, for being my source of inspiration.

Also, I would like to thank the staff of CreateSpace and Amazon.com for their great effort for the production and selling of this book.

Special dedications to my mother Erlinda, my dad Akmad, Sr. (deceased), to my sisters Eileen and Yasmin, to my brothers Akmad, Jr., Jamal, and Benjamin, furthermore, to my in-laws, Chaves Family, and relatives.

I am grateful to my boss, Peter G. Read, P.E., who is our regional manager in South Florida area, for giving me the opportunity to work at UES. Last but not least, thanks to Scott Rowe, P.E., our geotechnical manager, for his practical advice.

Introduction

Thank you for purchasing this book. If you are taking the PE Exam in civil engineering and want to store useful equations presented in this book to your HP 35s or HP 33s scientific calculator(s), then this book is for you.

The PE exam in civil engineering is an 8-hour open-book exam; 4 hours in the morning known as the "breadth" and 4 hours in the afternoon known as "depth".

The 4-hour exam in the morning contains 40 multiple-choice problems from all five fields of civil engineering (geotechnical, water resources and environmental, transportation, structural, and construction). Each field contains 8 problems ranging from easy to difficult. The 4-hour exam in the afternoon includes 40 multiple-choice problems that concentrate more on a single field of civil engineering. The examinee will choose from five "depth" modules: geotechnical, water resources and environmental, transportation, structural, and construction.

As of November 16, 2012 the HP 35s and HP 33s were two of the approved calculators in the civil PE exam. Please check the list of the approved calculators at the National Council of Examiners for Engineering and Surveying (NCEES) website at www.ncees.org as it is updated every year.

The equations can be stored in either HP 35s or HP 33s scientific calculators using the Equation mode. If you are not familiar with storing equations, you might want to consult the calculator's manual. The equations are organized by subject. Part I is geotechnical, Part II is water resources and environmental, Part III is transportation, and Part IV is structural. No equations are prepared for construction because it only requires basic knowledge of multiplication, division, addition, and subtraction.

There are 92 equations (Equation Nos. 1 through 92) for geotechnical that you might find useful for "breadth" and "depth" exams. Water resources and environmental has 63 equations (Equation Nos. 93 through 155) that are effective for "breadth" exam, transportation has 29 equations that are beneficial for "breadth" exam (Equation Nos. 156 through 184, with two "depth" equations, Equation Nos. 183 and 184), and structural has 16 equations (Equation Nos. 185 through 200) that are useful for the "breadth" exam. You may store all 200 equations in one calculator but it will take longer to scroll to find the equation you want to use. I stored all the geotechnical equations in one calculator because I took the geotechnical "depth" and the other subjects in another calculator.

Each equation consists of two lines. The first line is the equation number with an abbreviated description. The second line is the equation. A sample of the equation number and an abbreviated description is shown below (Equation No. 30). You can use the provided description or you can create your own. If the provided description is used, it will appear in the display screen as

for HP 35s and

for HP 33s

The description that is shown on the display screen is sufficient to recognize that this equation is for shallow foundation with water table at the ground surface (Terzaghi).

30SHALFWTSURF
(0.5(S−W)×B×N×I)+C×O×J+(S−W)×E(Q−1)=P÷B^2×F×Z

Where:

S = density of saturated soil γ_{sat} (lb/ft^3, kN/m^3)
W = unit weight of water γ_w (62.4 lb/ft^3, 9.81 kN/m^3)
B = width of square, continuous, or diameter of circular footing B (ft, m)
N = capacity factor N_γ
I = shape factor of N_γ (e.g., 0.85). The default value is 1.
C = cohesion c (lb/ft^2, kN/m^2)
O = capacity factor N_c
J = shape factor of N_c (e.g., 1.25). The default value is 1.
E = depth of footing D_f (ft, m)
Q = capacity factor N_q
P = total allowable load P (lb, kN)
F = factor of safety FS
Z = 1 for square or continuous footing, 1.2732 for circular footing Z

Equation No. 30 can be found on page 45 of Part I (geotechnical) and can used to solve the net or gross (ultimate) bearing capacity of square, continuous, and circular footings with water table at the ground surface (Terzaghi).

Some equation number has 2 or more equations as shown below (P, Y, and O).

52ACTWTSURCOHE
P=Q×X×TAN(45−A÷2)^2+0.5×D×X^2×TAN(45−A÷2)^2−2×C×X(TAN(45−A÷2)^2)^0.5
+((Q+D×X)×TAN(45−B÷2)^2−2×E(TAN(45−B÷2)^2)^0.5)×Z+0.5(S−W)×Z^2
×TAN(45−B÷2)^2+0.5×W×Z^2
Y=((Q×X×TAN(45−A÷2)^2(Z+X÷2)+(0.5×D×X^2×TAN(45−A÷2)^2−2×C×X(TAN(45−A÷2)^2)^
0.5)×(Z+X÷3)+((Q+D×X)×TAN(45−B÷2)^2−2×E(TAN(45−B÷2)^2)^0.5)×Z^2÷2+0.5(S−W)
×TAN(45−B÷2)^2×Z^3÷3+0.5×W×Z^3÷3)÷P
O=P×Y

Where:

P = total lateral force per unit length of wall P (lb/ft, kN/m)
Q = surcharge load Q (lb/ft^2, kN/m^2)
X = distance from top of backfill to water table X (ft, m)
A = angle of internal friction of moist soil ϕ_1
D = density of moist soil γ_m (lb/ft^3, kN/m^3)
C = cohesion of moist soil c_1 (lb/ft^2, kN/m^2)
B = angle of internal friction of saturated soil ϕ_2
E = cohesion of saturated soil c_2 (lb/ft^2, kN/m^2)
Z = distance from water table to bottom of backfill Z (ft, m)
S = density of saturated soil γ_{sat} (lb/ft^3, kN/m^3)
W = unit weight of water γ_w (62.4 lb/ft^3, 9.81 kN/m^3)
Y = location of resultant lateral force from the bottom of wall $\bar{y}$ (ft, m)
O = moment at the bottom of wall due to active lateral force O (ft-lb, kN-m)

Equation No. 52 can be found on page 94 of Part I (geotechnical) and can be used to calculate the total lateral force per unit length of wall (P), location of resultant lateral force from the bottom of wall (Y), and overturning moment (O) in an active condition with water table, surcharge load, and cohesion.

Each equation has keystrokes for HP 35s and HP 33s, checksum, and length of equation (CK and LN) in order to confirm that the equation is correctly entered. If you are using HP 35s, press [↰] then hold down the SHOW key to show its checksum and length of equation. If you are using HP 33s, press [↱] then hold down the SHOW key to show its checksum and length of equation. No keystrokes are provided for equation number and abbreviated description. However, the keystrokes for Equation No. 52's abbreviated description is

[5] [2] [RCL] [A] [RCL] [C] [RCL] [T] [RCL] [W] [RCL] [T] [RCL] [S] [RCL] [U] [RCL] [R] [RCL] [C] [RCL] [O] [RCL] [H] [RCL] [E] [ENTER]

Some keystrokes for HP 35s show different checksum and less length of equation than HP 33s because HP 35s is capable of multiplying a number or a character followed by a parenthesis without using × symbol. For example, HP 35s can do a multiplication of...0.425(S−W) while HP 33s can not. It needs a × symbol,...0.425×(S−W).

A couple of features you can do in HP 35s that you can't do in HP 33s are UNDO and EDIT.

UNDO: If you accidentally deleted an equation, you can recover the deleted equation by pressing [↰] then the UNDO key.

EDIT: You can edit any part of the equation without deleting any entered keys.

Programming Tips:

Enter all equations in Equation mode. To put HP 35s in Equation mode, press [EQN]. To put HP 33s in Equation mode, press [↱] [EQN]. Enter the equations using the provided keystrokes. Keystrokes are from left to right, top to bottom, and always end with ENTER.

For faster programming, use your left thumb only for RCL, A, B, E, H, I, SIN, COS, and ENTER keys for HP 35s, RCL, A, B, F, G, J, K, N, O, and SIN keys for HP 33s. Use your right thumb on other keys. It would take approximately 3 to 4 days to program all 200 equations, depending on how fast you program them. If you want to purchase a pre-programmed calculator, it is available at www.usefulequations.com.

Reverse Polish Notation (RPN):

Your calculator must be in RPN mode at all times. With RPN mode you can perform calculation when prompted in equation. Sometimes you need to calculate the saturated density of soil, buoyant unit weight of soil, dry density of soil, moisture content of soil, conversion of in/min to ft/day, gal/min to ft^3/sec, or lb/in^2 to lb/ft^2 before pressing R/S. Below are sample calculations using RPN.

Saturated density of soil given void ratio and specific gravity. $e = 1.2$, $G = 2.7$

Keys: 3.9 ENTER 62.4 × 2.2 ÷

$$\gamma_{sat} = \frac{(G+e)\gamma_w}{1+e}$$

$$\gamma_{sat} = \frac{(2.7+1.2)62.4\frac{lb}{ft^3}}{1+1.2}$$

$$\gamma_{sat} = 110.6182 \frac{lb}{ft^3}$$

Converting 1,200 gal/min to ft³/sec.

Keys: 1200 ENTER 7.48 ÷ 60 ÷

$$1{,}200 \frac{gal}{\text{min}} \times \frac{ft^3}{7.48\,gal} \times \frac{\text{min}}{60\,\text{sec}} = 2.6738 \frac{ft^3}{\text{sec}}$$

Converting 65 mi/hr to ft/sec.

Keys: 65 ENTER 3600 ÷ 5280 ×

$$65 \frac{mi}{hr} \times \frac{hr}{3600\,\text{sec}} \times \frac{5280\,ft}{mi} = 95.3333 \frac{ft}{\text{sec}}$$

References

Michael R. Lindeburg, PE "Civil Engineering Reference Manual for the PE Exam" 11th Edition

Braja M. Das, "Principles of Foundation Engineering" 5th Edition

Bruce A. Wolle, MSE, PE "Six-Minute Solutions for Civil PE Exam Geotechnical Problems"

Helpful Tips

- Tab your binders, books, this book, and your Civil Engineering Reference Manual (CERM). Tabs are color coded (e.g., blue for water resources, green for environmental, pink for geotechnical, etc...). (Refer to Photo 1). Other references that are useful are NCEES and Six-Minutes Solutions books. Tabbing your books and binders is like using a freeway instead of side streets or sending an email instead of mailing letters.
- Organize your notes, sample problems with solutions, formulas, and equations by subject in a 3-ring binder.
- Remove all loose papers from your books and binders. Loose papers are not allowed in the exam room.
- If you are taking the geotechnical "depth", I recommend Six-Minute Solutions by Bruce Wole, P.E., NCEES, CERM, Principles of Foundation Engineering by Braja Das, NAVFAC 7.01, 7.02, and 7.03. The NAVFAC 7.01 through 7.03 can be downloaded online for free. The NAVFAC DM 7.03 is a good reference for earthquake engineering and seismic analysis.
- Bring a couple of bookends to support your books and binders. House your books and binders in an upright position for easy access. Stacking them flat can be difficult to retrieve especially if the book or binder you want is at the bottom. (Refer to Photo 2).
- Bring snacks, sandwich, lunch, water, and leave your cell phone in your car.
- Bring sweater or cardigan because it might be cold in the exam room.
- Book a hotel near the exam site to avoid traffic.
- Bring your admission slip, driver's license, calculators with extra batteries, extra cash, etc...
- Bring 2 digital watches.
- You have 4 hours to answer 40 questions in each session (morning and afternoon) with an average time of 6 minutes per question. Some questions can be answered in less than 6 minutes or more than 6 minutes depending on the difficulty of the question.

At the beginning of each session, start the clock on your first digital watch. Answer all the easy questions first and mark them. Once you answered all the easy questions, make a quick count on how many questions you answered then multiply that by 6. Let's say you answered 25 easy questions at the elapsed time of 90 minutes, multiply that by 6 which is equal to 150 minutes, which means you have 60 minutes extra time for the remaining 15 difficult questions or an average time of 10 minutes per question. That's plenty of time for reading the question, analysis, calculations, and searching for a particular page in your book or binder.

As you start answering the remaining difficult questions, use your second digital watch. Start the clock and you must answer each difficult question in 10 minutes or less. If 10 minutes have passed and you did not come up with an answer, take a guess and move on to the next question. You can not be penalized for guessing. Reset the clock then start the clock again as you begin the next question. Repeat this exercise until all questions are answered. Check your first digital watch for the remaining time. If you still have time, review your work.

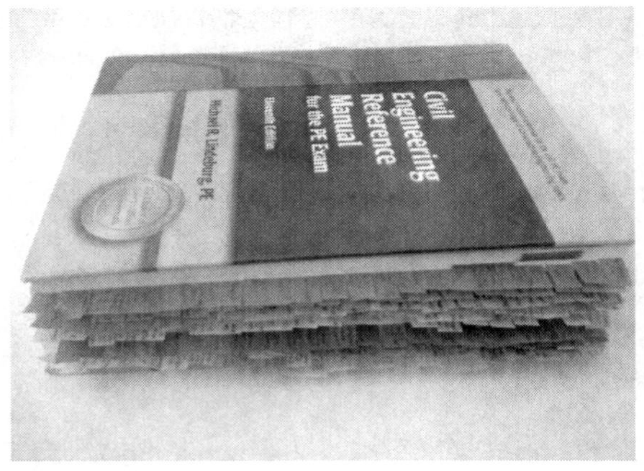

Photo 1 (CERM book with tabs)

Photo 2 (books and binders supported by bookends)

Interpolation Equation

The equation is entered as

INTERPOLATION
I=A+(E−D)÷((E−D)+(F−E))×(B−A)

Keystrokes

HP 35s Checksum; Length of Equation: **CK=C4ED; LN=29**

[RCL] [I] [↰] [=] [RCL] [A] [+] [()] [RCL] [E] [−] [RCL] [D] [>] [÷] [()] [()] [RCL] [E] [−] [RCL] [D] [>] [+] [()] [RCL] [F] [−] [RCL] [E] [>] [>] [×] [()] [RCL] [B] [−] [RCL] [A] [ENTER]

HP 33s Checksum; Length of Equation: **CK=C4ED; LN=29**

[RCL] [I] [↱] [=] [RCL] [A] [+] [↱] [(] [RCL] [E] [−] [RCL] [D] [↱] [)] [÷] [↱] [(] [↱] [(] [RCL] [E] [−] [RCL] [D] [↱] [)] [+] [↱] [(] [RCL] [F] [−] [RCL] [E] [↱] [)] [↱] [)] [×] [↱] [(] [RCL] [B] [−] [RCL] [A] [↱] [)] [ENTER]

Example:

Find the value of 4.

D = 1.0 ⟶ **A** = 0.5
E = 4.0 ⟶ **I** = ?
F = 10.0 ⟶ **B** = 1.0

F	**E**	**D**
10.0	4.0	1.0
1.0	?	0.5
B	**I**	**A**

Solution

Use the Interpolation Equation. Press ENTER.

Display	Keys	Description
A?	.5 R/S	Value of A
E?	4 R/S	Value of E
D?	1 R/S	Value of D
F?	10 R/S	Value of F
B?	1 R/S	Value of B
I = 0.6667	--	Interpolation value

Note: You can also use Linear Regression on page 11-7 of HP 33s manual or page 12-7 of HP 35s manual.

PART I: GEOTECHNICAL

CHAPTER 1: ENGINEERING PROPERTIES OF SOIL

1.1 Moisture Content of Soil

1.1.1 Moisture Content Given Weight or Mass of Wet and Dry Soil

$$\omega = \frac{Soil_{wet} - Soil_{dry}}{Soil_{dry}} \times 100\% \qquad \text{Equation No. 1}$$

The equation is entered as

1MOISTCONTENT
C=(T−U)÷U×100

Where:

C = moisture content ω (%)
T = weight or mass of wet soil $Soil_{wet}$ (lb, kN, N, g)
U = weight or mass of oven dry soil $Soil_{dry}$ (lb, kN, N, g)

Keystrokes

HP 35s Checksum; Length of Equation: **CK=F308; LN=13**

[RCL] [C] [↰] [=] [()] [RCL] [T] [−] [RCL] [U] [>] [÷] [RCL] [U] [×] [1] [0] [0] [ENTER]

HP 33s Checksum; Length of Equation: **CK=F308; LN=13**

[RCL] [C] [↱] [=] [↱] [(] [RCL] [T] [−] [RCL] [U] [↱] [)] [÷] [RCL] [U] [×] [1] [0] [0] [ENTER]

≈≈≈≈≈≈≈≈≈≈

1.2 Moist Density of Soil

1.2.1 Moist Density of Soil Given Dry Density and Moisture Content

$$\gamma_m = \gamma_d \left(1 + \frac{\omega}{100}\right) \qquad \text{Equation No. 2}$$

The equation is entered as

2MOISDENDDMC
E=D(1+C÷100)

Where:

E = moist density of soil γ_m (lb/ft^3, kN/m^3)
D = dry density of soil γ_d (lb/ft^3, kN/m^3)
C = moisture content ω (%)

Keystrokes

HP 35s Checksum; Length of Equation: **CK=718B; LN=12**

[RCL] [E] [↰] [=] [RCL] [D] [()] [1] [+] [RCL] [C] [÷] [1] [0] [0] [ENTER]

HP 33s Checksum; Length of Equation: **CK=D049; LN=13**

[RCL] [E] [↱] [=] [RCL] [D] [×] [↱] [(] [1] [+] [RCL] [C] [÷] [1] [0] [0] [↱] [)] [ENTER]

≈≈≈≈≈≈≈≈≈≈

1.2.2 Moist Density of Soil Given Specific Gravity, Degree of Saturation, and Void Ratio

$$\gamma_m = \frac{(G + Se)\gamma_w}{1 + e} \qquad \text{Equation No. 3}$$

The equation is entered as

3MOISDENGZV
E=(G+Z÷100×V)×W÷(1+V)

Where:

E = moist density of soil γ_m (lb/ft^3, kN/m^3)
G = specific gravity G
Z = degree of saturation S (%)
V = void ratio e (decimal)
W = unit weight of water γ_w (62.4 lb/ft^3, 9.81 kN/m^3)

Keystrokes

HP 35s Checksum; Length of Equation: **CK=8378; LN=21**

[RCL] [E] [↰] [=] [()] [RCL] [G] [+] [RCL] [Z] [÷] [1] [0] [0] [×] [RCL] [V] [>] [×] [RCL] [W] [÷] [()] [1] [+] [RCL] [V] [ENTER]

HP 33s Checksum; Length of Equation: **CK=8378; LN=21**

[RCL] [E] [↱] [=] [↱] [(] [RCL] [G] [+] [RCL] [Z] [÷] [1] [0] [0] [×] [RCL] [V] [↱] [)] [×] [RCL] [W] [÷] [↱] [(] [1] [+] [RCL] [V] [↱] [)] [ENTER]

≈≈≈≈≈≈≈≈≈≈

1.2.3 Moist Density of Soil Given Moisture Content, Specific Gravity, and Void Ratio

$$\gamma_m = \frac{\left(1+\frac{\omega}{100}\right)G\gamma_w}{1+e} \qquad \text{Equation No. 4}$$

The equation is entered as

4MOISDENMCGV
E=(1+C÷100)×G×W÷(1+V)

Where:

E = moist density of soil γ_m (lb/ft^3, kN/m^3)
C = moisture content ω (%)
G = specific gravity G
W = unit weight of water γ_w (62.4 lb/ft^3, 9.81 kN/m^3)
V = void ratio e (decimal)

Keystrokes

HP 35s Checksum; Length of Equation: **CK=38F3; LN=21**

[RCL] [E] [↰] [=] [()] [1] [+] [RCL] [C] [÷] [1] [0] [0] [>] [×] [RCL] [G] [×] [RCL] [W] [÷] [()] [1] [+] [RCL] [V] [ENTER]

HP 33s Checksum; Length of Equation: **CK=38F3; LN=21**

[RCL] [E] [↱] [=] [↱] [(] [1] [+] [RCL] [C] [÷] [1] [0] [0] [↱] [)] [×] [RCL] [G] [×] [RCL] [W] [÷] [↱] [(] [1] [+] [RCL] [V] [↱] [)] [ENTER]

≈≈≈≈≈≈≈≈≈≈

1.3 Saturated Density of Soil

1.3.1 Saturated Density of Soil Given Moisture Content and Specific Gravity

$$\gamma_{sat} = \frac{\left(1+\frac{\omega}{100}\right)G\gamma_w}{1+\frac{\omega}{100}G} \qquad \text{Equation No. 5}$$

The equation is entered as

5SATDENMCG
S=(1+C÷100)×G×W÷(1+C÷100×G)

Where:

S = saturated density of soil γ_{sat} (lb/ft^3, kN/m^3)
C = moisture content ω (%)
G = specific gravity G
W = unit weight of water γ_w (62.4 lb/ft^3, 9.81 kN/m^3)

Keystrokes

HP 35s Checksum; Length of Equation: **CK=D7F6; LN=27**

[RCL] [S] [↰] [=] [()] [1] [+] [RCL] [C] [÷] [1] [0] [0] [>] [×] [RCL] [G] [×] [RCL] [W] [÷] [()] [1] [+] [RCL] [C] [÷] [1] [0] [0] [×] [RCL] [G] [ENTER]

HP 33s Checksum; Length of Equation: **CK=D7F6; LN=27**

[RCL] [S] [↱] [=] [↱] [(] [1] [+] [RCL] [C] [÷] [1] [0] [0] [↱] [)] [×] [RCL] [G] [×] [RCL] [W] [÷] [↱] [(] [1] [+] [RCL] [C] [÷] [1] [0] [0] [×] [RCL] [G] [↱] [)] [ENTER]

≈≈≈≈≈≈≈≈≈≈

1.3.2 Saturated Density of Soil Given Specific Gravity and Void Ratio

$$\gamma_{sat} = \frac{(G+e)\gamma_w}{1+e} \qquad \text{Equation No. 6}$$

The equation is entered as

6SATDENGV
S=(G+V)×W÷(1+V)

Where:

S = saturated density of soil γ_{sat} (lb/ft^3, kN/m^3)
G = specific gravity G
V = void ratio e (decimal)
W = unit weight of water γ_w (62.4 lb/ft^3, 9.81 kN/m^3)

Keystrokes

HP 35s Checksum; Length of Equation: **CK=E5C0; LN=15**

[RCL] [S] [↰] [=] [()] [RCL] [G] [+] [RCL] [V] [>] [×] [RCL] [W] [÷] [()] [1] [+] [RCL] [V] [ENTER]

HP 33s Checksum; Length of Equation: **CK=E5C0; LN=15**

[RCL] [S] [↱] [=] [↱] [(] [RCL] [G] [+] [RCL] [V] [↱] [)] [×] [RCL] [W] [÷] [↱] [(] [1] [+] [RCL] [V] [↱] [)] [ENTER]

≈≈≈≈≈≈≈≈≈≈

1.4 Degree of Saturation

1.4.1 Degree of Saturation Given Void Ratio, Moisture Content, and Specific Gravity

$S = \dfrac{\omega G}{e}$ Equation No. 7

The equation is entered as

7DEGOFSATVCG
Z=C×G÷V

Where:

Z = degree of saturation S (%)
C = moisture content ω (%)
G = specific gravity G
V = void ratio e (decimal)

Keystrokes

HP 35s Checksum; Length of Equation: **CK=3D5B; LN=7**

[RCL] [Z] [↰] [=] [RCL] [C] [×] [RCL] [G] [÷] [RCL] [V] [ENTER]

HP 33s Checksum; Length of Equation: **CK=3D5B; LN=7**

[RCL] [Z] [↱] [=] [RCL] [C] [×] [RCL] [G] [÷] [RCL] [V] [ENTER]

Note: If the degree of saturation is expressed in decimal, divide the degree of saturation by 100.

1.5 Dry Density of Soil

1.5.1 Dry Density of Soil Given Specific Gravity and Void Ratio

$$\gamma_d = \frac{G\gamma_w}{1+e}$$ Equation No. 8

The equation is entered as

8DRYDENGV
D=G×W÷(1+V)

Where:

D = dry density of soil γ_d (lb/ft³, kN/m³)
G = specific gravity G
W = unit weight of water γ_w (62.4 lb/ft³, 9.81 kN/m³)
V = void ratio e (decimal)

Keystrokes

HP 35s Checksum; Length of Equation: **CK=F995; LN=11**

[RCL] [D] [↰] [=] [RCL] [G] [×] [RCL] [W] [÷] [()] [1] [+] [RCL] [V] [ENTER]

HP 33s Checksum; Length of Equation: **CK=F995; LN=11**

[RCL] [D] [↱] [=] [RCL] [G] [×] [RCL] [W] [÷] [↱] [(] [1] [+] [RCL] [V] [↱] [)] [ENTER]

≈≈≈≈≈≈≈≈≈≈

1.5.2 Dry Density of Soil Given Moist Density and Moisture Content

$$\gamma_d = \frac{\gamma_m}{1+\frac{\omega}{100}}$$ Equation No. 9

The equation is entered as

9DRYDENMOISDMC
D=E÷(1+C÷100)

Where:

D = dry density of soil γ_d (lb/ft³, kN/m³)
E = moist density of soil γ_m (lb/ft³, kN/m³)
C = moisture content ω (%)

Keystrokes

HP 35s Checksum; Length of Equation: **CK=FCAC; LN=13**

[RCL] [D] [↰] [=] [RCL] [E] [÷] [()] [1] [+] [RCL] [C] [÷] [1] [0] [0] [ENTER]

HP 33s Checksum; Length of Equation: **CK=FCAC; LN=13**

[RCL] [D] [↱] [=] [RCL] [E] [÷] [↱] [(] [1] [+] [RCL] [C] [÷] [1] [0] [0] [↱] [)] [ENTER]

≈≈≈≈≈≈≈≈≈≈

1.6 Porosity

1.6.1 Porosity Given Void Ratio

$\eta = \dfrac{e}{1+e}$ Equation No. 10

The equation is entered as

10POROSITYVOID
P=V÷(1+V)

Where:

P = porosity η (decimal)
V = void ratio e (decimal)

Keystrokes

HP 35s Checksum; Length of Equation: **CK=F10C; LN=9**

[RCL] [P] [↰] [=] [RCL] [V] [÷] [()] [1] [+] [RCL] [V] [ENTER]

HP 33s Checksum; Length of Equation: **CK=F10C; LN=9**

[RCL] [P] [↱] [=] [RCL] [V] [÷] [↱] [(] [1] [+] [RCL] [V] [↱] [)] [ENTER]

≈≈≈≈≈≈≈≈≈≈

1.7 Relative Density

1.7.1 Relative Density Given Void Ratio, Maximum and Minimum Void Ratios of Soil

$$D_r = \frac{e_{max} - e}{e_{max} - e_{min}} \times 100\% \qquad \text{Equation No. 11}$$

The equation is entered as

11RELDENVOID
R=(M−V)÷(M−N)×100

Where:

R = relative density of soil D_r (%)
M = maximum void ratio e_{max} (decimal)
V = void ratio e (decimal)
N = minimum void ratio e_{min} (decimal)

Keystrokes

HP 35s Checksum; Length of Equation: **CK=2AC0; LN=17**

[RCL] [R] [↰] [=] [()] [RCL] [M] [−] [RCL] [V] [>] [÷] [()] [RCL] [M] [−] [RCL] [N] [>] [×] [1] [0] [0] [ENTER]

HP 33s Checksum; Length of Equation: **CK=2AC0; LN=17**

[RCL] [R] [↱] [=] [↱] [(] [RCL] [M] [−] [RCL] [V] [↱] [)] [÷] [↱] [(] [RCL] [M] [−] [RCL] [N] [↱] [)] [×] [1] [0] [0] [ENTER]

≈≈≈≈≈≈≈≈≈≈

1.7.2 Relative Density Given Dry Density, Maximum and Minimum Dry Densities of Soil

$$D_r = \frac{\dfrac{1}{\gamma_{d(\min)}} - \dfrac{1}{\gamma_d}}{\dfrac{1}{\gamma_{d(\min)}} - \dfrac{1}{\gamma_{d(\max)}}} \times 100\% \qquad \text{Equation No. 12}$$

The equation is entered as

12RELDENDRYDEN
R=((1÷Q)−(1÷D))÷((1÷Q)−(1÷Y))×100

Where:

R = relative density of soil D_r (%)
Q = minimum dry density of soil $\gamma_{d(\min)}$ (lb/ft³, kN/m³)
D = dry density of soil γ_d (lb/ft³, kN/m³)
Y = maximum dry density of soil $\gamma_{d(\max)}$ (lb/ft³, kN/m³)

Keystrokes

HP 35s Checksum; Length of Equation: **CK=45B4; LN=33**

[RCL] [R] [↰] [=] [()] [()] [1] [÷] [RCL] [Q] [>] [−] [()] [1] [÷] [RCL] [D] [>] [>] [÷] [()] [()] [1] [÷] [RCL] [Q] [>] [−] [()] [1] [÷] [RCL] [Y] [>] [>] [×] [1] [0] [0] [ENTER]

HP 33s Checksum; Length of Equation: **CK=45B4; LN=33**

[RCL] [R] [↱] [=] [↱] [(] [↱] [(] [1] [÷] [RCL] [Q] [↱] [)] [−] [↱] [(] [1] [÷] [RCL] [D] [↱] [)] [↱] [)] [÷] [↱] [(] [↱] [(] [1] [÷] [RCL] [Q] [↱] [)] [−] [↱] [(] [1] [÷] [RCL] [Y] [↱] [)] [↱] [)] [×] [1] [0] [0] [ENTER]

≈≈≈≈≈≈≈≈≈≈

1.8 Laboratory Soil Compaction

1.8.1 Soil Compaction Using Standard or Modified Proctor

$$\gamma_d = \frac{Soil_{wet}}{(V_{mold})\left(1+\frac{\omega}{100}\right)}$$ Equation No. 13

The equation is entered as

13PROCTOR
D=T÷V÷(1+C÷100)

Where:

D = dry density of compacted soil γ_d (lb/ft³)
T = weight of wet soil $Soil_{wet}$ (lb)
V = volume of mold V_{mold} (0.0333 ft³ for standard proctor, 0.075 ft³ for modified proctor)
C = moisture content ω (%)

Keystrokes

HP 35s Checksum; Length of Equation: **CK=A5DE; LN=15**

RCL D ↰ = RCL T ÷ RCL V ÷ () 1 + RCL C ÷ 1 0 0 ENTER

HP 33s Checksum; Length of Equation: **CK=A5DE; LN=15**

RCL D ↱ = RCL T ÷ RCL V ÷ ↱ (1 + RCL C ÷ 1 0 0 ↱) ENTER

Notes: This equation shall be used to calculate the maximum dry density using standard or modified proctor. The water content of maximum dry density is the optimum moisture content.

≈≈≈≈≈≈≈≈≈≈

1.8.2 Zero Air Voids Density

$$\gamma_Z = \frac{\gamma_W}{\frac{\omega}{100} + \frac{1}{G}}$$ Equation No. 14

The equation is entered as

14ZEROAIRVOIDS
D=W÷(C÷100+(1÷G))

Where:

D = dry density of zero air voids γ_Z (lb/ft³, kN/m³)
W = unit weight of water γ_w (62.4 lb/ft³, 9.81 kN/m³)
C = moisture content ω (%)
G = specific gravity G

Keystrokes

HP 35s Checksum; Length of Equation: **CK=094C; LN=17**

RCL D ↰ = RCL W ÷ () RCL C ÷ 1 0 0 + () 1 ÷ RCL G ENTER

HP 33s Checksum; Length of Equation: **CK=094C; LN=17**

RCL D ↱ = RCL W ÷ (RCL C ÷ 1 0 0 + ↱ (1 ÷ RCL G ↱) ↱) ENTER

≈≈≈≈≈≈≈≈≈≈

1.9 Dry Density of Soil in the Field Using Sand Cone Method

1.9.1 Dry Density of Soil in the Field Using Sand Cone Method Given Moisture Content

$$\gamma_d = \frac{\dfrac{W\gamma_s}{I-F}}{1+\dfrac{\omega}{100}}$$ Equation No. 15

The equation is entered as

15SANDCONE
D=((W×S)÷(I−F))÷(1+C÷100)

Where:

D = dry density of soil γ_d (lb/ft^3, kN/m^3)
W = weight of wet soil removed from the hole W (lb, kN)
S = unit weight of dry test sand γ_s (lb/ft^3, kN/m^3)
I = initial weight of sand cone apparatus filled with dry test sand I (lb, kN)
F = final weight of sand cone apparatus after the sand filled the test hole F (lb, kN)
C = moisture content of soil removed from the hole ω (%)

Keystrokes

HP 35s Checksum; Length of Equation: **CK=F9D6; LN=25**

[RCL] [D] [↰] [=] [()] [()] [RCL] [W] [×] [RCL] [S] [>] [÷] [()] [RCL] [I] [−] [RCL] [F] [>] [>] [÷] [()] [1] [+] [RCL] [C] [÷] [1] [0] [0] [ENTER]

HP 33s Checksum; Length of Equation: **CK=F9D6; LN=25**

[RCL] [D] [↱] [=] [↱] [(] [↱] [(] [RCL] [W] [×] [RCL] [S] [↱] [)] [÷] [↱] [(] [RCL] [I] [−] [RCL] [F] [↱] [)] [↱] [)] [÷] [↱] [(] [1] [+] [RCL] [C] [÷] [1] [0] [0] [↱] [)] [ENTER]

Notes: If the moisture content of soil removed from the hole is not given and the weight of oven dry soil is given, the moisture content can be calculated using RPN mode or hand calculation by using W as the weight of wet soil. If initial and final weights of sand cone are not given and the weight of sand used is given, assign I as the weight of sand used and F is zero. For English units, if the weight of wet and oven dry soil are given in grams, convert it to lb.

≈≈≈≈≈≈≈≈≈≈

1.10 Borrow Soil

1.10.1 Volume of Soil Required for Embankment

$$V_{soil} = \frac{V_{embankment} \times MDD \times \%_{compaction}}{\gamma_d} \qquad \text{Equation No. 16}$$

The equation is entered as

16VOLOFSOILREQ
V=E×M×P÷100÷D

Where:

V = volume of soil required for embankment V_{soil} (ft³, m³)
E = volume of embankment $V_{embankment}$ (ft³, m³)
M = proctor's maximum dry density MDD (lb/ft³, kN/m³)
P = percent compaction of MDD $\%_{compaction}$ (%)
D = dry density of borrowed soil γ_d (lb/ft³, kN/m³)

Keystrokes

HP 35s Checksum; Length of Equation: **CK=1F53; LN=13**

[RCL] [V] [↰] [=] [RCL] [E] [×] [RCL] [M] [×] [RCL] [P] [÷] [1] [0] [0] [÷] [RCL] [D] [ENTER]

HP 33s Checksum; Length of Equation: **CK=1F53; LN=13**

[RCL] [V] [↱] [=] [RCL] [E] [×] [RCL] [M] [×] [RCL] [P] [÷] [1] [0] [0] [÷] [RCL] [D] [ENTER]

Note: This equation shall be used to determine the number of truckloads of soil from the borrow pit, where D is the dry density of soil during transport based on void ratio.

≈≈≈≈≈≈≈≈≈≈

1.10.2 Volume of Water Required to Achieve Optimum Moisture Content

$$V_{water} = \frac{V_{embankment} \times MDD \times \%_{compaction} \times \%_{moisture}}{8.33} \qquad \text{Equation No. 17}$$

The equation is entered as

17VOLOFWATEREQ
V=E×M×P×W÷10000÷8.33

Where:

V = volume of water required to achieve optimum moisture content V_{water} (gallons)
E = volume of embankment $V_{embankment}$ (ft^3)
M = proctor's maximum dry density MDD (lb/ft^3)
P = percent compaction of MDD $\%_{compaction}$ (%)
W = percentage of moisture required to achieve optimum moisture content $\%_{moisture}$ (%)

Keystrokes

HP 35s Checksum; Length of Equation: **CK=3615; LN=20**

[RCL] [V] [↰] [=] [RCL] [E] [×] [RCL] [M] [×] [RCL] [P] [×] [RCL] [W] [÷] [1] [0] [0] [0] [0] [÷] [8] [·] [3] [3] [ENTER]

HP 33s Checksum; Length of Equation: **CK=3615; LN=20**

[RCL] [V] [↱] [=] [RCL] [E] [×] [RCL] [M] [×] [RCL] [P] [×] [RCL] [W] [÷] [1] [0] [0] [0] [0] [÷] [8] [·] [3] [3] [ENTER]

≈≈≈≈≈≈≈≈≈≈

1.11 Hydraulic Conductivity of Soil

1.11.1 Darcy's Law

$Q = KiA$ Equation No. 18

The equation is entered as

18DARCYSLAW
Q=K×I×A

Where:

Q = flow rate of soil passing through permeable soil Q (ft^3/sec, m^3/s)
K = hydraulic conductivity K (ft/sec, m/s)
I = hydraulic gradient i
A= total cross-sectional area of permeable soil A (ft^2, m^2)

Keystrokes

HP 35s Checksum; Length of Equation: **CK=58DD; LN=7**

[RCL] [Q] [↰] [=] [RCL] [K] [×] [RCL] [I] [×] [RCL] [A] [ENTER]

HP 33s Checksum; Length of Equation: **CK=58DD; LN=7**

[RCL] [Q] [↱] [=] [RCL] [K] [×] [RCL] [I] [×] [RCL] [A] [ENTER]

1.11.2 Flow Net

$$Q = Kh\frac{N_f}{N_d}$$ Equation No. 19

The equation is entered as

19FLOWNET
Q=K×H×F÷D

Where:

Q = seepage rate per unit length of structure Q (ft^3/sec, ft^3/day, m^3/s)
K = hydraulic conductivity K (ft/sec, ft/day, m/s)
H = difference between upstream and downstream water levels h (ft, m)
F = number of flow channels N_f
D = number of equipotential drops N_d

Keystrokes

HP 35s Checksum; Length of Equation: **CK=92EE; LN=9**

[RCL] [Q] [↰] [=] [RCL] [K] [×] [RCL] [H] [×] [RCL] [F] [÷] [RCL] [D] [ENTER]

HP 33s Checksum; Length of Equation: **CK=92EE; LN=9**

[RCL] [Q] [↱] [=] [RCL] [K] [×] [RCL] [H] [×] [RCL] [F] [÷] [RCL] [D] [ENTER]

≈≈≈≈≈≈≈≈≈≈

1.12 Laboratory Permeability Tests

1.12.1 Constant Head

$$K = \frac{VL}{h\frac{\pi}{4}D^2T}$$ Equation No. 20

The equation is entered as

20CONSTANTHEAD
C=V×L÷(H×π÷4×D^2×T)

Where:

C = coefficient of permeability K (ft/sec, in/min, cm/s)
V = volume of water collected V (ft^3, cm^3)
L = length of soil sample L (in, ft, cm)
H = water level difference h (in, ft, cm)
D = diameter of soil sample D (in, ft, cm)
T = time it took for a volume of water percolated through a soil T (sec, min)

Keystrokes

HP 35s Checksum; Length of Equation: **CK=018A; LN=19**

[RCL] [C] [↰] [=] [RCL] [V] [×] [RCL] [L] [÷] [()] [RCL] [H] [×] [↰] [π] [÷] [4] [×] [RCL] [D] [y^x] [2] [×] [RCL] [T] [ENTER]

HP 33s Checksum; Length of Equation: **CK=018A; LN=19**

[RCL] [C] [↱] [=] [RCL] [V] [×] [RCL] [L] [÷] [↱] [(] [RCL] [H] [×] [↱] [π] [÷] [4] [×] [RCL] [D] [y^x] [2] [×] [RCL] [T] [↱] [)] [ENTER]

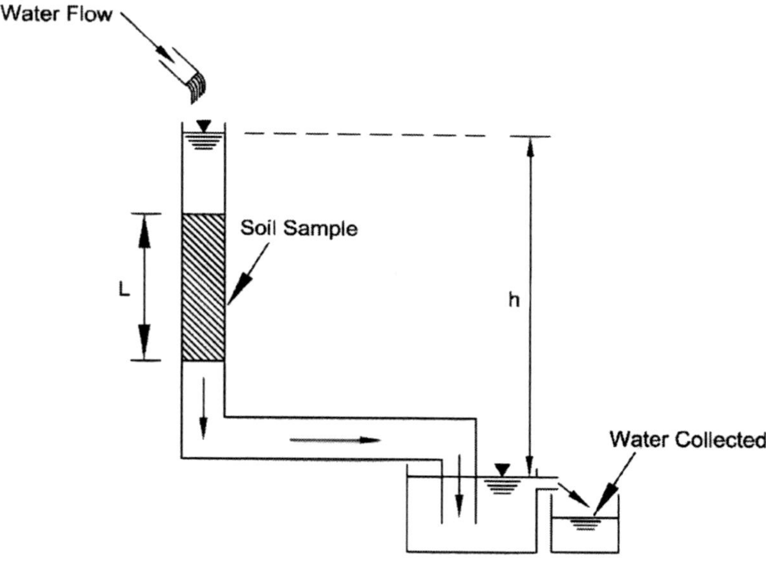

Figure 1-1 Constant Head

Notes: Be consistent with the units. If solving for coefficient of permeability K in ft/sec, the volume of water collected V must be in ft^3, length of soil sample, h, and diameter of soil sample must be in ft, and the time T must be in seconds.

≈≈≈≈≈≈≈≈≈≈

1.12.2 Falling Head

$$K = \frac{\frac{\pi}{4}B^2 L}{\frac{\pi}{4}D^2 T}\ln\frac{h_1}{h_2}$$ Equation No. 21

The equation is entered as

21FALLINGHEAD
F=π÷4×B^2×L÷(π÷4×D^2×T)×LN(Y÷Z)

Where:

F = coefficient of permeability K (ft/sec, in/min, cm/s)
B = diameter of burette B (in, cm)
L = length of soil sample L (in, cm)
D = diameter of soil sample D (in, cm)
T = time it took for the head to drop from h_1 to h_2 T (sec, min)
Y = h_1 (in, ft, cm)
Z = h_2 (in, ft, cm)

Keystrokes

HP 35s Checksum; Length of Equation: **CK=7437; LN=31**

[RCL] [F] [↰] [=] [↰] [π] [÷] [4] [×] [RCL] [B] [yˣ] [2] [×] [RCL] [L] [÷] [()] [↰] [π] [÷] [4] [×] [RCL] [D] [yˣ] [2] [×]
[RCL] [T] [>] [×] [↱] [LN] [RCL] [Y] [÷] [RCL] [Z] [ENTER]

HP 33s Checksum; Length of Equation: **CK=7437; LN=31**

[RCL] [F] [↱] [=] [↱] [π] [÷] [4] [×] [RCL] [B] [yˣ] [2] [×] [RCL] [L] [÷] [↱] [(] [↱] [π] [÷] [4] [×] [RCL] [D] [yˣ] [2] [×]
[RCL] [T] [↱] [)] [×] [LN] [RCL] [Y] [÷] [RCL] [Z] [↱] [)] [ENTER]

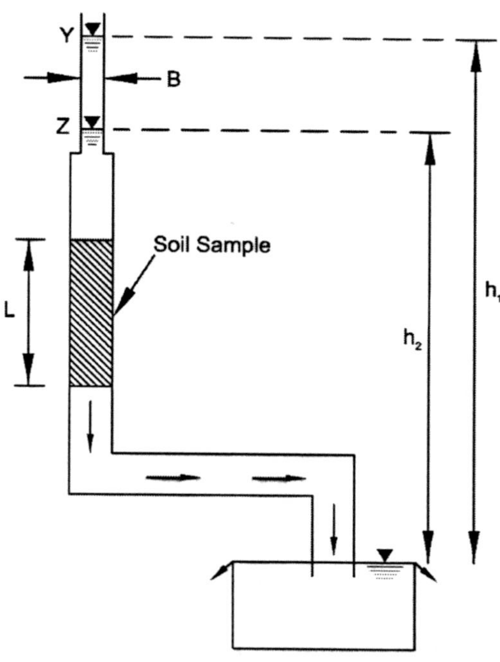

Figure 1-2 Falling Head

≈≈≈≈≈≈≈≈≈≈

1.13 Soil Classification

1.13.1 USCS Classification

$G = 100 - F$ Equation No. 22 (G)

$H = 100 - \left(G \times \frac{R}{100} \right)$ Equation No. 22 (H)

$PI = LL - PL$ Equation No. 22 (P)

$U = \frac{S}{T}$ Equation No. 22 (U)

$Z = \frac{Y^2}{T \times S}$ Equation No. 22 (Z)

The equations are entered as

22USCSCLASSIFF
G=100−F
H=100−(G×R÷100)
I=L−P
U=S÷T
Z=Y^2÷T÷S

Where:

G = percent by weight retained on no. 200 sieve (%)
F = percent by weight passed no. 200 sieve (%)
H = sand fraction (%)
R = percent by weight retained on no. 4 sieve (%)
I = plasticity index *PI*
L = liquid limit *LL*
P = plastic limit *PL*
U = uniformity coefficient *U*
S = the diameter, for which only 60% of the particles are finer (D_{60}) *S*
T = the diameter, for which only 10% of the particles are finer (D_{10}) *T*
Z = coefficient of curvature *Z*
Y = the diameter, for which only 30% of the particles are finer (D_{30}) *Y*

Keystrokes

G=100−F

HP 35s Checksum; Length of Equation: **CK=B22C; LN=7**

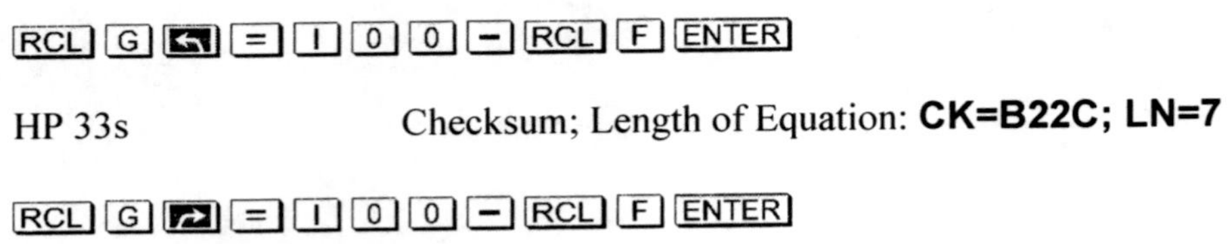

HP 33s Checksum; Length of Equation: **CK=B22C; LN=7**

H=100−(G×R÷100)

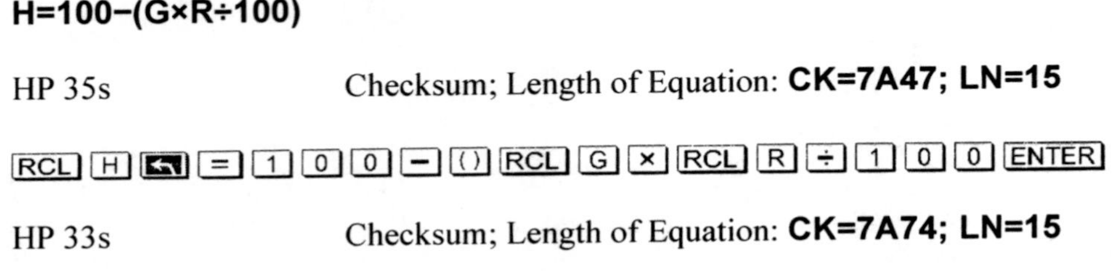

HP 35s Checksum; Length of Equation: **CK=7A47; LN=15**

HP 33s Checksum; Length of Equation: **CK=7A74; LN=15**

I=L−P

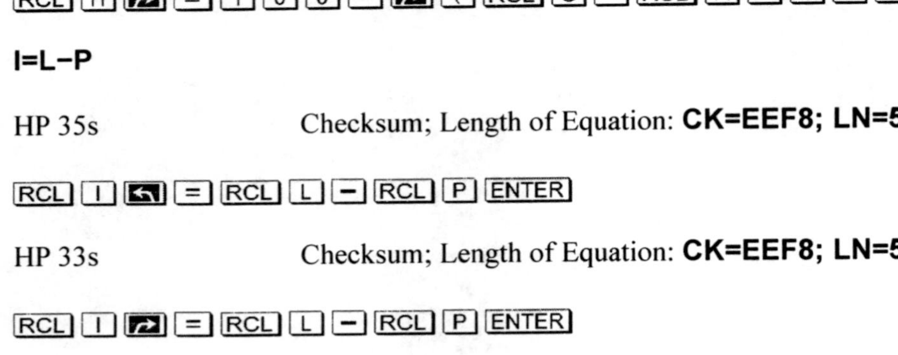

HP 35s Checksum; Length of Equation: **CK=EEF8; LN=5**

HP 33s Checksum; Length of Equation: **CK=EEF8; LN=5**

U=S÷T

HP 35s Checksum; Length of Equation: **CK=164C; LN=5**

[RCL] [U] [↰] [=] [RCL] [S] [÷] [RCL] [T] [ENTER]

HP 33s Checksum; Length of Equation: **CK=164C; LN=5**

[RCL] [U] [↱] [=] [RCL] [S] [÷] [RCL] [T] [ENTER]

Z=Y^2÷T÷S

HP 35s Checksum; Length of Equation: **CK=E1BB; LN=9**

[RCL] [Z] [↰] [=] [RCL] [Y] [y^x] [2] [÷] [RCL] [T] [÷] [RCL] [S] [ENTER]

HP 33s Checksum; Length of Equation: **CK=E1BB; LN=9**

[RCL] [Z] [↱] [=] [RCL] [Y] [y^x] [2] [÷] [RCL] [T] [÷] [RCL] [S] [ENTER]

≈≈≈≈≈≈≈≈≈≈

1.13.2 Group Index for A-1 through A-8 Type Soils

$$I_g = (F_{200} - 35)(0.2 + 0.005(LL - 40)) + 0.01(F_{200} - 15)(PI - 10) \qquad \text{Equation No. 23}$$

The equation is entered as

23GRPINDA1A8
G=(F−35)×(0.2+0.005(L−40))+0.01(F−15)×(I−10)

Where:

G = group index for A-1 through A-8 type soils I_g
F = percent passing no. 200 sieve F_{200} (e.g., 40)
L = liquid limit LL
I = plasticity index PI (LL – PL), PL is plastic limit.

Keystrokes

HP 35s Checksum; Length of Equation: **CK=97A9; LN=44**

[RCL] [G] [↰] [=] [()] [RCL] [F] [−] [3] [5] [>] [×] [()] [·] [2] [+] [·] [0] [0] [5] [()] [RCL] [L] [−] [4] [0] [>] [>] [+] [·] [0] [1] [()] [RCL] [F] [−] [1] [5] [>] [×] [()] [RCL] [I] [−] [1] [0] [ENTER]

HP 33s Checksum; Length of Equation: **CK=4EA4; LN=46**

[RCL] [G] [↱] [=] [↱] [(] [RCL] [F] [−] [3] [5] [↱] [)] [×] [↱] [(] [·] [2] [+] [·] [0] [0] [5] [×] [↱] [(] [RCL] [L] [−] [4] [0] [↱] [)] [↱] [)] [+] [·] [0] [1] [×] [↱] [(] [RCL] [F] [−] [1] [5] [↱] [)] [×] [↱] [(] [RCL] [I] [−] [1] [0] [↱] [)] [ENTER]

Notes: This equation shall be used to calculate the group index for A-1 through A-8 type soils classified using AASHTO method, given percent passing no. 200 sieve, liquid limit, and plasticity index. Round the group index to the nearest whole number.

≈≈≈≈≈≈≈≈≈≈

1.13.3 Group Index for A-2-6 and A-2-7 Type Soils

$I_g = 0.01(F_{200} - 15)(PI - 10)$ Equation No. 24

The equation is entered as

24GRPINDA26A27
G=0.01(F−15)×(I−10)

Where:

G = group index for A-2-6 and A-2-7 type soils I_g

F = percent passing no. 200 sieve F_{200} (e.g., 40)

I = plasticity index PI (LL – PL), PL is plastic limit.

Keystrokes

HP 35s Checksum; Length of Equation: **CK=5F5C; LN=19**

[RCL] [G] [↰] [=] [·] [0] [1] [()] [RCL] [F] [−] [1] [5] [>] [×] [()] [RCL] [I] [−] [1] [0] [ENTER]

HP 33s Checksum; Length of Equation: **CK=1013; LN=20**

[RCL] [G] [↱] [=] [·] [0] [1] [×] [↱] [(] [RCL] [F] [−] [1] [5] [↱] [)] [×] [↱] [(] [RCL] [I] [−] [1] [0] [↱] [)] [ENTER]

Notes: This equation shall be used to calculate the group index for A-2-6 and A-2-7 type soils classified using AASHTO method, given percent passing no. 200 sieve, liquid limit, and plasticity index. Round the group index to the nearest whole number.

≈≈≈≈≈≈≈≈≈≈

1.14 Effective Stress

1.14.1 Effective Stress of Soil up to 4 Layers

$\sigma' = \sigma - u$ Equation No. 25

The equation is entered as

25EFFECTSTRESS
S=A×E+B×F+C×G+D×H

Where:

S = effective stress (lb/ft², kN/m²)
A = buoyant unit weight of soil at layer 1 γ_{b_1} (lb/ft³, kN/m³)
E = thickness of layer 1 (ft, m)
B = buoyant unit weight of soil at layer 2 γ_{b_2} (lb/ft³, kN/m³)
F = thickness of layer 2 (ft, m)
C = buoyant unit weight of soil at layer 3 γ_{b_3} (lb/ft³, kN/m³)
G = thickness of layer 3 (ft, m)
D = buoyant unit weight of soil at layer 4 γ_{b_4} (lb/ft³, kN/m³)
H = thickness of layer 4 (ft, m)

Keystrokes

HP 35s Checksum; Length of Equation: **CK=4278; LN=17**

[RCL] [S] [↰] [=] [RCL] [A] [×] [RCL] [E] [+] [RCL] [B] [×] [RCL] [F] [+] [RCL] [C] [×] [RCL] [G] [+] [RCL] [D] [×] [RCL] [H] [ENTER]

HP 33s Checksum; Length of Equation: **CK=4278; LN=17**

[RCL] [S] [↱] [=] [RCL] [A] [×] [RCL] [E] [+] [RCL] [B] [×] [RCL] [F] [+] [RCL] [C] [×] [RCL] [G] [+] [RCL] [D] [×] [RCL] [H] [ENTER]

Note: If the soil layer is not submerged, use the moist density and consider it as an isolated layer.

≈≈≈≈≈≈≈≈≈≈

1.15 Shear Strength

1.15.1 Shear Strength of Soil with Normal Stress, Cohesion, and Angle of Internal Friction

$S = c + \sigma \tan\phi$ Equation No. 26

The equation is entered as

26SHEARSTRENGTH
S=C+N×TAN(A)

Where:

S = shear strength S (lb/ft², lb/in², KN/m²)
C = cohesion c (lb/ft², lb/in², KN/m²)
N = normal stress σ (lb/ft², lb/in², KN/m²)
A = angle of internal friction ϕ

Keystrokes

HP 35s Checksum; Length of Equation: **CK=5D1A; LN=12**

[RCL] [S] [↰] [=] [RCL] [C] [+] [RCL] [N] [×] [TAN] [RCL] [A] [ENTER]

HP 33s Checksum; Length of Equation: **CK=5D1A; LN=12**

[RCL] [S] [↱] [=] [RCL] [C] [+] [RCL] [N] [×] [TAN] [RCL] [A] [ENTER]

≈≈≈≈≈≈≈≈≈≈

1.16 Triaxial Test

1.16.1 Angle of Internal Friction

$$\phi = \arcsin\left(\frac{\dfrac{\sigma_1 - \sigma_3}{2}}{\sigma_3 + \dfrac{\sigma_1 - \sigma_3}{2}}\right)$$ Equation No. 27

The equation is entered as

27AOIFTRIAXIAL
A=ASIN(((B−D)÷2)÷(D+(B−D)÷2))

Where:

A = angle of internal friction ϕ
B = total vertical stress σ_1 (lb/ft², lb/in², KN/m²)
D = confining pressure σ_3 (lb/ft², lb/in², KN/m²)

Keystrokes

HP 35s Checksum; Length of Equation: **CK=70E8; LN=29**

[RCL] [A] [↰] [=] [↱] [ASIN] [()] [()] [RCL] [B] [−] [RCL] [D] [>] [÷] [2] [>] [÷] [()] [RCL] [D] [+] [()] [RCL] [B] [−] [RCL] [D] [>] [÷] [2] [ENTER]

HP 33s Checksum; Length of Equation: **CK=70E8; LN=29**

[RCL] [A] [↱] [=] [↰] [ASIN] [↱] [(] [↱] [(] [RCL] [B] [−] [RCL] [D] [↱] [)] [÷] [2] [↱] [)] [÷] [↱] [(] [RCL] [D] [+] [↱] [(] [RCL] [B] [−] [RCL] [D] [↱] [)] [÷] [2] [↱] [)] [↱] [)] [ENTER]

Note: Total vertical stress is the sum of deviator stress $\Delta\sigma$ and confining pressure σ_3.

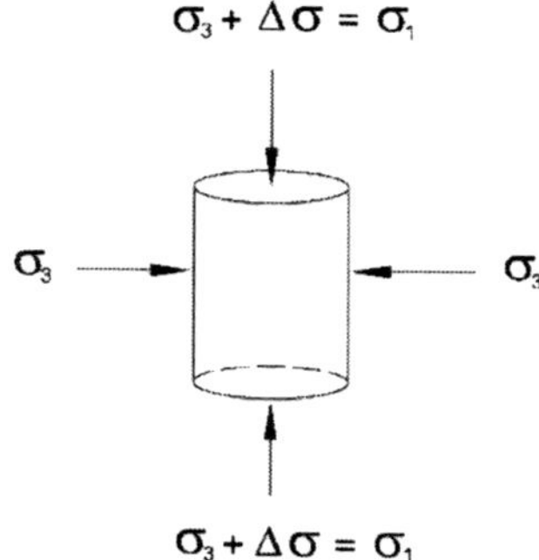

Figure 1-3 Triaxial Stress Test

Note: If solving for effective friction angle, subtract the pore water pressure from the vertical total stress σ_1 and confining pressure σ_3 before entering into equation.

≈≈≈≈≈≈≈≈≈≈

1.17 Mohr-Coulomb

1.17.1 Major and Minor Principal Effective Stresses with Effective Angle of Internal Friction and Cohesion

$$\sigma_1' = \sigma_3' \tan^2\left(45 + \frac{\phi'}{2}\right) + 2c\tan\left(45 + \frac{\phi'}{2}\right)$$ Equation No. 28

The equation is entered as

28MOHR−COULOMB
O=M(TAN(45+A÷2))^2+2×C×TAN(45+A÷2)

Where:

O = major principal effective stress, confining pressure σ_3' + deviator stress $\Delta\sigma = \sigma_1'$ (lb/ft², lb/in², KN/m²)

M = minor principal effective stress, confining pressure σ_3' (lb/ft², lb/in², KN/m²)

A = effective angle of internal friction ϕ'

C = cohesion c (lb/ft², lb/in², KN/m²)

Keystrokes

HP 35s Checksum; Length of Equation: **CK=5373; LN=34**

[RCL] [O] [↰] [=] [RCL] [M] [()] [TAN] [4] [5] [+] [RCL] [A] [÷] [2] [>] [>] [y^x] [2] [+] [2] [×] [RCL] [C] [×] [TAN] [4] [5] [+] [RCL] [A] [÷] [2] [ENTER]

HP 33s Checksum; Length of Equation: **CK=262E; LN=35**

[RCL] [O] [↱] [=] [RCL] [M] [×] [↱] [(] [TAN] [4] [5] [+] [RCL] [A] [÷] [2] [↱] [)] [↱] [)] [y^x] [2] [+] [2] [×] [RCL] [C] [×] [TAN] [4] [5] [+] [RCL] [A] [÷] [2] [↱] [)] [ENTER]

≈≈≈≈≈≈≈≈≈≈

Problem 1.1

A representative soil specimen collected from the field has a moist density of 115 lb/ft³. The moisture content as determined in the laboratory is 10% and the specific gravity is 2.7. The dry density, void ratio, porosity, and degree of saturation are most nearly

	Dry Density (lb/ft³)	Void Ratio	Porosity	Degree of Saturation (%)
(A)	100.0	0.4	0.3	40
(B)	102.5	0.5	0.35	42
(C)	104.5	0.61	0.38	45
(D)	105.5	0.72	0.45	60

Solution

a) Dry density

Calculate the dry density of soil with given moist density and moisture content. Use Equation No. 9, page 6. Press ENTER.

Display	Keys	Description
E?	115 R/S	Moist density of soil (lb/ft³)
C?	10 R/S	Moisture content (%)
D = 104.5455	--	Dry density of soil (lb/ft³)

b) Void ratio

The void ratio can be obtained using the dry density from previous calculation. Use Equation No. 8, page 6. Press SOLVE V.

Display	Keys	Description
D? 104.5455	R/S	Dry density of soil (lb/ft³)
G?	2.7 R/S	Specific gravity
W?	62.4 R/S	Unit weight of water (lb/ft³)
V = 0.6115	--	Void ratio

Notes: Pressing R/S means accepting the value you've just entered, or accepting the displayed value which is the result from previous calculation from different equation, or accepting the result of calculation using RPN. To use the SOLVE function on HP 35s, press the [↱] followed by SOLVE key. There will always be a displayed value from previous calculation. If you are using HP 35s and want to switch to another equation after each calculation, press the [EQN] key then [^] or [v] key. If you are using HP 33s and want to switch to another equation after each calculation, press the [↱] followed by [EQN] key, then the up or down large silver keys.

c) Porosity

Using the calculated void ratio, the porosity can be determined. Use Equation No. 10, page 7. Press ENTER.

Display	Keys	Description
V? 0.6115	R/S	Void ratio
P = 0.3795	--	Porosity

d) Degree of saturation

The values of moisture content and specific gravity are given, the void ratio was obtained. The degree of saturation can now be determined. Use Equation No. 7, page 5. Press ENTER.

Display	Keys	Description
C? 10.0000	R/S	Moisture content (%)
G? 2.7000	R/S	Specific gravity
V? 0.6115	R/S	Void ratio
Z = 44.1503	--	Degree of saturation (%)

The answer is (C).

Problem 1.2

A sandy soil was tested in the laboratory and found to have a maximum void ratio of 0.85 and a minimum void ratio of 0.35. Its porosity is 0.38. The relative density of the soil in the field is most nearly

(A) 40%
(B) 50%
(C) 60%
(D) 70%

Solution

To calculate the relative density with given maximum and minimum void ratios, and porosity, perform the following steps:

Step 1. Porosity is provided. Use Equation No. 10, page 7 to solve for the void ratio. Press SOLVE V.

Display	Keys	Description
P?	.38 R/S	Porosity
V = 0.6129	--	Void ratio

Step 2. The void ratio computed from the previous calculation shall be used to calculate the relative density. Use Equation No. 11, page 8. Press ENTER.

Display	Keys	Description
M?	.85 R/S	Maximum void ratio
V? 0.6129	R/S	Void ratio
N?	.35 R/S	Minimum void ratio
R = 47.4194	--	Relative density of soil (%)

The answer is (B).

Problem 1.3

A sandy soil was tested in the laboratory and found to have a maximum dry density of 120 lb/ft^3 and a minimum dry density of 110 lb/ft^3. Its moist density is 125 lb/ft^3 and relative density is 65%. The moisture content of soil is most nearly

(A) 8% (C) 12%
(B) 10% (D) 15%

Solution

Using the given values, the moisture content of soil can be calculated in the following manner:

Step 1. Calculate the dry density of soil with given relative density, maximum and minimum dry densities. Use Equation No. 12, page 8. Press SOLVE D.

Display	Keys	Description
R?	65 R/S	Relative density of soil (%)
Q?	110 R/S	Minimum dry density of soil (lb/ft^3)
Y?	120 R/S	Maximum dry density of soil (lb/ft^3)
D = 116.2996	--	Dry density of soil (lb/ft^3)

Step 2. Compute the moisture content given moist density of soil and calculated dry density. Use Equation No. 9, page 6. Press SOLVE C.

Display	Keys	Description
D? 116.2996	R/S	Dry density of soil (lb/ft^3)
E?	125 R/S	Moist density of soil (lb/ft^3)
C = 7.4811	--	Moisture content (%)

The answer is (A).

Problem 1.4

A soil sample was tested in the laboratory with given parameters below. The degree of saturation is most nearly

(A) 40% (C) 55%
(B) 50% (D) 60%

Sample diameter	3 in
Sample length	6 in
Sample weight before oven drying	2.9 lb
Sample weight after oven drying	2.6 lb
Specific gravity	2.65

Solution

Calculate the degree of saturation using the following procedure:

Step 1. Solve the void ratio. The dry density of soil is not given; it can be calculated within the equation using RPN method. Alternatively, it can be computed by hand calculation. Use Equation No. 8, page 6. Press SOLVE V.

Display	Keys	Description
D?	*	Dry density of soil (lb/ft³)
D? 105.9335	R/S	
G?	2.65 R/S	Specific gravity
W?	62.4 R/S	Unit weight of water (lb/ft³)
V = 0.5610	--	Void ratio

* Keys for calculating dry density using RPN:

2.6 ENTER [↰] [π] 1.5 [↱] [x²] × 144 ÷ .5 × ÷ (HP 35s)
2.6 ENTER [↱] [π] 1.5 [x²] × 144 ÷ .5 × ÷ (HP 33s)

Calculation of dry density of soil:

$$\gamma_d = \frac{2.6lb}{\pi \times (1.5in)^2 \times \frac{ft^2}{144in^2} \times 0.25\,ft} \qquad \gamma_d = 105.9335\frac{lb}{ft^3}$$

Step 2. The calculated void ratio shall be used to determine the degree of saturation. The moisture content is not given; it can be obtained by using RPN when prompted in the equation or as an alternative, it can be calculated separately before entering into the equation. Use Equation No. 7, page 5. Press ENTER.

Display	Keys	Description
C?	2.9 ENTER 2.6 – 2.6 ÷ 100 ×	Moisture content (%)
C? 11.5385	R/S	

Display	Keys	Description
G? 2.6500	R/S	Specific gravity
V? 0.5610	R/S	Void ratio
Z = 54.5064	--	Degree of saturation (%)

Calculation of moisture content:

$$\omega = \frac{2.9lb - 2.6lb}{2.6lb} \times 100\%$$

$$\omega = 11.5385\%$$

The answer is (C).

Problem 1.5

A soil sample is obtained from below the groundwater table. The soil has a void ratio of 0.72 and a specific gravity of 2.65. The buoyant unit weight in kN/m^3 is most nearly

(A) 9 kN/m^3
(B) 15 kN/m^3
(C) 17 kN/m^3
(D) 19 kN/m^3

Solution

Calculate the saturated density of soil with given void ratio and specific gravity. Use Equation No. 6, page 4. Press ENTER.

Display	Keys	Description
G?	2.65 R/S	Specific gravity of soil
V?	.72 R/S	Void ratio
W?	9.81 R/S	Unit weight of water (kN/m^3)
S = 19.2208	--	Saturated density of soil (kN/m^3)
--	9.81 –	Subtract the saturated density by 9.81 to calculate the buoyant unit weight
9.8100 9.4108 ←	←	Buoyant unit weight (kN/m^3)

The answer is (A).

Problem 1.6

A 5-point standard proctor compaction test was performed for a soil sample being used as backfill material. The soil sample data for each point are given below. After adequate compaction of the same backfill material at the jobsite, the dry density was 98 lb/ft^3. The maximum dry density of standard proctor compaction test and percent compaction of the soil at the jobsite are most nearly

	Standard Proctor Maximum Dry Density (lb/ft^3)	Percent Compaction (%)
(A)	98 lb/ft^3	95
(B)	101 lb/ft^3	97
(C)	105 lb/ft^3	100
(D)	110 lb/ft^3	102

Soil sample data:

Point No.	Moisture Content (%)	Weight of Moist Soil in Proctor Mold (lb)
1	12	3.57
2	14	3.77
3	16	3.90
4	18	3.87
5	20	3.67

Solution

The sequence of calculating the maximum dry density and percent compaction is as follows:

Step 1. Calculate the dry density of each moist soil with given moisture content. The volume of the standard proctor mold is 0.0333 ft^3. Use Equation No. 13, page 9. Press ENTER.

Display	Keys	Description
T?	3.57 R/S	Weight of moist soil for Point No. 1 (lb)
V?	.0333 R/S	Volume of mold for standard proctor (ft^3)
C?	12 R/S	Moisture content of soil for Point No. 1 (%)
D = 95.7207	--	Dry density of soil sample for Point No. 1 (lb/ft^3)

Step 2. Repeat the process for the remaining points and you'll get the results in the following order, 99.3098, 100.9630, 98.4883, and 91.8418. The maximum dry density is 100.9630 lb/ft^3.

Step 3. Compute the percent compaction using RPN. Press C.

$$\text{Percent Compaction} = \frac{\gamma_{d(field)}}{\gamma_{d(\max)proctor}} \times 100\%$$

Display	Keys	Description
20.0000 91.8418	98 ENTER	Dry density of soil in the field (lb/ft^3)
98.0000 98.0000	101 ÷	Divide the dry density of soil in the field by the maximum dry density of standard proctor test
91.8418 0.9703	100 ×	Convert the decimal to percent
91.8418 97.0297 ←		Percent compaction (%)

The answer is (B).

Problem 1.7

A falling-head permeability test was performed on a soil sample. After surcharging the soil, it took 6 minutes for the water level in the burette to drop from 30 inches to 10 inches. The coefficient of permeability of the soil in feet per day is most nearly

(A) 1.2×10^{-1} ft/day
(B) 1.2×10^{-3} ft/day
(C) 1.46 ft/day
(D) 14.6 ft/day

Soil sample data:

Sample diameter: 3 in
Sample length: 6 in
Burette diameter: 1 in

Solution

Calculate the coefficient of permeability of soil using falling-head method. Use Equation No. 21, page 16. Press ENTER.

Display	Keys	Description
B?	1 R/S	Diameter of burette (in)
L?	6 R/S	Length of soil sample (in)
D?	3 R/S	Diameter of soil sample (in)
T?	6 R/S	Time of test (min)
Y?	30 R/S	Water level in the burette at the beginning of the test (in)
Z?	10 R/S	Water level in the burette at the end of the test (in)
F = 0.1221	--	Coefficient of permeability of soil (in/min)

Display	Keys	Description
--	1440 × 12 ÷	Convert the in/min to ft/day
10.0000 14.6482 ←		Coefficient of permeability (ft/day)

Conversion of in/min to ft/day:

$$0.1221\frac{in}{\min}\times\frac{1440\min}{day}\times\frac{ft}{12in}=14.6482\frac{ft}{day}$$

The answer is (D).

Problem 1.8

A constant-head permeability test was performed on a soil sample. It took 5 minutes to collect 20 in^3 of water that passed through the soil sample. The coefficient of permeability of the soil in inch per minute is most nearly

(A) 1.1 x 10^{-1} in/min
(B) 2.1 x 10^{-1} in/min
(C) 1.7 x 10^{-1} in/min
(D) 2.1 x 10^{-3} in/min

Soil sample data:

Sample diameter:	3 inches
Sample length:	6 inches
h:	30 inches

Solution

Determine the soil permeability using constant-head method. Use Equation No. 20, page 14. Press ENTER.

Display	Keys	Description
V?	20 R/S	Volume of water collected (in^3)
L?	6 R/S	Length of soil sample (in)
H?	30 R/S	Water level difference (in)
D?	3 R/S	Diameter of soil sample (in)
T?	5 R/S	Time of test (min)
C = 0.1132	--	Coefficient of permeability of soil (in/min)

The answer is (A).

Problem 1.9

A constant-head permeability test was performed on a soil sample. The soil sample data are given below. The flow rate is most nearly

(A) 12 cm³/s (C) 36 cm³/s
(B) 25 cm³/s (D) 50 cm³/s

Soil sample data:

K:	0.2 cm/s
Sample diameter:	7 cm
Sample length:	15 cm
Constant head loss h:	70 cm

Solution

Calculate the flow rate using Darcy's Law. Use Equation No. 18, page 13. Press ENTER.

Display	Keys	Description
K?	.2 R/S	Hydraulic conductivity (cm/s)
I?	70 ENTER 15 ÷	Hydraulic gradient
I? 4.6667	R/S	
A?	*	Cross-sectional area (cm²)
A? 38.4845	R/S	
Q = 35.9189	--	Flow rate (cm³/s)

* Keys for calculating cross-sectional area using RPN:

[↰] [π] 3.5 [↱] [x²] × (HP 35s)
[↱] [π] 3.5 [x²] × (HP 33s)

$$Area = \pi(3.5cm)^2 = 38.4845cm^2$$

The answer is (C).

Problem 1.10

A sheet pile wall is driven in a pond maintaining a 10-foot water level difference between upstream and downstream by pumping. The hydraulic conductivity of soil underneath the pond is 0.02 ft/sec, the number of flow channels is 5, and the number of equipotential drops is 7. The flow rate per linear foot of sheet pile wall is most nearly

(A) 0.1 ft^3/sec
(B) 0.5 ft^3/sec
(C) 2 ft^3/sec
(D) 5 ft^3/sec

Solution

Determine the flow rate using the flow net. Use Equation No. 19, page 14. Press ENTER.

Display	Keys	Description
K?	.02 R/S	Hydraulic conductivity (ft/sec)
H?	10 R/S	Difference between upstream and downstream water levels (ft)
F?	5 R/S	Number of flow channels
D?	7 R/S	Number of equipotential drops
Q = 0.1429	--	Flow rate per linear foot of sheet pile (ft^3/sec)

The answer is (A).

Problem 1.11

A soil sample was tested in the laboratory with the following results:

Percent passing no. 200 sieve (based on dry weight)	40
Liquid limit	56
Plastic limit	47

Using the AASHTO soil classification system, the group index of this soil is most nearly

(A) 1
(B) 2
(C) 3
(D) 4

Solution

The AASHTO (American Association of State Highways and Transportation Officials) classification and group index of the soil can be obtained using the following exercise:

Step 1. Classify the soil according to AASHTO classification system. The percentage passing the no. 200 sieve is greater than 35%. Therefore, the soil sample is a silt-clay material. The liquid limit is greater than 41 and the plasticity index is 9. The soil sample meets the A-5 criteria.

Step 2. Calculate the group index. Use Equation No. 23, page 19. Press ENTER.

Display	Keys	Description
F?	40 R/S	Percent passing no. 200 sieve
L?	56 R/S	Liquid limit of soil sample
I?	56 ENTER 47 –	Plasticity index
I? 9.0000	R/S	
G = 1.1500	--	Group index is 1 by rounding to the nearest whole number

The answer is (A).

Problem 1.12

Classify the non-plastic soil sample with the following results after testing for sieve analysis:

Percent passing (by mass) 1 inch sieve	100
Percent passing (by mass) no. 4 sieve	90
Percent passing (by mass) no. 200 sieve	4
D_{60}	6.5 mm
D_{10}	0.5 mm
D_{30}	2.5 mm

(A) SM
(B) SP
(C) SW
(D) SP-SM

Solution

The USCS (Unified Soil Classification System) classification of this soil maybe obtained in the following manner:

Step 1. Calculate the percent retained on no. 200 sieve and determine whether the material is coarse-grained or fine grained soil. Use Equation No. 22 (G), page 17. Press ENTER.

Display	Keys	Description
F?	4 R/S	Percent passed no. 200 sieve (fine-grained material)
G = 96.0000	--	Percent retained on no. 200 sieve (coarse fraction) (The material is coarse-grained soil since more than 50% of the sample was retained on no. 200 sieve)

Step 2. Determine the sand fraction and gravel fraction. Use Equation No. 22 (H), page 17. Press ENTER.

Display	Keys	Description
G? 96.0000	R/S	Percent retained on no. 200 sieve (coarse-grained material)
R?	100 ENTER 90 –	Percent retained on no. 4 sieve
R? 10.0000	R/S	

Display	Keys	Description
H = 90.4000	--	Sand fraction (%) (The material is sandy soil since more than 50% of the coarse fraction is sand, 90.4% > 48%)
--	100 x<>y –	Gravel fraction calculation
10.0000		Percent retained on no. 4 sieve (gravel fraction)
9.6000 ←		Gravel fraction (%)

Step 3. Calculate the coefficient of uniformity. Use Equation No. 22 (U), page 17. Press ENTER.

Display	Keys	Description
S?	6.5 R/S	D_{60}
T?	.5 R/S	D_{10}
U = 13.0000	--	Coefficient of uniformity

Step 4. Compute the coefficient of curvature. Use Equation No. 22 (Z), page 17. Press ENTER.

Display	Keys	Description
Y?	2.5 R/S	D_{30}
T? 0.5000	R/S	D_{10}
S? 6.5000	R/S	D_{60}
Z = 1.9231	--	Coefficient of curvature

Notes: The soil is a coarse-grained material since more than 50% of the sample was retained on no. 200 sieve (100 – 4 = 96% > 50%). The gravel fraction (retained on no. 4 sieve) is 10% of the coarse fraction (10% × 96% = 9.6 %) which means 90.4% (100% – 9.6%) is the sand fraction. The sand fraction is greater than 50% of the coarse fraction. Therefore, the material is a sandy soil. The coefficient of uniformity is greater than 6 and the coefficient of curvature is between 1 and 3. Thus, meets the criteria of well-graded sand.

The answer is (C).

Problem 1.13

A subsurface exploration was conducted in a soil profile shown using a Standard Penetration Test (SPT) boring. The effective stress of soil in the middle of silty sand layer is most nearly

(A) 1,000 lb/ft^2
(B) 1,480 lb/ft^2
(C) 2,000 lb/ft^2
(D) 2,500 lb/ft^2

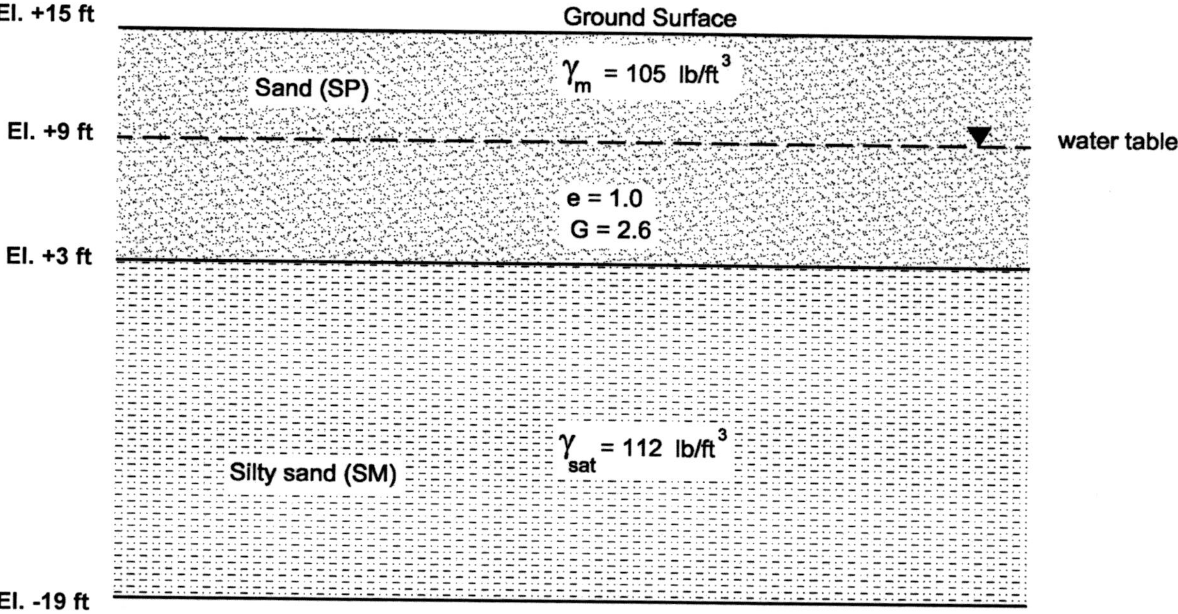

Solution

Option 1

Calculate the effective stress at the middle of silty sand layer. Assign the sand above water table as layer 1, the sand below water table as layer 2, and the silty sand as layer 3. Use Equation No. 25, page 20. Press ENTER.

Display	Keys	Description
A?	105 R/S	Moist density of soil above water table (layer 1) (lb/ft^3)
E?	6 R/S	Thickness of soil layer above water table (layer 1) (ft)
B?	3.6 ENTER 62.4 × 2 ÷ 62.4 –	Buoyant unit weight of soil at layer 2 (lb/ft^3)
B? 49.9200	R/S	
F?	6 R/S	Thickness of soil layer 2 (ft)
C?	112 ENTER 62.4 –	Buoyant unit weight of soil at layer 3 (lb/ft^3)
C? 49.6000	R/S	
G?	11 R/S	Distance from bottom of layer 2 to middle of layer 3 (ft)
D?	0 R/S	Buoyant unit weight of soil at layer 4 (lb/ft^3)
H?	0 R/S	Thickness of soil layer 4 (ft)
S = 1,475.1200	--	Effective stress in the middle of silty sand layer (lb/ft^2)

Calculation of buoyant unit weight of soil at layer 2:

$$\gamma_{sat} = \frac{(G+e)\gamma_w}{1+e} \qquad \gamma_b = 112.32\frac{lb}{ft^3} - 62.4\frac{lb}{ft^3}$$

$$\gamma_{sat} = \frac{(2.6+1)62.4\frac{lb}{ft^3}}{1+1} \qquad \gamma_b = 49.92\frac{lb}{ft^3}$$

$$\gamma_{sat} = 112.32\frac{lb}{ft^3}$$

Option 2

Use RPN. Press C.

105 ENTER 6 × 3.6 ENTER 62.4 × 2 ÷ 62.4 – 6 × + 112 ENTER 62.4 – 11 × +

The answer is (B).

Note: Use Option 2 if there are more than 4 layers of soil.

Problem 1.14

A saturated cohesionless soil was tested to failure in a triaxial test. The total vertical stress is 28 psi, the chamber pressure is 15 psi, and pore water pressure is 10 psi. Under drained conditions, the effective friction angle is most nearly

(A) 18°
(B) 30°
(C) 34°
(D) 44°

Solution

Determine the effective friction angle. Use Equation No. 27, page 22. Press ENTER.

Display	Keys	Description
B?	28 ENTER 10 –	Total vertical effective stress (psi)
B? 18.0000	R/S	
D?	15 ENTER 10 –	Effective confining pressure (psi)
D? 5.0000	R/S	
A = 34.4174	--	Effective friction angle

The answer is (C).

Note: The total vertical effective stress and effective confining pressure can be determined by subtracting the pore water pressure from the total vertical stress and chamber pressure, respectively.

Problem 1.15

A consolidated-drained triaxial test was performed on a clay sample. If the confining pressure, angle of internal friction, cohesion, and pore pressure were 2,500 lb/ft^2, 30°, 700 lb/ft^2, and 1,440 lb/ft^2, respectively. The major effective principal stress at failure is most nearly

(A) 5,600 lb/ft^2
(B) 7,500 lb/ft^2
(C) 9,500 lb/ft^2
(D) 10,000 lb/ft^2

Solution

Calculate the major principal stress at failure. Use Equation No. 28, page 23. Press ENTER.

Display	Keys	Description
M?	2500 ENTER 1440 –	Minor principal effective stress at failure (lb/ft^2)
M? 1,060.0000	R/S	
A?	30 R/S	Angle of internal friction
C?	700 R/S	Cohesion (lb/ft^2)
O = 5,604.8711	--	Major principal effective stress at failure (lb/ft^2)

The answer is (A).

Problem 1.16

A direct shear test was performed on a dry sand of area 4 in^2. The normal force and shear force at failure were 50 lb and 33 lb, respectively. The angle of internal friction angle is most nearly

(A) 28°
(B) 30°
(C) 33°
(D) 36°

Solution

Solve the angle of internal friction. Use Equation No. 26, page 21. Press SOLVE A.

Display	Keys	Description
S?	33 ENTER 4 ÷	Shear strength (psi)
S? 8.2500	R/S	
C?	0 R/S	Cohesion (psi)
N?	50 ENTER 4 ÷	Normal stress (psi)
N? 12.5000	R/S	
A = 33.4248	--	Angle of internal friction

The answer is (C).

Problem 1.17

An undivided, one-mile-long, multilane segment roadway is proposed. The segment has four 12-ft-wide lanes. The pavement sections consist of asphalt surface course, base, and stabilized subgrade. The base will be 10 inches thick and will be compacted to 98% of Modified Proctor maximum dry density. The Modified Proctor's maximum dry density is 120 lb/ft^3. The import material for base from a borrow pit has a moist density of 110 lb/ft^3, a moisture content of 10%, and a specific gravity of 2.7.

What is most nearly the amount of import material for base and the minimum number of truckloads if the volume per truckload is 5 yd^3 and the void ratio during transport is 1.3 assuming no waste?

	Import Material Required (yd^3)	Minimum Number of Truckloads
(A)	9,200 yd^3	2,560
(B)	14,000 yd^3	5,000
(C)	15,500 yd^3	10,800
(D)	340,000 yd^3	12,800

Solution

The import material required and minimum number of truckloads can be obtained using the following procedure:

Step 1. Calculate the volume required. Use Equation No. 16, page 12. Press ENTER.

Display	Keys	Description
E?	10 ENTER 12 ÷ 12 × 4 × 5280 ×	Volume of base material (ft^3)
E? 211,200.0000	R/S	
M?	120 R/S	Proctor's maximum dry density (lb/ft^3)

Display	Keys	Description
P?	98 R/S	Percent compaction of MDD (%)
D?	110 ENTER 1.1 ÷	Dry density of import material from borrow pit for base (lb/ft^3)
D? 100.0000	R/S	
V = 248,371.2000	--	Volume of import material required (ft^3)
--	27 ÷	Divide the volume of import material required by 27 to convert ft^3 to yd^3
100.0000 9,198.9333 ←		Volume of import material required (yd^3)

Step 2. Determine the number of truckloads for the base material. Use Equation No. 16, page 12. Press ENTER

Display	Keys	Description
E? 211,200.0000	R/S	Volume of base material (ft^3)
M? 120.0000	R/S	Proctor's maximum dry density (lb/ft^3)
P? 98.0000	R/S	Percent compaction of MDD (%)
D?	2.65 ENTER 62.4 × 2.3 ÷	Dry density of import material during transport based on void ratio (lb/ft^3)
D? 71.8957	R/S	
V = 345,460.6676	--	Volume of import material required (ft^3)
--	27 ÷	Divide the volume of import material required by 27 to convert ft^3 to yd^3
71.8957 12,794.8395	--	Volume of import material required (yd^3)
--	5 ÷	Divide the volume of import material required by 5yd^3 per truckload
71.8957 2,558.9679 ←		Minimum number of truckloads required

The answer is (A).

CHAPTER 2: SHALLOW FOUNDATION

2.1 Shallow Foundation without Water Table

$$\frac{1}{2}\gamma_m B N_\gamma + cN_c + (P_q + \gamma_m D_f)(N_q - 1) = \frac{P}{B^2} FS \times Z$$ Equation No. 29

The equation is entered as

29SHALFWOWT
(0.5×D×B×N×I)+C×O×J+(M+D×E)×(Q−1)=P÷B^2×F×Z

Where:

D = density of moist soil γ_m (lb/ft³, kN/m³)
B = width of square or continuous footing, or diameter of circular footing B (ft, m)
N = capacity factor N_γ
I = shape factor of N_γ (e.g., 0.85). The default value is 1.
C = cohesion c (lb/ft², kN/m²)
O = capacity factor N_c
J = shape factor of N_c (e.g., 1.25). The default value is 1.
M = surcharge P_q (lb/ft², kN/m²)
E = depth of footing D_f (ft, m)
Q = capacity factor N_q
P = total allowable load P (lb, kN)
F = factor of safety FS
Z = 1 for square or continuous footing, 1.2732 for circular footing Z

Keystrokes

HP 35s Checksum; Length of Equation: **CK=62EF; LN=43**

[()] [·] [5] [×] [RCL] [D] [×] [RCL] [B] [×] [RCL] [N] [×] [RCL] [I] [>] [+] [RCL] [C] [×] [RCL] [O] [×] [RCL] [J] [+] [()] [RCL] [M] [+] [RCL] [D] [×] [RCL] [E] [>] [×] [()] [RCL] [Q] [−] [1] [>] [↰] [=] [RCL] [P] [÷] [RCL] [B] [y^x] [2] [×] [RCL] [F] [×] [RCL] [Z] [ENTER]

HP 33s Checksum; Length of Equation: **CK=62EF; LN=43**

[↱] [(] [·] [5] [×] [RCL] [D] [×] [RCL] [B] [×] [RCL] [N] [×] [RCL] [I] [↱] [)] [+] [RCL] [C] [×] [RCL] [O] [×] [RCL] [J] [+] [↱] [(] [RCL] [M] [+] [RCL] [D] [×] [RCL] [E] [↱] [)] [×] [↱] [(] [RCL] [Q] [−] [1] [↱] [)] [↱] [=] [RCL] [P] [÷] [RCL] [B] [y^x] [2] [×] [RCL] [F] [×] [RCL] [Z] [ENTER]

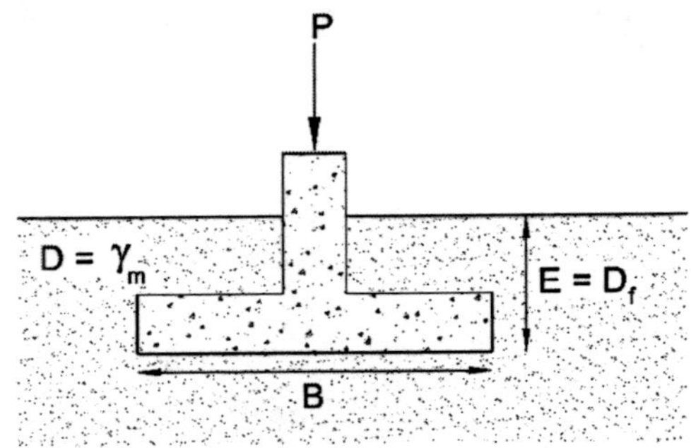

Figure 2-1 Shallow Foundation without Water Table

Notes: This equation, based on Terzaghi-Meyerhof theory, shall be used to calculate the net bearing capacity of square, continuous, and circular footings without water table. The net bearing capacity is the soil bearing pressure at the bottom of footing excluding the overburden pressure. The ultimate bearing capacity (this includes the overburden pressure) can be calculated by adding 1 to the N_q value before entering into the equation.

The net or ultimate bearing capacity (lb/ft^2, kN/m^2) can be calculated by using the following procedure:

Press ENTER, then enter the value of D, press R/S, enter the value of B, press R/S, enter the value of N, press R/S, enter the value of I, press R/S, enter the value of C, press R/S, enter the value of O, press R/S, enter the value of J, press R/S, enter the value of M, press R/S, enter the value of Q, press R/S, enter 0 for P, press R/S, enter 0 for F, press R/S, and finally enter 0 for Z. B is the width of square or continuous footings, or diameter of circular footing.

This equation can also be used to calculate the allowable load, width of square footing or diameter of circular footing, and factor of safety. To determine the width of square footing or diameter of circular footing, press SOLVE B then enter the values of D, N, I, C, O, J, M, E, Q, P, F, and Z. This equation is not applicable for solving the width, allowable load, and factor of safety of continuous footing. To solve the width of continuous footing, the equation must be altered by adding × B on the right side of the equation.

If the density of dry soil and moisture content are given, calculate the density of moist soil by using the equation $\gamma_m = \gamma_d(1+\omega)$.

≈≈≈≈≈≈≈≈≈≈

2.2 Shallow Foundation with Water Table at the Ground Surface

$$\frac{1}{2}\gamma_b B N_\gamma + cN_c + \gamma_b D_f (N_q - 1) = \frac{P}{B^2} FS \times Z \qquad \text{Equation No. 30}$$

in which $\gamma_b = \gamma_{sat} - \gamma_w$

The equation is entered as

30SHALFWTSURF
(0.5(S−W)×B×N×I)+C×O×J+(S−W)×E(Q−1)=P÷B^2×F×Z

Where:

S = density of saturated soil γ_{sat} (lb/ft³, kN/m³)
W = unit weight of water γ_w (62.4 lb/ft³, 9.81 kN/m³)
B = width of square or continuous footing, or diameter of circular footing B (ft, m)
N = capacity factor N_γ
I = shape factor of N_γ (e.g., 0.85). The default value is 1.
C = cohesion c (lb/ft², kN/m²)
O = capacity factor N_c
J = shape factor of N_c (e.g., 1.25). The default value is 1.
E = depth of footing D_f (ft, m)
Q = capacity factor N_q
P = total allowable load P (lb, kN)
F = factor of safety FS
Z = 1 for square or continuous footing, 1.2732 for circular footing Z

Keystrokes

HP 35s Checksum; Length of Equation: **CK=5FE5; LN=45**

[()] [.] [5] [()] [RCL] [S] [−] [RCL] [W] [>] [×] [RCL] [B] [×] [RCL] [N] [×] [RCL] [I] [>] [+] [RCL] [C] [×] [RCL] [O] [×] [RCL] [J] [+] [()] [RCL] [S] [−] [RCL] [W] [>] [×] [RCL] [E] [()] [RCL] [Q] [−] [1] [>] [left-shift] [=] [RCL] [P] [÷] [RCL] [B] [yˣ] [2] [×] [RCL] [F] [×] [RCL] [Z] [ENTER]

HP 33s Checksum; Length of Equation: **CK=D047; LN=47**

[right-shift] [(] [.] [5] [×] [right-shift] [(] [RCL] [S] [−] [RCL] [W] [right-shift] [)] [×] [RCL] [B] [×] [RCL] [N] [×] [RCL] [I] [right-shift] [)] [+] [RCL] [C] [×] [RCL] [O] [×] [RCL] [J] [+] [right-shift] [(] [RCL] [S] [−] [RCL] [W] [right-shift] [)] [×] [RCL] [E] [×] [right-shift] [(] [RCL] [Q] [−] [1] [right-shift] [)] [right-shift] [=] [RCL] [P] [÷] [RCL] [B] [yˣ] [2] [×] [RCL] [F] [×] [RCL] [Z] [ENTER]

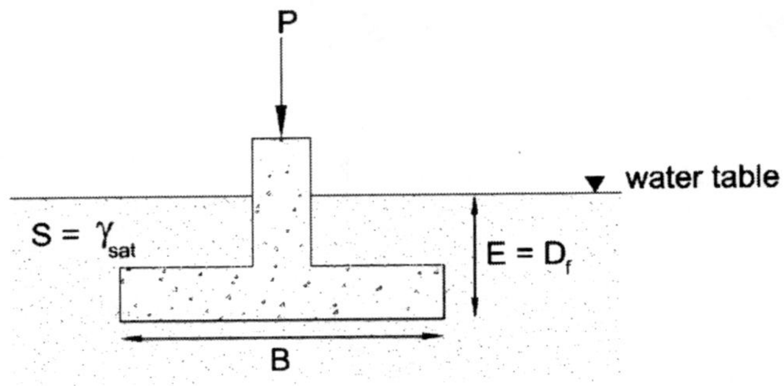

Figure 2-2 Shallow Foundation with Water Table at the Ground Surface

Notes: This equation, based on Terzaghi-Meyerhof theory, shall be used to calculate the net bearing capacity of square, continuous, and circular footings with water table at the ground surface. The net bearing capacity is the soil bearing pressure at the bottom of footing with the overburden pressure not taken into account. The ultimate bearing capacity (this includes the overburden pressure) can be obtained by adding 1 to the N_q value before entering into the equation.

The following procedure can be used to determine the net or ultimate bearing capacity (lb/ft^2, kN/m^2).

Press ENTER, then enter the value of D, press R/S, enter the value of B, press R/S, enter the value of N, press R/S, enter the value of I, press R/S, enter the value of C, press R/S, enter the value of O, press R/S, enter the value of J, press R/S, enter the value of M, press R/S, enter the value of Q, press R/S, enter 0 for P, press R/S, enter 0 for F, press R/S, and finally enter 0 for Z. B is the width of square or continuous footings, or diameter of circular footing.

This equation can also be used to calculate the allowable load, width of square footing or diameter of circular footing, and factor of safety. To determine the width of square footing or diameter of circular footing, press SOLVE B then enter the values of D, N, I, C, O, J, M, E, Q, P, F, and Z. This equation is not applicable for solving the width, allowable load, and factor of safety of continuous footing. To solve the width of continuous footing, the equation must be altered by adding × B on the right side of the equation.

If the buoyant unit weight of soil is given instead of the saturated density, assign S as the buoyant unit weight and W is zero. If the density of dry soil and moisture content are given, calculate the saturated density of soil by using the equation

$\gamma_{sat} = \gamma_d (1 + \omega)$.

≈≈≈≈≈≈≈≈≈≈

$$\frac{1}{2}\gamma_b BN_\gamma + cN_c + (P_q + \gamma_d D_f + \gamma_w (Y - D_f))(N_q - 1) = \frac{P}{B^2} FS \times Z \qquad \text{Equation No. 31}$$

in which $\gamma_b = \gamma_{sat} - \gamma_w$

The equation is entered as

31SHALFWTBETBS
(0.5(S−W)×B×N×I)+C×O×J+(M+D×E+W(Y−E))×(Q−1)=P÷B^2×F×Z

Where:

S = density of saturated soil γ_{sat} (lb/ft³, kN/m³)
W = unit weight of water γ_w (62.4 lb/ft³, 9.81 kN/m³)
B = width of square or continuous footing, or diameter of circular footing B (ft, m)
N = capacity factor N_γ
I = shape factor of N_γ (e.g., 0.85). The default value is 1.
C = cohesion c (lb/ft², kN/m²)
O = capacity factor N_c
J = shape factor of N_c (e.g., 1.25). The default value is 1.
M = surcharge P_q (lb/ft², kN/m²)
D = density of dry soil γ_d (lb/ft³, kN/m³)
E = depth of footing D_f (ft, m)
Y = distance from ground surface to water table Y (ft, m)
Q = capacity factor N_q
P = total allowable load P (lb, kN)
F = factor of safety FS
Z = 1 for square or continuous footing, 1.2732 for circular footing Z

Keystrokes

HP 35s Checksum; Length of Equation: **CK=5C02; LN=53**

[()] [·] [5] [()] [RCL] [S] [−] [RCL] [W] [>] [×] [RCL] [B] [×] [RCL] [N] [×] [RCL] [I] [>] [+] [RCL] [C] [×] [RCL] [O] [×] [RCL] [J] [+] [()] [RCL] [M] [+] [RCL] [D] [×] [RCL] [E] [+] [RCL] [W] [()] [RCL] [Y] [−] [RCL] [E] [>] [>] [×] [()] [RCL] [Q] [−] [1] [>] [↰] [=] [RCL] [P] [÷] [RCL] [B] [y^x] [2] [×] [RCL] [F] [×] [RCL] [Z] [ENTER]

HP 33s Checksum; Length of Equation: **CK=4682; LN=55**

[↱] [(] [·] [5] [×] [↱] [(] [RCL] [S] [−] [RCL] [W] [↱] [)] [×] [RCL] [B] [×] [RCL] [N] [×] [RCL] [I] [↱] [)] [+] [RCL] [C] [×] [RCL] [O] [×] [RCL] [J] [+] [↱] [(] [RCL] [M] [+] [RCL] [D] [×] [RCL] [E] [+] [RCL] [W] [×] [↱] [(] [RCL] [Y] [−] [RCL] [E] [↱] [)] [↱] [)] [×] [↱] [(] [RCL] [Q] [−] [1] [↱] [)] [↱] [=] [RCL] [P] [÷] [RCL] [B] [y^x] [2] [×] [RCL] [F] [×] [RCL] [Z] [ENTER]

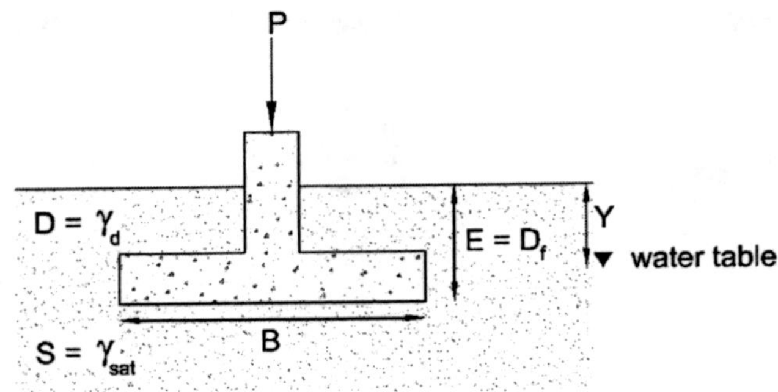

Figure 2-3 Shallow Foundation with Water Table Between the Bottom of Footing and Ground Surface

Notes: This equation, based on Terzaghi-Meyerhof theory, shall be used to calculate the net bearing capacity of square, continuous, and circular footings with water table between the bottom of footing and ground surface. The net bearing capacity is the soil bearing pressure at the bottom of footing neglecting the overburden pressure. The ultimate bearing capacity (this includes the overburden pressure) can be calculated by adding 1 to the N_q value before entering into equation.

The net or ultimate bearing capacity (lb/ft², kN/m²) can be computed by following these steps:

Press ENTER, then enter the value of D, press R/S, enter the value of B, press R/S, enter the value of N, press R/S, enter the value of I, press R/S, enter the value of C, press R/S, enter the value of O, press R/S, enter the value of J, press R/S, enter the value of M, press R/S, enter the value of Q, press R/S, enter 0 for P, press R/S, enter 0 for F, press R/S, and finally enter 0 for Z. B is the width of square or continuous footings, or diameter of circular footing.

This equation can also be used to calculate the allowable load, width of square footing or diameter of circular footing, and factor of safety. To determine the width of square footing or diameter of circular footing, press SOLVE B then enter the values of D, N, I, C, O, J, M, E, Q, P, F, and Z. This equation is not applicable for solving the width, allowable load, and factor of safety of continuous footing. To solve the width of continuous footing, the equation must be altered by adding × B on the right side of the equation.

If the buoyant unit weight of soil is given instead of the saturated density, transform the buoyant unit weight to saturated density by adding the unit weight of water (62.4 lb/ft³, 9.81 kN/m³). If the density of dry soil and moisture content are given, calculate the saturated density of soil by using the equation $\gamma_{sat} = \gamma_d(1+\omega)$.

≈≈≈≈≈≈≈≈≈≈

$$\frac{1}{2}\gamma_b BN_\gamma + cN_c + \gamma_d D_f (N_q - 1) = \frac{P}{B^2} FS \times Z \qquad \text{Equation No. 32}$$

in which $\gamma_b = \gamma_{sat} - \gamma_w$

The equation is entered as

32SHALFWTBOTT
(0.5(S−W)×B×N×I)+C×O×J+D×E(Q−1)=P÷B^2×F×Z

Where:

S = density of saturated soil γ_{sat} (lb/ft³, kN/m³)
W = unit weight of water γ_w (62.4 lb/ft³, 9.81 kN/m³)
B = width of square or continuous footing, or diameter of circular footing B (ft, m)
N = capacity factor N_γ
I = shape factor of N_γ (e.g., 0.85). The default value is 1.
C = cohesion c (lb/ft², kN/m²)
O = capacity factor N_c
J = shape factor of N_c (e.g., 1.25). The default value is 1.
D = density of dry soil γ_d (lb/ft³, kN/m³)
E = depth of footing D_f (ft, m)
Q = capacity factor N_q
P = total allowable load P (lb, kN)
F = factor of safety FS
Z = 1 for square or continuous footing, 1.2732 for circular footing Z

Keystrokes

HP 35s Checksum; Length of Equation: **CK=E23B; LN=41**

[()] [·] [5] [()] [RCL] [S] [−] [RCL] [W] [>] [×] [RCL] [B] [×] [RCL] [N] [×] [RCL] [I] [>] [+] [RCL] [C] [×] [RCL] [O] [×]
[RCL] [J] [+] [RCL] [D] [×] [RCL] [E] [()] [RCL] [Q] [−] [1] [>] [↰] [=] [RCL] [P] [÷] [RCL] [B] [y^x] [2] [×] [RCL] [F] [×]
[RCL] [Z] [ENTER]

HP 33s Checksum; Length of Equation: **CK=1C0C; LN=43**

[↱] [(] [·] [5] [×] [↱] [(] [RCL] [S] [−] [RCL] [W] [↱] [)] [×] [RCL] [B] [×] [RCL] [N] [×] [RCL] [I] [↱] [)] [+] [RCL]
[C] [×] [RCL] [O] [×] [RCL] [J] [+] [RCL] [D] [×] [RCL] [E] [×] [↱] [(] [RCL] [Q] [−] [1] [↱] [)] [↱] [=] [RCL] [P] [÷]
[RCL] [B] [y^x] [2] [×] [RCL] [F] [×] [RCL] [Z] [ENTER]

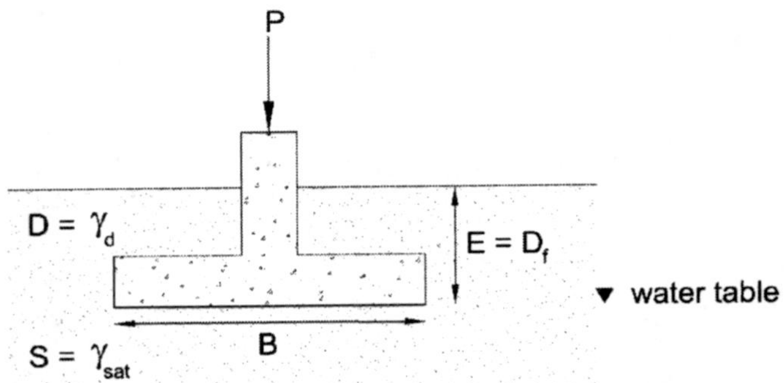

Figure 2-4 Shallow Foundation with Water Table at the Bottom of Footing

Notes: This equation, based on Terzaghi-Meyerhof theory, shall be used to calculate the net bearing capacity of square, continuous, and circular footings without water table. The net bearing capacity is the soil bearing pressure at the bottom of footing where the overburden pressure is insignificant. The ultimate bearing capacity (this includes the overburden pressure) can be calculated by adding 1 to the N_q value before entering into equation.

The net or ultimate bearing capacity (lb/ft^2, kN/m^2) can be obtained by executing the following exercise:

Press ENTER, then enter the value of D, press R/S, enter the value of B, press R/S, enter the value of N, press R/S, enter the value of I, press R/S, enter the value of C, press R/S, enter the value of O, press R/S, enter the value of J, press R/S, enter the value of M, press R/S, enter the value of Q, press R/S, enter 0 for P, press R/S, enter 0 for F, press R/S, and finally enter 0 for Z. B is the width of square or continuous footings, or diameter of circular footing.

This equation can also be used to calculate the allowable load, width of square footing or diameter of circular footing, and factor of safety. To determine the width of square footing or diameter of circular footing, press SOLVE B then enter the values of D, N, I, C, O, J, M, E, Q, P, F, and Z. This equation is not applicable for solving the width, allowable load, and factor of safety of continuous footing. To solve the width of continuous footing, the equation must be altered by adding × B on the right side of the equation.

If the buoyant unit weight of soil is given instead of the saturated density, assign S as the buoyant unit weight and W is zero. If the density of dry soil and moisture content are given, calculate the saturated density of soil by using the equation
$\gamma_{sat} = \gamma_d(1+\omega)$.

≈≈≈≈≈≈≈≈≈≈

2.5.1 One-way Eccentricity

$e = \frac{M}{P}$ Equation No. 33

in which $M = V \times Y + M$

The equation is entered as

33ELOADSQFTNG
E=(V×Y+M)÷P

Where:

E = eccentricity e (ft)
V = horizontal load V (kips)
Y = distance from horizontal load to bottom of footing Y (ft)
M = moment on column M (ft-kips)
P = load on column P (kips)

Keystrokes

HP 35s Checksum; Length of Equation: **CK=07E1; LN=11**

[RCL] [E] [↰] [=] [()] [RCL] [V] [×] [RCL] [Y] [+] [RCL] [M] [>] [÷] [RCL] [P] [ENTER]

HP 33s Checksum; Length of Equation: **CK=07E1; LN=11**

[RCL] [E] [↱] [=] [↱] [(] [RCL] [V] [×] [RCL] [Y] [+] [RCL] [M] [↱] [)] [÷] [RCL] [P] [ENTER]

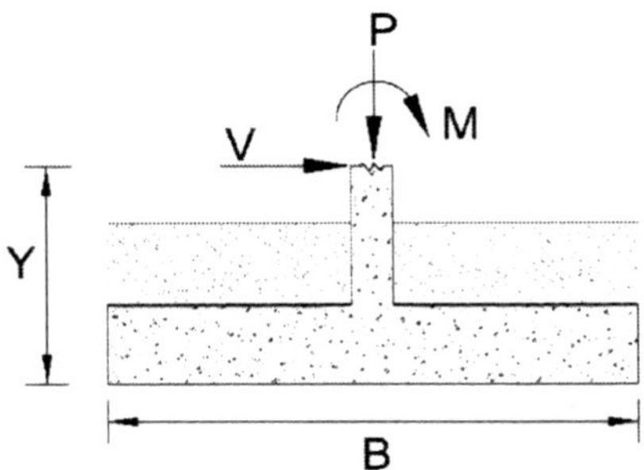

Figure 2-5a Eccentric Load on Square Footing (Elevation)

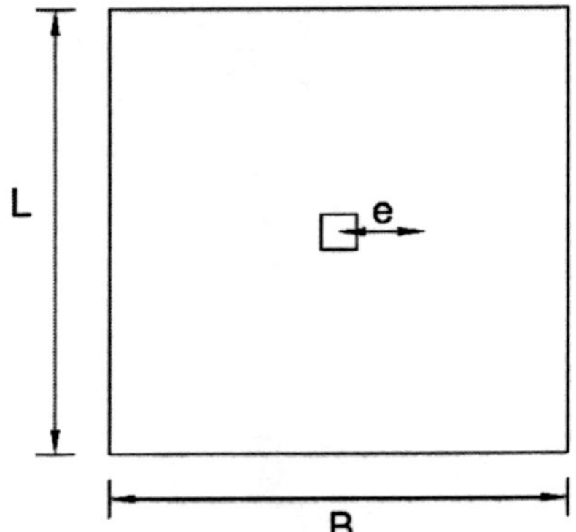

Figure 2-5b Eccentric Load on Square Footing (Plan)

≈≈≈≈≈≈≈≈≈≈

2.5.2 Maximum Contact Pressure on the Soil with Kern Greater Than Eccentricity

To calculate the maximum contact pressure on the soil for square footing with Kern (B/6) greater than eccentricity e, use the equation below.

$$Q_{\max} = \frac{P}{BL}\left(1 + \frac{6e}{B}\right)$$ Equation No. 34

The equation is entered as

34MAXSTKERNGTE
Q=P÷B÷L(1+6×E÷B)

Where:

Q = maximum contact pressure on the soil $Q_{\max}$ (kips/ft^2)
P = load on column P (kips)
B = width of footing B (ft)
L = length of footing L (ft)
E = eccentricity e (ft)

Keystrokes

HP 35s Checksum; Length of Equation: **CK=AA88; LN=16**

[RCL] [Q] [↰] [=] [RCL] [P] [÷] [RCL] [B] [÷] [RCL] [L] [()] [1] [+] [6] [×] [RCL] [E] [÷] [RCL] [B] [ENTER]

HP 33s Checksum; Length of Equation: **CK=F8CB; LN=17**

[RCL] [Q] [↱] [=] [RCL] [P] [÷] [RCL] [B] [÷] [RCL] [L] [×] [↱] [(] [1] [+] [6] [×] [RCL] [E] [÷] [RCL] [B] [↱] [)] [ENTER]

≈≈≈≈≈≈≈≈≈≈

2.5.3 Maximum Contact Pressure on the Soil with Kern Less Than Eccentricity

The maximum contact pressure on the soil for square footing with Kern (B/6) less than eccentricity e can be calculated using the equation below.

$$Q_{max} = \frac{4P}{3L(B-2e)}$$ Equation No. 35

The equation is entered as

35MAXSTKERNLTE
Q=4×P÷3÷L÷(B−2×E)

Where:

Q = maximum stress in soil Q_{max} (kips/ft²)
P = load on column P (kips)
L = length of footing L (ft)
B = width of footing B (ft)
E = eccentricity e (ft)

Keystrokes

HP 35s Checksum; Length of Equation: **CK=9CF1; LN=17**

[RCL] [Q] [↰] [=] [4] [×] [RCL] [P] [÷] [3] [÷] [RCL] [L] [÷] [()] [RCL] [B] [−] [2] [×] [RCL] [E] [ENTER]

HP 33s Checksum; Length of Equation: **CK=9CF1; LN=17**

[RCL] [Q] [↱] [=] [4] [×] [RCL] [P] [÷] [3] [÷] [RCL] [L] [÷] [↱] [(] [RCL] [B] [−] [2] [×] [RCL] [E] [↱] [)] [ENTER]

≈≈≈≈≈≈≈≈≈≈

Problem 2.1

The square footing shown below is required to support a structural dead plus live load of 100 kips. Consider the weight of a 4-inch thick concrete slab (not shown) with a unit weight of 150 lb/ft^3. The factor of safety with respect to net bearing capacity (using Terzaghi factors) is most nearly

Use 0.85 as shape factor of N_γ and 1.25 as shape factor of N_c

(A) 0.5
(B) 2
(C) 3
(D) 4

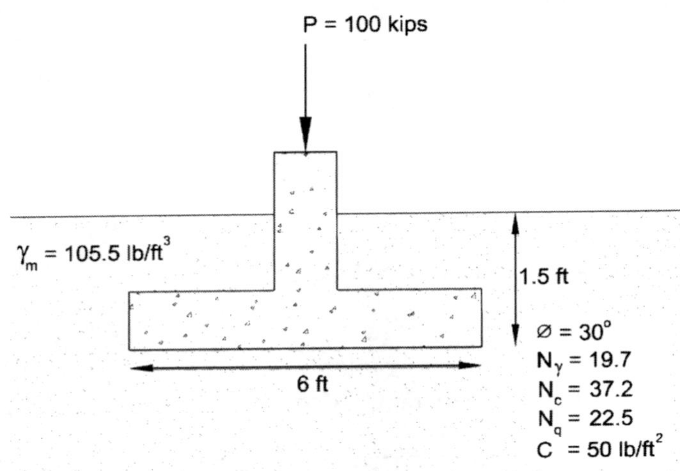

Solution

Calculate the factor of safety. Use Equation No. 29, page 43. Press SOLVE F.

Display	Keys	Description
D?	105.5 R/S	Density of moist soil γ_m (lb/ft^3)
B?	6 R/S	Width of footing (ft)
N?	19.7 R/S	Bearing capacity factor N_γ
I?	.85 R/S	Shape factor of N_γ
C?	50 R/S	Cohesion (lb/ft^2)
O?	37.2 R/S	Bearing capacity factor N_c
J?	1.25 R/S	Shape factor of N_c

Display	Keys	Description
M?	4 ENTER 12 ÷ 150 ×	Surcharge (lb/ft²)
M? 50.0000	R/S	
E?	1.5 R/S	Depth of footing (ft)
Q?	22.5 R/S	Bearing capacity factor N_q
P?	100000 R/S	Total load (lb)
Z?	1 R/S	1 for square footing
F = 4.3568	--	Factor of safety

The answer is (D).

Note: In the case of bearing capacity factors not given, they can be obtained from published tables based on the phi angle.

Problem 2.2

The allowable net bearing capacity of the square footing shown with a factor of safety of 3 is most nearly

(A) 5 kips/ft²
(B) 6 kips/ft²
(C) 7 kips/ft²
(D) 16 kips/ft²

Use a factor of safety of 3, 0.8 as shape factor of N_γ, and 1.3 as shape factor of N_c

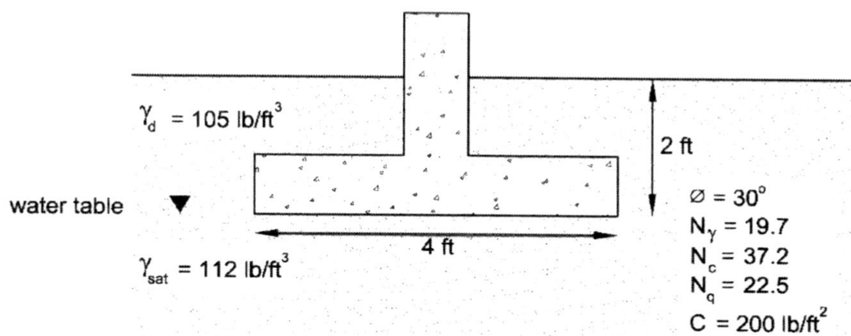

Solution

To calculate the allowable net bearing capacity of square footing with water table at the bottom of footing, first compute the net bearing capacity, and then divide the net bearing capacity by the factor of safety. Use Equation No. 32, page 49. Press ENTER.

Display	Keys	Description
S?	112 R/S	Saturated density of backfill soil (lb/ft^3)
W?	62.4 R/S	Unit weight of water (lb/ft^3)
B?	4 R/S	Width of footing (ft)
N?	19.7 R/S	Bearing capacity factor N_γ
I?	.8 R/S	Shape factor of N_γ
C?	200 R/S	Cohesion (lb/ft^2)
O?	37.2 R/S	Bearing capacity factor N_c
J?	1.3 R/S	Shape factor of N_c
D?	105 R/S	Dry density of backfill soil (lb/ft^3)
E?	2 R/S	Depth of footing (ft)
Q?	22.5 R/S	Bearing capacity factor N_q
P?	0 R/S	Column load set to zero
F?	0 R/S	Factor of safety set to zero
Z?	1 R/S	1 for square footing
1.0000 15,750.3920	--	Net bearing capacity of footing (lb/ft^2)
--	3 ÷	Divide the net bearing capacity by the factor of safety of 3
1.0000 5,250.1307 ←		Allowable net bearing capacity of footing (lb/ft^2)

The answer is (A).

Problem 2.3

Determine the width of the shallow square footing shown. The footing is to support a structural load of 100 kips with a factor of safety of 2. Ignore the correction for overburden.

(A) 3 ft
(B) 6 ft
(C) 7 ft
(D) 8 ft

Use 0.85 as shape factor of N_γ and 1.25 as shape factor of N_c

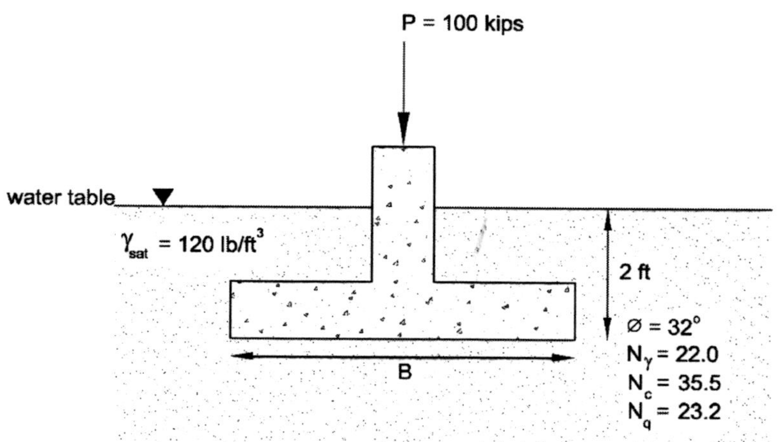

Solution

Solve the width of the ultimate bearing capacity of square footing with water table at the ground surface. Use Equation No. 30, page 45. Press SOLVE B.

Display	Keys	Description
S?	120 R/S	Saturated density of backfill soil (lb/ft³)
W?	62.4 R/S	Unit weight of water (lb/ft³)
N?	22 R/S	Bearing capacity factor N_γ
I?	.85 R/S	Shape factor of N_γ
C?	0 R/S	Cohesion (lb/ft²)
O?	35.5 R/S	Bearing capacity factor N_c
J?	1.25 R/S	Shape factor of N_c
E?	2 R/S	Depth of footing (ft)
Q?	24.2 R/S	Bearing capacity factor N_q
P?	100000 R/S	Column load (lb)
F?	2 R/S	Factor of safety
Z?	1 R/S	1 for square footing
B = 5.8583	--	Width of square footing (ft)

Note: The problem stated to ignore the correction for overburden. This means that the weight of the soil above the footing must be added (ultimate). Therefore, add 1 to the bearing capacity factor (N_q) before entering into equation (23.2 + 1).

The answer is (B).

Problem 2.4

A continuous footing is constructed 2 feet below the ground surface. The net bearing capacity (lb/ft²) using Terzaghi factors is most nearly

(A) 9 kips/ft²
(B) 10 kips/ft²
(C) 13 kips/ft²
(D) 15 kips/ft²

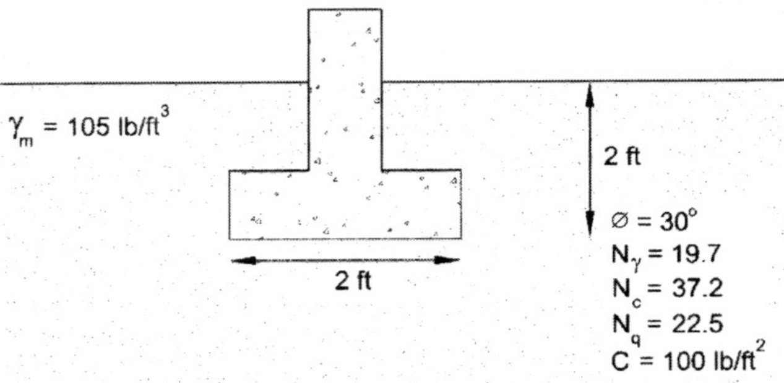

Solution

Calculate the net bearing capacity of continuous footing. Use Equation No. 29, page 43. Press ENTER.

Display	Keys	Description
D?	105 R/S	Density of moist soil γ_m (lb/ft³)
B?	2 R/S	Width of footing (ft)
N?	19.7 R/S	Bearing capacity factor N_γ
I?	1 R/S	Shape factor of N_γ
C?	100 R/S	Cohesion (lb/ft²)
O?	37.2 R/S	Bearing capacity factor N_c
J?	1 R/S	Shape factor of N_c
M?	0 R/S	Surcharge (lb/ft²)
E?	2 R/S	Depth of footing (ft)
Q?	22.5 R/S	Bearing capacity factor N_q
P?	0 R/S	Total load (lb)
F?	0 R/S	Factor of safety
Z?	1 R/S	1 for continuous footing
1.0000 10,303.5000 ◄	———	Net bearing capacity (lb/ft²)

The answer is (B).

Problem 2.5

A circular footing is designed to support 100 kips of column load. Assuming the water table will rise 1 foot above the bottom of footing. The overburden is insignificant. Use 2 as factor of safety, 0.85 as shape factor of N_γ, and 1.25 as shape factor of N_c. The diameter of the circular footing is most nearly

(A) 3 ft
(B) 6 ft
(C) 7 ft
(D) 8 ft

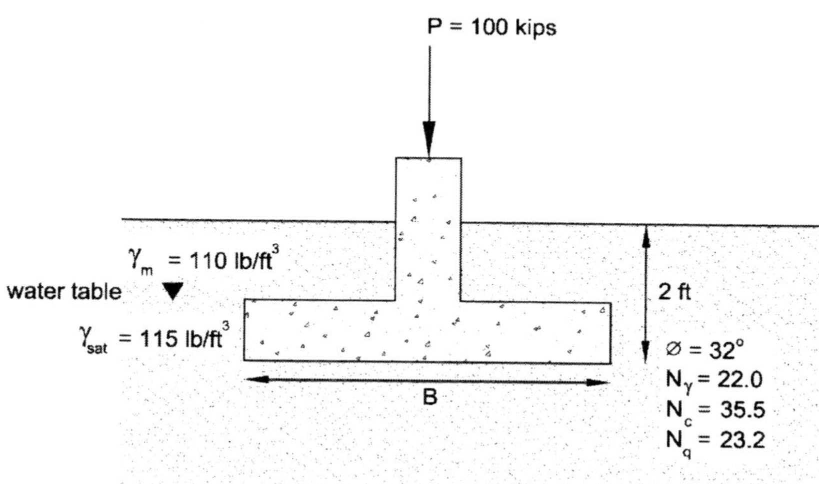

Solution

Solve the diameter of the circular footing with water table between the ground surface and the bottom of footing. Use Equation No. 31, page 47. Press SOLVE B.

Display	Keys	Description
S?	115 R/S	Saturated density of backfill soil (lb/ft^3)
W?	62.4 R/S	Unit weight of water (lb/ft^3)
N?	22 R/S	Bearing capacity factor N_γ
I?	.85 R/S	Shape factor of N_γ
C?	0 R/S	Cohesion (lb/ft^2)
O?	35.5 R/S	Bearing capacity factor N_c
J?	1.25 R/S	Shape factor of N_c
M?	0 R/S	Surcharge (lb/ft^2)
D?	110 R/S	Density of moist soil γ_m (lb/ft^3)
E?	2 R/S	Depth of footing (ft)
Y?	1 R/S	Distance from ground surface to water table Y (ft)

Display	Keys	Description
Q?	23.2 R/S	Bearing capacity factor N_q
P?	100000 R/S	Column load (lb)
F?	2 R/S	Factor of safety
Z?	1.2732 R/S	1.2732 for circular footing
B = 6.2292	--	Diameter of circular footing (ft)

The answer is (B).

Problem 2.6

A one-foot-thick square footing carries a dead load, a live load, and moments due to wind load and horizontal force. Use 150 lb/ft^3 for the density of concrete. The actual maximum contact pressure (lb/ft^2) on the soil including the weight of the footing is most nearly

(A) 4 kips/ft^2
(B) 6 kips/ft^2
(C) 8 kips/ft^2
(D) 10 kips/ft^2

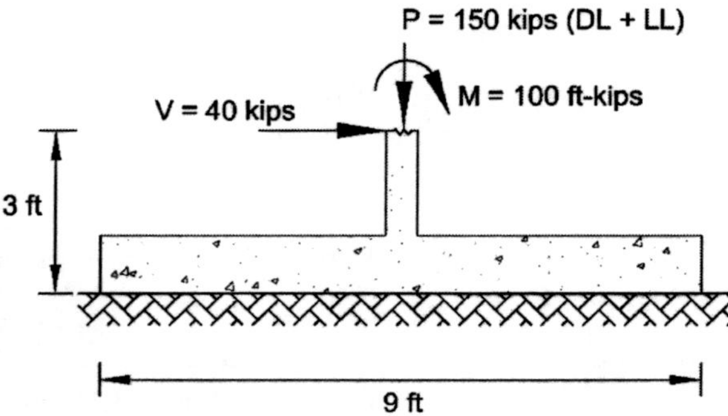

Solution

The following procedure can be used to calculate the maximum contact pressure on the soil.

Step 1. Calculate the eccentricity. Use Equation No. 33, page 51. Press ENTER.

Display	Keys	Description
V?	40000 R/S	Horizontal force (lb)
Y?	3 R/S	Distance from bottom of footing to horizontal force (ft)
M?	100000 R/S	Moment at the column (ft-lb)
P?	150000 ENTER 150 ENTER 9 × 9 × 1 × +	Dead load + live load + weight of footing (lb)
P? 162,150.0000	R/S	
E = 1.3568	--	Eccentricity (ft)

Step 2. Determine the Kern (B/6)

Kern = 9 ft / 6
Kern = 1.5 ft
Kern > e
1.5 ft > 1.3568 ft (compression will develop)

Step 3. Compute the maximum contact pressure on the soil. Use Equation No. 34, page 52. Press ENTER.

Display	Keys	Description
P? 162,150.0000	R/S	Dead load + live load + weight of footing (lb)
B?	9 R/S	Width of footing (ft)
L?	9 R/S	Length of footing (ft)
E? 1.3915	R/S	Eccentricity (ft)
Q = 3,812.5514	--	Maximum contact pressure on the soil (lb/ft^2)

The answer is (A).

Problem 2.7

A one-foot-thick square footing shown carries a dead load and live load of 150 kips and a moment due to wind load of 250 ft-kips. Use 150 lb/ft^3 for the density of concrete. The actual maximum contact pressure (lb/ft^2) on the soil including the weight of the footing is most nearly

(A) 4 kips/ft^2
(B) 6 kips/ft^2
(C) 8 kips/ft^2
(D) 12 kips/ft^2

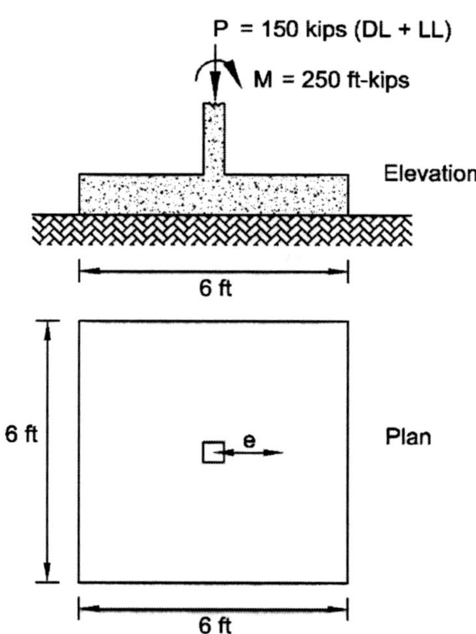

Solution

The step-by-step procedure for obtaining the maximum contact pressure is as follows:

Step 1. Calculate the eccentricity. Use Equation No. 33, page 51. Press ENTER.

Display	Keys	Description
V?	0 R/S	Horizontal force (lb)
Y?	0 R/S	Distance from bottom of footing to horizontal force (ft)
M?	250000 R/S	Moment at the column (ft-lb)
P?	150000 ENTER 150 ENTER 6 × 6 × 1 × +	Dead load + live load + weight of footing (lb)
P? 155,400.0000	R/S	
E = 1.6088	--	Eccentricity (ft)

Step 2. Determine the Kern (B/6)

Kern = 6 ft / 6
Kern = 1.0 ft
Kern < e
1.0 ft < 1.6088 ft (tension will develop)

Step 3. Compute the maximum contact pressure on the soil. Use Equation No. 35, page 53. Press ENTER.

Display	Keys	Description
P? 155,400.0000	R/S	Dead load + live load + weight of footing (lb)
L?	6 R/S	Length of footing (ft)
B?	6 R/S	Width of footing (ft)
E? 1.6088	R/S	Eccentricity (ft)
Q = 12,410.9158	--	Maximum contact pressure on the soil (lb/ft^2)

The answer is (D).

CHAPTER 3: MAT FOUNDATION

3.1 Gross Ultimate Bearing Capacity in Saturated Clay

$$Q_{ult} = 5.14c_u\left(1+\frac{0.195B}{L}\right)\left(1+\frac{0.4D_f}{B}\right)+q \qquad \text{Equation No. 36}$$

The equation is entered as

36MATSATCLAYGROSS
U=5.14×C(1+0.195×B÷L)×(1+0.4×E÷B)+D×E

Where:

U = gross ultimate bearing capacity Q_{ult} (lb/ft², kN/m²)

C = undrained cohesion of saturated clay c_u (lb/ft², kN/m²)

B = width of footing B (ft, m)
L = length of footing L (ft, m)
E = depth of mat foundation D_f (ft, m)

D = saturated soil density γ_{sat} (lb/ft³, kN/m³)

Keystrokes

HP 35s Checksum; Length of Equation: **CK=7028; LN=37**

[RCL] [U] [left-shift] [=] [5] [.] [1] [4] [×] [RCL] [C] [()] [1] [+] [.] [1] [9] [5] [×] [RCL] [B] [÷] [RCL] [L] [>] [×] [()] [1] [+] [.] [4] [×] [RCL] [E] [÷] [RCL] [B] [>] [+] [RCL] [D] [×] [RCL] [E] [ENTER]

HP 33s Checksum; Length of Equation: **CK=6689; LN=38**

[RCL] [U] [right-shift] [=] [5] [.] [1] [4] [×] [RCL] [C] [×] [right-shift] [(] [1] [+] [.] [1] [9] [5] [×] [RCL] [B] [÷] [RCL] [L] [right-shift] [)] [×] [right-shift] [(] [1] [+] [right-shift] [(] [.] [4] [×] [RCL] [E] [÷] [RCL] [B] [right-shift] [)] [+] [RCL] [D] [×] [RCL] [E] [ENTER]

Note: To solve for the net ultimate bearing capacity, D is zero.

≈≈≈≈≈≈≈≈≈≈

3.2 Depth of Fully Compensated Mat Foundation

$$D_f = \frac{Q}{BL\gamma}$$ Equation No. 37

The equation is entered as

37FULCOMPMATFOUND
E=Q÷B÷L÷D

Where:

E = depth of fully compensated foundation D_f (ft, m)
Q = total live load and dead load Q (lb, kN)
B = width of mat foundation B (ft, m)
L = length of mat foundation L (ft, m)
D = density of soil γ (lb/ft³, kN/m³)

Keystrokes

HP 35s Checksum; Length of Equation: **CK=4D99; LN=9**

[RCL] [E] [↰] [=] [RCL] [Q] [÷] [RCL] [B] [÷] [RCL] [L] [÷] [RCL] [D] [ENTER]

HP 33s Checksum; Length of Equation: **CK=4D99; LN=9**

[RCL] [E] [↱] [=] [RCL] [Q] [÷] [RCL] [B] [÷] [RCL] [L] [÷] [RCL] [D] [ENTER]

Notes: Fully compensated foundation is when the total load of the building including the mat foundation is equal to the weight of the excavated soil. This equation is applicable only for one type of soil without water table.

≈≈≈≈≈≈≈≈≈≈

Problem 3.1

What is most nearly the gross ultimate bearing capacity of a mat foundation with dimensions of 100 ft x 50 ft resting on saturated clay with a density of 115 lb/ft^3 and cohesion of 1,000 lb/ft^2? The depth of the mat is 7 feet below land surface.

(A) 6 kips/ft^2
(B) 7 kips/ft^2
(C) 8 kips/ft^2
(D) 9 kips/ft^2

Solution

Calculate the gross ultimate bearing capacity on saturated clay. Use Equation No. 36, page 63. Press ENTER.

Display	Keys	Description
C?	1000 R/S	Cohesion of saturated clay (lb/ft^2)
B?	50 R/S	Width of mat foundation (ft)
L?	100 R/S	Length of mat foundation (ft)
E?	7 R/S	Depth of mat foundation (ft)
D?	115 R/S	Density of saturated clay (lb/ft^3)
U = 6,762.0544	--	Gross ultimate bearing capacity (lb/ft^2)

The answer is (B).

Problem 3.2

What is most nearly the net ultimate bearing capacity of a mat foundation with dimensions of 90 ft × 55 ft resting on saturated clay with c_u of 800 lb/ft^2? The depth of the mat is 8 feet below land surface.

(A) 5 kips/ft^2
(B) 6 kips/ft^2
(C) 7 kips/ft^2
(D) 8 kips/ft^2

Solution

Compute the net ultimate bearing capacity on saturated clay. Use Equation No. 36, page 63. Press ENTER.

Display	Keys	Description
C?	800 R/S	Cohesion of saturated clay (lb/ft^2)
B?	55 R/S	Width of mat foundation (ft)
L?	90 R/S	Length of mat foundation (ft)
E?	8 R/S	Depth of mat foundation (ft)
D?	0 R/S	Density of saturated clay (lb/ft^3)
N = 4,869.7668	--	Net ultimate bearing capacity (lb/ft^2)

The answer is (A).

Problem 3.3

Determine the depth for a fully compensated mat foundation with dimensions of 100 ft x 100 ft constructed on clayey sand with a uniform density of 119 lb/ft^3. The total dead load and live load is 20,000 kips.

(A) 10 ft
(B) 12 ft
(C) 15 ft
(D) 17 ft

Solution

Calculate the depth for a fully compensated foundation. Use Equation No. 37, page 64. Press ENTER.

Display	Keys	Description
Q?	20000000 R/S	Total dead load and live load (lb)
B?	100 R/S	Width of mat foundation (ft)
L?	100 R/S	Length of mat foundation (ft)
D?	119 R/S	Density of clayey sand (lb/ft^3)
E = 16.8067	--	Depth of fully compensated foundation (ft)

The answer is (D).

CHAPTER 4: CONSOLIDATION SETTLEMENT

4.1 Settlement of Normally Consolidated Clay with up to 4 Layers of Soil Given Surcharge Load

$$S_{primary} = \frac{HC_c \log_{10}\left(\dfrac{p'_o + \Delta p'_v}{p'_o}\right)}{1 + e_o} \qquad \text{Equation No. 38}$$

The equation is entered as

38PRICONSET4LAYERS
S=T×U÷(1+V)×LOG((A×E+B×F+C×G+D×H+R)÷(A×E+B×F+C×G+D×H))

Where:

S = settlement $S_{primary}$ (ft, m)
T = thickness of clay layer H (ft, m)
U = compression index of clay layer C_c
V = void ratio of clay layer e_o
A = buoyant unit weight of soil at layer 1 γ_{b_1} (lb/ft^3, kN/m^3)
E = thickness of layer 1 (ft, m)
B = buoyant unit weight of soil at layer 2 γ_{b_2} (lb/ft^3, kN/m^3)
F = thickness of layer 2 (ft, m) (If this is the clay layer, use half of thickness)
C = buoyant unit weight of soil at layer 3 γ_{b_3} (lb/ft^3, kN/m^3)
G = thickness of layer 3 (ft, m) (If this is the clay layer, use half of thickness)
D = buoyant unit weight of soil at layer 4 γ_{b_4} (lb/ft^3, kN/m^3)
H = thickness of layer 4 (ft, m) (If this is the clay layer, use half of thickness)
R = surcharge stress due to fill (lb/ft^2, kN/m^2)

Keystrokes

HP 35s Checksum; Length of Equation: **CK=7E4B; LN=54**

[RCL] [S] [↰] [=] [RCL] [T] [×] [RCL] [U] [÷] [()] [1] [+] [RCL] [V] [>] [×] [↰] [LOG] [()] [RCL] [A] [×] [RCL] [E] [+] [RCL]
[B] [×] [RCL] [F] [+] [RCL] [C] [×] [RCL] [G] [+] [RCL] [D] [×] [RCL] [H] [+] [RCL] [R] [>] [÷] [()] [RCL] [A] [×] [RCL] [E]
[+] [RCL] [B] [×] [RCL] [F] [+] [RCL] [C] [×] [RCL] [G] [+] [RCL] [D] [×] [RCL] [H] [ENTER]

HP 33s Checksum; Length of Equation: **CK=7E4B; LN=54**

[RCL] [S] [↱] [=] [RCL] [T] [×] [RCL] [U] [÷] [↱] [(] [1] [+] [RCL] [V] [↱] [)] [×] [↰] [LOG] [↱] [(] [RCL] [A] [×] [RCL]
[E] [+] [RCL] [B] [×] [RCL] [F] [+] [RCL] [C] [×] [RCL] [G] [+] [RCL] [D] [×] [RCL] [H] [+] [RCL] [R] [↱] [)] [÷] [↱] [(]
[RCL] [A] [×] [RCL] [E] [+] [RCL] [B] [×] [RCL] [F] [+] [RCL] [C] [×] [RCL] [G] [+] [RCL] [D] [×] [RCL] [H] [↱] [)] [↱] [)]
[ENTER]

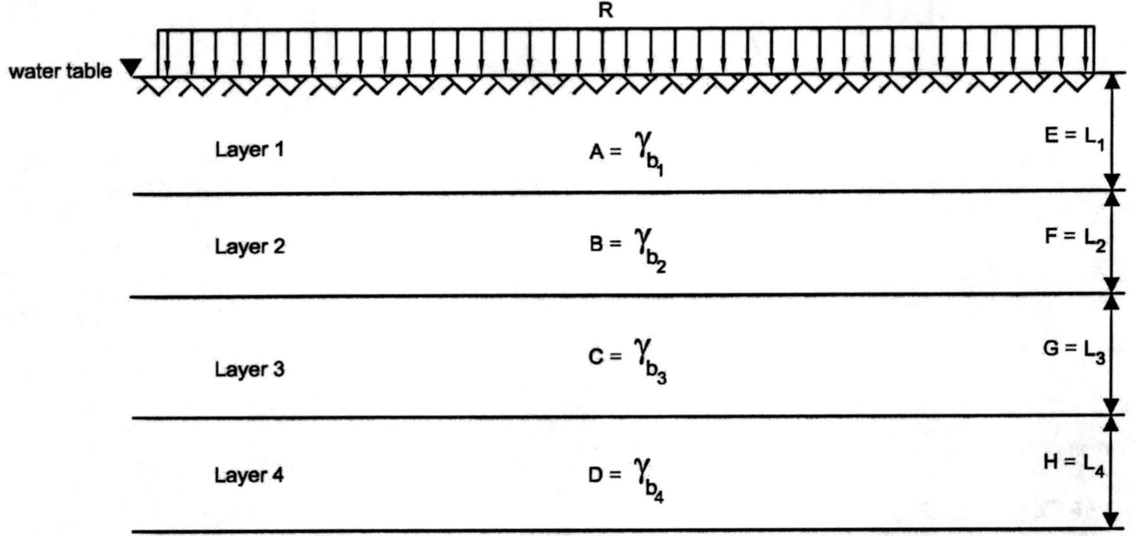

Figure 4-1 Consolidation Settlement with Surcharge Load

Note: If the soil layer is not submerged, use the moist unit weight.

≈≈≈≈≈≈≈≈≈≈

4.2 Settlement of Normally Consolidated Clay Given Overburden Pressure and Surcharge Load

$$S_{primary} = \frac{HC_c \log_{10}\left(\frac{p'_o + \Delta p'_v}{p'_o}\right)}{1 + e_o}$$ Equation No. 39

The equation is entered as

39PRICONSETOPSL
S=T×U÷(1+V)×LOG((O+R)÷O)

Where:

S = settlement $S_{primary}$ (ft, m)
T = thickness of clay layer H (ft, m)
U = compression index of clay layer C_c
V = void ratio of clay layer e_o
O = effective overburden stress at the middle of the clay layer P'_o (lb/ft², kN/m²)
R = stress increase due to surcharge $\Delta P'_v$ (lb/ft², kN/m²)

Keystrokes

HP 35s Checksum; Length of Equation: **CK=82CE; LN=24**

[RCL] [S] [←] [=] [RCL] [T] [×] [RCL] [U] [÷] [()] [1] [+] [RCL] [V] [>] [×] [←] [LOG] [()] [RCL] [O] [+] [RCL] [R] [>] [÷] [RCL] [O] [ENTER]

HP 33s Checksum; Length of Equation: **CK=82CE; LN=24**

[RCL] [S] [→] [=] [RCL] [T] [×] [RCL] [U] [÷] [→] [(] [1] [+] [RCL] [V] [→] [)] [×] [←] [LOG] [→] [(] [RCL] [O] [+] [RCL] [R] [→] [)] [÷] [RCL] [O] [→] [)] [ENTER]

≈≈≈≈≈≈≈≈≈≈

4.3 Settlement of Normally Consolidated Clay Layer after Lowering Water Table

$$S_{primary} = \frac{HC_c \log_{10}\left(\frac{p}{p'_o}\right)}{1+e_o} \quad \text{Equation No. 40}$$

The equation is entered as

40PRICONSETLOWT
S=T×U÷(1+V)×LOG(R÷O)

Where:

S = settlement $S_{primary}$ (ft, m)
T = thickness of clay layer H (ft, m)
U = compression index of clay layer C_c
V = void ratio of clay layer e_o
R = effective overburden stress at the middle of the clay layer after lowering water table p (lb/ft^2, kN/m^2)
O = effective overburden stress at the middle of the clay layer before lowering water table P'_o (lb/ft^2, kN/m^2)

Keystrokes

HP 35s Checksum; Length of Equation: **CK=526F; LN=20**

[RCL] [S] [←] [=] [RCL] [T] [×] [RCL] [U] [÷] [()] [1] [+] [RCL] [V] [>] [×] [←] [LOG] [RCL] [R] [÷] [RCL] [O] [ENTER]

HP 33s Checksum; Length of Equation: **CK=526F; LN=20**

[RCL] [S] [→] [=] [RCL] [T] [×] [RCL] [U] [÷] [→] [(] [1] [+] [RCL] [V] [→] [)] [×] [←] [LOG] [RCL] [R] [÷] [RCL] [O] [→] [)] [ENTER]

≈≈≈≈≈≈≈≈≈≈

4.4 Settlement of Mat Foundation on Normally Consolidated Clay

4.4.1 Settlement at the Center of Buried Mat Foundation

$$S_{center} = \frac{HC_c \log_{10}\left(\frac{p'_o + \Delta p'_v}{p'_o}\right)}{1+e_o} \qquad \text{Equation No. 41}$$

The equations are entered as

41MATSETCLCENTER
M=K÷2÷Y
N=L÷2÷Y
S=T×U÷(1+V)×LOG((A×E+B×F+C×G+D×H+(R−O)×4×I)÷(A×E+B×F+C×G+D×H))

Where:

M = m_1
K = width of mat (ft, m)
Y = distance from bottom of mat to center of clay layer (ft, m)
N = n_1
L = length of mat (ft, m)
S = settlement S_{center} (ft, m)
T = thickness of clay layer H (ft, m)
U = compression index of clay layer C_c
V = void ratio of clay layer e_o
A = total unit weight of soil at layer 1 γ (lb/ft^3, kN/m^3)
E = thickness of layer 1 (ft, m)
B = buoyant unit weight of soil at layer 2 γ_{b_2} (lb/ft^3, kN/m^3)
F = thickness of layer 2 (ft, m) (If this is the clay layer, use half of thickness)
C = buoyant unit weight of soil at layer 3 γ_{b_3} (lb/ft^3, kN/m^3)
G = thickness of layer 3 (ft, m) (If this is the clay layer, use half of thickness)
D = buoyant unit weight of soil at layer 4 γ_{b_4} (lb/ft^3, kN/m^3)
H = thickness of layer 4 (ft, m) (If this is the clay layer, use half of thickness)
R = uniform stress of mat (lb/ft^2, kN/m^2)
O = overburden pressure due to excavation (lb/ft^2, kN/m^2)
I = influence value (from published table based on m_1 and n_1)

Keystrokes

M=K÷2÷Y

HP 35s Checksum; Length of Equation: **CK=4882; LN=7**

[RCL] [M] [↰] [=] [RCL] [K] [÷] [2] [÷] [RCL] [Y] [ENTER]

HP 33s Checksum; Length of Equation: **CK=4882; LN=7**

[RCL] [M] [↱] [=] [RCL] [K] [÷] [2] [÷] [RCL] [Y] [ENTER]

N=L÷2÷Y

HP 35s Checksum; Length of Equation: **CK=F7D4; LN=7**

[RCL] [N] [↰] [=] [RCL] [L] [÷] [2] [÷] [RCL] [Y] [ENTER]

HP 33s Checksum; Length of Equation: **CK=F7D4; LN=7**

[RCL] [N] [↱] [=] [RCL] [L] [÷] [2] [÷] [RCL] [Y] [ENTER]

S=T×U÷(1+V)×LOG((A×E+B×F+C×G+D×H+(R−O)×4×I)÷(A×E+B×F+C×G+D×H))

HP 35s Checksum; Length of Equation: **CK=9905; LN=62**

[RCL] [S] [↰] [=] [RCL] [T] [×] [RCL] [U] [÷] [()] [1] [+] [RCL] [V] [>] [×] [↰] [LOG] [()] [RCL] [A] [×] [RCL] [E] [+] [RCL] [B] [×] [RCL] [F] [+] [RCL] [C] [×] [RCL] [G] [+] [RCL] [D] [×] [RCL] [H] [+] [()] [RCL] [R] [−] [RCL] [O] [>] [×] [4] [×] [RCL] [I] [>] [÷] [()] [RCL] [A] [×] [RCL] [E] [+] [RCL] [B] [×] [RCL] [F] [+] [RCL] [C] [×] [RCL] [G] [+] [RCL] [D] [×] [RCL] [H] [ENTER]

HP 33s Checksum; Length of Equation: **CK=9905; LN=62**

[RCL] [S] [↱] [=] [RCL] [T] [×] [RCL] [U] [÷] [↱] [(] [1] [+] [RCL] [V] [↱] [)] [×] [↰] [LOG] [↱] [(] [RCL] [A] [×] [RCL] [E] [+] [RCL] [B] [×] [RCL] [F] [+] [RCL] [C] [×] [RCL] [G] [+] [RCL] [D] [×] [RCL] [H] [+] [↱] [(] [RCL] [R] [−] [RCL] [O] [↱] [)] [×] [4] [×] [RCL] [I] [↱] [)] [÷] [↱] [(] [RCL] [A] [×] [RCL] [E] [+] [RCL] [B] [×] [RCL] [F] [+] [RCL] [C] [×] [RCL] [G] [+] [RCL] [D] [×] [RCL] [H] [↱] [)] [↱] [)] [ENTER]

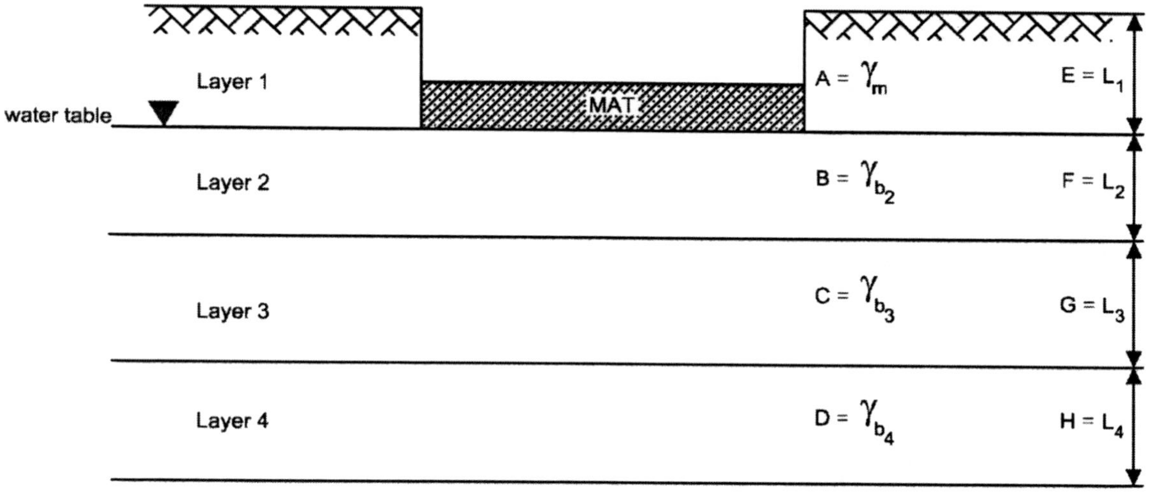

Figure 4-2 Mat Foundation Settlement on Normally Consolidated Clay

Notes: In the case of mat foundation not being buried, A, E, and O are zero. If the soil layer is not submerged, use the moist unit weight.

≈≈≈≈≈≈≈≈≈≈

4.4.2 Settlement at the Corner of Buried Mat Foundation

$$S_{corner} = \frac{HC_c \log_{10}\left(\frac{p'_o + \Delta p'_v}{p'_o}\right)}{1 + e_o}$$ Equation No. 42

The equations are entered as

42MATSETCLCORNER
M=K÷Y
N=L÷Y
S=T×U÷(1+V)×LOG((A×E+B×F+C×G+D×H+(R−O)×I)÷(A×E+B×F+C×G+D×H))

Where:

M = m_1
K = width of mat (ft, m)
Y = distance from bottom of mat to center of clay layer (ft, m)
N = n_1
L = length of mat (ft, m)
S = settlement S_{corner} (ft, m)
T = thickness of clay layer H (ft, m)
U = compression index of clay layer C_c
V = void ratio of clay layer e_o
A = total unit weight of soil at layer 1 γ (lb/ft^3, kN/m^3)
E = thickness of layer 1 (ft, m)
B = buoyant unit weight of soil at layer 2 γ_{b_2} (lb/ft^3, kN/m^3)
F = thickness of layer 2 (ft, m) (If this is the clay layer, use half of thickness)
C = buoyant unit weight of soil at layer 3 γ_{b_3} (lb/ft^3, kN/m^3)
G = thickness of layer 3 (ft, m) (If this is the clay layer, use half of thickness)
D = buoyant unit weight of soil at layer 4 γ_{b_4} (lb/ft^3, kN/m^3)
H = thickness of layer 4 (ft, m) (If this is the clay layer, use half of thickness)
R = uniform stress of mat (lb/ft^2, kN/m^2)
O = overburden pressure due to excavation (lb/ft^2, kN/m^2)
I = influence value (from published table based on m_1 and n_1)

Keystrokes

M=K÷Y

HP 35s Checksum; Length of Equation: **CK=2B54; LN=5**

[RCL] [M] [↰] [=] [RCL] [K] [÷] [RCL] [Y] [ENTER]

HP 33s Checksum; Length of Equation: **CK=2B54; LN=5**

[RCL] [M] [↱] [=] [RCL] [K] [÷] [RCL] [Y] [ENTER]

N=L÷Y

HP 35s Checksum; Length of Equation: **CK=4016; LN=5**

[RCL] [N] [↰] [=] [RCL] [L] [÷] [RCL] [Y] [ENTER]

HP 33s Checksum; Length of Equation: **CK=4016; LN=5**

[RCL] [N] [↱] [=] [RCL] [L] [÷] [RCL] [Y] [ENTER]

S=T×U÷(1+V)×LOG((A×E+B×F+C×G+D×H+(R−O)×I)÷(A×E+B×F+C×G+D×H))

HP 35s Checksum; Length of Equation: **CK=CC58; LN=60**

[RCL] [S] [↰] [=] [RCL] [T] [×] [RCL] [U] [÷] [()] [1] [+] [RCL] [V] [>] [×] [↰] [LOG] [()] [RCL] [A] [×] [RCL] [E] [+] [RCL] [B] [×] [RCL] [F] [+] [RCL] [C] [×] [RCL] [G] [+] [RCL] [D] [×] [RCL] [H] [+] [()] [RCL] [R] [−] [RCL] [O] [>] [×] [RCL] [I] [>] [÷] [()] [RCL] [A] [×] [RCL] [E] [+] [RCL] [B] [×] [RCL] [F] [+] [RCL] [C] [×] [RCL] [G] [+] [RCL] [D] [×] [RCL] [H] [ENTER]

HP 33s Checksum; Length of Equation: **CK=CC58; LN=60**

[RCL] [S] [↱] [=] [RCL] [T] [×] [RCL] [U] [÷] [↱] [(] [1] [+] [RCL] [V] [↱] [)] [×] [↰] [LOG] [↱] [(] [RCL] [A] [×] [RCL] [E] [+] [RCL] [B] [×] [RCL] [F] [+] [RCL] [C] [×] [RCL] [G] [+] [RCL] [D] [×] [RCL] [H] [+] [↱] [(] [RCL] [R] [−] [RCL] [O] [↱] [)] [×] [RCL] [I] [↱] [)] [÷] [↱] [(] [RCL] [A] [×] [RCL] [E] [+] [RCL] [B] [×] [RCL] [F] [+] [RCL] [C] [×] [RCL] [G] [+] [RCL] [D] [×] [RCL] [H] [↱] [)] [↱] [)] [ENTER]

Notes: If the mat foundation is not buried, A, E, and O are zero. If the soil layer is not submerged, use the moist unit weight.

≈≈≈≈≈≈≈≈≈≈

4.5 Time Rate of Settlement

$$t = \frac{T_v H^2}{C_v}$$ Equation No. 43

The equation is entered as

43TIMERATESET
T=V×H^2÷C

Where:

T = time t (sec, min, hour, day, year)
V = time factor T_v
H = thickness of clay layer, full layer if single-drained, half layer if double-drained H (ft, m)
C = coefficient of consolidation C_v (ft²/sec, m²/s)

Keystrokes

HP 35s Checksum; Length of Equation: **CK=AB4D; LN=9**

[RCL] [T] [↰] [=] [RCL] [V] [×] [RCL] [H] [y^x] [2] [÷] [RCL] [C] [ENTER]

HP 33s Checksum; Length of Equation: **CK=AB4D; LN=9**

[RCL] [T] [↱] [=] [=] [RCL] [V] [×] [RCL] [H] [y^x] [2] [÷] [RCL] [C] [ENTER]

≈≈≈≈≈≈≈≈≈≈

4.6 Slope Stability in Saturated Clay

$$F_{cohesive} = \frac{N_o c}{\gamma_{eff} H}$$ Equation No. 44

The equation is entered as

44SLOPESTABSCLAY
F=N×C÷S÷H

Where:

F = factor of safety $F_{cohesive}$

N = stability number N_o

C = cohesion of clay c (lb/ft^2, kN/m^2)

S = effective unit weight of saturated clay γ_{eff} (lb/ft^3, kN/m^3)

H = depth of the cut H (ft, m)

Keystrokes

HP 35s Checksum; Length of Equation: **CK=1720; LN=9**

[RCL] [F] [↰] [=] [RCL] [N] [×] [RCL] [C] [÷] [RCL] [S] [÷] [RCL] [H] [ENTER]

HP 33s Checksum; Length of Equation: **CK=1720; LN=9**

[RCL] [F] [↱] [=] [RCL] [N] [×] [RCL] [C] [÷] [RCL] [S] [÷] [RCL] [H] [ENTER]

≈≈≈≈≈≈≈≈≈≈

4.7 Cyclic Stress Ratio

$$\frac{\tau_{h,ave}}{\sigma'_o} \approx 0.65\left(\frac{a_{\max}}{g}\right)\left(\frac{\sigma_o}{\sigma'_o}\right)r_d \qquad \text{Equation No. 45}$$

The equation is entered as

45CYCLICSTRESS
C=0.65×A(T÷O)×R

Where:

C = cyclic stress ratio $\frac{\tau_{h,ave}}{\sigma'_o}$
A = maximum acceleration
T = total overburden pressure σ_o (lb/ft², kN/m²)
O = initial effective overburden stress σ'_o (lb/ft², kN/m²)
R = stress reduction factor r_d

Keystrokes

HP 35s Checksum; Length of Equation: **CK=B558; LN=15**

[RCL] [C] [↰] [=] [.] [6] [5] [×] [RCL] [A] [()] [RCL] [T] [÷] [RCL] [O] [>] [×] [RCL] [R] [ENTER]

HP 33s Checksum; Length of Equation: **CK=29F2; LN=16**

[RCL] [C] [↱] [=] [.] [6] [5] [×] [RCL] [A] [×] [↱] [(] [RCL] [T] [÷] [RCL] [O] [↱] [)] [×] [RCL] [R] [ENTER]

≈≈≈≈≈≈≈≈≈≈

Sample Problems

Problem 4.1

An embankment with a uniform vertical stress is to be placed to consolidate the clay layer in the soil profile shown. Assuming the clay layer is normally consolidated, what is most nearly the settlement of the embankment in inches?

(A) 12 in (C) 20 in
(B) 15 in (D) 22 in

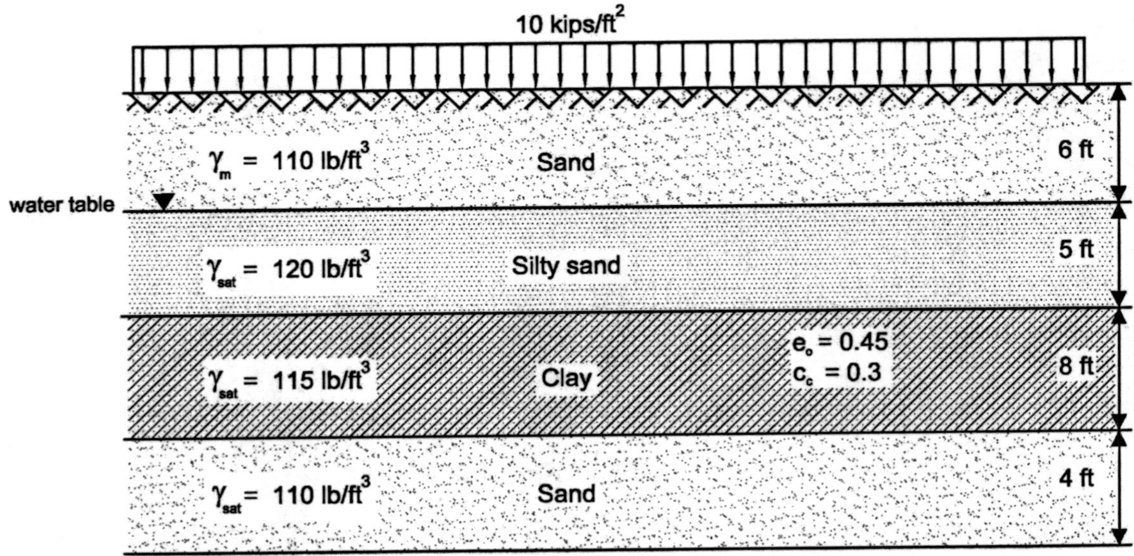

Solution

Option 1

Calculate the settlement of the embankment. Use Equation No. 38, page 67. Press ENTER.

Display	Keys	Description
T?	8 R/S	Thickness of clay layer (ft)
U?	.3 R/S	Compression index of clay layer
V?	.45 R/S	Void ratio of clay layer
A?	110 R/S	Moist unit weight of soil at layer 1 (lb/ft³)
E?	6 R/S	Thickness of layer 1 (ft)
B?	120 ENTER 62.4 –	Buoyant unit weight of soil at layer 2 (lb/ft³)
B? 57.6000	R/S	
F?	5 R/S	Thickness of layer 2 (ft)
C?	115 ENTER 62.4 –	Buoyant unit weight of soil at layer 3 (lb/ft³)
C? 52.6000	R/S	

Display	Keys	Description
G?	4 R/S	This is the clay layer, therefore use half of thickness (ft)
D?	0 R/S	Buoyant unit weight of soil at layer 4 (ignored)
H?	0 R/S	Thickness of layer 4 (ignored)
R?	10000 R/S	Stress increase due to embankment (lb/ft^2)
S = 1.6283	--	Settlement of embankment (ft)
--	12 ×	Multiply the settlement by 12 to convert ft to in
10,000.0000 19.5392 ←		Settlement of embankment (inches)

Option 2

Calculate the settlement of embankment. Use Equation No. 39, page 68. Press ENTER.

Display	Keys	Description
T?	8 R/S	Thickness of clay layer (ft)
U?	.3 R/S	Compression index of clay layer
V?	.45 R/S	Void ratio of clay layer
O?	110 ENTER 6 × 120 ENTER 62.4 – 5 × + 115 ENTER 62.4 – 4 × +	Effective overburden stress at the middle of the clay layer (lb/ft^2)
O? 1,158.4000	R/S	
R?	10000 R/S	Stress increase due to embankment (lb/ft^2)
S = 1.6283	--	Settlement of embankment (ft)
--	12 ×	Multiply the settlement by 12 to convert ft to in
10,000.0000 19.5392 ←		Settlement of embankment (inches)

The answer is (C).

Problem 4.2

An embankment is to be placed to consolidate the clay layer in the soil profile shown. Assume that the effective overburden stress at the middle of the clay layer is 2,000 lb/ft². The vertical pressure is expected to increase by 1,500 lb/ft². The settlement of the embankment in inches is most nearly

(A) 4 in (C) 8 in
(B) 6 in (D) 9 in

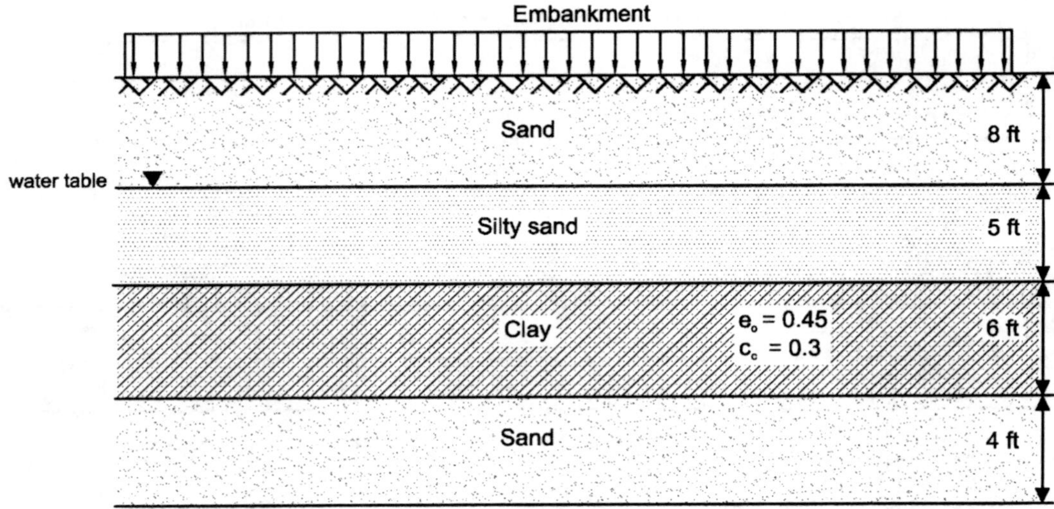

Solution

Compute the settlement of the embankment. Use Equation No. 39, page 68. Press ENTER.

Display	Keys	Description
T?	6 R/S	Thickness of clay layer (ft)
U?	.3 R/S	Compression index of clay layer
V?	.45 R/S	Void ratio of clay layer
O?	2000 R/S	Effective overburden stress at the middle of the clay layer (lb/ft²)
R?	1500 R/S	Vertical pressure increase (lb/ft²)
S = 0.3017	--	Settlement of embankment (ft)
--	12 ×	Multiply the settlement by 12 to convert ft to in
1,500.0000 3.6204 ←		 Settlement of embankment (inches)

The answer is (A).

Problem 4.3

A mat foundation 100 ft × 100 ft will be constructed 6 feet below the ground surface. The mat foundation will have a uniform stress load of 5,000 lb/ft². The clay is normally consolidated. The settlement in inches of the mat foundation directly below the center is most nearly

(A) 4 in (C) 8 in
(B) 6 in (D) 9 in

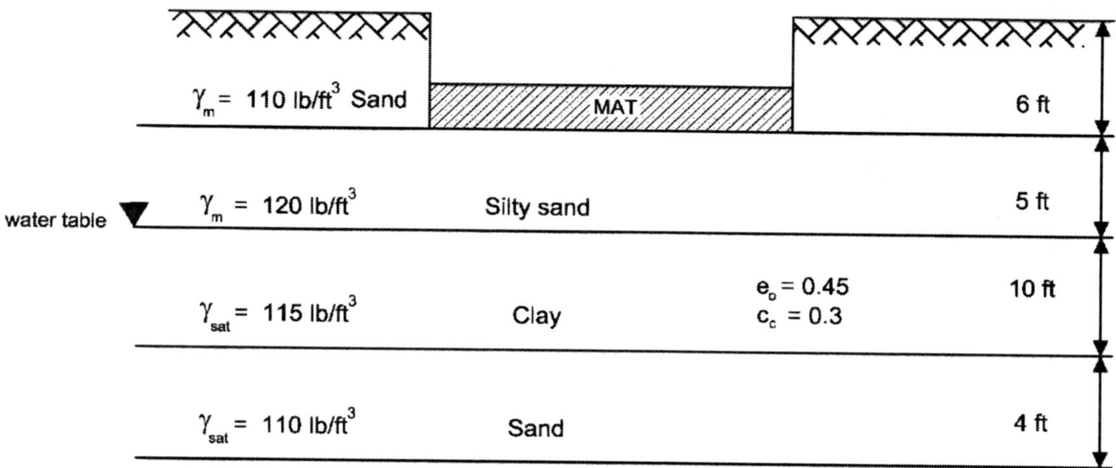

Solution

The settlement of mat foundation directly below the center can be calculated using the following procedure:

Step 1. Determine m_l. Use Equation No. 41 (M), page 70. Press ENTER.

Display	Keys	Description
K?	100 R/S	Width of mat foundation (ft)
Y?	10 R/S	Distance from the bottom of foundation to the center of clay layer (ft)
M = 5.0000	--	m_l

Step 2. Determine n_l. Use Equation No. 41 (N), page 70. Press ENTER.

Display	Keys	Description
L?	100 R/S	Length of mat foundation (ft)
Y? 10.0000	R/S	Distance from the bottom of foundation to the center of clay layer (ft)
N = 5.0000	--	n_l

Step 3. As the results of m_l and n_l values, the influence value is 0.24857 from published tables or charts.

Step 4. Calculate the settlement directly below the center of the mat foundation. Use Equation No. 41 (S), page 70. Press ENTER.

Display	Keys	Description
T?	10 R/S	Thickness of clay layer (ft)
U?	.3 R/S	Compression index of clay layer
V?	.45 R/S	Void ratio of clay layer
A?	110 R/S	Moist unit weight of soil at layer 1 (lb/ft³)
E?	6 R/S	Thickness of layer 1 (ft)
B?	120 R/S	Moist unit weight of soil at layer 2 (lb/ft³)
F?	5 R/S	Thickness of layer 2 (ft)
C?	115 ENTER 62.4 –	Buoyant unit weight of soil at layer 3 (lb/ft³)
C? 52.6000	R/S	
G?	5 R/S	This is the clay layer, therefore use half of the thickness (ft)
D?	0 R/S	Buoyant unit weight of soil at layer 4 (ignored)
H?	0 R/S	Thickness of layer 4 (ignored)
R?	5000 R/S	Uniform stress load (lb/ft²)
O?	5000 ENTER 110 ENTER 6 × –	Applied pressure minus overburden pressure (lb/ft²)
O? 4,340.0000	R/S	
I?	.24857 R/S	Influence value from published table based on m_1 and n_1
S = 0.3219	--	Settlement directly below the center of mat foundation (ft)
--	12 ×	Multiply the settlement by 12 to convert ft to in
0.2486 3.8632 ←		Settlement directly below the center of mat foundation (in)

The answer is (A).

Problem 4.4

The water table will be lowered to elevation +8 by dewatering. The soil above the water table once it is lowered is 105 lb/ft^3. The compression index and void ratio of the clay layer are 0.35 and 1.5, respectively. The settlement of the ground surface after lowering the water table is most nearly

(A) 3.2 in (C) 8 in
(A) 5 in (C) 9 in

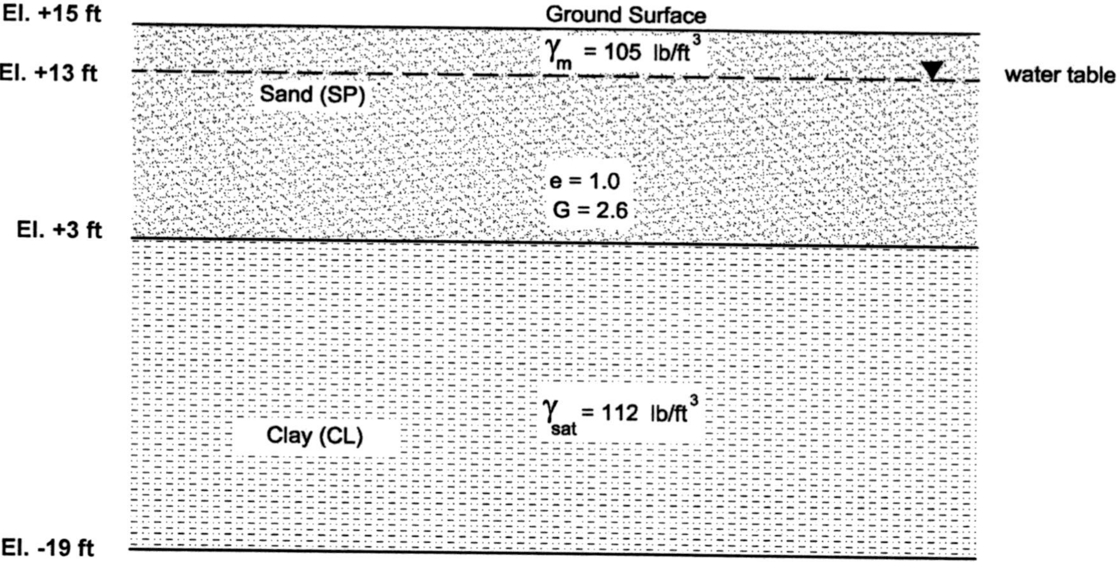

Solution

Calculate the settlement of the ground surface. Use Equation No. 40, page 69. Press ENTER.

Display	Keys	Description
T?	22 R/S	Thickness of the clay layer (ft)
U?	.35 R/S	Compression index of clay layer
V?	1.5 R/S	Void ratio of clay layer
R?	*	Effective overburden stress at the middle of the clay layer after lowering water table (lb/ft^2)
R? 1,530.2000	R/S	
O?	**	Effective overburden stress at the middle of the clay layer before lowering water table (lb/ft^2)
O? 1,254.8000	R/S	
S = 0.2654	--	Settlement of the ground surface (ft)
--	12 ×	Multiply the settlement by 12 to convert ft to in
1,254.8000 3.1850 ←		Settlement of the ground surface (inches)

* Keys for calculating effective stress after lowering water table using RPN:

105 ENTER 7 × 3.6 ENTER 62.4 × 2 ÷ 62.4 – 5 × + 112 ENTER 62.4 – 11 × +

** Keys for calculating effective stress before lowering water table using RPN:

105 ENTER 2 × 3.6 ENTER 62.4 × 2 ÷ 62.4 – 10 × + 112 ENTER 62.4 – 11 × +

The answer is (A).

Problem 4.5

A 6-foot-thick clay layer lies between two sand layers in the field that will be subject to consolidation. A clay sample was collected for consolidation test. At the laboratory, a 3-inch-thick clay sample yielded 85% consolidation in 10 minutes. The time for the 6-foot-thick clay layer to achieve 85% consolidation is most nearly

(A) 3 days
(B) 4 days
(C) 6 days
(D) 10 days

Solution

The following procedure can be used to determine the time for the clay layer to achieve 85% consolidation.

Step 1. Determine the coefficient of consolidation of the clay sample from the consolidation test. Use Equation No. 43, page 73. Press SOLVE C.

Display	Keys	Description
T?	600 R/S	Time for the 3-inch-thick clay sample to achieve 85% consolidation (sec)
V?	.684 R/S	Time factor for 85% consolidation
H?	3 ENTER 12 ÷ 2 ÷	Thickness of the clay sample in the laboratory, double-drained (ft)
H? 0.1250	R/S	
C = 1.7813E⁻5	--	Coefficient of consolidation (ft^2/sec)

Step 2. Calculate the time for the 6-foot-thick clay layer to achieve 85% consolidation. Use Equation No. 43, page 73. Press ENTER.

Display	Keys	Description
V? 0.6840	R/S	Time factor for 85% consolidation
H?	6 ENTER 2 ÷	Thickness of the clay layer in the field, double-drained (ft)
H? 3.0000	R/S	
C = 1.7813E⁻5	R/S	Coefficient of consolidation (ft^2/sec)

Display	Keys	Description
T = 345,600.0000	--	Time for the 6-foot-thick clay sample to achieve 85% consolidation (sec)
--	86400 ÷	Divide the time for consolidation by 86400 to convert sec to days
1.7813E⁻5 4.0000 ←		Time for the 6-foot-thick clay sample to achieve 85% consolidation (days)

The answer is (B).

Problem 4.6

The factor of safety for the slope stability shown below is most nearly

(A) 1
(B) 1.5
(C) 2
(D) 2.5

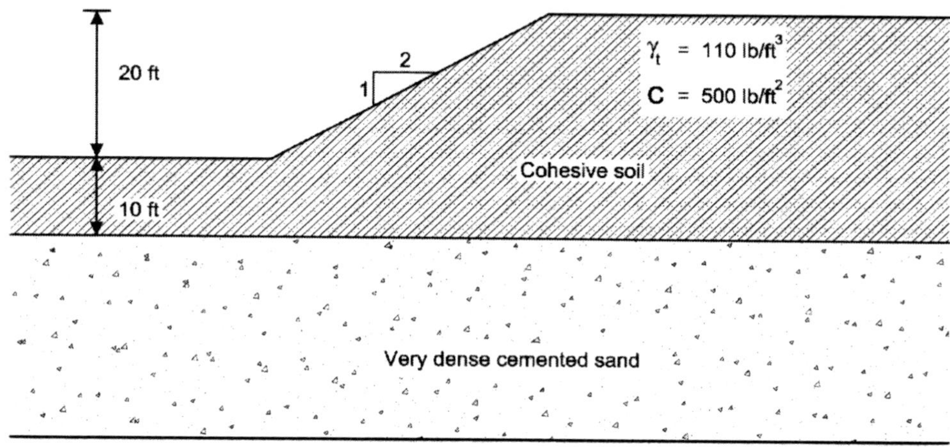

Solution

Calculate the factor of safety. Use Equation No. 44, page 74. Press ENTER.

Display	Keys	Description
N?	10 ENTER 20 ÷	Stability number (6.6) obtained from Taylor chart with the slope angle of 26.6° and depth ratio of 0.5
N? 0.5000	6.6 R/S	
C?	500 R/S	Cohesion of soil (lb/ft²)
S?	110 R/S	Density of soil (lb/ft³)
H?	20 R/S	Height of cut (ft)
F = 1.5	--	Factor of safety

The answer is (B).

Problem 4.7

A subsurface profile shown is located within an earthquake prone area. What is most nearly the cyclic stress ratio within the middle of silty sand layer if the ground surface experiences a peak acceleration of 0.42g and a stress reduction factor of 0.9?

(A) 0.2
(B) 0.3
(C) 0.4
(D) 0.5

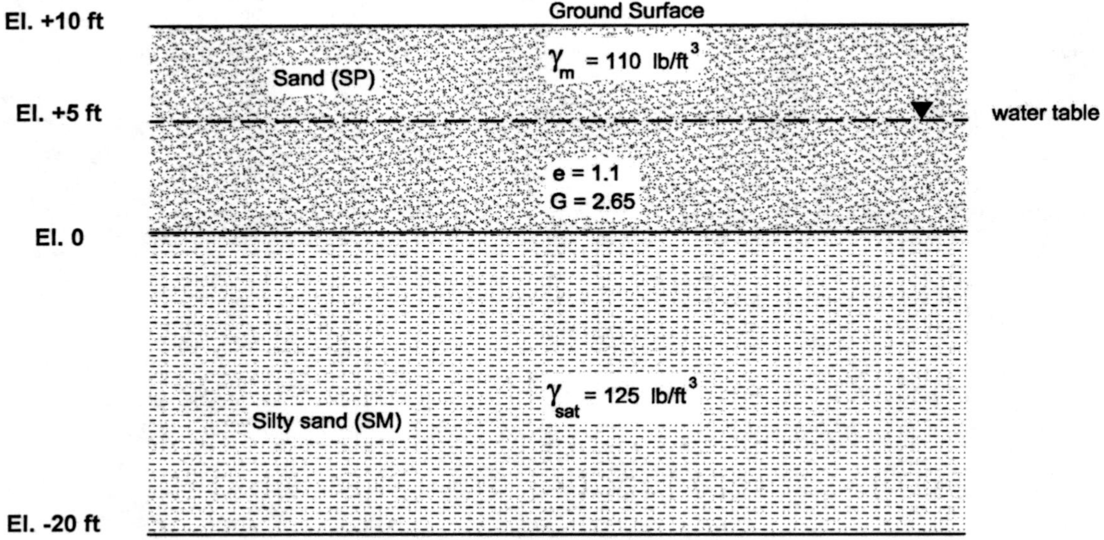

Solution

Compute the cyclic stress ratio. Use Equation No. 45, page 75. Press ENTER.

Display	Keys	Description
A?	.42 R/S	Peak acceleration
T?	*	Total overburden pressure at the middle of the silty sand layer (lb/ft^2)
T? 2,357.1429	R/S	
O?	**	Initial effective overburden stress at the middle of the silty sand layer (lb/ft^2)
O? 1,421.1429	R/S	
R?	.9 R/S	Stress reduction factor
C = 0.4075	--	Cyclic stress ratio

The answer is (C).

* Keys for calculating total overburden pressure using RPN:

110 ENTER 5 × 3.75 ENTER 62.4 × 2.1 ÷ 5 × + 125 ENTER 10 × +

$$\sigma = \left(110\frac{lb}{ft^3}\right)(5\,ft) + \left(\frac{(1.1+2.65)\left(62.4\frac{lb}{ft^3}\right)}{1+1.1}\right)(5\,ft) + \left(125\frac{lb}{ft^3}\right)(10\,ft)$$

$$\sigma = 2{,}357.1429\frac{lb}{ft^2}$$

** Keys for calculating initial effective stress using RPN:

R↓ 62.4 ENTER 15 × −

$$\sigma' = 2{,}357.1429\frac{lb}{ft^2} - \left(62.4\frac{lb}{ft^3}\right)(15\,ft)$$

$$\sigma' = 1{,}421.1429\frac{lb}{ft^2}$$

CHAPTER 5: LATERAL EARTH PRESSURE

5.1 Lateral Force Given Equivalent Fluid Pressures of Backfill

Equation No. 46 below has 3 equations; P is the total lateral force per unit length of wall, $\bar{y}$ is the location of resultant lateral force from the bottom of wall, and O is the moment from the bottom of wall. Equivalent fluid pressures can be active, passive, or at-rest.

$$P = QX + \frac{1}{2}AX^2 + QZ + AXZ + \frac{1}{2}BZ^2 + \frac{1}{2}\gamma_w Z^2$$ Equation No. 46 (P)

$$\bar{y} = \frac{QX\left(Z + \frac{X}{2}\right) + \frac{1}{2}AX^2\left(Z + \frac{X}{3}\right) + QZ\left(\frac{Z}{2}\right) + AXZ\left(\frac{Z}{3}\right) + \frac{1}{2}BZ^2\left(\frac{Z}{3}\right) + \frac{1}{2}\gamma_w Z^2\left(\frac{Z}{3}\right)}{P}$$ Equation No. 46 (Y)

$$O = P\bar{y}$$ Equation No. 46 (O)

The equations are entered as

46LATFOREQFLUID
P=Q×X+0.5×A×X^2+Q×Z+A×X×Z+0.5×B×Z^2+0.5×W×Z^2
Y=(Q×X(Z+X÷2)+0.5×A×X^2(Z+X÷3)+Q×Z^2÷2+A×X×Z^2÷3+0.5×B×Z^3÷3+0.5×W×Z^3÷3)÷P
O=P×Y

Where:

P = total lateral force per unit length of wall P (lb/ft, kN/m)
Q = surcharge load Q (lb/ft^2, kN/m^2)
X = distance from top of backfill to water table X (ft, m)
A = equivalent fluid pressure of backfill above water table A (lb/ft^3, kN/m^3)
Z = distance from water table to the bottom of wall Z (ft, m)
B = equivalent fluid pressure of backfill below water table B (lb/ft^3, kN/m^3)
W = unit weight of water γ_w (62.4 lb/ft^3, 9.81 kN/m^3)
Y = location of resultant lateral force from the bottom of wall $\bar{y}$ (ft, m)
O = moment at the bottom of wall O (ft-lb, kN-m)

Keystrokes

P=Q×X+0.5×A×X^2+Q×Z+A×X×Z+0.5×B×Z^2+0.5×W×Z^2

HP 35s Checksum; Length of Equation: **CK=6649; LN=45**

[RCL] [P] [↰] [=] [RCL] [Q] [×] [RCL] [X] [+] [·] [5] [×] [RCL] [A] [×] [RCL] [X] [y^x] [2] [+] [RCL] [Q] [×] [RCL] [Z] [+]
[RCL] [A] [×] [RCL] [X] [×] [RCL] [Z] [+] [·] [5] [×] [RCL] [B] [×] [RCL] [Z] [y^x] [2] [+] [·] [5] [×] [RCL] [W] [×] [RCL] [Z]
[y^x] [2] [ENTER]

HP 33s Checksum; Length of Equation: **CK=6649; LN=45**

[RCL] [P] [↱] [=] [RCL] [Q] [×] [RCL] [X] [+] [·] [5] [×] [RCL] [A] [×] [RCL] [X] [y^x] [2] [+] [RCL] [Q] [×] [RCL] [Z] [+]
[RCL] [A] [×] [RCL] [X] [×] [RCL] [Z] [+] [·] [5] [×] [RCL] [B] [×] [RCL] [Z] [y^x] [2] [+] [·] [5] [×] [RCL] [W] [×] [RCL] [Z]
[y^x] [2] [ENTER]

Y=(Q×X(Z+X÷2)+0.5×A×X^2(Z+X÷3)+Q×Z^2÷2+A×X×Z^2÷3+0.5×B×Z^3÷3+0.5×W×Z^3÷3)÷P

HP 35s Checksum; Length of Equation: **CK=BAD0; LN=75**

[RCL] [Y] [↰] [=] [()] [RCL] [Q] [×] [RCL] [X] [()] [RCL] [Z] [+] [RCL] [X] [÷] [2] [>] [+] [·] [5] [×] [RCL] [A] [×] [RCL]
[X] [y^x] [2] [()] [RCL] [Z] [+] [RCL] [X] [÷] [3] [>] [+] [RCL] [Q] [×] [RCL] [Z] [y^x] [2] [÷] [2] [+] [RCL] [A] [×] [RCL] [X]
[×] [RCL] [Z] [y^x] [2] [÷] [3] [+] [·] [5] [×] [RCL] [B] [×] [RCL] [Z] [y^x] [3] [÷] [3] [+] [·] [5] [×] [RCL] [W] [×] [RCL] [Z]
[y^x] [3] [÷] [3] [>] [÷] [RCL] [P] [ENTER]

HP 33s Checksum; Length of Equation: **CK=1A32; LN=77**

[RCL] [Y] [↱] [=] [↱] [(] [RCL] [Q] [×] [RCL] [X] [×] [↱] [(] [RCL] [Z] [+] [RCL] [X] [÷] [2] [↱] [)] [+] [·] [5] [×]
[RCL] [A] [×] [RCL] [X] [y^x] [2] [×] [↱] [(] [RCL] [Z] [+] [RCL] [X] [÷] [3] [↱] [)] [+] [RCL] [Q] [×] [RCL] [Z] [y^x] [2] [÷]
[2] [+] [RCL] [A] [×] [RCL] [X] [×] [RCL] [Z] [y^x] [2] [÷] [3] [+] [·] [5] [×] [RCL] [B] [×] [RCL] [Z] [y^x] [3] [÷] [3] [+] [·]
[5] [×] [RCL] [W] [×] [RCL] [Z] [y^x] [3] [÷] [3] [↱] [)] [÷] [RCL] [P] [ENTER]

O=P×Y

HP 35s Checksum; Length of Equation: **CK=8916; LN=5**

[RCL] [O] [↰] [=] [RCL] [P] [×] [RCL] [Y] [ENTER]

HP 33s Checksum; Length of Equation: **CK=8916; LN=5**

[RCL] [O] [↱] [=] [RCL] [P] [×] [RCL] [Y] [ENTER]

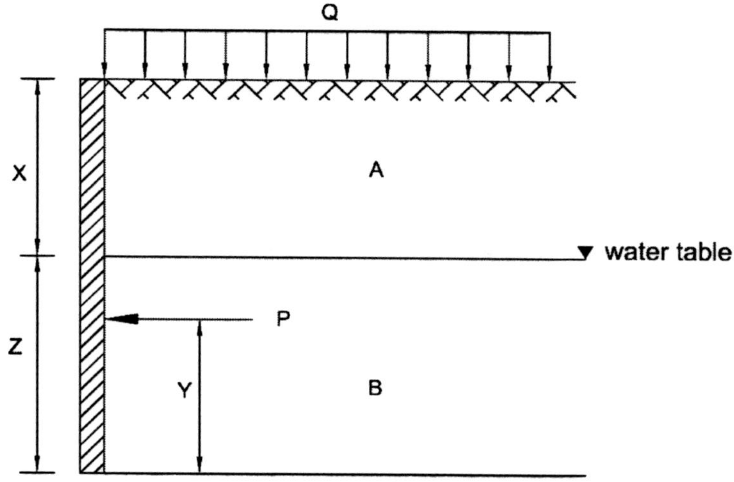

Figure 5-1 Lateral Force Given Equivalent Fluid Pressures of Backfill

Notes: If there is no surcharge load, then Q is zero. If there is no water table, then W is zero.

≈≈≈≈≈≈≈≈≈≈

5.2 Active Earth Pressure Coefficient

5.2.1 Rankine Active Earth Pressure Coefficient for Horizontal Backfill and Vertical Wall

$$K_a = \tan^2\left(45 - \frac{\phi}{2}\right)$$ Equation No. 47

The equation is entered as

47RANACTCOEFFI
K=TAN(45−A÷2)^2

Where:

K = Rankine active earth pressure coefficient K_a
A = angle of internal friction of backfill ϕ

Keystrokes

HP 35s Checksum; Length of Equation: **CK=8CDE; LN=15**

[RCL] [K] [↰] [=] [TAN] [4] [5] [−] [RCL] [A] [÷] [2] [>] [y^x] [2] [ENTER]

HP 33s Checksum; Length of Equation: **CK=8CDE; LN=15**

[RCL] [K] [↱] [=] [TAN] [4] [5] [−] [RCL] [A] [÷] [2] [↱] [ )] [y^x] [2] [ENTER]

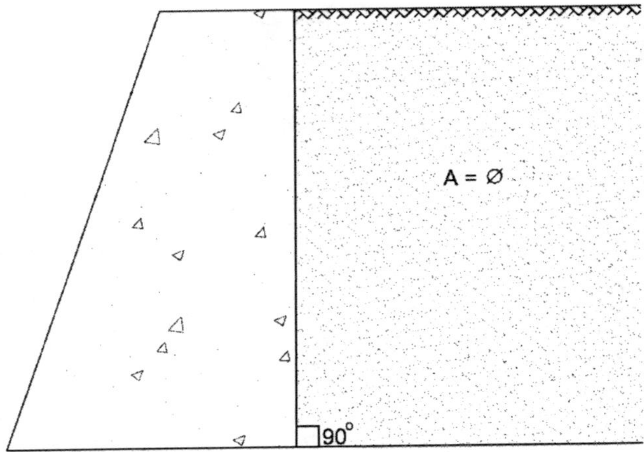

Figure 5-2 Rankine Active Earth Pressure with Horizontal Backfill and Vertical Wall

≈≈≈≈≈≈≈≈≈≈

5.2.2 Rankine Active Earth Pressure Coefficient for Sloping Backfill and Frictionless Vertical Wall

$$K_a = \cos\alpha \frac{\cos\alpha - \sqrt{\cos^2\alpha - \cos^2\phi}}{\cos\alpha + \sqrt{\cos^2\alpha - \cos^2\phi}}$$ Equation No. 48

The equation is entered as

48RANACTCOSBVW
K=COS(I)×(COS(I)−(COS(I)^2−COS(A)^2)^0.5)÷(COS(I)+(COS(I)^2−COS(A)^2)^0.5)

Where:

K = Rankine active earth pressure coefficient K_a
I = angle of sloping backfill from horizontal α
A = angle of internal friction of backfill ϕ

Keystrokes

HP 35s Checksum; Length of Equation: **CK=A1C8; LN=74**

[RCL] [K] [↰] [=] [COS] [RCL] [I] [>] [×] [()] [COS] [RCL] [I] [>] [−] [()] [COS] [RCL] [I] [>] [yˣ] [2] [−] [COS] [RCL] [A] [>] [yˣ] [2] [>] [yˣ] [.] [5] [>] [÷] [()] [COS] [RCL] [I] [>] [+] [()] [COS] [RCL] [I] [>] [yˣ] [2] [−] [COS] [RCL] [A] [>] [yˣ] [2] [>] [yˣ] [.] [5] [ENTER]

HP 33s Checksum; Length of Equation: **CK=FCB3; LN=74**

[RCL] [K] [↱] [=] [COS] [RCL] [I] [↱] [)] [×] [↱] [(] [COS] [RCL] [I] [↱] [)] [−] [↱] [(] [COS] [RCL] [I] [↱] [)] [yˣ] [2] [−] [COS] [RCL] [A] [↱] [)] [yˣ] [2] [↱] [)] [yˣ] [.] [5] [↱] [)] [÷] [↱] [(] [COS] [RCL] [I] [↱] [)] [+] [↱] [(] [COS] [RCL] [I] [↱] [)] [yˣ] [2] [−] [COS] [RCL] [A] [↱] [)] [yˣ] [2] [↱] [)] [yˣ] [.] [5] [↱] [)] [ENTER]

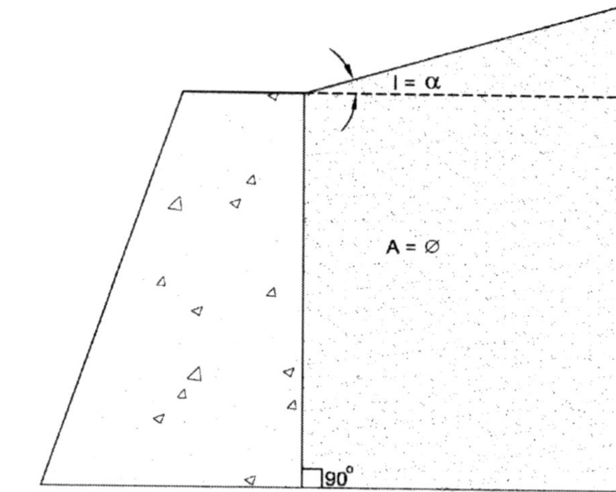

Figure 5-3 Rankine Active Earth Pressure with Sloping Backfill and Vertical Wall

≈≈≈≈≈≈≈≈≈≈

5.3 Active Earth Pressure

5.3.1 Active Earth Pressure for Horizontal Backfill and Vertical Wall

$\sigma_a = \gamma H K_a - 2c\sqrt{K_a}$ Equation No. 49

The equation is entered as

49ACTEARTHPRESS
P=S×H×K−2×C×K^0.5

Where:

P = active earth pressure per unit length of wall σ_a (lb/ft^2, kN/m^2)
S = density of backfill γ (lb/ft^3, kN/m^3)
H = height of backfill H (ft, m)
K = Rankine active earth pressure coefficient K_a
C = cohesion of backfill c (lb/ft^2, kN/m^2)

Keystrokes

HP 35s Checksum; Length of Equation: **CK=7824; LN=17**

[RCL] [P] [↰] [=] [RCL] [S] [×] [RCL] [H] [×] [RCL] [K] [−] [2] [×] [RCL] [C] [×] [RCL] [K] [yˣ] [·] [5] [ENTER]

HP 33s Checksum; Length of Equation: **CK=7824; LN=17**

[RCL] [P] [↱] [=] [RCL] [S] [×] [RCL] [H] [×] [RCL] [K] [−] [2] [×] [RCL] [C] [×] [RCL] [K] [yˣ] [·] [5] [ENTER]

≈≈≈≈≈≈≈≈≈≈

5.4 Active Lateral Force

5.4.1 Active Lateral Force

$$P_a = \frac{1}{2}\gamma H^2 K_a \qquad \text{Equation No. 50}$$

The equation is entered as

50ACTLATFORCE
P=0.5×S×H^2×K

Where:

P = active lateral force per unit length of wall P_a (lb/ft, kN/m)
S = density of backfill γ (lb/ft^3, kN/m^3)
H = height of backfill H (ft, m)
K = Rankine active earth pressure coefficient K_a

Keystrokes

HP 35s Checksum; Length of Equation: **CK=880B; LN=13**

[RCL] [P] [↰] [=] [·] [5] [×] [RCL] [S] [×] [RCL] [H] [y^x] [2] [×] [RCL] [K] [ENTER]

HP 33s Checksum; Length of Equation: **CK=880B; LN=13**

[RCL] [P] [↱] [=] [·] [5] [×] [RCL] [S] [×] [RCL] [H] [y^x] [2] [×] [RCL] [K] [ENTER]

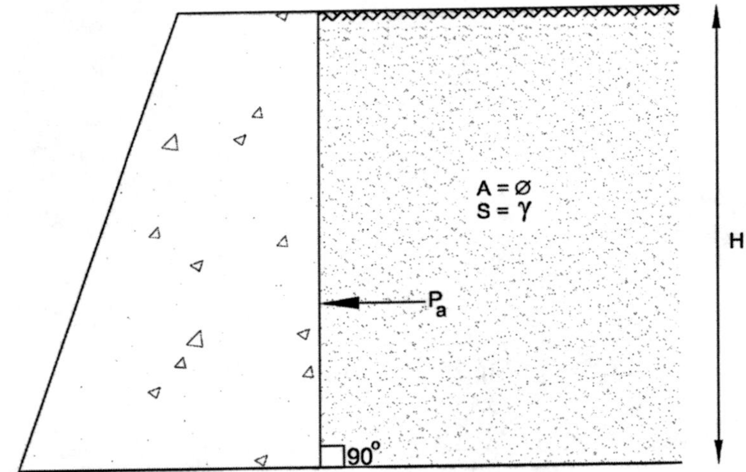

Figure 5-4 Active Lateral Force with Horizontal Backfill and Vertical Wall

Notes: The active lateral force per unit length of vertical wall with sloping backfill can be obtained by first calculating the Rankine active earth pressure coefficient using Equation No. 48. Then, use Equation No. 50.

≈≈≈≈≈≈≈≈≈≈

5.4.2 Active Lateral Force with Sloping Backfill and Inclined Wall

$$P_a = \frac{1}{2}\gamma H^2 \frac{\sin^2(\beta+\phi)}{\sin^2\beta\sin(\beta-\delta)\left[1+\sqrt{\frac{\sin(\phi+\delta)\sin(\phi-\alpha)}{\sin(\beta-\delta)\sin(\alpha+\beta)}}\right]^2} \qquad \text{Equation No. 51}$$

The equation is entered as

51ACTLATFORSBIW
P=0.5×S×H^2×SIN(A+B)^2÷SIN(B)^2÷SIN(B−C)÷(1+(SIN(A+C)×SIN(A−I)÷SIN(B−C)÷SIN(I+B))^0.5)^2

Where:

P = active lateral force per unit length of wall P_a (lb/ft, kN/m)
S = density of backfill γ (lb/ft³, kN/m³)
H = height of wall H (ft, m)
A = angle of internal friction of backfill ϕ
B = angle of inclined wall from horizontal β
C = angle of friction between the soil and wall face δ
I = angle of sloping backfill from horizontal α

Keystrokes

HP 35s Checksum; Length of Equation: **CK=C108; LN=88**

[RCL] [P] [↰] [=] [.] [5] [×] [RCL] [S] [×] [RCL] [H] [y^x] [2] [×] [SIN] [RCL] [A] [+] [RCL] [B] [>] [y^x] [2] [÷] [SIN] [RCL] [B] [>] [y^x] [2] [÷] [SIN] [RCL] [B] [−] [RCL] [C] [>] [÷] [()] [1] [+] [()] [SIN] [RCL] [A] [+] [RCL] [C] [>] [×] [SIN] [RCL] [A] [−] [RCL] [I] [>] [÷] [SIN] [RCL] [B] [−] [RCL] [C] [>] [÷] [SIN] [RCL] [I] [+] [RCL] [B] [>] [>] [y^x] [.] [5] [>] [y^x] [2] [ENTER]

HP 33s Checksum; Length of Equation: **CK=CC66; LN=88**

[RCL] [P] [↱] [=] [.] [5] [×] [RCL] [S] [×] [RCL] [H] [y^x] [2] [×] [SIN] [RCL] [A] [+] [RCL] [B] [↱] [)] [y^x] [2] [÷] [SIN] [RCL] [B] [↱] [)] [y^x] [2] [÷] [SIN] [RCL] [B] [−] [RCL] [C] [↱] [)] [÷] [↱] [(] [1] [+] [↱] [(] [SIN] [RCL] [A] [+] [RCL] [C] [↱] [)] [×] [SIN] [RCL] [A] [−] [RCL] [I] [↱] [)] [÷] [SIN] [RCL] [B] [−] [RCL] [C] [↱] [)] [÷] [SIN] [RCL] [I] [+] [RCL] [B] [↱] [)] [↱] [)] [y^x] [.] [5] [↱] [)] [y^x] [2] [ENTER]

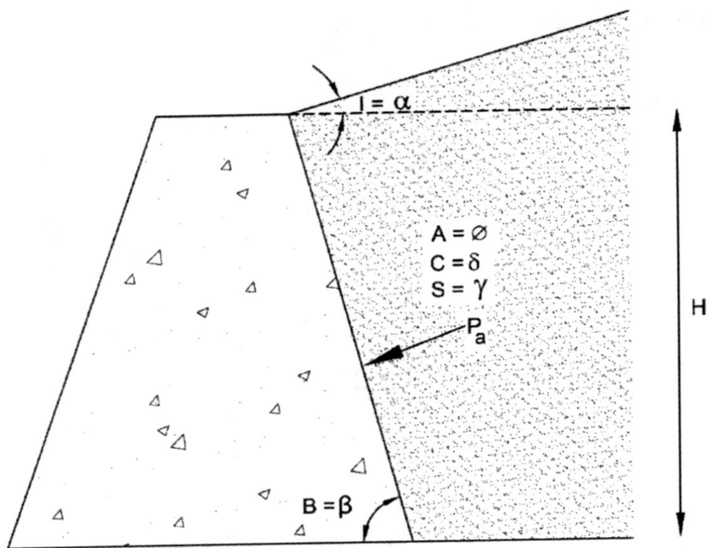

Figure 5-5 Active Lateral Force with Sloping Backfill and Inclined Wall

Notes: The last term of the equation is the Coulomb equation. To calculate only the earth pressure coefficient K_a, assign S and H as 1 then multiply the result by 2.

≈≈≈≈≈≈≈≈≈≈

5.4.3 Active Lateral Force with Water Table Between Top and Bottom of Wall, Surcharge Load, and Cohesion

$$P_a = QXK_{a_1} + \frac{1}{2}\gamma_m X^2 K_{a_1} - 2c_1 X\sqrt{K_{a_1}} + \left((Q+\gamma_m X)K_{a_2} - 2c_2\sqrt{K_{a_2}}\right)Z + \frac{1}{2}\gamma_b Z^2 K_{a_2} + \frac{1}{2}\gamma_w Z^2$$

Equation No. 52 (P)

The Rankine active earth pressure coefficients are

$$K_{a_1} = \tan^2\left(45 - \frac{\phi_1}{2}\right) \text{ and } K_{a_2} = \tan^2\left(45 - \frac{\phi_2}{2}\right)$$

Where $\gamma_b = \gamma_{sat} - \gamma_w$

$$\bar{y} = \frac{\left(QXK_{a_1}\right)\left(Z + \frac{X}{2}\right) + \left(\frac{1}{2}\gamma_m X^2 K_{a_1} - 2c_1 X\sqrt{K_{a_1}}\right)\left(Z + \frac{X}{3}\right) + \left((Q+\gamma_m X)ZK_{a_2} - 2c_2 Z\sqrt{K_{a_2}}\right)\left(\frac{Z}{2}\right)}{P_a} \cdots$$

$$\cdots \frac{+\left(\frac{1}{2}\gamma_b K_{a_2} Z^2\right)\left(\frac{Z}{3}\right) + \left(\frac{1}{2}\gamma_w Z^2\right)\left(\frac{Z}{3}\right)}{}$$ Equation No. 52 (Y)

$O = P_a \bar{y}$ Equation No. 52 (O)

The equations are entered as

52ACTWTSURCOHE
P=Q×X×TAN(45−A÷2)^2+0.5×D×X^2×TAN(45−A÷2)^2−2×C×X(TAN(45−A÷2)^2)^0.5
+((Q+D×X)×TAN(45−B÷2)^2−2×E(TAN(45−B÷2)^2)^0.5)×Z+0.5(S−W)×Z^2
×TAN(45−B÷2)^2+0.5×W×Z^2
Y=(Q×X×TAN(45−A÷2)^2(Z+X÷2)+(0.5×D×X^2×TAN(45−A÷2)^2−2×C×X(TAN(45−A÷2)^2)^
0.5)×(Z+X÷3)+((Q+D×X)×TAN(45−B÷2)^2−2×E(TAN(45−B÷2)^2)^0.5)×Z^2÷2+0.5(S−W)
×TAN(45−B÷2)^2×Z^3÷3+0.5×W×Z^3÷3)÷P
O=P×Y

Where:

P = total active lateral force per unit length of wall P_a (lb/ft, kN/m)
Q = surcharge load Q (lb/ft², kN/m²)
X = distance from top of backfill to water table X (ft, m)
A = angle of internal friction of moist soil ϕ_1
D = density of moist soil γ_m (lb/ft³, kN/m³)
C = cohesion of moist soil c_1 (lb/ft², kN/m²)
B = angle of internal friction of saturated soil ϕ_2
E = cohesion of saturated soil c_2 (lb/ft², kN/m²)
Z = distance from water table to the bottom of wall Z (ft, m)
S = density of saturated soil γ_{sat} (lb/ft³, kN/m³)
W = unit weight of water γ_w (62.4 lb/ft³, 9.81 kN/m³)
Y = location of resultant lateral force from the bottom of wall $\bar{y}$ (ft, m)
O = moment at the bottom of wall due to active lateral force O (ft-lb, kN-m)

Keystrokes

P=Q×X×TAN(45−A÷2)^2+0.5×D×X^2×TAN(45−A÷2)^2−2×C×X(TAN(45−A÷2)^2)^0.5
+((Q+D×X)×TAN(45−B÷2)^2−2×E(TAN(45−B÷2)^2)^0.5)×Z+0.5(S−W)×Z^2
×TAN(45−B÷2)^2+0.5×W×Z^2

HP 35s Checksum; Length of Equation: **CK=8CAA; LN=154**

[RCL] [P] [↰] [=] [RCL] [Q] [×] [RCL] [X] [×] [TAN] [4] [5] [−] [RCL] [A] [÷] [2] [>] [yˣ] [2] [+] [·] [5] [×] [RCL] [D] [×]
[RCL] [X] [yˣ] [2] [×] [TAN] [4] [5] [−] [RCL] [A] [÷] [2] [>] [yˣ] [2] [−] [2] [×] [RCL] [C] [×] [RCL] [X] [()] [TAN] [4] [5]
[−] [RCL] [A] [÷] [2] [>] [yˣ] [2] [>] [yˣ] [·] [5] [+] [()] [()] [RCL] [Q] [+] [RCL] [D] [×] [RCL] [X] [>] [×] [TAN] [4] [5] [−]
[RCL] [B] [÷] [2] [>] [yˣ] [2] [−] [2] [×] [RCL] [E] [()] [TAN] [4] [5] [−] [RCL] [B] [÷] [2] [>] [yˣ] [2] [>] [yˣ] [·] [5] [>]
[×] [RCL] [Z] [+] [·] [5] [()] [RCL] [S] [−] [RCL] [W] [>] [×] [RCL] [Z] [yˣ] [2] [×] [TAN] [4] [5] [−] [RCL] [B] [÷] [2] [>]
[yˣ] [2] [+] [·] [5] [×] [RCL] [W] [×] [RCL] [Z] [yˣ] [2] [ENTER]

HP 33s Checksum; Length of Equation: **CK=57D9; LN=157**

[RCL] [P] [↱] [=] [RCL] [Q] [×] [RCL] [X] [×] [TAN] [4] [5] [−] [RCL] [A] [÷] [2] [↱] [)] [y^x] [2] [+] [·] [5] [×] [RCL] [D]
[×] [RCL] [X] [y^x] [2] [×] [TAN] [4] [5] [−] [RCL] [A] [÷] [2] [↱] [)] [y^x] [2] [−] [2] [×] [RCL] [C] [×] [RCL] [X] [×] [↱]
[(] [TAN] [4] [5] [−] [RCL] [A] [÷] [2] [↱] [)] [y^x] [2] [↱] [)] [y^x] [·] [5] [+] [↱] [(] [↱] [(] [RCL] [Q] [+] [RCL] [D] [×]
[RCL] [X] [↱] [)] [×] [TAN] [4] [5] [−] [RCL] [B] [÷] [2] [↱] [)] [y^x] [2] [−] [2] [×] [RCL] [E] [×] [↱] [(] [TAN] [4] [5]
[−] [RCL] [B] [÷] [2] [↱] [)] [y^x] [2] [↱] [)] [y^x] [·] [5] [↱] [)] [×] [RCL] [Z] [+] [·] [5] [×] [(] [RCL] [S] [−] [RCL] [W]
[↱] [)] [×] [RCL] [Z] [y^x] [2] [×] [TAN] [4] [5] [−] [RCL] [B] [÷] [2] [↱] [)] [y^x] [2] [+] [·] [5] [×] [RCL] [W] [×] [RCL]
[Z] [y^x] [2] [ENTER]

Y=(Q×X×TAN(45−A÷2)^2(Z+X÷2)+(0.5×D×X^2×TAN(45−A÷2)^2−2×C×X(TAN(45−A÷2)^2)^0.5)×(Z+X÷3)+((Q+D×X)×TAN(45−B÷2)^2−2×E(TAN(45−B÷2)^2)^0.5)×Z^2÷2+0.5(S−W)×TAN(45−B÷2)^2×Z^3÷3+0.5×W×Z^3÷3)÷P

HP 35s Checksum; Length of Equation: **CK=39E6; LN=183**

[RCL] [Y] [↰] [=] [()] [RCL] [Q] [×] [RCL] [X] [×] [TAN] [4] [5] [−] [RCL] [A] [÷] [2] [>] [y^x] [2] [()] [RCL] [Z] [+] [RCL]
[X] [÷] [2] [>] [+] [()] [·] [5] [×] [RCL] [D] [×] [RCL] [X] [y^x] [2] [×] [TAN] [4] [5] [−] [RCL] [A] [÷] [2] [>] [y^x] [2] [−]
[2] [×] [RCL] [C] [×] [RCL] [X] [()] [TAN] [4] [5] [−] [RCL] [A] [÷] [2] [>] [y^x] [2] [>] [y^x] [·] [5] [>] [×] [()] [RCL] [Z] [+]
[RCL] [X] [÷] [3] [>] [+] [()] [()] [RCL] [Q] [+] [RCL] [D] [×] [RCL] [X] [>] [×] [TAN] [4] [5] [−] [RCL] [B] [÷] [2] [>] [y^x]
[2] [−] [2] [×] [RCL] [E] [()] [TAN] [4] [5] [−] [RCL] [B] [÷] [2] [>] [y^x] [2] [>] [y^x] [·] [5] [>] [×] [RCL] [Z] [y^x] [2] [÷]
[2] [+] [·] [5] [()] [RCL] [S] [−] [RCL] [W] [>] [×] [TAN] [4] [5] [−] [RCL] [B] [÷] [2] [>] [y^x] [2] [×] [RCL] [Z] [y^x] [3] [÷]
[3] [+] [·] [5] [×] [RCL] [W] [×] [RCL] [Z] [y^x] [3] [÷] [3] [>] [÷] [RCL] [P] [ENTER]

HP 33s Checksum; Length of Equation: **CK=B6A4; LN=187**

[RCL] [Y] [↱] [=] [↱] [(] [RCL] [Q] [×] [RCL] [X] [×] [TAN] [4] [5] [−] [RCL] [A] [÷] [2] [↱] [)] [y^x] [2] [×] [↱] [(]
[RCL] [Z] [+] [RCL] [X] [÷] [2] [↱] [)] [+] [↱] [(] [·] [5] [×] [RCL] [D] [×] [RCL] [X] [y^x] [2] [×] [TAN] [4] [5] [−] [RCL]
[A] [÷] [2] [↱] [)] [y^x] [2] [−] [2] [×] [RCL] [C] [×] [RCL] [X] [×] [↱] [(] [TAN] [4] [5] [−] [RCL] [A] [÷] [2] [↱] [)] [y^x]
[2] [↱] [)] [y^x] [·] [5] [↱] [)] [×] [↱] [(] [RCL] [Z] [+] [RCL] [X] [÷] [3] [↱] [)] [+] [↱] [(] [↱] [(] [RCL] [Q] [+]
[RCL] [D] [×] [RCL] [X] [↱] [)] [×] [TAN] [4] [5] [−] [RCL] [B] [÷] [2] [↱] [)] [y^x] [2] [−] [2] [×] [RCL] [E] [×] [↱] [(]
[TAN] [4] [5] [−] [RCL] [B] [÷] [2] [↱] [)] [y^x] [2] [↱] [)] [y^x] [·] [5] [↱] [)] [×] [RCL] [Z] [y^x] [2] [÷] [2] [+] [·] [5]
[×] [↱] [(] [RCL] [S] [−] [RCL] [W] [↱] [)] [×] [TAN] [4] [5] [−] [RCL] [B] [÷] [2] [↱] [)] [y^x] [2] [×] [RCL] [Z] [y^x] [3]
[÷] [3] [+] [·] [5] [×] [RCL] [W] [×] [RCL] [Z] [y^x] [3] [÷] [3] [↱] [)] [÷] [RCL] [P] [ENTER]

O=P×Y

HP 35s Checksum; Length of Equation: **CK=8916; LN=5**

[RCL] [O] [↰] [=] [RCL] [P] [×] [RCL] [Y] [ENTER]

HP 33s Checksum; Length of Equation: **CK=8916; LN=5**

[RCL] [O] [↱] [=] [RCL] [P] [×] [RCL] [Y] [ENTER]

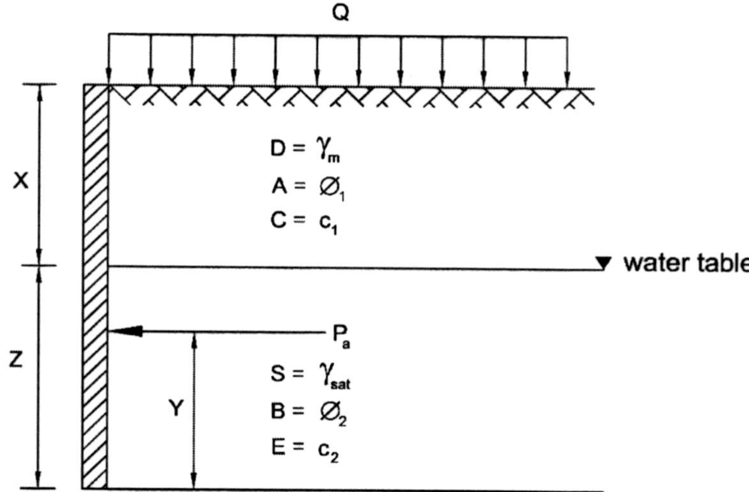

Figure 5-6 Active Lateral Force with Water Table Between Top and Bottom of Wall, Surcharge Load, and Cohesion

Notes: The above equations are not applicable for overconsolidated clay backfill. If there is no surcharge load, then Q is zero. In the absence of water table, W is zero. For 1 layer unsaturated soil, B, E, Z, S, and W are zero. Rankine active earth pressure coefficients and buoyant unit weight of saturated soil are automatically calculated. In the case of Rankine active earth pressure coefficients being given instead of friction angles, calculate the angles of internal friction by using Equation No. 47. If buoyant unit weight is given instead of saturated density, transform the buoyant unit weight to a saturated density by adding the unit weight of water (62.4 lb/ft^3, 9.81 kN/m^3).

If the density of dry soils and moisture contents are given, calculate the densities of moist and saturated soils by using the equations $\gamma_m = \gamma_d(1+\omega)$ and $\gamma_{sat} = \gamma_d(1+\omega)$, respectively.

≈≈≈≈≈≈≈≈≈≈

5.4.4 Active Lateral Force with Water Table at the Surface, Cohesion, Surcharge Load, and 1 Type of Soil

$$P_a = QHK_{a_1} + \frac{1}{2}\gamma_b H^2 K_{a_1} - 2c_1 H\sqrt{K_{a1}} + \frac{1}{2}\gamma_w H^2 \qquad \text{Equation No. 53 (P)}$$

Where $\gamma_b = \gamma_{sat} - \gamma_w$

$$\bar{y} = \frac{\left(QHK_{a_1}\right)\left(\frac{H}{2}\right) + \left(\frac{1}{2}\gamma_b H^2 K_{a_1} - 2c_1 H\sqrt{K_{a_1}}\right)\left(\frac{H}{3}\right) + \left(\frac{1}{2}\gamma_w H^2\right)\left(\frac{H}{3}\right)}{P_a} \qquad \text{Equation No. 53 (Y)}$$

$O = P_a\bar{y}$ Equation No. 53 (O)

The equations are entered as

53ACTWTSURFCO1SOIL
P=Q×H×TAN(45−A÷2)^2+0.5(S−W)×H^2×TAN(45−A÷2)^2−2×C×H(TAN(45−A÷2)^2)^0.5+0.5×W×H^2
Y=(Q×TAN(45−A÷2)^2×H^2÷2+(0.5(S−W)×H^2×TAN(45−A÷2)^2−2×C×H(TAN(45−A÷2)^2)^0.5)×H÷3+ 0.5×W×H^3÷3)÷P
O=P×Y

Where:

P = total active lateral force per unit length of wall P_a (lb/ft, kN/m)
Q = surcharge load Q (lb/ft^2, kN/m^2)
H = height of backfill H (ft, m)
A = angle of internal friction of soil ϕ_1
S = density of saturated soil γ_{sat} (lb/ft^3, kN/m^3)
W = unit weight of water γ_w (62.4 lb/ft^3, 9.81 kN/m^3)
C = cohesion of soil c_1 (lb/ft^2, kN/m^2)
Y = location of resultant lateral force from the bottom of wall $\bar{y}$ (ft, m)
O = moment at the bottom of wall due to active lateral force O (ft-lb, kN-m)

Keystrokes

P=Q×H×TAN(45−A÷2)^2+0.5(S−W)×H^2×TAN(45−A÷2)^2−2×C×H(TAN(45−A÷2)^2)^0.5 +0.5×W×H^2

HP 35s Checksum; Length of Equation: **CK=1C78; LN=81**

[RCL] [P] [↰] [=] [RCL] [Q] [×] [RCL] [H] [×] [TAN] [4] [5] [−] [RCL] [A] [÷] [2] [>] [y^x] [2] [+] [.] [5] [()] [RCL] [S] [−]
[RCL] [W] [>] [×] [RCL] [H] [y^x] [2] [×] [TAN] [4] [5] [−] [RCL] [A] [÷] [2] [>] [y^x] [2] [−] [2] [×] [RCL] [C] [×] [RCL] [H]
[()] [TAN] [4] [5] [−] [RCL] [A] [÷] [2] [>] [y^x] [2] [>] [y^x] [.] [5] [+] [.] [5] [×] [RCL] [W] [×] [RCL] [H] [y^x] [2] [ENTER]

HP 33s Checksum; Length of Equation: **CK=FDA0; LN=83**

[RCL] [P] [↱] [=] [RCL] [Q] [×] [RCL] [H] [×] [TAN] [4] [5] [−] [RCL] [A] [÷] [2] [↱] [)] [y^x] [2] [+] [.] [5] [×] [↱] [(]
[RCL] [S] [−] [RCL] [W] [↱] [)] [×] [RCL] [H] [y^x] [2] [×] [TAN] [4] [5] [−] [RCL] [A] [÷] [2] [↱] [)] [y^x] [2] [−] [2] [×]
[RCL] [C] [×] [RCL] [H] [×] [↱] [(] [TAN] [4] [5] [−] [RCL] [A] [÷] [2] [↱] [)] [y^x] [2] [↱] [)] [y^x] [.] [5] [+] [.] [5] [×]
[RCL] [W] [×] [RCL] [H] [y^x] [2] [ENTER]

Y=(Q×TAN(45−A÷2)^2×H^2÷2+(0.5(S−W)×H^2×TAN(45−A÷2)^2−2×C×H(TAN(45−A÷2)^2)^0.5)×H÷3+ 0.5×W×H^3÷3)÷P

HP 35s Checksum; Length of Equation: **CK=9642; LN=97**

[RCL] [Y] [↰] [=] [()] [RCL] [Q] [×] [TAN] [4] [5] [−] [RCL] [A] [÷] [2] [>] [y^x] [2] [×] [RCL] [H] [y^x] [2] [÷] [2] [+] [()] [.]
[5] [()] [RCL] [S] [−] [RCL] [W] [>] [×] [RCL] [H] [y^x] [2] [×] [TAN] [4] [5] [−] [RCL] [A] [÷] [2] [>] [y^x] [2] [−] [2] [×]
[RCL] [C] [×] [RCL] [H] [()] [TAN] [4] [5] [−] [RCL] [A] [÷] [2] [>] [y^x] [2] [>] [y^x] [.] [5] [>] [×] [RCL] [H] [÷] [3] [+] [.]
[5] [×] [RCL] [W] [×] [RCL] [H] [y^x] [3] [÷] [3] [>] [÷] [RCL] [P] [ENTER]

HP 33s Checksum; Length of Equation: **CK=F049; LN=99**

[RCL] [Y] [↱] [=] [↱] [(] [RCL] [Q] [×] [TAN] [4] [5] [−] [RCL] [A] [÷] [2] [↱] [)] [y^x] [2] [×] [RCL] [H] [y^x] [2] [÷] [2]
[+] [↱] [(] [.] [5] [×] [↱] [(] [RCL] [S] [−] [RCL] [W] [↱] [)] [×] [RCL] [H] [y^x] [2] [×] [TAN] [4] [5] [−] [RCL] [A] [÷]
[2] [↱] [)] [y^x] [2] [−] [2] [×] [RCL] [C] [×] [RCL] [H] [×] [↱] [(] [TAN] [4] [5] [−] [RCL] [A] [÷] [2] [↱] [)] [y^x] [2] [↱]
[)] [y^x] [.] [5] [↱] [)] [×] [RCL] [H] [÷] [3] [+] [.] [5] [×] [RCL] [W] [×] [RCL] [H] [y^x] [3] [÷] [3] [↱] [)] [÷] [RCL] [P]
[ENTER]

O=P×Y

HP 35s Checksum; Length of Equation: **CK=8916; LN=5**

[RCL] [O] [↰] [=] [RCL] [P] [×] [RCL] [Y] [ENTER]

HP 33s Checksum; Length of Equation: **CK=8916; LN=5**

[RCL] [O] [↱] [=] [RCL] [P] [×] [RCL] [Y] [ENTER]

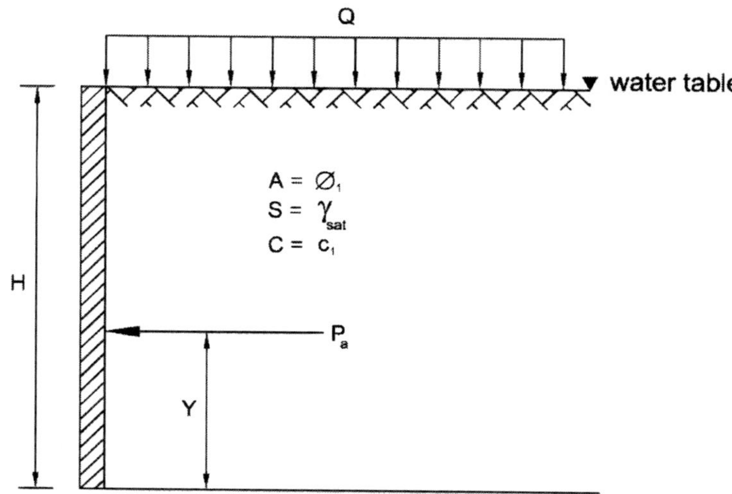

Figure 5-7 Active Lateral Force with Water Table at the Surface, Cohesion, Surcharge Load, and 1 Type of Soil

Notes: The above equations are not applicable for overconsolidated clay backfill. If there is no surcharge load, then Q is zero. For cohesionless backfill, C is zero. Rankine active earth pressure coefficient and buoyant unit weight of saturated soil are automatically calculated. If Rankine active earth pressure coefficient is given instead of friction angle, the angle of internal friction can be calculated by using Equation No. 47. If there is no water table, then W is zero and use S as the dry or moist density of soil. If the buoyant unit weight is given instead of the saturated density, transform the buoyant unit weight to a saturated density by adding the unit weight of water (62.4 lb/ft^3, 9.81 kN/m^3).

If the density of dry soil and moisture content are given, calculate the saturated density of soil by using the equation $\gamma_{sat} = \gamma_d (1 + \omega)$.

≈≈≈≈≈≈≈≈≈≈

5.5 Passive Earth Pressure Coefficient

5.5.1 Rankine Passive Earth Pressure Coefficient for Horizontal Backfill and Vertical Wall

$$K_p = \tan^2\left(45 + \frac{\phi}{2}\right)$$ Equation No. 54

The equation is entered as

54RANPASCOEFFI
K=TAN(45+A÷2)^2

Where:

K = Rankine passive earth pressure coefficient K_p
A = angle of internal friction of backfill ϕ

Keystrokes

HP 35s Checksum; Length of Equation: **CK=2DFB; LN=15**

[RCL] [K] [↰] [=] [TAN] [4] [5] [+] [RCL] [A] [÷] [2] [>] [y^x] [2] [ENTER]

HP 33s Checksum; Length of Equation: **CK=2DFB; LN=15**

[RCL] [K] [↱] [=] [TAN] [4] [5] [+] [RCL] [A] [÷] [2] [↱] [)] [y^x] [2] [ENTER]

≈≈≈≈≈≈≈≈≈≈

5.5.2 Rankine Passive Earth Pressure Coefficient for Sloping Backfill and Frictionless Vertical Wall

$$K_p = \cos\alpha \frac{\cos\alpha + \sqrt{\cos^2\alpha - \cos^2\phi}}{\cos\alpha - \sqrt{\cos^2\alpha - \cos^2\phi}}$$ Equation No. 55

The equation is entered as

55RANPASCOSBVW
K=COS(I)×(COS(I)+(COS(I)^2−COS(A)^2)^0.5)÷(COS(I)−(COS(I)^2−COS(A)^2)^0.5)

Where:

K = Rankine passive earth pressure coefficient K_p
I = angle of sloping backfill from horizontal α
A = angle of internal friction of backfill ϕ

Keystrokes

HP 35s Checksum; Length of Equation: **CK=29E9; LN=74**

[RCL] [K] [↰] [=] [COS] [RCL] [I] [>] [×] [()] [COS] [RCL] [I] [>] [+] [()] [COS] [RCL] [I] [>] [y^x] [2] [−] [COS] [RCL] [A] [>] [y^x] [2] [>] [y^x] [.] [5] [>] [÷] [()] [COS] [RCL] [I] [>] [−] [()] [COS] [RCL] [I] [>] [y^x] [2] [−] [COS] [RCL] [A] [>] [y^x] [2] [>] [y^x] [.] [5] [ENTER]

 Checksum; Length of Equation: **CK=32BD; LN=74**

RCL K ↱ = COS RCL I ↱) × ↱ (COS RCL I ↱) + ↱ (COS RCL I ↱) yˣ 2 − COS RCL A ↱) yˣ 2 ↱) yˣ · 5 ↱) ÷ ↱ (COS RCL I ↱) − ↱ (COS RCL I ↱) yˣ 2 − COS RCL A ↱) yˣ 2 ↱) yˣ · 5 ↱) ENTER

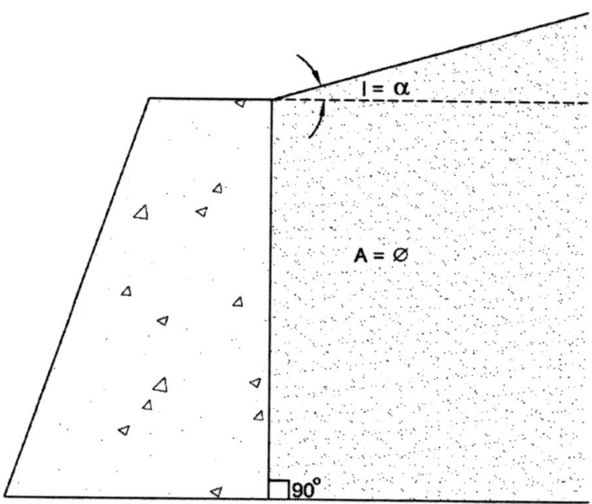

Figure 5-8 Rankine Passive Earth Pressure with Sloping Backfill and Vertical Wall

≈≈≈≈≈≈≈≈≈≈

5.6 Passive Earth Pressure

5.6.1 Passive Earth Pressure for Horizontal Backfill and Vertical Wall

$\sigma_p = \gamma H K_p + 2c\sqrt{K_p}$ Equation No. 56

The equation is entered as

56PASEARTHPRESS
P=S×H×K+2×C×K^0.5

Where:

P = passive earth pressure per unit length of wall σ_p (lb/ft², kN/m²)
S = density of backfill γ (lb/ft³, kN/m³)
H = height of backfill H (ft, m)
K = Rankine active earth pressure coefficient K_p
C = cohesion of backfill c (lb/ft², kN/m²)

Keystrokes

HP 35s Checksum; Length of Equation: **CK=0B9B; LN=17**

[RCL] [P] [↰] [=] [RCL] [S] [×] [RCL] [H] [×] [RCL] [K] [+] [2] [×] [RCL] [C] [×] [RCL] [K] [y^x] [.] [5] [ENTER]

HP 33s Checksum; Length of Equation: **CK=0B9B; LN=17**

[RCL] [P] [↱] [=] [RCL] [S] [×] [RCL] [H] [×] [RCL] [K] [+] [2] [×] [RCL] [C] [×] [RCL] [K] [y^x] [.] [5] [ENTER]

≈≈≈≈≈≈≈≈≈≈

5.7 Passive Lateral Force

5.7.1 Passive Lateral Force

$$P_p = \frac{1}{2}\gamma H^2 K_p$$ Equation No. 57

The equation is entered as

57PASLATFORCE
P=0.5×S×H^2×K

Where:

P = passive lateral force per unit length of wall P_p (lb/ft, kN/m)
S = density of backfill γ (lb/ft^3, kN/m^3)
H = height of backfill H (ft, m)
K = Rankine passive earth pressure coefficient K_p

Keystrokes

HP 35s Checksum; Length of Equation: **CK=880B; LN=13**

[RCL] [P] [↰] [=] [.] [5] [×] [RCL] [S] [×] [RCL] [H] [y^x] [2] [×] [RCL] [K] [ENTER]

HP 33s Checksum; Length of Equation: **CK=880B; LN=13**

[RCL] [P] [↱] [=] [.] [5] [×] [RCL] [S] [×] [RCL] [H] [y^x] [2] [×] [RCL] [K] [ENTER]

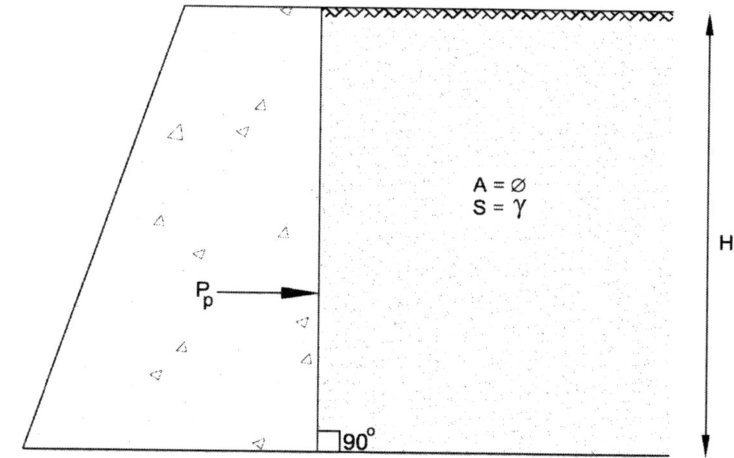

Figure 5-9 Passive Lateral Force with Horizontal Backfill and Vertical Wall

≈≈≈≈≈≈≈≈≈≈

5.7.2 Passive Lateral Force with Sloping Backfill and Inclined Wall

$$P_p = \frac{1}{2}\gamma H^2 \frac{\sin^2(\beta - \phi)}{\sin^2\beta \sin(\beta + \delta)\left[1 - \sqrt{\frac{\sin(\phi + \delta)\sin(\phi + \alpha)}{\sin(\beta + \delta)\sin(\beta + \alpha)}}\right]^2}$$

Equation No. 58

The equation is entered as

58PASLATFORSBIW
P=0.5×S×H^2×SIN(B−A)^2÷SIN(B)^2÷SIN(B+C)÷(1−(SIN(A+C)×SIN(A+I)÷SIN(B+C)÷SIN(B+I))^0.5)^2

Where:

P = passive lateral force per unit length of wall P_p (lb/ft, kN/m)
S = density of backfill γ (lb/ft³, kN/m³)
H = height of wall H (ft, m)
B = angle of inclined wall from horizontal β
A = angle of internal friction of backfill ϕ
C = angle of friction between the soil and wall face δ
I = angle of sloping backfill from horizontal α

Keystrokes

HP 35s Checksum; Length of Equation: **CK=9D92; LN=88**

[RCL] [P] [↰] [=] [·] [5] [×] [RCL] [S] [×] [RCL] [H] [y^x] [2] [×] [SIN] [RCL] [B] [−] [RCL] [A] [>] [y^x] [2] [÷] [SIN] [RCL]
[B] [>] [y^x] [2] [÷] [SIN] [RCL] [B] [+] [RCL] [C] [>] [÷] [()] [1] [−] [()] [SIN] [RCL] [A] [+] [RCL] [C] [>] [×] [SIN] [RCL]
[A] [+] [RCL] [I] [>] [÷] [SIN] [RCL] [B] [+] [RCL] [C] [>] [÷] [SIN] [RCL] [B] [+] [RCL] [I] [>] [>] [y^x] [·] [5] [>] [y^x] [2]
[ENTER]

HP 33s Checksum; Length of Equation: **CK=3E4F; LN=88**

[RCL] [P] [↱] [=] [·] [5] [×] [RCL] [S] [×] [RCL] [H] [y^x] [2] [×] [SIN] [RCL] [B] [−] [RCL] [A] [↱] [)] [y^x] [2] [÷] [SIN]
[RCL] [B] [↱] [)] [y^x] [2] [÷] [SIN] [RCL] [B] [+] [RCL] [C] [↱] [)] [÷] [↱] [(] [1] [−] [↱] [(] [SIN] [RCL] [A] [+] [RCL]
[C] [↱] [)] [×] [SIN] [RCL] [A] [+] [RCL] [I] [↱] [)] [÷] [SIN] [RCL] [B] [+] [RCL] [C] [↱] [)] [÷] [SIN] [RCL] [B] [+]
[RCL] [I] [↱] [)] [↱] [)] [y^x] [·] [5] [↱] [)] [y^x] [2] [ENTER]

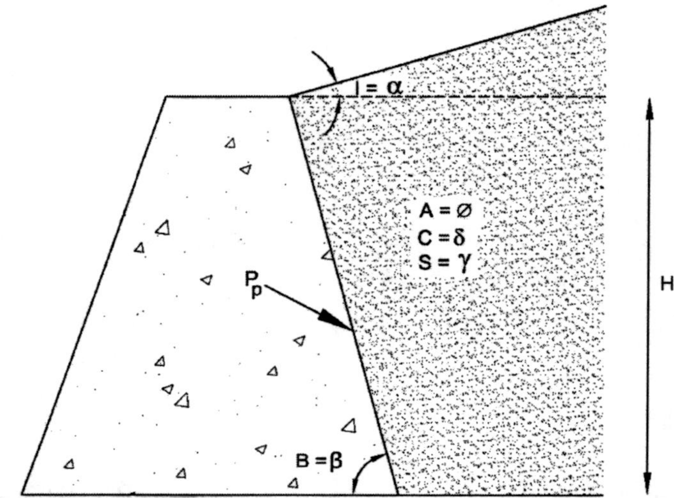

Figure 5-10 Passive Lateral Force with Sloping Backfill and Inclined Wall

Notes: The last term of the equation is the Coulomb equation. To calculate only the earth pressure coefficient K_p, assign S and H as 1 then multiply the result by 2.

≈≈≈≈≈≈≈≈≈≈

5.7.3 Passive Lateral Force with Water Table Between Top and Bottom of Wall, Surcharge Load, and Cohesion

$$P_p = QXK_{p_1} + \frac{1}{2}\gamma_m X^2 K_{p_1} + 2c_1 X\sqrt{K_{p_1}} + \left(QK_{p_2} + \gamma_m XK_{p_2} + 2c_2\sqrt{K_{p_2}}\right)Z + \frac{1}{2}\gamma_b Z^2 K_{p_2} + \frac{1}{2}\gamma_w Z^2$$

Equation No. 59 (P)

The Rankine passive earth pressure coefficients are

$$K_{p_1} = \tan^2\left(45 + \frac{\phi_1}{2}\right) \text{ and } K_{p_2} = \tan^2\left(45 + \frac{\phi_2}{2}\right)$$

Where: $\gamma_b = \gamma_{sat} - \gamma_w$

$$\bar{y} = \frac{\left(QXK_{P_1}\right)\left(Z+\frac{X}{2}\right)+\left(\frac{1}{2}\gamma_m X^2 K_{P_1}+2c_1 X\sqrt{K_{P_1}}\right)\left(Z+\frac{X}{3}\right)+\left((Q+\gamma_m X)ZK_{P_2}+2c_2 Z\sqrt{K_{P_2}}\right)\left(\frac{Z}{2}\right)}{P_p} \cdots$$

$$\cdots \frac{+\left(\frac{1}{2}\gamma_b K_{P_2} Z^2\right)\left(\frac{Z}{3}\right)+\left(\frac{1}{2}\gamma_w Z^2\right)\left(\frac{Z}{3}\right)}{} \quad \text{Equation No. 59 (Y)}$$

$O = P_p \bar{y}$ Equation No. 59 (O)

The equations are entered as

59PASWTSURCOHE
P=Q×X×TAN(45+A÷2)^2+0.5×D×X^2×TAN(45+A÷2)^2+2×C×X(TAN(45+A÷2)^2)^0.5+((Q+D×X)×TAN(45+B÷2)^2+2×E(TAN(45+B÷2)^2)^0.5)×Z+0.5(S−W)×Z^2×TAN(45+B÷2)^2+0.5×W×Z^2
Y=(Q×X×TAN(45+A÷2)^2(Z+X÷2)+(0.5×D×X^2×TAN(45+A÷2)^2+2×C×X(TAN(45+A÷2)^2)^0.5)×(Z+X÷3)+((Q+D×X)×TAN(45+B÷2)^2+2×E(TAN(45+B÷2)^2)^0.5)×Z^2÷2+0.5(S−W)×TAN(45+B÷2)^2×Z^3÷3+0.5×W×Z^3÷3)÷P
O=P×Y

Where:

P = total passive lateral force per unit length of wall P_p (lb/ft, kN/m)
Q = surcharge load Q (lb/ft^2, kN/m^2)
X = distance from top of backfill to water table X (ft, m)
A = angle of internal friction of moist soil ϕ_1
D = density of moist soil γ_m (lb/ft^3, kN/m^3)
C = cohesion of moist soil c_1 (lb/ft^2, kN/m^2)
B = angle of internal friction of saturated soil ϕ_2
E = cohesion of saturated soil c_2 (lb/ft^2, kN/m^2)
Z = distance from water table to the bottom of wall Z (ft, m)
S = density of saturated soil γ_{sat} (lb/ft^3, kN/m^3)
W = unit weight of water γ_w (62.4 lb/ft^3, 9.81 kN/m^3)
Y = location of resultant lateral force from the bottom of wall $\bar{y}$ (ft, m)
O = moment at the bottom of wall due to passive lateral force O (ft-lb, kN-m)

Keystrokes

P=Q×X×TAN(45+A÷2)^2+0.5×D×X^2×TAN(45+A÷2)^2+2×C×X(TAN(45+A÷2)^2)^0.5+((Q+D×X)×TAN(45+B÷2)^2+2×E(TAN(45+B÷2)^2)^0.5)×Z+0.5(S−W)×Z^2×TAN(45+B÷2)^2+0.5×W×Z^2

HP 35s Checksum; Length of Equation: **CK=EDF6; LN=154**

[RCL] [P] [↰] [=] [RCL] [Q] [×] [RCL] [X] [×] [TAN] [4] [5] [+] [RCL] [A] [÷] [2] [>] [y^x] [2] [+] [·] [5] [×] [RCL] [D] [×]
[RCL] [X] [y^x] [2] [×] [TAN] [4] [5] [+] [RCL] [A] [÷] [2] [>] [y^x] [2] [+] [2] [×] [RCL] [C] [×] [RCL] [X] [()] [TAN] [4] [5]
[+] [RCL] [A] [÷] [2] [>] [y^x] [2] [>] [y^x] [·] [5] [+] [()] [()] [RCL] [Q] [+] [RCL] [D] [×] [RCL] [X] [>] [×] [TAN] [4] [5] [+]
[RCL] [B] [÷] [2] [>] [y^x] [2] [+] [2] [×] [RCL] [E] [()] [TAN] [4] [5] [+] [RCL] [B] [÷] [2] [>] [y^x] [2] [>] [y^x] [·] [5] [>]
[×] [RCL] [Z] [+] [·] [5] [()] [RCL] [S] [−] [RCL] [W] [>] [×] [RCL] [Z] [y^x] [2] [×] [TAN] [4] [5] [+] [RCL] [B] [÷] [2] [>]
[y^x] [2] [+] [·] [5] [×] [RCL] [W] [×] [RCL] [Z] [y^x] [2] [ENTER]

HP 33s Checksum; Length of Equation: **CK=DA3E; LN=157**

[RCL] [P] [↱] [=] [RCL] [Q] [×] [RCL] [X] [×] [TAN] [4] [5] [+] [RCL] [A] [÷] [2] [↱] [)] [y^x] [2] [+] [·] [5] [×] [RCL] [D]
[×] [RCL] [X] [y^x] [2] [×] [TAN] [4] [5] [+] [RCL] [A] [÷] [2] [↱] [)] [y^x] [2] [+] [2] [×] [RCL] [C] [×] [RCL] [X] [×] [↱]
[(] [TAN] [4] [5] [+] [RCL] [A] [÷] [2] [↱] [)] [y^x] [2] [↱] [)] [y^x] [·] [5] [+] [↱] [(] [↱] [(] [RCL] [Q] [+] [RCL] [D] [×]
[RCL] [X] [↱] [)] [×] [TAN] [4] [5] [+] [RCL] [B] [÷] [2] [↱] [)] [y^x] [2] [+] [2] [×] [RCL] [E] [×] [↱] [(] [TAN] [4] [5]
[+] [RCL] [B] [÷] [2] [↱] [)] [y^x] [2] [↱] [)] [y^x] [·] [5] [↱] [)] [×] [RCL] [Z] [+] [·] [5] [×] [↱] [(] [RCL] [S] [−] [RCL]
[W] [↱] [)] [×] [RCL] [Z] [y^x] [2] [×] [TAN] [4] [5] [+] [RCL] [B] [÷] [2] [↱] [)] [y^x] [2] [+] [·] [5] [×] [RCL] [W] [×]
[RCL] [Z] [y^x] [2] [ENTER]

Y=(Q×X×TAN(45+A÷2)^2(Z+X÷2)+(0.5×D×X^2×TAN(45+A÷2)^2+2×C×X(TAN(45+A÷2)^2)^0.5)×(Z+X÷3)+((Q+D×X)×TAN(45+B÷2)^2+2×E(TAN(45+B÷2)^2)^0.5)×Z^2÷2+0.5(S−W)×TAN(45+B÷2)^2×Z^3÷3+0.5×W×Z^3÷3)÷P

HP 35s Checksum; Length of Equation: **CK=A5D5; LN=183**

[RCL] [Y] [↰] [=] [()] [RCL] [Q] [×] [RCL] [X] [×] [TAN] [4] [5] [+] [RCL] [A] [÷] [2] [>] [y^x] [2] [()] [RCL] [Z] [+] [RCL]
[X] [÷] [2] [>] [+] [()] [·] [5] [×] [RCL] [D] [×] [RCL] [X] [y^x] [2] [×] [TAN] [4] [5] [+] [RCL] [A] [÷] [2] [>] [y^x] [2] [+]
[2] [×] [RCL] [C] [×] [RCL] [X] [()] [TAN] [4] [5] [+] [RCL] [A] [÷] [2] [>] [y^x] [2] [>] [y^x] [·] [5] [>] [×] [()] [RCL] [Z] [+]
[RCL] [X] [÷] [3] [>] [+] [()] [()] [RCL] [Q] [+] [RCL] [D] [×] [RCL] [X] [>] [×] [TAN] [4] [5] [+] [RCL] [B] [÷] [2] [>] [y^x]
[2] [+] [2] [×] [RCL] [E] [()] [TAN] [4] [5] [+] [RCL] [B] [÷] [2] [>] [y^x] [2] [>] [y^x] [·] [5] [>] [×] [RCL] [Z] [y^x] [2] [÷]
[2] [+] [·] [5] [()] [RCL] [S] [−] [RCL] [W] [>] [×] [TAN] [4] [5] [+] [RCL] [B] [÷] [2] [>] [y^x] [2] [×] [RCL] [Z] [y^x] [3] [÷]
[3] [+] [·] [5] [×] [RCL] [W] [×] [RCL] [Z] [y^x] [3] [÷] [3] [>] [÷] [RCL] [P] [ENTER]

HP 33s Checksum; Length of Equation: **CK=7A7F; LN=187**

[RCL] [Y] [↱] [=] [↱] [(] [RCL] [Q] [×] [RCL] [X] [×] [TAN] [4] [5] [+] [RCL] [A] [÷] [2] [↱] [)] [y^x] [2] [×] [↱] [(]
[RCL] [Z] [+] [RCL] [X] [÷] [2] [↱] [)] [+] [↱] [(] [·] [5] [×] [RCL] [D] [×] [RCL] [X] [y^x] [2] [×] [TAN] [4] [5] [+] [RCL]
[A] [÷] [2] [↱] [)] [y^x] [2] [+] [2] [×] [RCL] [C] [×] [RCL] [X] [×] [↱] [(] [TAN] [4] [5] [+] [RCL] [A] [÷] [2] [↱] [)] [y^x]
[2] [↱] [)] [y^x] [·] [5] [↱] [)] [×] [↱] [(] [RCL] [Z] [+] [RCL] [X] [÷] [3] [↱] [)] [+] [↱] [(] [↱] [(] [RCL] [Q] [+]
[RCL] [D] [×] [RCL] [X] [↱] [)] [×] [TAN] [4] [5] [+] [RCL] [B] [÷] [2] [↱] [)] [y^x] [2] [+] [2] [×] [RCL] [E] [×] [↱] [(]
[TAN] [4] [5] [+] [RCL] [B] [÷] [2] [↱] [)] [y^x] [2] [↱] [)] [y^x] [·] [5] [↱] [)] [×] [RCL] [Z] [y^x] [2] [÷] [2] [+] [·] [5]
[×] [↱] [(] [RCL] [S] [−] [RCL] [W] [↱] [)] [×] [TAN] [4] [5] [+] [RCL] [B] [÷] [2] [↱] [)] [y^x] [2] [×] [RCL] [Z] [y^x] [3]
[÷] [3] [+] [·] [5] [×] [RCL] [W] [×] [RCL] [Z] [y^x] [3] [÷] [3] [↱] [)] [÷] [RCL] [P] [ENTER]

O=P×Y

HP 35s Checksum; Length of Equation: **CK=8916; LN=5**

RCL O ↰ = RCL P × RCL Y ENTER

HP 33s Checksum; Length of Equation: **CK=8916; LN=5**

RCL O ↱ = RCL P × RCL Y ENTER

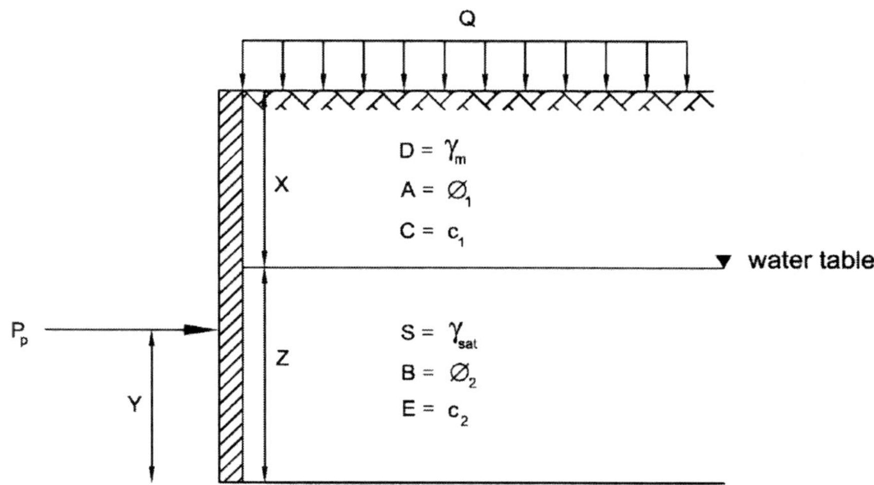

Figure 5-11 Passive Lateral Force with Water Table Between Top and Bottom of Wall, Surcharge Load, and Cohesion

Notes: The above equations are not applicable for overconsolidated clay backfill. If the surcharge load is neglected, then Q is zero. If there is no water table, W is zero. In the case of 1 layer unsaturated soil, B, E, Z, S, and W are zero. Rankine passive earth pressure coefficients and buoyant unit weight of saturated soil are automatically calculated. If the Rankine passive earth pressure coefficients are given instead of friction angles, calculate the angles of internal friction by using Equation No. 54. If the buoyant unit weight is given instead of saturated density, transform the buoyant unit weight to a saturated density by adding the unit weight of water (62.4 lb/ft^3, 9.81 kN/m^3).

If the density of dry soils and moisture contents are given, calculate the densities of moist and saturated soils by using the equations $\gamma_m = \gamma_d(1+\omega)$ and $\gamma_{sat} = \gamma_d(1+\omega)$, respectively.

≈≈≈≈≈≈≈≈≈≈

5.7.4 Passive Lateral Force with Water Table at the Surface, Cohesion, Surcharge Load, and 1 Type of Soil

$$P_p = QHK_{p_1} + \frac{1}{2}\gamma_b H^2 K_{p_1} + 2c_1 H\sqrt{K_{p_1}} + \frac{1}{2}\gamma_w H^2$$ Equation No. 60 (P)

Where $\gamma_b = \gamma_{sat} - \gamma_w$

$$\bar{y} = \frac{\left(QHK_{p_1}\right)\left(\frac{H}{2}\right) + \left(\frac{1}{2}\gamma_b H^2 K_{p_1} + 2c_1 H\sqrt{K_{p_1}}\right)\left(\frac{H}{3}\right) + \left(\frac{1}{2}\gamma_w H^2\right)\left(\frac{H}{3}\right)}{P_p}$$ Equation No. 60 (Y)

$$O = P_p\bar{y}$$ Equation No. 60 (O)

The equations are entered as

60PASWTSURFCO1SOIL
P=Q×H×TAN(45+A÷2)^2+0.5(S−W)×H^2×TAN(45+A÷2)^2+2×C×H(TAN(45+A÷2)^2)^0.5 +0.5×W×H^2
Y=(Q×TAN(45+A÷2)^2×H^2÷2+(0.5(S−W)×H^2×TAN(45+A÷2)^2+2×C×H(TAN(45+A÷2)^2)^0.5)×H÷3+ 0.5×W×H^3÷3)÷P
O=P×Y

Where:

P = total passive lateral force per unit length of wall P_p (lb/ft, kN/m)
Q = surcharge load Q (lb/ft², kN/m²)
H = height of backfill H (ft, m)
A = angle of internal friction of soil ϕ_1
S = density of saturated soil γ_{sat} (lb/ft³, kN/m³)
W = unit weight of water γ_w (62.4 lb/ft³, 9.81 kN/m³)
C = cohesion of soil c_1 (lb/ft², kN/m²)
Y = location of resultant lateral force from the bottom of wall $\bar{y}$ (ft, m)
O = moment at the bottom of wall due to passive lateral force O (ft-lb, kN-m)

Keystrokes

P=Q×H×TAN(45+A÷2)^2+0.5(S−W)×H^2×TAN(45+A÷2)^2+2×C×H(TAN(45+A÷2)^2)^0.5 +0.5×W×H^2

HP 35s Checksum; Length of Equation: **CK=53AF; LN=81**

[RCL] [P] [↰] [=] [RCL] [Q] [×] [RCL] [H] [×] [TAN] [4] [5] [+] [RCL] [A] [÷] [2] [>] [y^x] [2] [+] [.] [5] [()] [RCL] [S] [−] [RCL] [W] [>] [×] [RCL] [H] [y^x] [2] [×] [TAN] [4] [5] [+] [RCL] [A] [÷] [2] [>] [y^x] [2] [+] [2] [×] [RCL] [C] [×] [RCL] [H] [()] [TAN] [4] [5] [+] [RCL] [A] [÷] [2] [>] [y^x] [2] [>] [y^x] [.] [5] [+] [.] [5] [×] [RCL] [W] [×] [RCL] [H] [y^x] [2] [ENTER]

HP 33s Checksum; Length of Equation: **CK=1905; LN=83**

[RCL] [P] [↱] [=] [RCL] [Q] [×] [RCL] [H] [×] [TAN] [4] [5] [+] [RCL] [A] [÷] [2] [↱] [)] [y^x] [2] [+] [.] [5] [×] [↱] [(] [RCL] [S] [−] [RCL] [W] [↱] [)] [×] [RCL] [H] [y^x] [2] [×] [TAN] [4] [5] [+] [RCL] [A] [÷] [2] [↱] [)] [y^x] [2] [+] [2] [×] [RCL] [C] [×] [RCL] [H] [×] [↱] [(] [TAN] [4] [5] [+] [RCL] [A] [÷] [2] [↱] [)] [y^x] [2] [↱] [)] [y^x] [.] [5] [+] [.] [5] [×] [RCL] [W] [×] [RCL] [H] [y^x] [2] [ENTER]

Y=(Q×TAN(45+A÷2)^2×H^2÷2+(0.5(S−W)×H^2×TAN(45+A÷2)^2+2×C×H(TAN(45+A÷2)^2)^0.5)×H÷3+ 0.5×W×H^3÷3)÷P

HP 35s Checksum; Length of Equation: **CK=71DC; LN=97**

[RCL] [Y] [↰] [=] [()] [RCL] [Q] [×] [TAN] [4] [5] [+] [RCL] [A] [÷] [2] [>] [y^x] [2] [×] [RCL] [H] [y^x] [2] [÷] [2] [+] [()] [.] [5] [()] [RCL] [S] [−] [RCL] [W] [>] [×] [RCL] [H] [y^x] [2] [×] [TAN] [4] [5] [+] [RCL] [A] [÷] [2] [>] [y^x] [2] [+] [2] [×] [RCL] [C] [×] [RCL] [H] [()] [TAN] [4] [5] [+] [RCL] [A] [÷] [2] [>] [y^x] [2] [>] [y^x] [.] [5] [>] [×] [RCL] [H] [÷] [3] [+] [.] [5] [×] [RCL] [W] [×] [RCL] [H] [y^x] [3] [÷] [3] [>] [÷] [RCL] [P] [ENTER]

HP 33s Checksum; Length of Equation: **CK=18A1; LN=99**

[RCL] [Y] [↱] [=] [↱] [(] [RCL] [Q] [×] [TAN] [4] [5] [+] [RCL] [A] [÷] [2] [↱] [)] [y^x] [2] [×] [RCL] [H] [y^x] [2] [÷] [2] [+] [↱] [(] [·] [5] [×] [↱] [(] [RCL] [S] [−] [RCL] [W] [↱] [)] [×] [RCL] [H] [y^x] [2] [×] [TAN] [4] [5] [+] [RCL] [A] [÷] [2] [↱] [)] [y^x] [2] [+] [2] [×] [RCL] [C] [×] [RCL] [H] [×] [↱] [(] [TAN] [4] [5] [+] [RCL] [A] [÷] [2] [↱] [)] [y^x] [2] [↱] [)] [y^x] [·] [5] [↱] [)] [×] [RCL] [H] [÷] [3] [+] [·] [5] [×] [RCL] [W] [×] [RCL] [H] [y^x] [3] [÷] [3] [↱] [)] [÷] [RCL] [P] [ENTER]

O=P×Y

HP 35s Checksum; Length of Equation: **CK=8916; LN=5**

[RCL] [O] [↰] [=] [RCL] [P] [×] [RCL] [Y] [ENTER]

HP 33s Checksum; Length of Equation: **CK=8916; LN=5**

[RCL] [O] [↱] [=] [RCL] [P] [×] [RCL] [Y] [ENTER]

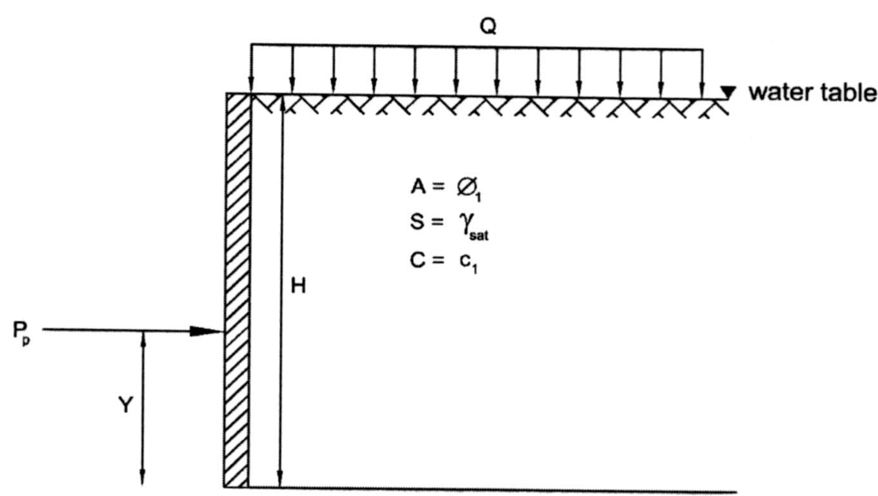

Figure 5-12 Passive Lateral Force with Water Table at the Surface, Cohesion, Surcharge Load, and 1 Type of Soil

Notes: The above equations are not applicable for overconsolidated clay backfill. If there is no surcharge load, then Q is zero. For cohesionless backfill, C is zero. The Rankine passive earth pressure coefficient and buoyant unit weight of saturated soil are automatically calculated. If the Rankine passive earth pressure coefficient is given instead of the friction angle, calculate the angle of internal friction by using Equation No. 54. In the absence of water table, W is zero and use S as the dry or moist density of soil. If the buoyant unit weight is given instead of the saturated density, transform the buoyant unit weight to a saturated density by adding the unit weight of water (62.4 lb/ft^3, 9.81 kN/m^3).

If the density of dry soil and moisture content are given, calculate the saturated density of soil by using the equation $\gamma_{sat} = \gamma_d(1+\omega)$.

≈≈≈≈≈≈≈≈≈≈

5.8 At-rest Earth Pressure Coefficient

5.8.1 Rankine At-rest Earth Pressure Coefficient for Horizontal Backfill and Vertical Wall

$K_o = 1 - \sin\phi$ Equation No. 61

The equation is entered as

61RANATRESCOEF
K=1−SIN(A)

Where:

K = Rankine at-rest earth pressure coefficient K_o
A = angle of internal friction of backfill ϕ

Keystrokes

HP 35s Checksum; Length of Equation: **CK=C92B; LN=10**

[RCL] [K] [↰] [=] [1] [−] [SIN] [RCL] [A] [ENTER]

HP 33s Checksum; Length of Equation: **CK=C92B; LN=10**

[RCL] [K] [↱] [=] [1] [−] [SIN] [RCL] [A] [↱] [)] [ENTER]

≈≈≈≈≈≈≈≈≈≈

5.9 At-rest Earth Pressure

5.9.1 At-rest Lateral Force

$P_o = \frac{1}{2}\gamma H^2 K_o$ Equation No. 62

The equation is entered as

62ATRESTLATFORCE
P=0.5×S×H^2×K

Where:

P = at-rest lateral force per unit length of wall P_o (lb/ft, kN/m)
S = density of backfill γ (lb/ft^3, kN/m^3)
H = height of backfill H (ft, m)
K = at-rest earth pressure coefficient K_o

Keystrokes

HP 35s Checksum; Length of Equation: **CK=880B; LN=13**

RCL P ⬏ = . 5 × RCL S × RCL H y^x 2 × RCL K ENTER

HP 33s Checksum; Length of Equation: **CK=880B; LN=13**

RCL P ⬏ = . 5 × RCL S × RCL H y^x 2 × RCL K ENTER

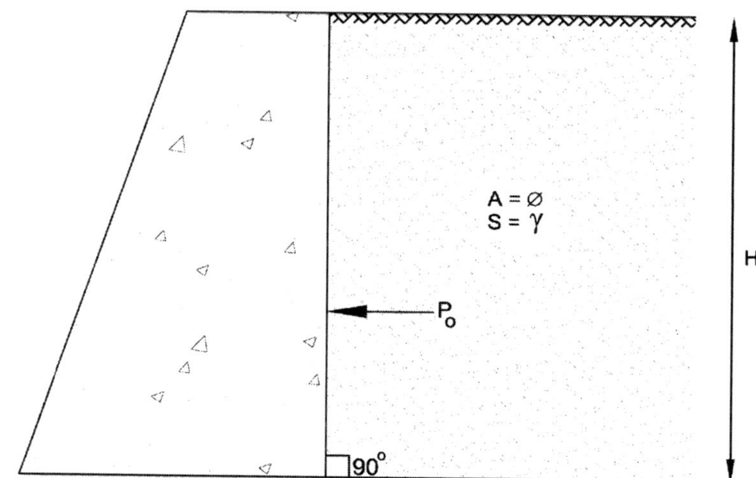

Figure 5-13 At-rest Lateral Force with Horizontal Backfill and Vertical Wall

≈≈≈≈≈≈≈≈≈≈

5.9.2 At-rest Lateral Force with Water Table Between Top and Bottom of Wall, and Surcharge Load

$$P_o = QXK_{o_1} + \frac{1}{2}\gamma_m X^2 K_{o_1} + (Q + \gamma_m X)ZK_{o_2} + \frac{1}{2}\gamma_b Z^2 K_{o_2} + \frac{1}{2}\gamma_w Z^2$$ Equation No. 63 (P)

The Rankine at-rest earth pressure coefficients are

$K_{o_1} = 1 - \sin\phi_1$ and $K_{o_2} = 1 - \sin\phi_2$

Where $\gamma_b = \gamma_{sat} - \gamma_w$

$$\bar{y} = \frac{(QXK_{o_1})\left(Z + \frac{X}{2}\right) + \left(\frac{1}{2}\gamma_m X^2 K_{o_1}\right)\left(Z + \frac{X}{3}\right) + (Q + \gamma_m X)K_{o_2} Z\left(\frac{Z}{2}\right) + \left(\frac{1}{2}\gamma_b K_{o_2} Z^2\right)\left(\frac{Z}{3}\right) + \left(\frac{1}{2}\gamma_w Z^2\right)\left(\frac{Z}{3}\right)}{P_o}$$

Equation No. 63 (Y)

$O = P_o\bar{y}$ Equation No. 63 (O)

The equations are entered as

63ATRESTWTSURCHARJ
P=Q×X(1−SIN(A))+0.5×D×X^2(1−SIN(A))+(Q+D×X)×Z(1−SIN(B))+0.5(S−W)×Z^2(1−SIN(B))
+0.5×W×Z^2
Y=(Q×X(1−SIN(A))×(Z+X÷2)+0.5×D×X^2(1−SIN(A))×(Z+X÷3)+(Q+D×X)×(1−SIN(B))×Z^2÷2
+0.5(S−W)×(1−SIN(B))×Z^3÷3+0.5×W×Z^3÷3)÷P
O=P×Y

Where:

P = total at-rest lateral force per unit length of wall P_o (lb/ft, kN/m)
Q = surcharge load Q (lb/ft², kN/m²)
X = distance from the top of backfill to water table X (ft, m)
A = angle of internal friction of moist soil ϕ_1
D = density of moist soil γ_m (lb/ft³, kN/m³)
Z = distance from water table to bottom of backfill Z (ft, m)
B = angle of internal friction of saturated soil ϕ_2
S = density of saturated soil γ_{sat} (lb/ft³, kN/m³)
W = unit weight of water γ_w (62.4 lb/ft³, 9.81 kN/m³)
Y = location of resultant lateral force from the bottom of wall $\bar{y}$ (ft, m)
O = moment at the bottom of wall due to at-rest lateral force O (ft-lb, kN-m)

Keystrokes

P=Q×X(1−SIN(A))+0.5×D×X^2(1−SIN(A))+(Q+D×X)×Z(1−SIN(B))+0.5(S−W)×Z^2(1−SIN(B))
+0.5×W×Z^2

HP 35s Checksum; Length of Equation: **CK=B609; LN=88**

[RCL] [P] [↰] [=] [RCL] [Q] [×] [RCL] [X] [()] [1] [−] [SIN] [RCL] [A] [>] [>] [+] [·] [5] [×] [RCL] [D] [×] [RCL] [X] [y^x]
[2] [()] [1] [−] [SIN] [RCL] [A] [>] [>] [+] [()] [RCL] [Q] [+] [RCL] [D] [×] [RCL] [X] [>] [×] [RCL] [Z] [()] [1] [−] [SIN]
[RCL] [B] [>] [>] [+] [·] [5] [()] [RCL] [S] [−] [RCL] [W] [>] [×] [RCL] [Z] [y^x] [2] [()] [1] [−] [SIN] [RCL] [B] [>] [>] [+]
[·] [5] [×] [RCL] [W] [×] [RCL] [Z] [y^x] [2] [ENTER]

HP 33s Checksum; Length of Equation: **CK=1F04; LN=93**

[RCL] [P] [↱] [=] [RCL] [Q] [×] [RCL] [X] [×] [↱] [(] [1] [−] [SIN] [RCL] [A] [↱] [)] [↱] [)] [+] [·] [5] [×] [RCL] [D]
[×] [RCL] [X] [y^x] [2] [×] [↱] [(] [1] [−] [SIN] [RCL] [A] [↱] [)] [↱] [)] [+] [↱] [(] [RCL] [Q] [+] [RCL] [D] [×] [RCL]
[X] [↱] [)] [×] [RCL] [Z] [×] [↱] [(] [1] [−] [SIN] [RCL] [B] [↱] [)] [↱] [)] [+] [·] [5] [×] [↱] [(] [RCL] [S] [−] [RCL]
[W] [↱] [)] [×] [RCL] [Z] [y^x] [2] [×] [↱] [(] [1] [−] [SIN] [RCL] [B] [↱] [)] [↱] [)] [+] [·] [5] [×] [RCL] [W] [×] [RCL]
[Z] [y^x] [2] [ENTER]

Y=(Q×X(1−SIN(A))×(Z+X÷2)+0.5×D×X^2(1−SIN(A))×(Z+X÷3)+(Q+D×X)×(1−SIN(B))×Z^2÷2 +0.5(S−W)×(1−SIN(B))×Z^3÷3+0.5×W×Z^3÷3)÷P

HP 35s Checksum; Length of Equation: **CK=F93E; LN=118**

[RCL] [Y] [↰] [=] [()] [RCL] [Q] [×] [RCL] [X] [()] [1] [−] [SIN] [RCL] [A] [>] [>] [×] [()] [RCL] [Z] [+] [RCL] [X] [÷] [2]
[>] [+] [.] [5] [×] [RCL] [D] [×] [RCL] [X] [y^x] [2] [()] [1] [−] [SIN] [RCL] [A] [>] [>] [×] [()] [RCL] [Z] [+] [RCL] [X] [÷]
[3] [>] [+] [()] [RCL] [Q] [+] [RCL] [D] [×] [RCL] [X] [>] [×] [()] [1] [−] [SIN] [RCL] [B] [>] [>] [×] [RCL] [Z] [y^x] [2] [÷]
[2] [+] [.] [5] [()] [RCL] [S] [−] [RCL] [W] [>] [×] [()] [1] [−] [SIN] [RCL] [B] [>] [>] [×] [RCL] [Z] [y^x] [3] [÷] [3] [+] [.]
[5] [×] [RCL] [W] [×] [RCL] [Z] [y^x] [3] [÷] [3] [>] [÷] [RCL] [P] [ENTER]

HP 33s Checksum; Length of Equation: **CK=4134; LN=121**

[RCL] [Y] [↱] [=] [↱] [(] [RCL] [Q] [×] [RCL] [X] [×] [↱] [(] [1] [−] [SIN] [RCL] [A] [↱] [)] [↱] [)] [×] [↱] [(] [RCL]
[Z] [+] [RCL] [X] [÷] [2] [↱] [)] [+] [.] [5] [×] [RCL] [D] [×] [RCL] [X] [y^x] [2] [×] [↱] [(] [1] [−] [SIN] [RCL] [A] [↱]
[)] [↱] [)] [×] [↱] [(] [RCL] [Z] [+] [RCL] [X] [÷] [3] [↱] [)] [+] [↱] [(] [RCL] [Q] [+] [RCL] [D] [×] [RCL] [X] [↱] [)]
[×] [↱] [(] [1] [−] [SIN] [RCL] [B] [↱] [)] [↱] [)] [×] [RCL] [Z] [y^x] [2] [÷] [2] [+] [.] [5] [×] [↱] [(] [RCL] [S] [−]
[RCL] [W] [↱] [)] [×] [↱] [(] [1] [−] [SIN] [RCL] [B] [↱] [)] [↱] [)] [×] [RCL] [Z] [y^x] [3] [÷] [3] [+] [.] [5] [×] [RCL]
[W] [×] [RCL] [Z] [y^x] [3] [÷] [3] [↱] [)] [÷] [RCL] [P] [ENTER]

O=P×Y

HP 35s Checksum; Length of Equation: **CK=8916; LN=5**

[RCL] [O] [↰] [=] [RCL] [P] [×] [RCL] [Y] [ENTER]

HP 33s Checksum; Length of Equation: **CK=8916; LN=5**

[RCL] [O] [↱] [=] [RCL] [P] [×] [RCL] [Y] [ENTER]

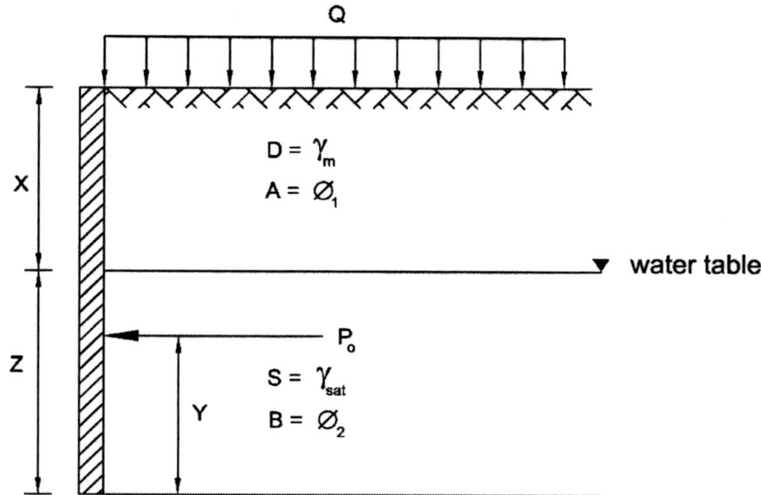

Figure 5-14 At-rest Lateral Force with Water Table Between Top and Bottom of Wall, and Surcharge Load

Notes: The above equations are not applicable for overconsolidated clay backfill. If surcharge load is neglected, Q is zero. If there is no water table, then W is zero. For 1 layer unsaturated soil, B, E, Z, S, and W are zero. The Rankine at-rest earth pressure coefficients and buoyant unit weight of saturated soil are automatically calculated. If the Rankine at-rest earth pressure coefficients are given instead of the friction angles, calculate the angles of internal friction by using Equation No. 61. If the buoyant unit weight is given instead of the saturated density, transform the buoyant unit weight to a saturated density by adding the unit weight of water (62.4 lb/ft^3, 9.81 kN/m^3).

If the density of dry soils and moisture contents are given, calculate the densities of moist and saturated soils by using the equations $\gamma_m = \gamma_d(1+\omega)$ and $\gamma_{sat} = \gamma_d(1+\omega)$, respectively.

≈≈≈≈≈≈≈≈≈≈

5.9.3 At-rest Lateral Force with Water Table at the Surface, Surcharge Load, and 1 Type of Soil

$$P_o = QHK_o + \frac{1}{2}\gamma_b H^2 K_o + \frac{1}{2}\gamma_w H^2 \quad \text{Equation No. 64 (P)}$$

Where $\gamma_b = \gamma_{sat} - \gamma_w$

$$\bar{y} = \frac{(QHK_o)\left(\frac{H}{2}\right) + \left(\frac{1}{2}\gamma_b K_o H^2\right)\left(\frac{H}{3}\right) + \left(\frac{1}{2}\gamma_w H^2\right)\left(\frac{H}{3}\right)}{P_o} \quad \text{Equation No. 64 (Y)}$$

$$O = P_o \bar{y} \quad \text{Equation No. 64 (O)}$$

The equations are entered as

```
64ATRESTWTSURF1SOIL
P=Q×H(1−SIN(A))+0.5(S−W)×H^2(1−SIN(A))+0.5×W×H^2
Y=(Q(1−SIN(A))×H^2÷2+0.5(S−W)×(1−SIN(A))×H^3÷3+0.5×W×H^3÷3)÷P
O=P×Y
```

Where:

P = total at-rest lateral force per unit length of wall P_o (lb/ft, kN/m)
Q = surcharge load Q (lb/ft^2, kN/m^2)
H = height of backfill H (ft, m)
A = angle of internal friction of soil ϕ_1
S = density of saturated soil γ_{sat} (lb/ft^3, kN/m^3)
W = unit weight of water γ_w (62.4 lb/ft^3, 9.81 kN/m^3)
Y = location of resultant lateral force from the bottom of wall $\bar{y}$ (ft, m)
O = moment at the bottom of wall due to at-rest lateral force O (ft-lb, kN-m)

Keystrokes

P=Q×H(1−SIN(A))+0.5(S−W)×H^2(1−SIN(A))+0.5×W×H^2

HP 35s Checksum; Length of Equation: **CK=429D; LN=48**

[RCL] [P] [↰] [=] [RCL] [Q] [×] [RCL] [H] [()] [1] [−] [SIN] [RCL] [A] [>] [>] [+] [·] [5] [()] [RCL] [S] [−] [RCL] [W] [>]
[×] [RCL] [H] [y^x] [2] [()] [1] [−] [SIN] [RCL] [A] [>] [>] [+] [·] [5] [×] [RCL] [W] [×] [RCL] [H] [y^x] [2] [ENTER]

HP 33s Checksum; Length of Equation: **CK=76E2; LN=51**

[RCL] [P] [↱] [=] [RCL] [Q] [×] [RCL] [H] [×] [↱] [(] [1] [−] [SIN] [RCL] [A] [↱] [)] [↱] [)] [+] [·] [5] [×] [↱] [(]
[RCL] [S] [−] [RCL] [W] [↱] [)] [×] [RCL] [H] [y^x] [2] [×] [↱] [(] [1] [−] [SIN] [RCL] [A] [↱] [)] [↱] [)] [+] [·] [5] [×]
[RCL] [W] [×] [RCL] [H] [y^x] [2] [ENTER]

Y=(Q(1−SIN(A))×H^2÷2+0.5(S−W)×(1−SIN(A))×H^3÷3+0.5×W×H^3÷3)÷P

HP 35s Checksum; Length of Equation: **CK=B903; LN=61**

[RCL] [Y] [↰] [=] [()] [RCL] [Q] [()] [1] [−] [SIN] [RCL] [A] [>] [>] [×] [RCL] [H] [y^x] [2] [÷] [2] [+] [·] [5] [()] [RCL] [S]
[−] [RCL] [W] [>] [×] [()] [1] [−] [SIN] [RCL] [A] [>] [>] [×] [RCL] [H] [y^x] [3] [÷] [3] [+] [·] [5] [×] [RCL] [W] [×] [RCL]
[H] [y^x] [3] [÷] [3] [>] [÷] [RCL] [P] [ENTER]

HP 33s Checksum; Length of Equation: **CK=27E5; LN=63**

[RCL] [Y] [↱] [=] [↱] [(] [RCL] [Q] [×] [↱] [(] [1] [−] [SIN] [RCL] [A] [↱] [)] [↱] [)] [×] [RCL] [H] [y^x] [2] [÷] [2] [+]
[·] [5] [×] [↱] [(] [RCL] [S] [−] [RCL] [W] [↱] [)] [×] [↱] [(] [1] [−] [SIN] [RCL] [A] [↱] [)] [↱] [)] [×] [RCL] [H] [y^x]
[3] [÷] [3] [+] [·] [5] [×] [RCL] [W] [×] [RCL] [H] [y^x] [3] [÷] [3] [↱] [)] [÷] [RCL] [P] [ENTER]

O=P×Y

HP 35s Checksum; Length of Equation: **CK=8916; LN=5**

[RCL] [O] [↰] [=] [RCL] [P] [×] [RCL] [Y] [ENTER]

HP 33s Checksum; Length of Equation: **CK=8916; LN=5**

[RCL] [O] [↱] [=] [RCL] [P] [×] [RCL] [Y] [ENTER]

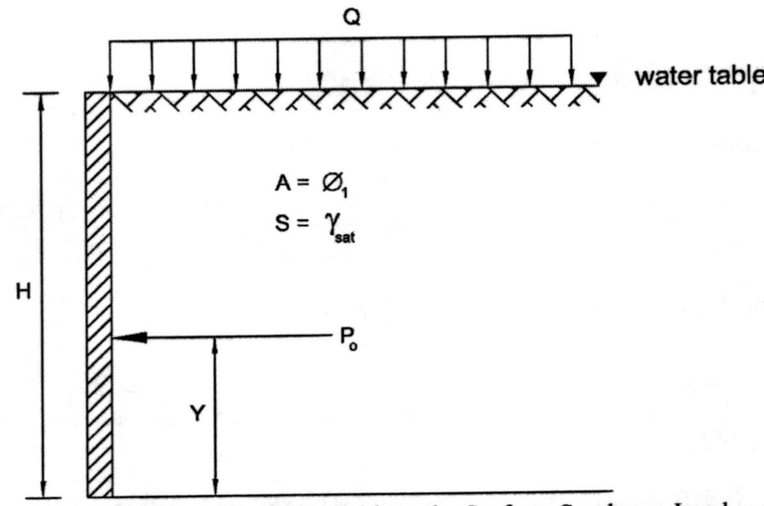

Figure 5-15 At-rest Lateral Force with Water Table at the Surface, Surcharge Load, and 1 Type of Soil

Notes: The above equations are not applicable for overconsolidated clay backfill. If there is no surcharge load, then Q is zero. The Rankine at-rest earth pressure coefficient and the buoyant unit weight of saturated soil are automatically calculated. If the Rankine at-rest earth pressure coefficient is given instead of the friction angle, calculate the angle of internal friction by using Equation No. 61. If there is no water table, then W is zero and use S as the dry or moist density of soil. If the buoyant unit weight is given instead of the saturated density, transform the buoyant unit weight to a saturated density by adding the unit weight of water (62.4 lb/ft^3, 9.81 kN/m^3).

If the density of dry soil and moisture content are given, calculate the density of saturated soil by using the equation $\gamma_{sat} = \gamma_d(1+\omega)$.

≈≈≈≈≈≈≈≈≈≈

Problem 5.1

A gravity retaining wall is supporting a cohesionless soil. The active lateral force per linear foot of the retaining wall is most nearly

(A) 5,000 lb/ft
(B) 6,000 lb/ft
(C) 7,200 lb/ft
(D) 8,500 lb/ft

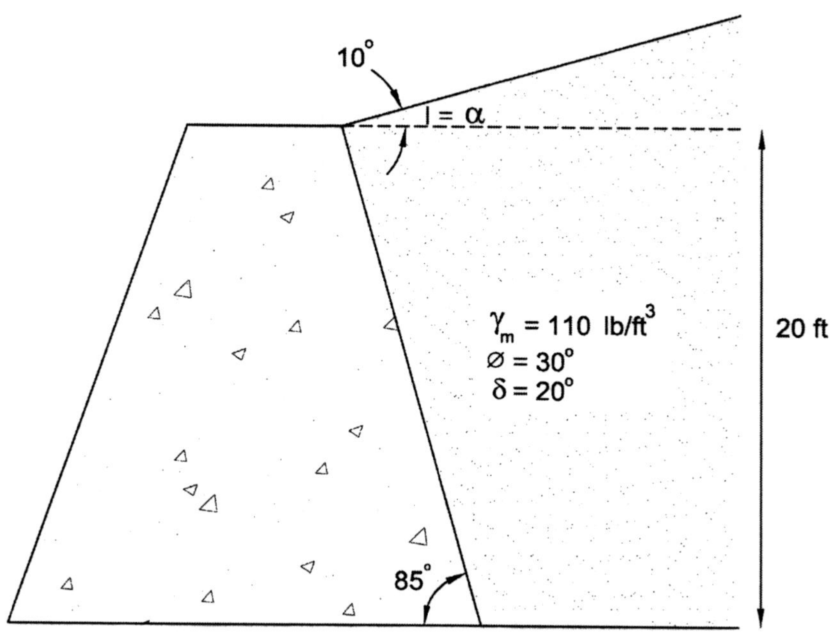

Solution

Compute the lateral force per linear foot with sloping backfill and inclined wall. Use Equation No. 51, page 93. Press ENTER.

Display	Keys	Description
S?	110 R/S	Density of backfill (lb/ft³)
H?	20 R/S	Height of wall (ft)
A?	30 R/S	Angle of internal friction of backfill
B?	85 R/S	Angle of inclined wall from horizontal
C?	20 R/S	Angle of friction between the soil and wall face
I?	10 R/S	Angle of sloping backfill from horizontal
P = 8,486.0369	--	Active lateral force per linear foot of the wall (lb/ft)

The answer is (D).

Problem 5.2

A ten-foot-high retaining wall is supporting a sand backfill. The elevation of the sand backfill equals the top elevation of the retaining wall. The angle of internal friction and dry density of the backfill are 31° and 110 lb/ft^3, respectively. The active lateral force per linear foot of the retaining wall is most nearly

(A) 1,700 lb/ft (C) 2,200 lb/ft
(B) 1,800 lb/ft (D) 3,500 lb/ft

Solution

The procedure for calculating the active lateral force per linear foot is as follows:

Step 1. Calculate the Rankine active earth pressure coefficient. Use Equation No. 47, page 89. Press ENTER.

Display	Keys	Description
A?	31 R/S	Angle of internal friction of backfill
K = 0.3201	--	Rankine active earth pressure coefficient

Step 2. Compute the active lateral force per linear foot of the retaining wall. Use Equation No. 50, page 92. Press ENTER.

Display	Keys	Description
S?	110 R/S	Density of backfill (lb/ft^3)
H?	10 R/S	Height of the wall (ft)
K? 0.3201	R/S	Rankine active earth pressure coefficient
P = 1,760.5436	--	Total active lateral force per unit length of the wall (lb/ft)

The answer is (A).

Problem 5.3

A retaining wall is supporting an 8-foot-high clayey sand backfill. The angle of internal friction of the backfill is 20°, the density is 100 lb/ft^3, and the cohesion is 100 lb/ft^2. The active earth pressure per unit length of wall is most nearly

(A) 250 lb/ft^2 (C) 400 lb/ft^2
(B) 300 lb/ft^2 (D) 700 lb/ft^2

Solution

Calculate the active earth pressure per unit length of the wall. Use Equation No. 49, page 91. Press ENTER.

Display	Keys	Description
S?	100 R/S	Density of clayey sand backfill (lb/ft^3)
H?	8 R/S	Height of backfill (ft)
K?	*	Rankine active earth pressure coefficient
K? 0.4903	R/S	
C?	100 R/S	Cohesion of clayey sand backfill (lb/ft^2)
P = 252.1910	--	Active earth pressure per unit length of the wall (lb/ft^2)

* Keys for calculating Rankine active earth pressure coefficient using RPN:

45 ENTER 20 ENTER 2 ÷ – TAN [↱] [x^2] (HP 35s)
45 ENTER 20 ENTER 2 ÷ – TAN [x^2] (HP 33s)

The answer is (A).

Problem 5.4

The retaining wall shown is supporting a sandy soil with an active equivalent fluid pressure of 38 lb/ft^3 and 31 lb/ft^3 above the water table and below the water table, respectively. The total active lateral force at the retaining wall is most nearly

(A) 5,200 lb/ft
(B) 6,000 lb/ft
(C) 6,200 lb/ft
(D) 7,000 lb/ft

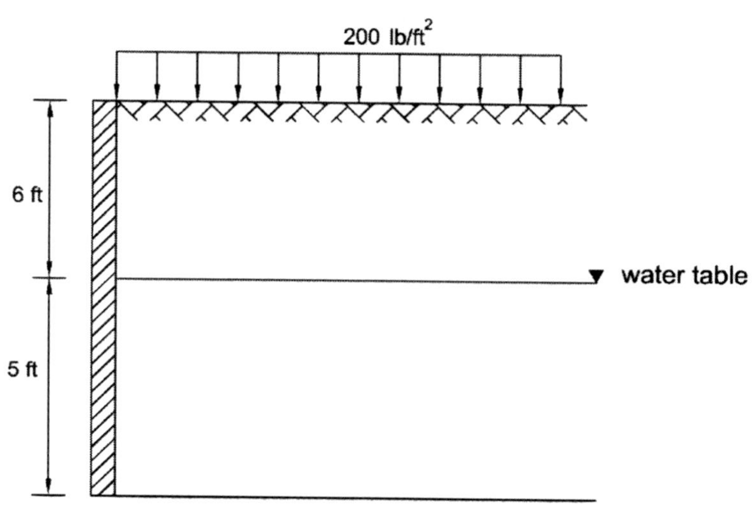

Solution

Compute the lateral force with given equivalent fluid pressures. Use Equation No. 46 (P), page 87. Press ENTER.

Display	Keys	Description
Q?	200 R/S	Surcharge load (lb/ft^2)
X?	6 R/S	Distance from top of backfill to water table (ft)
A?	38 R/S	Equivalent fluid pressure above water table (lb/ft^3)
Z?	5 R/S	Distance from water table to bottom of the wall (ft)
B?	31 R/S	Equivalent fluid pressure below water table (lb/ft^3)
W?	62.4 R/S	Unit weight of water (lb/ft^3)
P = 5,191.5000	--	Total active lateral force per unit length of the wall (lb/ft)

The answer is (A).

Problem 5.5

The retaining wall shown can yield sufficiently to develop an active state. The overturning moment per unit length of wall at point A is most nearly

(A) 16,000 ft-lb
(B) 22,000 ft-lb
(C) 25,000 ft-lb
(D) 27,000 ft-lb

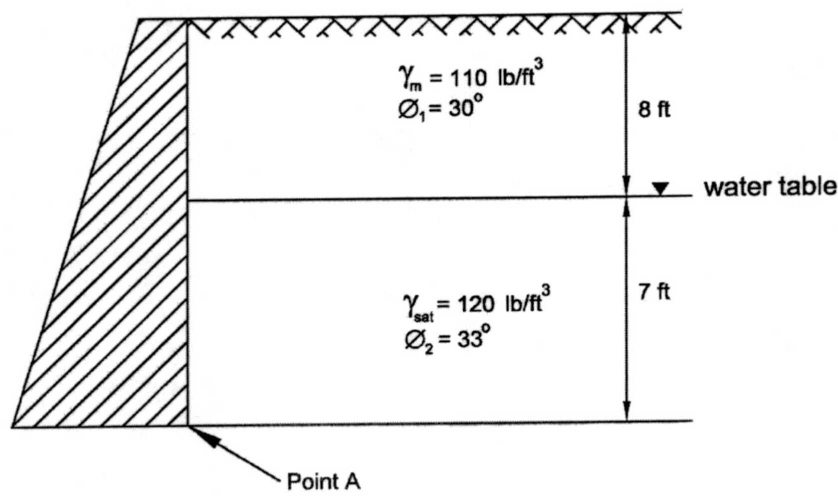

Solution

The calculation involves the following steps.

Step 1. Calculate the Rankine active force per unit length of the wall. Use Equation No. 52 (P), page 94. Press ENTER.

Display	Keys	Description
Q?	0 R/S	Surcharge load (lb/ft^2)
X?	8 R/S	Distance from top of backfill to water table (ft)
A?	30 R/S	Angle of internal friction of moist soil
D?	110 R/S	Density of moist soil (lb/ft^3)
C?	0 R/S	Cohesion of moist soil (lb/ft^2)
B?	33 R/S	Angle of internal friction of saturated soil
E?	0 R/S	Cohesion of saturated soil (lb/ft^2)
Z?	7 R/S	Distance from water table to bottom of retaining wall (ft)
S?	120 R/S	Density of saturated soil (lb/ft^3)
W?	62.4 R/S	Unit weight of water (lb/ft^3)
P = 4,934.1298	--	Rankine active force per unit length of the wall (lb/ft)

Step 2. Compute the location of resultant line of action from the bottom of the wall. Use Equation No. 52 (Y), page 94. Press ENTER. Press R/S every time you are prompted. You'll get Y = 4.5066 (ft).

Step 3. Calculate the overturning moment at point A. Use Equation No. 52 (O), page 94. Press ENTER. Press R/S every time you are prompted. You'll get O = 22,236.0498 (ft-lb).

The answer is (B).

Problem 5.6

The active resultant force and its location from the bottom of the wall are most nearly

	Active Resultant Force (lb/ft)	$\bar{y}$ (ft)
(A)	3,500	3
(B)	5,000	4
(C)	5,800	5
(D)	6,400	5

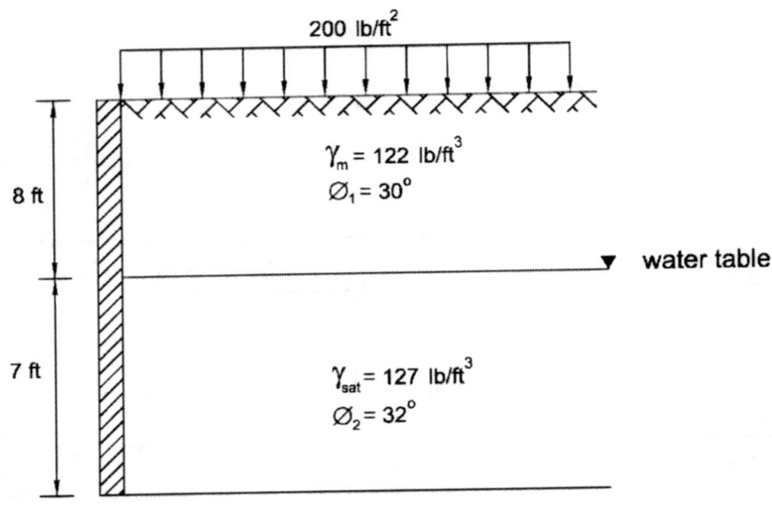

Solution

The following steps can be used to obtain the active force per unit length of the wall and the resultant line of action.

Step 1. Calculate the Rankine active lateral force. Use Equation No. 52 (P), page 94. Press ENTER.

Display	Keys	Description
Q?	200 R/S	Surcharge load (lb/ft^2)
X?	8 R/S	Distance from top of backfill to water table (ft)
A?	30 R/S	Angle of internal friction of moist soil
D?	122 R/S	Density of moist soil (lb/ft^3)
C?	0 R/S	Cohesion of moist soil (lb/ft^2)
B?	32 R/S	Angle of internal friction of saturated soil
E?	0 R/S	Cohesion of saturated soil (lb/ft^2)
Z?	7 R/S	Distance from water table to bottom of the wall (ft)
S?	127	Density of saturated soil (lb/ft^3)
W?	62.4 R/S	Unit weight of water (lb/ft^3)
P = 6,379.1169	--	Rankine active force per unit length of the wall (lb/ft)

Step 2. Compute the location of resultant line of action from the bottom of the wall. Use Equation No. 52 (Y), page 94. Press ENTER. Press R/S every time you are prompted. You'll get Y = 5.0165 (ft).

The answer is (D).

CHAPTER 6: RETAINING WALL

6.1 Retaining Wall with Sloping Backfill or Surcharge

6.1.1 Rankine Active Earth Pressure Coefficient for Sloping Backfill and Vertical Wall

$$K_a = \cos\alpha \frac{\cos\alpha - \sqrt{\cos^2\alpha - \cos^2\phi}}{\cos\alpha + \sqrt{\cos^2\alpha - \cos^2\phi}}$$ Equation No. 65

The equation is entered as

65RANACTCOSBVW
K=COS(I)×(COS(I)−(COS(I)^2−COS(A)^2)^0.5)÷(COS(I)+(COS(I)^2−COS(A)^2)^0.5)

Where:

K = Rankine active earth pressure coefficient K_a
I = angle of sloping backfill from horizontal α
A = angle of internal friction of backfill ϕ

Keystrokes

HP 35s Checksum; Length of Equation: **CK=A1C8; LN=74**

RCL K ↰ = COS RCL I > × () COS RCL I > − () COS RCL I > yˣ 2 − COS RCL A > yˣ 2 > yˣ · 5 > ÷ () COS RCL I > + () COS RCL I > yˣ 2 − COS RCL A > yˣ 2 > yˣ · 5 ENTER

HP 33s Checksum; Length of Equation: **CK=FCB3; LN=74**

RCL K ↱ = COS RCL I ↱) × ↱ (COS RCL I ↱) − ↱ (COS RCL I ↱) yˣ 2 − COS RCL A ↱) yˣ 2 ↱) yˣ · 5 ↱) ÷ ↱ (COS RCL I ↱) + ↱ (COS RCL I ↱) yˣ 2 − COS RCL A ↱) yˣ 2 ↱) yˣ · 5 ↱) ENTER

Notes: This equation is identical to Equation No. 48 on page 90. I recommend placing this equation in this chapter for quick access to calculate the Rankine active earth pressure coefficient for sloping backfill.

≈≈≈≈≈≈≈≈≈≈

6.1.2 Resisting Moment

$$\Sigma M_R = WY\gamma_c\left(B - E - \frac{W}{2}\right) + \frac{1}{2}(U - W)Y\gamma_c\left(B - E - W - \frac{(U - W)}{3}\right) + TB\gamma_c\left(\frac{B}{2}\right)$$
$$+ E(Y - H)\gamma_1\left(B - \frac{E}{2}\right) + EZ\left(B - \frac{E}{2}\right) + \frac{1}{2}E^2 \tan\alpha\gamma_1\left(B - \frac{E}{3}\right) + G(B - E - U)\gamma_2\left(\frac{B - E - U}{2}\right)$$
$$+ \frac{1}{2}\gamma_1(T + Y - H + \tan\alpha E)^2 K_a \sin\alpha B \qquad \text{Equation No. 66}$$

The equation is entered as

66RESISTMOMENT
R=W×Y×C(B−E−W÷2)+0.5(U−W)×Y×C(B−E−W−(U−W)÷3)+0.5×T×B^2×C+E(Y−H)×S(B−E÷2)+E×Z(B−E÷2)+0.5×E^2×TAN(I)×S(B−E÷3)+0.5×G(B−E−U)^2×D+0.5×S(T+Y−H+TAN(I)×E)^2×K×SIN(I)×B

Where:

R = resisting moment about the toe ΣM_R (ft-lb, kN-m)
W = stem thickness at the top W (ft, m)
Y = height of stem Y (ft, m)
C = density of concrete γ_c (lb/ft^3, kN/m^3)
B = length of base B (ft, m)
E = length of heel E (ft, m)
U = stem thickness at the bottom U (ft, m)
T = thickness of base footing T (ft, m)
H = vertical distance from top of stem to backfill H (ft, m)
S = density of backfill behind the wall γ_1 (lb/ft^3, kN/m^3)
Z = surcharge load Z (lb/ft^2, kN/m^2)
I = angle of sloping backfill from horizontal α
G = thickness of backfill from mudline to top of toe G (ft, m)
D = density of backfill at the toe γ_2 (lb/ft^3, kN/m^3)
K = Rankine active earth pressure coefficient for sloping backfill K_a

Keystrokes

HP 35s Checksum; Length of Equation: **CK=F836; LN=159**

[RCL] [R] [↰] [=] [RCL] [W] [×] [RCL] [Y] [×] [RCL] [C] [()] [RCL] [B] [−] [RCL] [E] [−] [RCL] [W] [÷] [2] [>] [+] [·] [5]
[()] [RCL] [U] [−] [RCL] [W] [>] [×] [RCL] [Y] [×] [RCL] [C] [()] [RCL] [B] [−] [RCL] [E] [−] [RCL] [W] [−] [()] [RCL] [U] [−]
[RCL] [W] [>] [÷] [3] [>] [+] [·] [5] [×] [RCL] [T] [×] [RCL] [B] [y^x] [2] [×] [RCL] [C] [+] [RCL] [E] [()] [RCL] [Y] [−]
[RCL] [H] [>] [×] [RCL] [S] [()] [RCL] [B] [−] [RCL] [E] [÷] [2] [>] [+] [RCL] [E] [×] [RCL] [Z] [()] [RCL] [B] [−] [RCL] [E]
[÷] [2] [>] [+] [·] [5] [×] [RCL] [E] [y^x] [2] [×] [TAN] [RCL] [I] [>] [×] [RCL] [S] [()] [RCL] [B] [−] [RCL] [E] [÷] [3] [>]
[+] [·] [5] [×] [RCL] [G] [()] [RCL] [B] [−] [RCL] [E] [−] [RCL] [U] [>] [y^x] [2] [×] [RCL] [D] [+] [·] [5] [×] [RCL] [S] [()]
[RCL] [T] [+] [RCL] [Y] [−] [RCL] [H] [+] [TAN] [RCL] [I] [>] [×] [RCL] [E] [>] [y^x] [2] [×] [RCL] [K] [×] [SIN] [RCL] [I]
[>] [×] [RCL] [B] [ENTER]

Checksum; Length of Equation: **CK=C5C0; LN=168**

[RCL] [R] [↱] [=] [RCL] [W] [×] [RCL] [Y] [×] [RCL] [C] [×] [↱] [(] [RCL] [B] [−] [RCL] [E] [−] [RCL] [W] [÷] [2] [↱] [)]
[+] [·] [5] [×] [↱] [(] [RCL] [U] [−] [RCL] [W] [↱] [)] [×] [RCL] [Y] [×] [RCL] [C] [×] [↱] [(] [RCL] [B] [−] [RCL] [E] [−]
[RCL] [W] [−] [↱] [(] [RCL] [U] [−] [RCL] [W] [↱] [)] [÷] [3] [↱] [)] [+] [·] [5] [×] [RCL] [T] [×] [RCL] [B] [y^x] [2] [×]
[RCL] [C] [+] [RCL] [E] [×] [↱] [(] [RCL] [Y] [−] [RCL] [H] [↱] [)] [×] [RCL] [S] [×] [↱] [(] [RCL] [B] [−] [RCL] [E] [÷]
[2] [↱] [)] [+] [RCL] [E] [×] [RCL] [Z] [×] [↱] [(] [RCL] [B] [−] [RCL] [E] [÷] [2] [↱] [)] [+] [·] [5] [×] [RCL] [E] [y^x]
[2] [×] [TAN] [RCL] [I] [↱] [)] [×] [RCL] [S] [×] [↱] [(] [RCL] [B] [−] [RCL] [E] [÷] [3] [↱] [)] [+] [·] [5] [×] [RCL] [G]
[×] [↱] [(] [RCL] [B] [−] [RCL] [E] [−] [RCL] [U] [↱] [)] [y^x] [2] [×] [RCL] [D] [+] [·] [5] [×] [RCL] [S] [×] [↱] [(] [RCL]
[T] [+] [RCL] [Y] [−] [RCL] [H] [+] [TAN] [RCL] [I] [↱] [)] [×] [RCL] [E] [↱] [)] [y^x] [2] [×] [RCL] [K] [×] [SIN] [RCL] [I]
[↱] [)] [×] [RCL] [B] [ENTER]

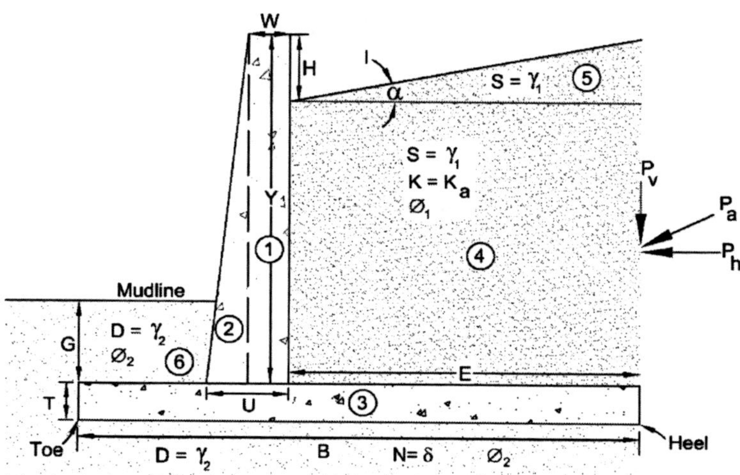

Figure 6-1 Retaining Wall with Sloping Backfill

Notes: If backfill is horizontal, I is zero. If the backfill extends to the top of stem, H is zero.

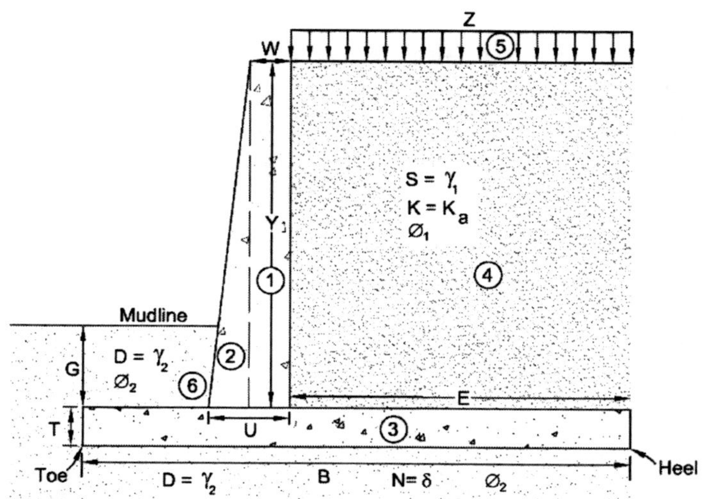

Figure 6-2 Retaining Wall with Surcharge Load

≈≈≈≈≈≈≈≈≈≈

6.1.3 Overturning Moment

$$\Sigma M_O = \frac{1}{2}\left(Z + \gamma_1\left(\frac{T + Y - H + \tan\alpha E}{3}\right)\right)(T + Y - H + \tan\alpha E)^2 K_a \cos\alpha \qquad \text{Equation No. 67}$$

The equation is entered as

67OTMOMENT
O=0.5(Z+S(T+Y−H+TAN(I)×E)÷3)×(T+Y−H+TAN(I)×E)^2×K×COS(I)

Where:

O = overturning moment about the toe ΣM_O (ft-lb, kN-m)
Z = surcharge load Z (lb/ft², kN/m²)
S = density of backfill behind the wall γ_1 (lb/ft³, kN/m³)
T = thickness of base footing T (ft, m)
Y = height of stem Y (ft, m)
H = vertical distance from top of stem to backfill H (ft, m)
I = angle of sloping backfill from horizontal α
E = length of heel E (ft, m)
K = Rankine active earth pressure coefficient for sloping backfill K_a

Keystrokes

HP 35s Checksum; Length of Equation: **CK=FD39; LN=56**

[RCL] [O] [↰] [=] [·] [5] [()] [RCL] [Z] [+] [RCL] [S] [()] [RCL] [T] [+] [RCL] [Y] [−] [RCL] [H] [+] [TAN] [RCL] [I] [>] [×]
[RCL] [E] [>] [÷] [3] [>] [×] [()] [RCL] [T] [+] [RCL] [Y] [−] [RCL] [H] [+] [TAN] [RCL] [I] [>] [×] [RCL] [E] [>] [y^x] [2]
[×] [RCL] [K] [×] [COS] [RCL] [I] [ENTER]

HP 33s Checksum; Length of Equation: **CK=E1F2; LN=58**

[RCL] [O] [↱] [=] [·] [5] [×] [↱] [(] [RCL] [Z] [+] [RCL] [S] [×] [↱] [(] [RCL] [T] [+] [RCL] [Y] [−] [RCL] [H] [+] [TAN]
[RCL] [I] [↱] [)] [×] [RCL] [E] [↱] [)] [÷] [3] [↱] [)] [×] [↱] [(] [RCL] [T] [+] [RCL] [Y] [−] [RCL] [H] [+] [TAN] [RCL]
[I] [↱] [)] [×] [RCL] [E] [↱] [)] [y^x] [2] [×] [RCL] [K] [×] [COS] [RCL] [I] [↱] [)] [ENTER]

≈≈≈≈≈≈≈≈≈≈

6.1.4 Factor of Safety against Overturning

$$L = \frac{\Sigma M_R}{\Sigma M_O} \qquad \text{Equation No. 68}$$

The equation is entered as

68FSAGOVERTURN
L=R÷O

Where:

L = factor of safety against overturning L
R = resisting moment about the toe ΣM_R (ft-lb, kN-m)
O = overturning moment about the toe ΣM_O (ft-lb, kN-m)

Keystrokes

HP 35s Checksum; Length of Equation: **CK=2E00; LN=5**

[RCL] [L] [↰] [=] [RCL] [R] [÷] [RCL] [O] [ENTER]

HP 33s Checksum; Length of Equation: **CK=2E00; LN=5**

[RCL] [L] [↱] [=] [RCL] [R] [÷] [RCL] [O] [ENTER]

≈≈≈≈≈≈≈≈≈≈

6.1.5 Total Weight

$$\Sigma V = WY\gamma_c + \frac{1}{2}(U-W)Y\gamma_c + TB\gamma_c + E(Y-H)\gamma_1 + EZ + \frac{1}{2}E^2 \tan\alpha\gamma_1 + G(B-E-U)\gamma_2$$
$$+\frac{1}{2}\gamma_1(T+Y-H+\tan\alpha E)^2 K_a \sin\alpha \qquad \text{Equation No. 69}$$

The equation is entered as

69TOTALWT
V=W×Y×C+0.5(U−W)×Y×C+T×B×C+E(Y−H)×S+E×Z+0.5×E^2×TAN(I)×S+G(B−E−U)×D +0.5×S(T+Y−H+TAN(I)×E)^2×K×SIN(I)

Where:

V = total weight of retaining wall including backfill soils ΣV (lb, kN)
W = stem thickness at the top W (ft, m)
Y = height of stem Y (ft, m)
C = density of concrete γ_c (lb/ft^3, kN/m^3)
U = stem thickness at the bottom U (ft, m)
T = thickness of base footing T (ft, m)
B = length of base B (ft, m)
E = length of heel E (ft, m)
H = vertical distance from top of stem to backfill H (ft, m)
S = density of backfill behind the wall γ_1 (lb/ft^3, kN/m^3)
Z = surcharge load Z (lb/ft^2, kN/m^2)
I = angle of sloping backfill from horizontal α
G = thickness of backfill from mudline to top of toe G (ft, m)
D = density of backfill at the toe γ_2 (lb/ft^3, kN/m^3)
K = Rankine active earth pressure coefficient for sloping backfill K_a

Keystrokes

HP 35s Checksum; Length of Equation: **CK=8588; LN=100**

[RCL] [V] [↰] [=] [RCL] [W] [×] [RCL] [Y] [×] [RCL] [C] [+] [·] [5] [()] [RCL] [U] [−] [RCL] [W] [>] [×] [RCL] [Y] [×] [RCL] [C] [+] [RCL] [T] [×] [RCL] [B] [×] [RCL] [C] [+] [RCL] [E] [()] [RCL] [Y] [−] [RCL] [H] [>] [×] [RCL] [S] [+] [RCL] [E] [×] [RCL] [Z] [+] [·] [5] [×] [RCL] [E] [y^x] [2] [×] [TAN] [RCL] [I] [>] [×] [RCL] [S] [+] [RCL] [G] [()] [RCL] [B] [−] [RCL] [E] [−] [RCL] [U] [>] [×] [RCL] [D] [+] [·] [5] [×] [RCL] [S] [()] [RCL] [T] [+] [RCL] [Y] [−] [RCL] [H] [+] [TAN] [RCL] [I] [>] [×] [RCL] [E] [>] [y^x] [2] [×] [RCL] [K] [×] [SIN] [RCL] [I] [ENTER]

HP 33s Checksum; Length of Equation: **CK=9C12; LN=104**

[RCL] [V] [↱] [=] [RCL] [W] [×] [RCL] [Y] [×] [RCL] [C] [+] [·] [5] [×] [↱] [(] [RCL] [U] [−] [RCL] [W] [↱] [)] [×] [RCL] [Y] [×] [RCL] [C] [+] [RCL] [T] [×] [RCL] [B] [×] [RCL] [C] [+] [RCL] [E] [×] [↱] [(] [RCL] [Y] [−] [RCL] [H] [↱] [)] [×] [RCL] [S] [+] [RCL] [E] [×] [RCL] [Z] [+] [·] [5] [×] [RCL] [E] [y^x] [2] [×] [TAN] [RCL] [I] [↱] [)] [×] [RCL] [S] [+] [RCL] [G] [×] [↱] [(] [RCL] [B] [−] [RCL] [E] [−] [RCL] [U] [↱] [)] [×] [RCL] [D] [+] [·] [5] [×] [RCL] [S] [×] [↱] [(] [RCL] [T] [+] [RCL] [Y] [−] [RCL] [H] [+] [TAN] [RCL] [I] [↱] [)] [×] [RCL] [E] [↱] [)] [y^x] [2] [×] [RCL] [K] [×] [SIN] [RCL] [I] [↱] [)] [ENTER]

≈≈≈≈≈≈≈≈≈≈

6.1.6 Factor of Safety against Sliding

$$M = \frac{\Sigma V \tan\delta + BC_A + \frac{1}{2}K_p\gamma_2(G+T)^2 + 2c\sqrt{K_p}(G+T)}{\frac{1}{2}\gamma_1(T+Y-H+\tan\alpha E)^2 K_a \cos\alpha + Z(T+Y)K_a}$$ Equation No. 70

The equation is entered as

70FSAGSLIDING
M=(V×TAN(N)+B×F+(0.5×P×D(G+T)^2+2×X×P^0.5(G+T)))÷(0.5×S(T+Y−H+TAN(I)×E)^2×K ×COS(I)+Z(T+Y)×K)

Where:

M = factor of safety against sliding M
V = total weight of retaining wall including backfill soils ΣV (lb, kN)
N = angle of external friction between soil and concrete δ
B = length of base B (ft, m)
F = adhesion C_A (lb/ft^2, kN/m^2)
P = Rankine passive earth pressure coefficient for backfill at the toe K_p
D = density of soil at the base and toe of retaining wall γ_2 (lb/ft^3, kN/m^3)
G = thickness of backfill from mudline to top of toe G (ft, m)
T = thickness of base footing T (ft, m)
X = cohesion of soil at the toe c (lb/ft^2, kN/m^2)
S = density of soil backfill behind the wall γ_1 (lb/ft^3, kN/m^3)
Y = height of stem Y (ft, m)
H = vertical distance from top of stem to backfill H (ft, m)
I = angle of sloping backfill from horizontal α

E = length of heel E (ft, m)
K = Rankine active earth pressure coefficient with sloping backfill K_a
Z = surcharge load Z (lb/ft², kN/m²)

Keystrokes

HP 35s Checksum; Length of Equation: **CK=A83A; LN=92**

[RCL] [M] [↰] [=] [()] [RCL] [V] [×] [TAN] [RCL] [N] [>] [+] [RCL] [B] [×] [RCL] [F] [+] [()] [·] [5] [×] [RCL] [P] [×] [RCL] [D] [()] [RCL] [G] [+] [RCL] [T] [>] [yˣ] [2] [+] [2] [×] [RCL] [X] [×] [RCL] [P] [yˣ] [·] [5] [()] [RCL] [G] [+] [RCL] [T] [>] [>] [>] [÷] [()] [·] [5] [×] [RCL] [S] [()] [RCL] [T] [+] [RCL] [Y] [−] [RCL] [H] [+] [TAN] [RCL] [I] [>] [×] [RCL] [E] [>] [yˣ] [2] [×] [RCL] [K] [×] [COS] [RCL] [I] [>] [+] [RCL] [Z] [()] [RCL] [T] [+] [RCL] [Y] [>] [×] [RCL] [K] [ENTER]

HP 33s Checksum; Length of Equation: **CK=99B2; LN=96**

[RCL] [M] [↱] [=] [↱] [(] [RCL] [V] [×] [TAN] [RCL] [N] [↱] [)] [+] [RCL] [B] [×] [RCL] [F] [+] [↱] [(] [·] [5] [×] [RCL] [P] [×] [RCL] [D] [×] [↱] [(] [RCL] [G] [+] [RCL] [T] [↱] [)] [yˣ] [2] [+] [2] [×] [RCL] [X] [×] [RCL] [P] [yˣ] [·] [5] [×] [↱] [(] [RCL] [G] [+] [RCL] [T] [↱] [)] [↱] [)] [↱] [)] [÷] [↱] [(] [·] [5] [×] [RCL] [S] [×] [↱] [(] [RCL] [T] [+] [RCL] [Y] [−] [RCL] [H] [+] [TAN] [RCL] [I] [↱] [)] [×] [RCL] [E] [↱] [)] [yˣ] [2] [×] [RCL] [K] [×] [COS] [RCL] [I] [↱] [)] [+] [RCL] [Z] [↱] [(] [RCL] [T] [+] [RCL] [Y] [↱] [)] [×] [RCL] [K] [↱] [)] [ENTER]

Notes: If the angle of external friction between soil and concrete (δ) is not given and the coefficient of friction between soil and concrete is given (e.g. 0.4), use the inverse tangent function of your calculator to calculate the angle of external friction between soil and concrete (δ). For example, if the coefficient of friction is given as 0.4, by using the inverse tangent of your calculator, .4 [↱] [ATAN] for HP 35s, .4 [↰] [ATAN] for the HP 33s, the inverse tangent is 21.8014° which is equivalent to the angle of internal friction between soil and concrete.

If solving only for factor of safety against sliding, skip the resisting moment and the overturning moment process. If ignoring the weight of soil above the toe for resisting moment, then G is zero. If ignoring the passive resistance to calculate the factor of safety against sliding, then P is zero. If the equivalent fluid pressure (lb/ft³, kN/m³) for active side is given, enter 1 for K (active lateral coefficient) and set S as the equivalent fluid pressure (lb/ft³, kN/m³). If the equivalent fluid pressure (lb/ft³, kN/m³) for passive side is given, enter 1 for P (passive lateral coefficient) and set D as the equivalent fluid pressure (lb/ft³, kN/m³).

The above equations can not be used if the lateral force (lb, kN) is given. The hydrostatic pressure behind the retaining wall and key resistance against sliding are not considered.

≈≈≈≈≈≈≈≈≈≈

6.1.7 Eccentricity

$$J = \frac{B}{2} - \frac{\Sigma M_R - \Sigma M_O}{\Sigma V}$$ Equation No. 71

The equation is entered as

71ECCENTRICITY
J=B÷2−(R−O)÷V

Where:

J = eccentricity J (ft, m)
B = length of base B (ft, m)
R = resisting moment about the toe ΣM_R (ft-lb)
O = overturning moment about the toe ΣM_O (ft-lb)
V = total weight of retaining wall including backfill soils ΣV (lb, kN)

Keystrokes

HP 35s Checksum; Length of Equation: **CK=7835; LN=13**

[RCL] [J] [↰] [=] [RCL] [B] [÷] [2] [−] [()] [RCL] [R] [−] [RCL] [O] [>] [÷] [RCL] [V] [ENTER]

HP 33s Checksum; Length of Equation: **CK=7835; LN=13**

[RCL] [J] [↱] [=] [RCL] [B] [÷] [2] [−] [↱] [(] [RCL] [R] [−] [RCL] [O] [↱] [)] [÷] [RCL] [V] [ENTER]

≈≈≈≈≈≈≈≈≈≈

6.1.8 Maximum Stress of Soil at the Toe

This equation is only applicable if the Kern $\left(\frac{B}{6}\right)$ is greater than eccentricity J.

$$Q_{(\max)_{toe}} = \frac{\Sigma V}{B}\left(1 + \frac{6J}{B}\right) \quad \text{Equation No. 72}$$

The equation is entered as

72QMAX
Q=V÷B(1+6×J÷B)

Where:

Q = maximum stress of soil at the toe $Q_{(\max)_{toe}}$ (lb/ft^2, kN/m^2)
V = total weight of retaining wall including backfill soils ΣV (lb, kN)
B = length of base B (ft, m)
J = eccentricity J (ft, m)

Keystrokes

HP 35s Checksum; Length of Equation: **CK=406F; LN=14**

[RCL] [Q] [↰] [=] [RCL] [V] [÷] [RCL] [B] [()] [1] [+] [6] [×] [RCL] [J] [÷] [RCL] [B] [ENTER]

HP 33s Checksum; Length of Equation: **CK=F2B8; LN=15**

[RCL] [Q] [↱] [=] [RCL] [V] [÷] [RCL] [B] [×] [↱] [(] [1] [+] [6] [×] [RCL] [J] [÷] [RCL] [B] [↱] [)] [ENTER]

6.1.9 Minimum Stress of Soil at the Heel

This equation is only applicable if the Kern $\left(\frac{B}{6}\right)$ is greater than eccentricity J.

$$Q_{(\min)_{heel}} = \frac{\Sigma V}{B}\left(1 - \frac{6J}{B}\right)$$ Equation No. 73

The equation is entered as

73QMIN
Q=V÷B(1−6×J÷B)

Where:

Q = minimum stress of soil at the heel $Q_{(\min)_{heel}}$ (lb/ft², kN/m²)
V = total weight of retaining wall including backfill soils ΣV (lb, kN)
B = length of base B (ft, m)
J = eccentricity J (ft, m)

Keystrokes

HP 35s Checksum; Length of Equation: **CK=E14A; LN=14**

[RCL] [Q] [↰] [=] [RCL] [V] [÷] [RCL] [B] [()] [1] [−] [6] [×] [RCL] [J] [÷] [RCL] [B] [ENTER]

HP 33s Checksum; Length of Equation: **CK=539D; LN=15**

[RCL] [Q] [↱] [=] [RCL] [V] [÷] [RCL] [B] [×] [↱] [(] [1] [−] [6] [×] [RCL] [J] [÷] [RCL] [B] [↱] [)] [ENTER]

≈≈≈≈≈≈≈≈≈≈

Problem 6.1

The cross section of cantilever retaining wall is show below. The angle of external friction between concrete and base soil is 20°, the adhesion is 100 lb/ft², and cohesion is 200 lb/ft². The density of concrete is 150 lb/ft³. The factor of safety against overturning, factor of safety against sliding, maximum stress at the toe, and minimum stress at the heel are most nearly

	Factor of Safety against Overturning	Factor of Safety against Sliding	Maximum Stress at the Toe (lb/ft²)	Minimum Stress at the Heel (lb/ft²)
(A)	2.5	1.9	3,000	500
(B)	3.2	2.3	4,200	700
(C)	3.8	2.5	5,000	1,000
(D)	4	3	6,000	2,000

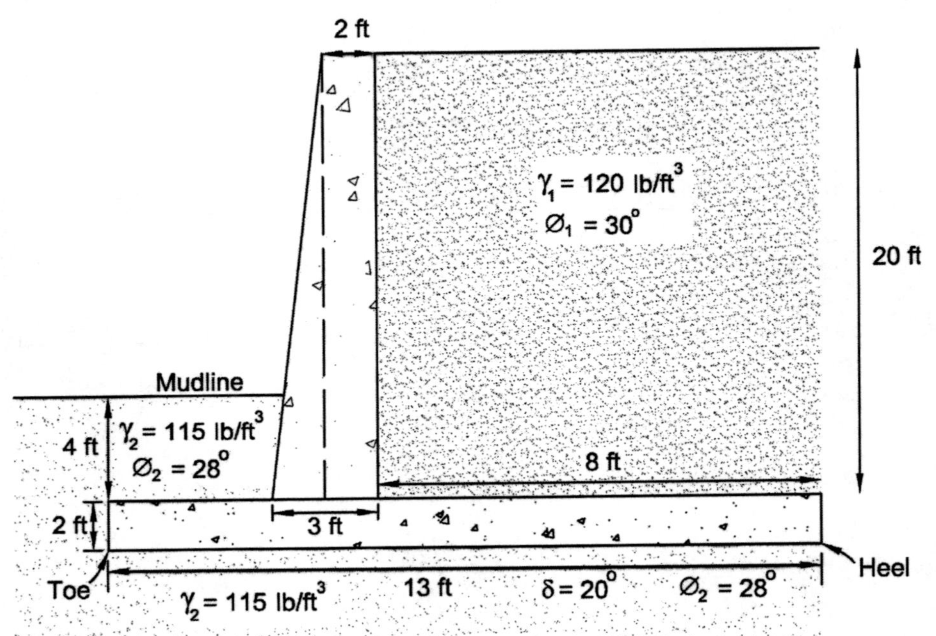

Solution

The following procedure can be used to analyze the retaining wall with given dimensions and soil parameters.

a) Factor of safety against overturning

Step 1. Calculate the Rankine active earth coefficient with horizontal backfill and vertical wall. Use Equation No. 65, page 123. Press ENTER.

Display	Keys	Description
I?	0 R/S	Angle of sloping backfill with respect to horizontal
A?	30 R/S	Angle of internal friction of soil
K = 0.3333	--	Rankine active pressure coefficient

Step 2. Compute the resisting moment about the toe. Use Equation No. 66, page 124. Press ENTER.

Display	Keys	Description
W?	2 R/S	Stem thickness at the top (ft)
Y?	20 R/S	Height of stem (ft)
C?	150 R/S	Density of concrete (lb/ft^3)
B?	13 R/S	Length of base (ft)
E?	8 R/S	Length of heel (ft)
U?	3 R/S	Stem thickness at the bottom (ft)
T?	2 R/S	Thickness of base footing (ft)
H?	0 R/S	Vertical distance from top of stem to backfill (ft)
S?	120 R/S	Density of backfill (lb/ft^3)
Z?	0 R/S	Surcharge load (lb/ft^2)
I? 0.0000	R/S	Angle of sloping backfill with respect to horizontal
G?	4 R/S	Thickness of backfill from mudline to top of toe (ft)
D?	115 R/S	Density of soil at the toe (lb/ft^3)
K? 0.3333	R/S	Rankine active pressure coefficient
R = 227,070.0000	--	Resisting moment about the toe (ft-lb)

Step 3. Calculate the overturning moment. Use Equation No. 67, page 126. Press ENTER. Press R/S every time you are prompted. You'll get O = 70,986.6667 (ft-lb).

Step 4. Compute the factor of safety against overturning. Use Equation No. 68, page 126. Press ENTER. Press R/S every time you are prompted. You'll get L = 3.1988.

b) Factor of safety against sliding

Step 1. Calculate the total weight. Use Equation No. 69, page 127. Press ENTER. Press R/S every time you are prompted. You'll get V = 31,520.0000 lb/ft.

Step 2. Compute the factor of safety against sliding. Use Equation No. 70, page 128. Press ENTER.

Display	Keys	Description
V? 31,520.0000	R/S	Total weight (lb/ft)
N?	20 R/S	Angle of external friction between soil and concrete
B? 13.0000	R/S	Length of base (ft)
F?	100 R/S	Adhesion of soil at the base (lb/ft²)
P?	*	Rankine passive coefficient of soil at the base
P? 2.7698	R/S	
D? 115.0000	R/S	Density of soil at the toe (lb/ft³)
G? 4.0000	R/S	Thickness of backfill from mudline to top of toe (ft)
T? 2.0000	R/S	Thickness of base footing (ft)
X?	200 R/S	Cohesion of soil at the base (lb/ft²)
S? 120.0000	R/S	Density of backfill (lb/ft³)
Y? 20.0000	R/S	Height of stem (ft)
H? 0.0000	R/S	Vertical distance from top of stem to backfill (ft)
I? 0.0000	R/S	Angle of sloping backfill with respect to horizontal
E? 8.0000	R/S	Length of heel (ft)
K? 0.3333	R/S	Rankine active earth pressure coefficient
Z? 0.0000	R/S	Surcharge load (lb/ft²)
M = 2.3244	--	Factor of safety against sliding

* Keys for calculating Rankine passive earth pressure coefficient of soil at the base using RPN:

45 ENTER 28 ENTER 2 ÷ + [TAN] [↱] [x^2] (HP 35s)
45 ENTER 28 ENTER 2 ÷ + [TAN] [x^2] (HP 33s)

$$K_p = \tan^2\left(45 + \frac{28}{2}\right)$$

c) Maximum stress at the toe

Step 1. Calculate the eccentricity. Use Equation No. 71, page 129. Press ENTER. Press R/S every time you are prompted. You'll get J = 1.5481 for the eccentricity (ft). B/6 (13 ft/6 = 2.167 ft) is greater than the eccentricity.

Step 2. Compute the maximum stress at the toe. Use Equation No. 72, page 130. Press ENTER. Press R/S every time you are prompted. You'll get Q = 4,157.0414 for maximum stress at the toe (lb/ft²).

d) Minimum stress at the heel

Calculate the minimum stress at the heel. Use Equation No. 73, page 131. Press ENTER. Press R/S every time you are prompted. You'll get Q = 692.1893 for minimum stress at the heel (lb/ft²).

The answer is (B).

Notes: If the stem is not tapered, the stem thickness at the bottom (U) is 2 feet. In case there is no backfill soil at the toe, (G) and (D) are zero.

Problem 6.2

A reinforced concrete retaining wall is holding a sandy soil with an inclined backfill of 15° from horizontal. The angle of external friction between concrete and base soil is 20°, adhesion is 100 lb/ft², and cohesion is 200 lb/ft². The density of concrete is 150 lb/ft³. Ignore the passive resistance of soil below the mudline. The factor of safety against overturning and sliding are most nearly

	Factor of Safety against Overturning	Factor of Safety against Sliding
(A)	2.8	1.1
(B)	3.1	1.5
(C)	3.5	2
(D)	4	2.5

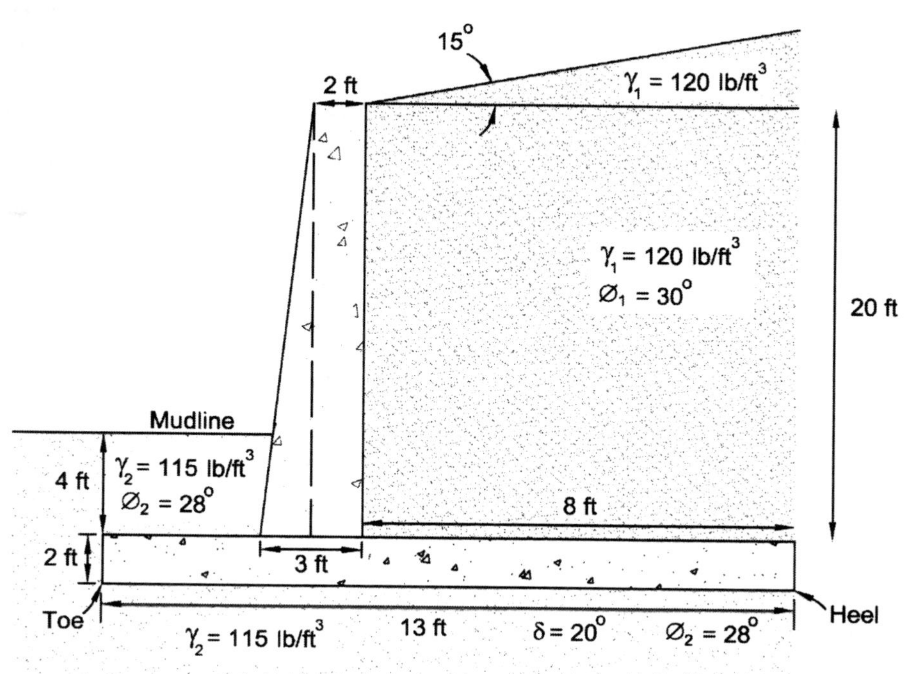

Solution

The factor of safety against overturning and sliding can be obtained in the following steps:

a) Factor of safety against overturning

Step 1. Calculate the Rankine active earth coefficient with sloping backfill and vertical wall. Use Equation No. 65, page 123. Press ENTER.

Display	Keys	Description
I?	15 R/S	Angle of sloping backfill with respect to horizontal
A?	30 R/S	Angle of internal friction of soil
K = 0.3729	--	Rankine active pressure coefficient

Step 2. Compute the resisting moment about the toe. Use Equation No. 66, page 124. Press ENTER.

Display	Keys	Description
W?	2 R/S	Stem thickness at the top (ft)
Y?	20 R/S	Height of stem (ft)
C?	150 R/S	Density of concrete (lb/ft^3)
B?	13 R/S	Length of base (ft)
E?	8 R/S	Length of heel (ft)
U?	3 R/S	Stem thickness at the bottom (ft)
T?	2 R/S	Thickness of base footing (ft)
H?	0 R/S	Vertical distance from top of stem to backfill (ft)
S?	120 R/S	Density of backfill (lb/ft^3)
Z?	0 R/S	Surcharge load (lb/ft^2)
I? 15.0000	R/S	Angle of sloping backfill with respect to horizontal
G?	0 R/S	Thickness of backfill from mudline to top of toe (ft) (ignored)
D?	115 R/S	Density of soil at the toe (lb/ft^3)
K? 0.3729	R/S	Rankine active pressure coefficient
R = 280,670.1544	--	Resisting moment about the toe (ft-lb)

Step 3. Calculate the overturning moment. Use Equation No. 67, page 126. Press ENTER. Press R/S every time you are prompted. You'll get O = 101,398.1318 ft-lb.

Step 4. Determine the factor of safety against overturning. Use Equation No. 68, page 126. Press ENTER. Press R/S every time you are prompted. You'll get L = 2.7680.

b) Factor of safety against sliding

Step 1. Calculate the total weight. Use Equation No. 69, page 127. Press ENTER. Press R/S every time you are prompted. You'll get V = 35,004.9195 (lb/ft).

Step 2. Compute the factor of safety against sliding. Use Equation No. 70, page 128. Press ENTER.

Display	Keys	Description
V? 35,004.9195	R/S	Total weight (lb/ft)
N?	20 R/S	Angle of external friction between soil and concrete
B? 13.0000	R/S	Length of base (ft)
F?	100 R/S	Adhesion of soil at the base (lb/ft^2)
P?	0 R/S	Rankine passive coefficient of soil at the base and toe (ignored)
D? 115.0000	R/S	Density of soil at the toe (lb/ft^3)
G? 0.0000	R/S	Thickness of backfill from mudline to top of toe (ft) (ignored)
T? 2.0000	R/S	Thickness of base footing (ft)
X?	200 R/S	Cohesion of soil at the base (lb/ft^2)
S? 120.0000	R/S	Density of backfill (lb/ft^3)
Y? 20.0000	R/S	Height of stem (ft)
H? 0.0000	R/S	Vertical distance from top of stem to backfill (ft)
I? 15.0000	R/S	Angle of sloping backfill with respect to horizontal
E? 8.0000	R/S	Length of heel (ft)
K? 0.3729	R/S	Rankine active pressure coefficient of backfill
Z? 0.0000	R/S	Surcharge load (lb/ft^2, kN/m^2)
M = 1.1144	--	Factor of safety against sliding

The answer is (A).

Notes: If the stem is not tapered, stem thickness at the bottom (U) is 2 feet. If no backfill soil at the toe, (G) and (D) are zero.

Problem 6.3

A reinforced concrete retaining wall is supporting a sandy soil backfill with surcharge. The angle of external friction between concrete and base soil is 20°, adhesion is 300 lb/ft², and cohesion is 100 lb/ft². The density of concrete is 150 lb/ft³. Include the passive resistance of soil below the mudline. The factor of safety against overturning and sliding are most nearly

	Factor of Safety against Overturning	Factor of Safety against Sliding
(A)	2.5	1.0
(B)	3	1.5
(C)	4	2.5
(D)	5	2.7

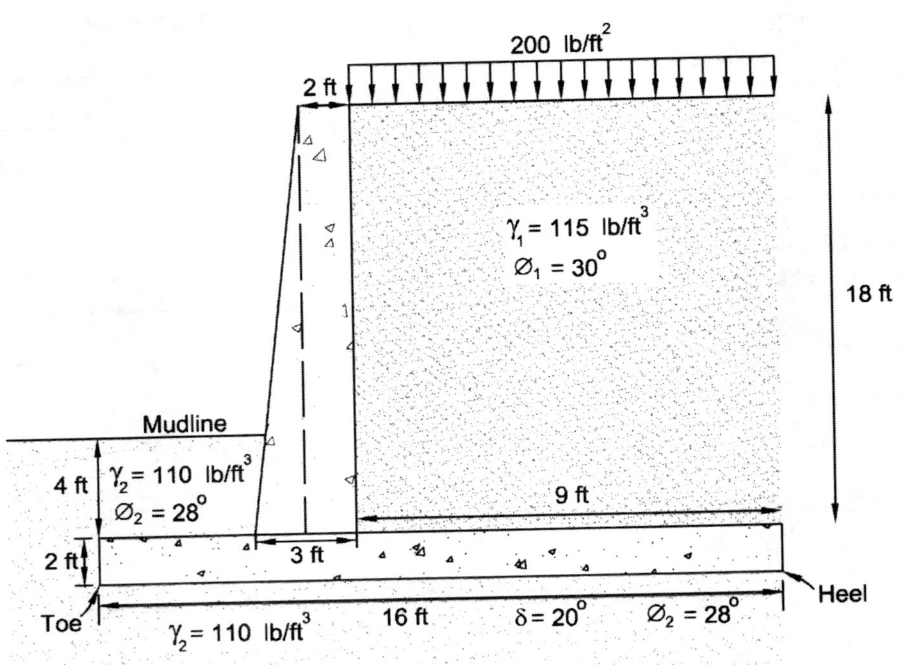

Solution

The calculations involving factor of safety against overturning and sliding are as follows:

a) Factor of safety against overturning

Step 1. Determine the Rankine active earth coefficient with sloping backfill and vertical wall. Use Equation No. 65, page 123. Press ENTER.

Display	Keys	Description
I?	0 R/S	Angle of sloping backfill with respect to horizontal
A?	30 R/S	Angle of internal friction of soil

Display	Keys	Description
K = 0.3333	--	Rankine active pressure coefficient

Step 2. Calculate the resisting moment about the toe. Use Equation No. 66, page 124. Press ENTER.

Display	Keys	Description
W?	2 R/S	Stem thickness at the top (ft)
Y?	18 R/S	Height of stem (ft)
C?	150 R/S	Density of concrete (lb/ft³)
B?	16 R/S	Length of base (ft)
E?	9 R/S	Length of heel (ft)
U?	3 R/S	Stem thickness at the bottom (ft)
T?	2 R/S	Thickness of base footing (ft)
H?	0 R/S	Vertical distance from top of stem to backfill (ft)
S?	115 R/S	Density of backfill (lb/ft³)
Z?	200 R/S	Surcharge load (lb/ft²)
I? 0.0000	R/S	Angle of sloping backfill with respect to horizontal
G?	4 R/S	Thickness of backfill from mudline to top of toe (ft)
D?	110 R/S	Density of soil at the toe (lb/ft³)
K? 0.3333	R/S	Rankine active pressure coefficient
R = 315,565.0000	--	Resisting moment about the toe (ft-lb)

Step 3. Compute the overturning moment. Use Equation No. 67, page 126. Press ENTER. Press R/S every time you are prompted. You'll get O = 64,444.4444 ft-lb.

Step 4. Calculate the factor of safety against overturning. Use Equation No. 68, page 126. Press ENTER. Press R/S every time you are prompted. You'll get L = 4.8967.

b) Factor of safety against sliding

Step 1. Calculate the total weight. Use Equation No. 69, page 127. Press ENTER. Press R/S every time you are prompted. You'll get V = 33,740.0000 (lb/ft).

Step 2. Compute the factor of safety against sliding. Use Equation No. 70, page 128. Press ENTER.

Display	Keys	Description
V? 33,740.0000	R/S	Total weight (lb/ft)
N?	20 R/S	Angle of external friction between soil and concrete

Display	Keys	Description
B? 16.0000	R/S	Length of base (ft)
F?	300 R/S	Adhesion of soil at the base (lb/ft^2)
P?	*	Rankine passive coefficient of soil at the base and toe
P? 2.7698	R/S	
D? 110.0000	R/S	Density of soil at the toe (lb/ft^3)
G? 4.0000	R/S	Thickness of backfill from mudline to top of toe (ft)
T? 2.0000	R/S	Thickness of base footing (ft)
X?	100 R/S	Cohesion of soil at the base (lb/ft^2)
S? 115.0000	R/S	Density of backfill (lb/ft^3)
Y? 18.0000	R/S	Height of stem (ft)
H? 0.0000	R/S	Vertical distance from top of stem to backfill (ft)
I? 0.0000	R/S	Angle of sloping backfill with respect to horizontal
E? 9.0000	R/S	Length of heel (ft)
K? 0.3333	R/S	Rankine active pressure coefficient of backfill
Z? 200.0000	R/S	Surcharge load (lb/ft^2, kN/m^2)
M = 2.7291	--	Factor of safety against sliding

* Keys for calculating Rankine passive earth pressure coefficient of soil at the base using RPN:

45 ENTER 28 ENTER 2 ÷ + TAN ↱ x^2 (HP 35s)
45 ENTER 28 ENTER 2 ÷ + TAN x^2 (HP 33s)

The answer is (D).

Problem 6.4

A gravity retaining wall is holding a backfill. The coefficient of friction between concrete and soil is 0.5. The factor of safety against overturning, factor of safety against sliding, and maximum stress at the toe are most nearly

	Factor of Safety against Overturning	Factor of Safety against Sliding	Maximum Stress at the Toe (lb/ft^2)
(A)	2.0	1.0	1,500
(B)	2.2	1.2	1,700
(C)	2.5	1.5	2,000
(D)	3.2	1.8	3,500

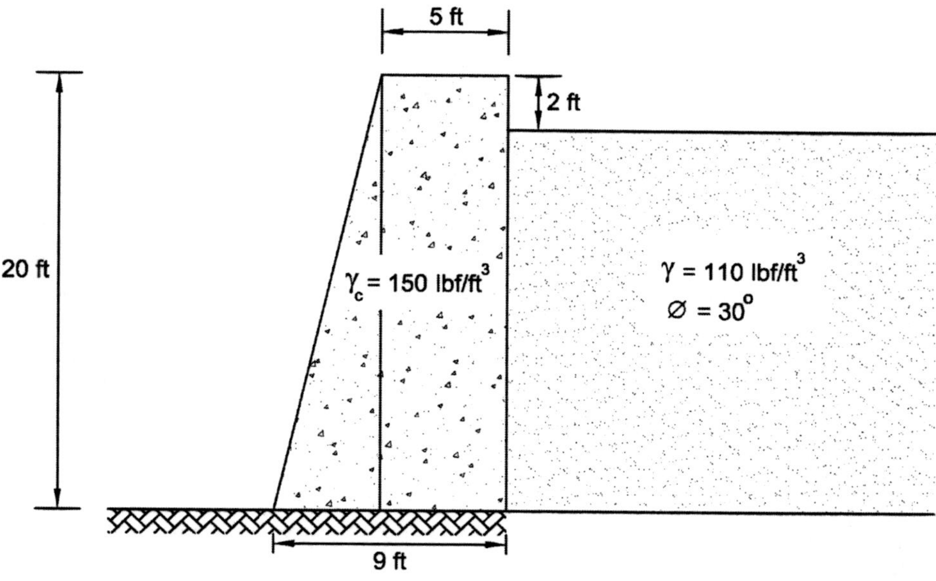

Solution

The computations for factors of safety against overturning and sliding, and maximum stress at the toe are in the following order:

a) Factor of safety against overturning

Step 1. Calculate the Rankine active earth pressure coefficient for horizontal backfill and vertical wall. Use Equation No. 65, page 123. Press ENTER.

Display	Keys	Description
I?	0 R/S	Angle of sloping backfill with respect to horizontal
A?	30 R/S	Angle of internal friction of soil
K = 0.3333	--	Rankine active pressure coefficient

Step 2. Determine the resisting moment about the toe. Use Equation No. 66, page 124. Press ENTER.

Display	Keys	Description
W?	5 R/S	Stem thickness at the top (ft)
Y?	20 R/S	Height of stem (ft)
C?	150 R/S	Density of concrete (lb/ft^3)
B?	9 R/S	Length of base (ft)
E?	0 R/S	Length of heel (ft)
U?	9 R/S	Stem thickness at the bottom (ft)
T?	0 R/S	Thickness of base footing (ft)
H?	2 R/S	Vertical distance from top of stem to backfill (ft)
S?	110 R/S	Density of backfill (lb/ft^3)

Display	Keys	Description
Z?	0 R/S	Surcharge load (lb/ft², kN/m²)
I? 0.0000	R/S	Angle of sloping backfill with respect to horizontal
G?	0 R/S	Thickness of backfill from mudline to top of toe (ft)
D?	0 R/S	Density of soil at the toe (lb/ft³)
K? 0.3333	R/S	Rankine active pressure coefficient
R = 113,500.0000	--	Resisting moment about the toe (ft-lb)

Step 3. Calculate the overturning moment. Use Equation No. 67, page 126. Press ENTER. Press R/S every time you are prompted. You'll get O = 35,640.0000 ft-lb.

Step 4. Compute the factor of safety against overturning. Use Equation No. 68, page 126. Press ENTER. Press R/S every time you are prompted. You'll get L = 3.1846.

b) Factor of safety against sliding

Step 1. Calculate the total weight. Use Equation No. 69, page 127. Press ENTER. Press R/S every time you are prompted. You'll get V = 21,000.0000 (lb/ft).

Step 2. Compute the factor of safety against sliding. Use Equation No. 70, page 128. Press ENTER.

Display	Keys	Description
V? 21,000.0000	R/S	Total weight (lb/ft)
N?	*	Angle of external friction between concrete and soil, equivalent of 0.5 coefficient of friction
N? 26.5651	R/S	
B? 9.0000	R/S	Length of base (ft)
F?	0 R/S	Adhesion of soil at the base (lb/ft²)
P?	0 R/S	Rankine passive coefficient of soil at the base and toe
D? 0.0000	R/S	Density of soil at the toe (lb/ft³)
G? 0.0000	R/S	Thickness of backfill from mudline to top of toe (ft)
T? 0.0000	R/S	Thickness of base footing (ft)
X?	0 R/S	Cohesion of soil at the base (lb/ft²)
S? 110.0000	R/S	Density of backfill (lb/ft³)
Y? 20.0000	R/S	Height of stem (ft)
H? 2.0000	R/S	Vertical distance from top of stem to backfill (ft)
I? 0.0000	R/S	Angle of sloping backfill with respect to horizontal
E? 0.0000	R/S	Length of heel (ft)
K? 0.3333	R/S	Rankine active pressure coefficient of backfill

Display	Keys	Description
Z? 0.0000	R/S	Surcharge load (lb/ft², kN/m²)
M = 1.7677	--	Factor of safety against sliding

* Keys for calculating angle of external friction between concrete and soil:

.5 [↱] [ATAN] (HP 35s)
.5 [↰] [ATAN] (HP 33s)

c) Maximum stress at the toe

Step 1. Calculate the eccentricity. Use Equation No. 71, page 129. Press ENTER. Press R/S every time you are prompted. You'll get J = 0.7924 for eccentricity (ft). B/6 (9 ft/6 = 1.5 ft) is greater than the eccentricity.

Step 2. Determine the maximum stress at the toe. Use Equation No. 72, page 130. Press ENTER. Press R/S every time you are prompted. You'll get Q = 3,565.9259 for maximum stress at the toe (lb/ft²).

The answer is (D).

Note: If the stem is not tapered, the stem thickness at the bottom (U) is 5 feet.

CHAPTER 7: BRACED CUT

7.1 Braced Cut in Sand

7.1.1 Two Struts Solving A

The lateral pressure for sand is

$$\sigma_a = 0.65\gamma H K_a$$

The Rankine active earth pressure coefficient is

$$K_a = \tan^2\left(45 - \frac{\phi}{2}\right)$$

To solve A, sum all moments at B, taking clockwise moments as positive.

$$\sum M_B = 0$$

$$AY + 0.65\gamma H K_a \frac{(H - X - Y)^2}{2} L = 0.65\gamma H K_a \frac{(X + Y)^2}{2} L \qquad \text{Equation No. 74}$$

The equation is entered as

BRACECUTSAND2STRUT
74SOLVINGA
A×Y+0.325×S×H×K(H−X−Y)^2×L=0.325×S×H×K(X+Y)^2×L

Where:

A = force at Strut 1 A (lb, kN)
Y = distance between Struts 1 and 2 Y (ft, m)
S = density of sand γ (lb/ft^3, kN/m^3)
H = height of cut H (ft, m)
K = Rankine active earth pressure coefficient of sand K_a
X = distance from top of cut to Strut 1 X (ft, m)
L = horizontal center-to-center spacing of struts L (ft, m)

Keystrokes

HP 35s Checksum; Length of Equation: **CK=E600; LN=47**

[RCL] [A] [×] [RCL] [Y] [+] [·] [3] [2] [5] [×] [RCL] [S] [×] [RCL] [H] [×] [RCL] [K] [()] [RCL] [H] [−] [RCL] [X] [−] [RCL] [Y] [>] [yˣ] [2] [×] [RCL] [L] [↰] [=] [·] [3] [2] [5] [×] [RCL] [S] [×] [RCL] [H] [×] [RCL] [K] [()] [RCL] [X] [+] [RCL] [Y] [>] [yˣ] [2] [×] [RCL] [L] [ENTER]

HP 33s Checksum; Length of Equation: **CK=DA2E; LN=49**

[RCL] [A] [×] [RCL] [Y] [+] [·] [3] [2] [5] [×] [RCL] [S] [×] [RCL] [H] [×] [RCL] [K] [×] [↱] [(] [RCL] [H] [−] [RCL] [X] [−] [RCL] [Y] [↱] [)] [y^x] [2] [×] [RCL] [L] [↱] [=] [·] [3] [2] [5] [×] [RCL] [S] [×] [RCL] [H] [×] [RCL] [K] [×] [↱] [(] [RCL] [X] [+] [RCL] [Y] [↱] [)] [y^x] [2] [×] [RCL] [L] [ENTER]

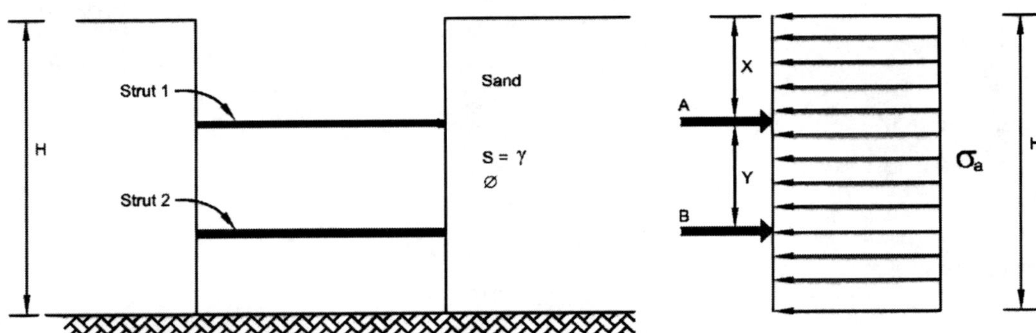

Figure 7-1 Braced Cut in Sand with Two Struts

≈≈≈≈≈≈≈≈≈≈

7.1.2 Two Struts Solving B

To solve B, sum all horizontal forces.

$$\sum F_H = 0$$

$$A + B = 0.65\gamma H^2 K_a L$$ Equation No. 75

The equation is entered as

75SOLVINGB
A+B=0.65×S×H^2×K×L

Where:

A = force at Strut 1 A (lb, kN)
B = force at Strut 2 B (lb, kN)
S = density of sand γ (lb/ft^3, kN/m^3)
H = height of cut H (ft, m)
K = Rankine active earth pressure coefficient of sand K_a
L = horizontal center-to-center spacing of struts L (ft, m)

Keystrokes

HP 35s Checksum; Length of Equation: **CK=ECF7; LN=18**

[RCL] [A] [+] [RCL] [B] [↰] [=] [·] [6] [5] [×] [RCL] [S] [×] [RCL] [H] [y^x] [2] [×] [RCL] [K] [×] [RCL] [L] [ENTER]

HP 33s Checksum; Length of Equation: **CK=ECF7; LN=18**

RCL A + RCL B [↱] = . 6 5 × RCL S × RCL H yˣ 2 × RCL K × RCL L ENTER

Note: If Strut 1 is located on top of cut, X is zero.

≈≈≈≈≈≈≈≈≈≈

7.2 Braced Cut in Soft to Medium Clay

$\frac{\gamma H}{c} \geq 4$ For soft to medium clay

where γ = the density of clay

H = the height of cut

c = cohesion of clay.

7.2.1 Two Struts Solving A, Strut 1 Within 0.25H

For maximum lateral pressure P, use the larger value between

$\sigma_a = 0.3\gamma H$ and $\sigma_a = \gamma H\left[1 - \left(\frac{4c}{\gamma H}\right)\right]$ Equation No. 76

The equations are entered as

SOFTMEDCLAY2STRUTS
76S1WI0.25HSOLP
P=0.3×S×H
P=S×H(1−4×E÷S÷H)

Where:

P = maximum lateral pressure P (lb/ft^2, kN/m^2)
S = density of clay γ (lb/ft^3, kN/m^3)
H = height of cut H (ft, m)
E = cohesion of clay c (lb/ft^2, kN/m^2)

Keystrokes

P=0.3×S×H

HP 35s Checksum; Length of Equation: **CK=917D; LN=9**

RCL P [↰] = . 3 × RCL S × RCL H ENTER

HP 33s Checksum; Length of Equation: **CK=917D; LN=9**

[RCL] [P] [↱] [=] [.] [3] [×] [RCL] [S] [×] [RCL] [H] [ENTER]

P=S×H(1−4×E÷S÷H)

HP 35s Checksum; Length of Equation: **CK=34AF; LN=16**

[RCL] [P] [↰] [=] [RCL] [S] [×] [RCL] [H] [()] [1] [−] [4] [×] [RCL] [E] [÷] [RCL] [S] [÷] [RCL] [H] [ENTER]

HP 33s Checksum; Length of Equation: **CK=22CE; LN=17**

[RCL] [P] [↱] [=] [RCL] [S] [×] [RCL] [H] [×] [↱] [(] [1] [−] [4] [×] [RCL] [E] [÷] [RCL] [S] [÷] [RCL] [H] [↱] [)]
[ENTER]

To solve A, sum all moments at B, taking clockwise moments as positive.

$$\sum M_B = 0$$

$$AY + \frac{1}{2}(H - X - Y)^2 PL = \frac{1}{2}(0.25H)P\left(X + Y - (0.25H) + \frac{0.25H}{3}\right)L + \frac{1}{2}(X + Y - 0.25H)^2 PL$$ Equation No. 77

The equation is entered as

77SOLVINGA
A×Y+0.5(H−X−Y)^2×P×L=0.125×H×P(X+Y−0.25×H+0.25×H÷3)×L+0.5(X+Y−0.25×H)^2×P×L

Where:

A = force at Strut 1 A (lb, kN)
Y = distance between Struts 1 and 2 Y (ft, m)
H = height of cut H (ft, m)
X = distance from top of cut to Strut 1 X (ft, m)
P = maximum lateral pressure P (lb/ft^2, kN/m^2)
L = horizontal center-to-center spacing of struts L (ft, m)

Keystrokes

HP 35s Checksum; Length of Equation: **CK=568C; LN=75**

[RCL] [A] [×] [RCL] [Y] [+] [.] [5] [()] [RCL] [H] [−] [RCL] [X] [−] [RCL] [Y] [>] [y^x] [2] [×] [RCL] [P] [×] [RCL] [L] [↰]
[=] [.] [1] [2] [5] [×] [RCL] [H] [×] [RCL] [P] [()] [RCL] [X] [+] [RCL] [Y] [−] [.] [2] [5] [×] [RCL] [H] [+] [.] [2] [5] [×]
[RCL] [H] [÷] [3] [>] [×] [RCL] [L] [+] [.] [5] [()] [RCL] [X] [+] [RCL] [Y] [−] [.] [2] [5] [×] [RCL] [H] [>] [y^x] [2] [×]
[RCL] [P] [×] [RCL] [L] [ENTER]

HP 33s Checksum; Length of Equation: **CK=68C6; LN=78**

[RCL] [A] [×] [RCL] [Y] [+] [.] [5] [×] [↱] [(] [RCL] [H] [−] [RCL] [X] [−] [RCL] [Y] [↱] [)] [y^x] [2] [×] [RCL] [P] [×]
[RCL] [L] [↱] [=] [.] [1] [2] [5] [×] [RCL] [H] [×] [RCL] [P] [×] [↱] [(] [RCL] [X] [+] [RCL] [Y] [−] [.] [2] [5] [×] [RCL]
[H] [+] [.] [2] [5] [×] [RCL] [H] [÷] [3] [↱] [)] [×] [RCL] [L] [+] [.] [5] [×] [↱] [(] [RCL] [X] [+] [RCL] [Y] [−] [.] [2]
[5] [×] [RCL] [H] [↱] [)] [y^x] [2] [×] [RCL] [P] [×] [RCL] [L] [ENTER]

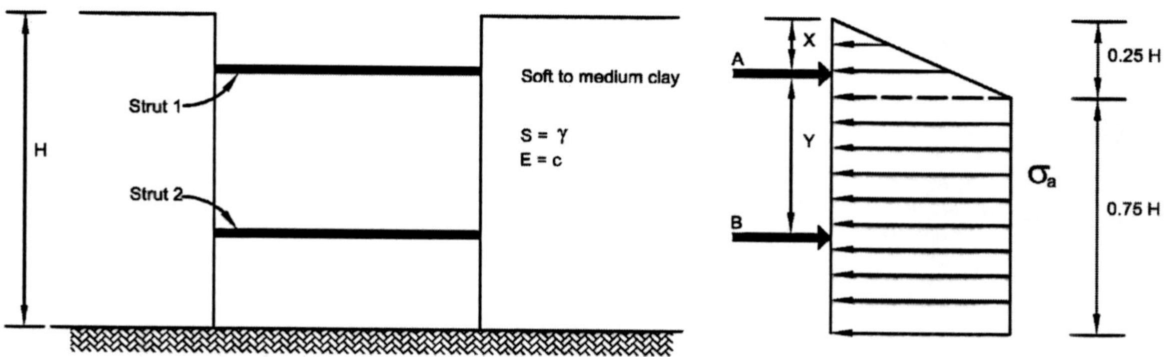

Figure 7-2 Braced Cut in Soft to Medium Clay with Two Struts, Strut 1 within 0.25H

≈≈≈≈≈≈≈≈≈≈

7.2.2 Two Struts Solving B, Strut 1 Within 0.25H

To solve B, sum all horizontal forces.

$$\sum F_H = 0$$

$$A + B = 0.75HPL + \frac{1}{2}(0.25H)PL \qquad \text{Equation No. 78}$$

The equation is entered as

78SOLVINGB
A+B=0.875(H×P×L)

Where:

A = force at Strut 1 A (lb, kN)
B = force at Strut 2 B (lb, kN)
H = height of cut H (ft, m)
P = maximum lateral pressure P (lb/ft^2, kN/m^2)
L = horizontal center-to-center spacing of struts L (ft, m)

Keystrokes

HP 35s Checksum; Length of Equation: **CK=FD17; LN=16**

[RCL] [A] [+] [RCL] [B] [⬑] [=] [.] [8] [7] [5] [()] [RCL] [H] [×] [RCL] [P] [×] [RCL] [L] [ENTER]

HP 33s Checksum; Length of Equation: **CK=FF67; LN=17**

[RCL] [A] [+] [RCL] [B] [⬏] [=] [.] [8] [7] [5] [×] [⬏] [(] [RCL] [H] [×] [RCL] [P] [×] [RCL] [L] [⬏] [)] [ENTER]

Notes: If Strut 1 is located at the bottom of 0.25H, X is equal to 0.25H. If Strut 1 is located on top of cut, X is zero.

≈≈≈≈≈≈≈≈≈≈

$\frac{\gamma H}{c} \leq 4$ For stiff clay

where γ = the density of clay

H = height of cut

c = cohesion of clay

7.3.1 Two Struts Solving A, Strut 1 Above 0.5H, and Strut 2 at the Bottom of 0.5H

For maximum lateral pressure P, use $\sigma_a = 0.3\gamma H$ Equation No. 79

The equation is entered as

STIFFCLAY2STRUTS
79S1ABV0.5HSOLP
P=0.3×S×H

Where:

P = maximum lateral pressure P (lb/ft², kN/m²)
S = density of clay γ (lb/ft³, kN/m³)
H = height of cut H (ft, m)

Keystrokes

HP 35s Checksum; Length of Equation: **CK=917D; LN=9**

[RCL] [P] [↰] [=] [·] [3] [×] [RCL] [S] [×] [RCL] [H] [ENTER]

HP 33s Checksum; Length of Equation: **CK=917D; LN=9**

[RCL] [P] [↱] [=] [·] [3] [×] [RCL] [S] [×] [RCL] [H] [ENTER]

To solve A, sum all moments at B, taking clockwise moments as positive.

$\sum M_B = 0$

$$AY + \frac{1}{2}(0.25H)P\left(\frac{0.25H}{3}\right)L = \frac{1}{2}(0.25H)P\left(0.5H + \frac{0.25H}{3}\right)L + \frac{1}{2}(0.5H)^2 PL$$ Equation No. 80

The equation is entered as

80SOLVINGA
A×Y+0.125×H×P(0.25×H÷3)×L=0.125×H×P(0.5×H+0.25×H÷3)×L+0.125×H^2×P×L

Where:

A = force at Strut 1 A (lb, kN)
Y = distance between Struts 1 and 2 Y (ft, m)
H = height of cut H (ft, m)
P = maximum lateral pressure P (lb/ft^2, kN/m^2)
L = horizontal center-to-center spacing of struts L (ft, m)

Keystrokes

HP 35s Checksum; Length of Equation: **CK=6172; LN=67**

RCL A × RCL Y + · 1 2 5 × RCL H × RCL P ( ) · 2 5 × RCL H ÷ 3 > × RCL L ↰ = · 1 2 5 × RCL H × RCL P ( ) · 5 × RCL H + · 2 5 × RCL H ÷ 3 > × RCL L + · 1 2 5 × RCL H yˣ 2 × RCL P × RCL L ENTER

HP 33s Checksum; Length of Equation: **CK=776C; LN=69**

RCL A × RCL Y + · 1 2 5 × RCL H × RCL P × ↱ (· 2 5 × RCL H ÷ 3 ↱) × RCL L ↱ = · 1 2 5 × RCL H × RCL P × ↱ (· 5 × RCL H + · 2 5 × RCL H ÷ 3 ↱) × RCL L + · 1 2 5 × RCL H yˣ 2 × RCL P × RCL L ENTER

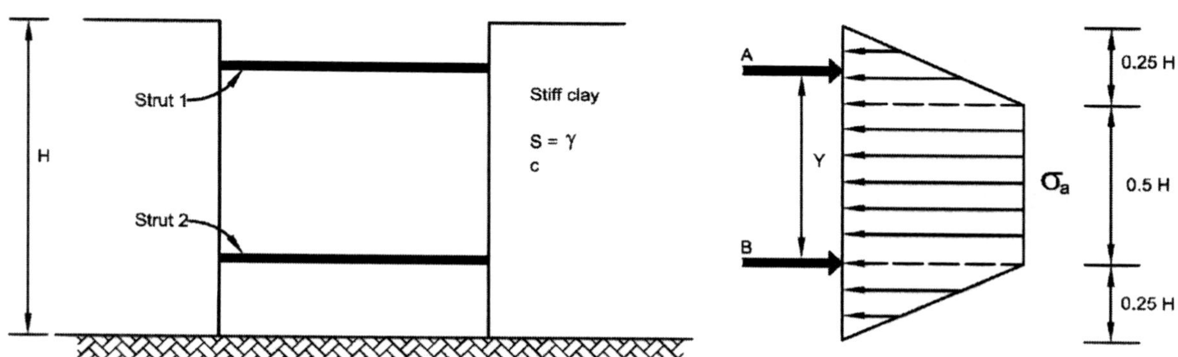

Figure 7-3 Braced Cut in Stiff Clay with Two Struts, Strut 1 Above 0.5H, and Strut 2 at the Bottom of 0.5H

≈≈≈≈≈≈≈≈≈≈

7.3.2 Two Struts Solving B, Strut 1 Above 0.5H, and Strut 2 at the Bottom of 0.5H

To solve B, sum all horizontal forces.

$$\sum F_H = 0$$

$$A + B = 0.75HPL$$ Equation No. 81

The equation is entered as

81SOLVINGB
A+B=0.75×H×P×L

Where:

A = force at Strut 1 A (lb, kN)
B = force at Strut 2 B (lb, kN)
H = height of cut H (ft, m)
P = maximum lateral pressure P (lb/ft^2, kN/m^2)
L = horizontal center-to-center spacing of struts L (ft, m)

Keystrokes

HP 35s Checksum; Length of Equation: **CK=B8D3; LN=14**

[RCL] [A] [+] [RCL] [B] [↰] [=] [.] [7] [5] [×] [RCL] [H] [×] [RCL] [P] [×] [RCL] [L] [ENTER]

HP 33s Checksum; Length of Equation: **CK=B8D3; LN=14**

[RCL] [A] [+] [RCL] [B] [↱] [=] [.] [7] [5] [×] [RCL] [H] [×] [RCL] [P] [×] [RCL] [L] [ENTER]

Notes: If Strut 1 is located on top of 0.5H, Y is equal to 0.5H. If Strut 1 is located on top of cut, Y is equal to 0.75H.

≈≈≈≈≈≈≈≈≈≈

7.3.3 Two Struts Solving B, Strut 1 on Top of 0.5H, and Strut 2 Below 0.5H

For maximum lateral pressure P, use $\sigma_a = 0.3\gamma H$ Equation No. 82

The equation is entered as

STIFFCLAY2STRUTS
82S2BEL0.5HSOLP
P=0.3×S×H

Where:

P = maximum lateral pressure P (lb/ft^2, kN/m^2)
S = density of clay γ (lb/ft^3, kN/m^3)
H = height of cut H (ft, m)

Keystrokes

HP 35s Checksum; Length of Equation: **CK=917D; LN=9**

[RCL] [P] [↰] [=] [.] [3] [×] [RCL] [S] [×] [RCL] [H] [ENTER]

HP 33s Checksum; Length of Equation: **CK=917D; LN=9**

[RCL] [P] [↱] [=] [.] [3] [×] [RCL] [S] [×] [RCL] [H] [ENTER]

To solve B, sum all moments at A, taking clockwise moments as positive.

$$\sum M_A = 0$$

$$\frac{1}{2}(0.5H)^2 PL + \frac{1}{2}(0.25H)P\left(0.5H + \frac{0.25H}{3}\right)L = BY + \frac{1}{2}(0.25H)P\left(\frac{0.25H}{3}\right)L \qquad \text{Equation No. 83}$$

The equation is entered as

83SOLVINGB
0.125×H^2×P×L+0.125×H×P(0.5×H+0.25×H÷3)×L=B×Y+0.125×H×P(0.25×H÷3)×L

Where:

H = height of cut H (ft, m)
P = maximum lateral pressure P (lb/ft^2, kN/m^2)
L = horizontal center-to-center spacing of struts L (ft, m)
B = force at Strut 2 B (lb, kN)
Y = distance between Struts 1 and 2 Y (ft, m)

Keystrokes

HP 35s Checksum; Length of Equation: **CK=896C; LN=67**

[·] [1] [2] [5] [×] [RCL] [H] [yˣ] [2] [×] [RCL] [P] [×] [RCL] [L] [+] [·] [1] [2] [5] [×] [RCL] [H] [×] [RCL] [P] [()] [·] [5]
[×] [RCL] [H] [+] [·] [2] [5] [×] [RCL] [H] [÷] [3] [>] [×] [RCL] [L] [◄] [=] [RCL] [B] [×] [RCL] [Y] [+] [·] [1] [2] [5]
[×] [RCL] [H] [×] [RCL] [P] [()] [·] [2] [5] [×] [RCL] [H] [÷] [3] [>] [×] [RCL] [L] [ENTER]

HP 33s Checksum; Length of Equation: **CK=87C5; LN=69**

[·] [1] [2] [5] [×] [RCL] [H] [yˣ] [2] [×] [RCL] [P] [×] [RCL] [L] [+] [·] [1] [2] [5] [×] [RCL] [H] [×] [RCL] [P] [×] [►] [(]
[·] [5] [×] [RCL] [H] [+] [·] [2] [5] [×] [RCL] [H] [÷] [3] [►] [)] [×] [RCL] [L] [►] [=] [RCL] [B] [×] [RCL] [Y] [+] [·]
[1] [2] [5] [×] [RCL] [H] [×] [RCL] [P] [×] [►] [(] [·] [2] [5] [×] [RCL] [H] [÷] [3] [►] [)] [×] [RCL] [L] [ENTER]

≈≈≈≈≈≈≈≈≈≈

7.3.4 Two Struts Solving A, Strut 1 on Top of 0.5H, and Strut 2 Below 0.5H

To solve A, sum all horizontal forces.

$$\sum F_H = 0$$

$$A + B = 0.75HPL \qquad \text{Equation No. 84}$$

The equation is entered as

84SOLVINGA
A+B=0.75×H×P×L

Where:

A = force at Strut 1 A (lb, kN)
B = force at Strut 2 B (lb, kN)
H = height of cut H (ft, m)
P = maximum lateral pressure P (lb/ft^2, kN/m^2)
L = horizontal center-to-center spacing of struts L (ft, m)

Keystrokes

HP 35s Checksum; Length of Equation: **CK=B8D3; LN=14**

[RCL] [A] [+] [RCL] [B] [↰] [=] [·] [7] [5] [×] [RCL] [H] [×] [RCL] [P] [×] [RCL] [L] [ENTER]

HP 33s Checksum; Length of Equation: **CK=B8D3; LN=14**

[RCL] [A] [+] [RCL] [B] [↱] [=] [·] [7] [5] [×] [RCL] [H] [×] [RCL] [P] [×] [RCL] [L] [ENTER]

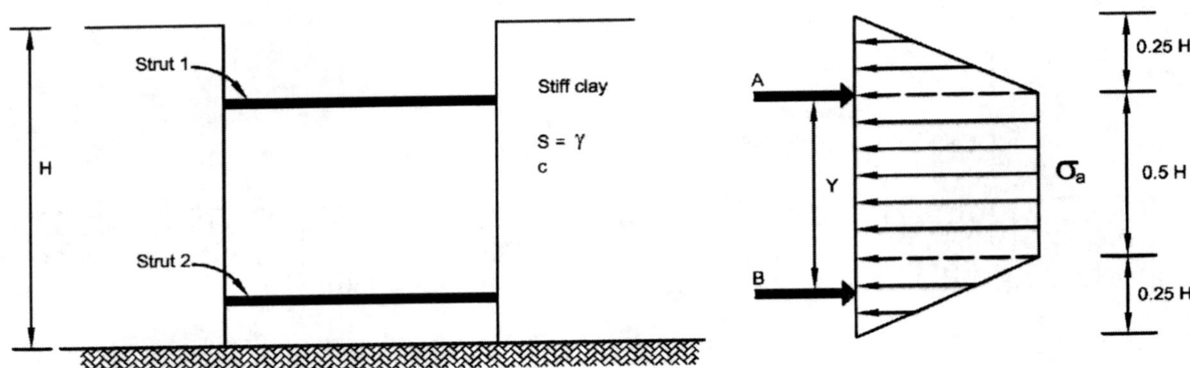

Figure 7-4 Braced Cut in Stiff Clay with Two Struts, Strut 1 on Top of 0.5H, and Strut 2 below 0.5H

Note: If Strut 2 is located at the bottom of cut, Y is equal to 0.75H.

≈≈≈≈≈≈≈≈≈≈

Problem 7.1

A braced cut in sand is shown below. The horizontal center-to-center spacing of struts is 10 feet. The forces at Struts 1 and 2 are most nearly

	Force at Strut 1 (lb)	Force at Strut 2 (lb)
(A)	10,000	15,000
(B)	13,000	18,000
(C)	15,000	20,000
(D)	18,000	21,000

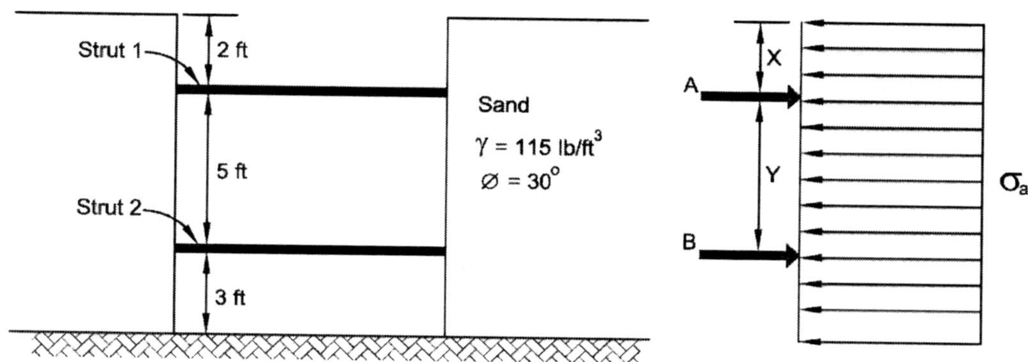

Solution

The forces at Struts 1 and 2 can be calculated using the following steps:

Step 1. Solve the force at Strut 1. Use Equation No. 74, page 145. Press SOLVE A.

Display	Keys	Description
Y?	5 R/S	Distance between Struts 1 and 2 (ft)
S?	115 R/S	Density of sand (lb/ft³)
H?	10 R/S	Height of cut (ft)
K?	*	Rankine active earth pressure coefficient
K? 0.3333	R/S	
X?	2 R/S	Distance from top of cut to Strut 1 (ft)
L?	10 R/S	Horizontal center-to-center spacing of struts (ft)
A = 9,966.6667	--	Force at Strut 1 (lb)

* Keys for calculating Rankine active earth pressure coefficient of soil at the base using RPN:

45 ENTER 30 ENTER 2 ÷ – TAN ↱ x^2 (HP 35s)
45 ENTER 30 ENTER 2 ÷ – TAN x^2 (HP 33s)

$$K_a = \tan^2\left(45 - \frac{30}{2}\right)$$

Step 2. Solve the force at Strut 2. Use Equation No. 75, page 146. Press SOLVE B. Press R/S every time you are prompted. You'll get B = 14,950.0000 for the force at Strut 2 (lb).

The answer is (A).

Problem 7.2

A braced cut in soft to medium clay has 2 struts with horizontal center-to-center spacing of 12 feet. The forces at Struts 1 and 2 are most nearly

	Force at Strut 1 (lb)	Force at Strut 2 (lb)
(A)	8,500	25,000
(B)	10,300	26,500
(C)	11,000	27,800
(D)	12,000	29,000

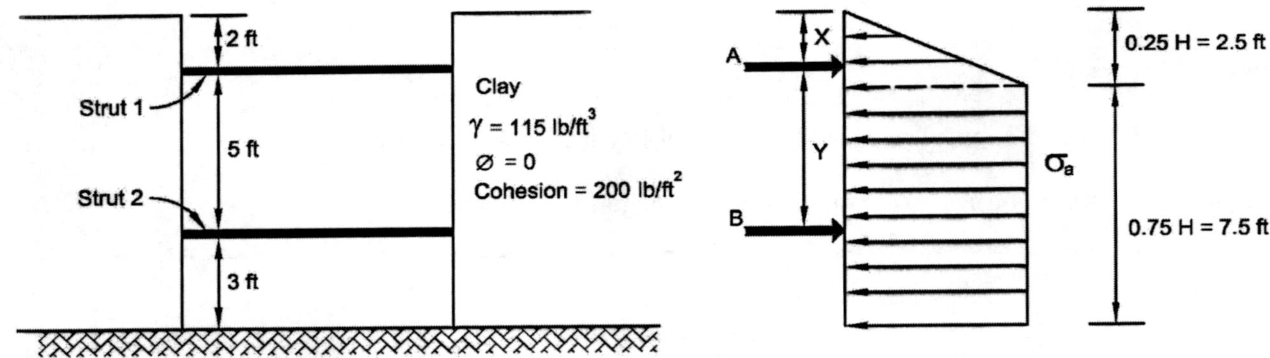

Solution

The following steps are shown in calculating the forces at Struts 1 and 2.

The clay is soft to medium proving $\dfrac{\gamma H}{cohesion} > 4$. (5.75 > 4). Strut 1 is within 0.25H.

Step 1. Calculate the maximum lateral pressure P use the larger value between $\sigma_a = 0.3\gamma H$ and $\sigma_a = \gamma H\left[1 - \left(\dfrac{4c}{\gamma H}\right)\right]$. Use Equation No. 76, page 147. For the first P, Press ENTER.

Display	Keys	Description
S?	115 R/S	Density of clay (lb/ft³)
H?	10 R/S	Height of cut (ft)
P = 345.0000	--	Lateral pressure (lb/ft²)

Step 2. Calculate the second P. Press ENTER.

Display	Keys	Description
S? 115.0000	R/S	Density of clay (lb/ft³)
H? 10.0000	R/S	Height of cut (ft)
E?	200 R/S	Cohesion of clay (lb/ft²)
P = 350.0000	--	Lateral pressure (lb/ft²). Use this value.

Step 3. Solve the force at Strut 1. Use Equation No. 77, page 148. Press SOLVE A.

Display	Keys	Description
Y?	5 R/S	Distance between Struts 1 and 2 (ft)
H? 10.0000	R/S	Height of cut (ft)
X?	2 R/S	Distance from top of cut to Strut 1 (ft)
P? 350.0000	R/S	Maximum lateral pressure (lb/ft²)
L?	12 R/S	Horizontal center-to-center spacing of struts (ft)
A = 10,325.0000	--	Force at Strut 1 (lb)

Step 4. Solve the force at Strut 2. Use Equation No. 78, page 149. Press SOLVE B. Press R/S every time you are prompted. You'll get B = 26,425.0000 for the force at Strut 2 (lb).

The answer is (B).

Problem 7.3

A braced cut in clay has 2 struts with horizontal center-to-center spacing of 12 feet. The forces at Struts 1 and 2 are most nearly

	Force at Strut 1 (lb)	Force at Strut 2 (lb)
(A)	10,000	14,000
(B)	11,000	15,000
(C)	14,000	17,000
(D)	15,000	20,000

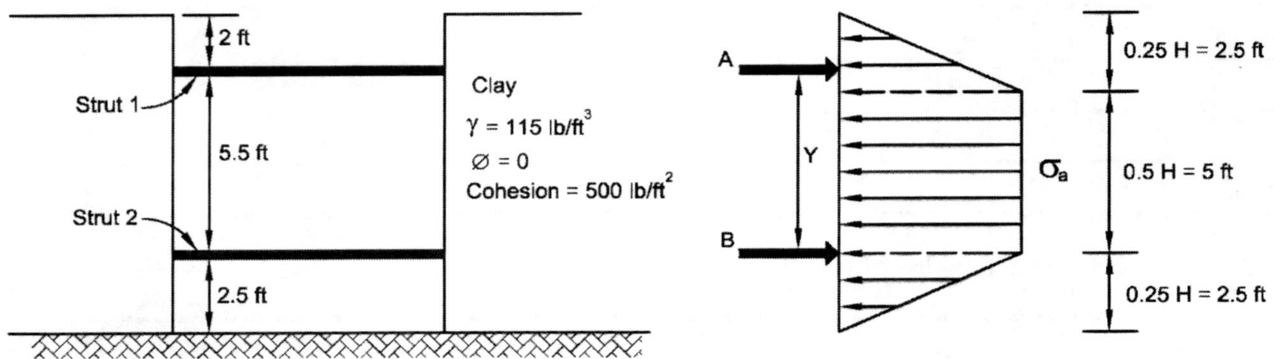

Solution

The strut loads can be calculated using the given dimensions and soil parameters.

The clay is stiff proving $\dfrac{\gamma H}{cohesion} < 4$. (2.3 < 4). Strut 1 is within 0.25H.

Step 1. Calculate the maximum lateral pressure P . $\sigma_a = 0.3\gamma H$. Use Equation No. 79, page 150. Press ENTER.

Display	Keys	Description
S?	115 R/S	Density of clay (lb/ft^3)
H?	10 R/S	Height of cut (ft)
P = 345.0000	--	Maximum lateral pressure (lb/ft^2)

Step 2. Solve the force at Strut 1. Use Equation No. 80, page 150. Press SOLVE A.

Display	Keys	Description
Y?	5.5 R/S	Distance between Struts 1 and 2 (ft)
H? 10.0000	R/S	Height of cut (ft)
P? 345.0000	R/S	Maximum lateral pressure (lb/ft^2)
L?	12 R/S	Horizontal center-to-center spacing of struts (ft)
A = 14,113.6364	--	Force at Strut 1 (lb)

Step 3. Solve the force at Strut 2. Use Equation No. 81, page 151. Press SOLVE B. Press R/S every time you are prompted. You'll get B = 16,936.3636 for the force at Strut 2 (lb).

The answer is (C).

CHAPTER 8: DEEP FOUNDATION

8.1 Skin Friction Resistance of Pile in Sand

8.1.1 Using Critical Depth Ratio for Circular Pile in 1 Layer of Sand

$$Q_s = \frac{C^2 D^2 \gamma k \tan \delta \pi D}{2} + CD\gamma k \tan \delta \pi D(L - CD) \qquad \text{Equation No. 85}$$

The effective vertical stress is $\sigma_o' = \gamma CD$

The equation is entered as

85CDEP1LAYSAND
S=C^2×D^2×M×K×TAN(A)÷2×π×D+C×D×M×K×TAN(A)×π×D(L−C×D)

Where:

S = skin friction resistance Q_s (lb, kN)
C = critical depth ratio C 10 to 20
D = diameter or width of pile D (ft, m)
M = density of sand γ (lb/ft^3, kN/m^3)
K = earth pressure coefficient of sand k (1.0 – 1.5)
A = soil-pile friction angle of sand δ
L = length of pile L (ft, m)

Keystrokes

HP 35s Checksum; Length of Equation: **CK=19DE; LN=52**

[RCL] [S] [↰] [=] [RCL] [C] [y^x] [2] [×] [RCL] [D] [y^x] [2] [×] [RCL] [M] [×] [RCL] [K] [×] [TAN] [RCL] [A] [>] [÷] [2] [×] [↰] [π] [×] [RCL] [D] [+] [RCL] [C] [×] [RCL] [D] [×] [RCL] [M] [×] [RCL] [K] [×] [TAN] [RCL] [A] [>] [×] [↰] [π] [×] [RCL] [D] [()] [RCL] [L] [−] [RCL] [C] [×] [RCL] [D] [ENTER]

HP 33s Checksum; Length of Equation: **CK=6DE7; LN=53**

[RCL] [S] [↱] [=] [RCL] [C] [y^x] [2] [×] [RCL] [D] [y^x] [2] [×] [RCL] [M] [×] [RCL] [K] [×] [TAN] [RCL] [A] [↱] [)] [÷] [2] [×] [↱] [π] [×] [RCL] [D] [+] [RCL] [C] [×] [RCL] [D] [×] [RCL] [M] [×] [RCL] [K] [×] [TAN] [RCL] [A] [↱] [)] [×] [↱] [π] [×] [RCL] [D] [×] [↱] [(] [RCL] [L] [−] [RCL] [C] [×] [RCL] [D] [↱] [)] [ENTER]

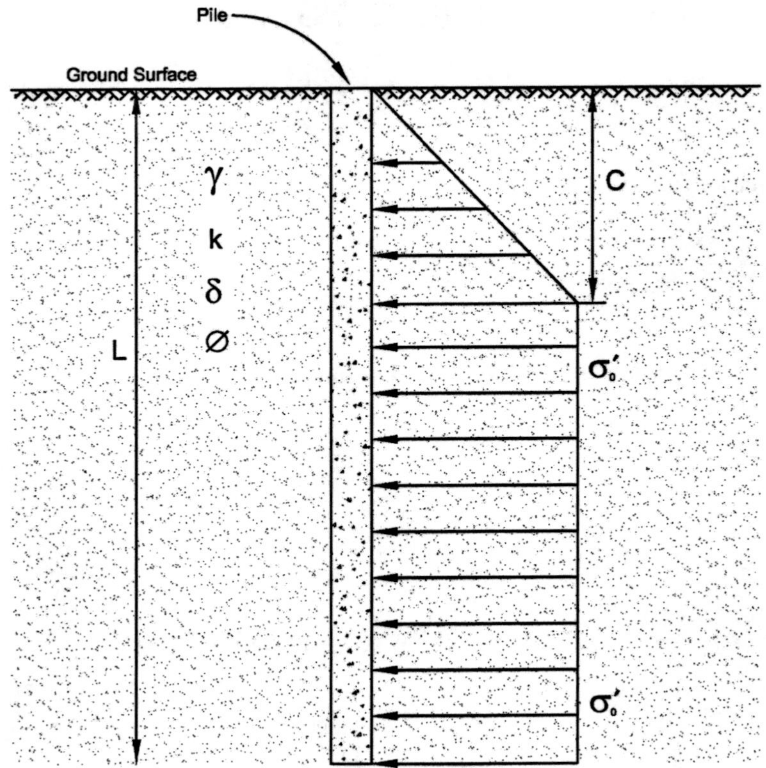

Figure 8-1 Pile on Homogeneous Sand

Note: To calculate the skin friction resistance of a square pile, multiply the skin friction resistance of circular pile by 1.273.

≈≈≈≈≈≈≈≈≈≈

8.1.2 Mohr-Coulomb Method for Circular Pile with up to 4 Layers of Sand with Clay

$$Q_s = \left(k_1 \tan\delta_1 \gamma_{b_1}\left(\frac{L_1}{2}\right) + c_{A_1}\right)\pi D L_1 + \left(k_2 \tan\delta_2\left(\gamma_{b_1} L_1 + \gamma_{b_2}\left(\frac{L_2}{2}\right)\right) + c_{A_2}\right)\pi D L_2$$

$$+\left(k_3 \tan\delta_3\left(\gamma_{b_1} L_1 + \gamma_{b_2} L_2 + \gamma_{b_3}\left(\frac{L_3}{2}\right)\right) + c_{A_3}\right)\pi D L_3 + \left(k_4 \tan\delta_4\left(\gamma_{b_1} L_1 + \gamma_{b_2} L_2 + \gamma_{b_3} L_3 + \gamma_{b_4}\left(\frac{L_4}{2}\right)\right) + c_{A_4}\right)\pi D L_4$$

Equation No. 86

The equation is entered as

86MOHRCIRC4LAYERS
S=(A×TAN(E)×I×O÷2+W)×π×D×O+(B×TAN(F)×(I×O+J×P÷2)+X)×π×D×P+(C×TAN(G)×(I×O+J×P+K×Q ÷2)+Y)×π×D×Q+(V×TAN(H)×(I×O+J×P+K×Q+L×R÷2)+Z)×π×D×R

Where:

S = skin friction resistance Q_s (lb, kN)

A = earth pressure coefficient of layer 1 k_1 (1.0 – 1.5)

E = soil pile friction angle of layer 1 δ_1

I = buoyant unit weight of soil at layer 1 γ_{b_1} (lb/ft^3, kN/m^3). Use moist unit weight if not submerged.

O = thickness of layer 1 that is in contact with the pile L_1 (ft, m)

W = adhesion of clay for layer 1 c_{A_1} (lb/ft^2, kN/m^2)

D = diameter of pile D (ft, m)

B = earth pressure coefficient of layer 2 k_2 (1.0 – 1.5)

F = soil pile friction angle of layer 2 δ_2

J = buoyant unit weight of soil at layer 2 γ_{b_2} (lb/ft^3, kN/m^3). Use moist unit weight if not submerged.

P = thickness of layer 2 that is in contact with the pile L_2 (ft, m)

X = adhesion of clay for layer 2 c_{A_2} (lb/ft^2, kN/m^2)

C = earth pressure coefficient of layer 3 k_3 (1.0 – 1.5)

G = soil pile friction angle of layer 3 δ_3

K = buoyant unit weight of soil at layer 3 γ_{b_3} (lb/ft^3, kN/m^3). Use moist unit weight if not submerged.

Q = thickness of layer 3 that is in contact with the pile L_3 (ft, m)

Y = adhesion of clay for layer 3 c_{A_3} (lb/ft^2, kN/m^2)

V = earth pressure coefficient of layer 4 k_4 (1.0 – 1.5)

H = soil pile friction angle of layer 4 δ_4

L = buoyant unit weight of soil at layer 4 γ_{b_4} (lb/ft^3, kN/m^3). Use moist unit weight if not submerged.

R = thickness of layer 4 that is in contact with the pile L_4 (ft, m)

Z = adhesion of clay for layer 4 c_{A_4} (lb/ft^2, kN/m^2)

Keystrokes

HP 35s Checksum; Length of Equation: **CK=7D67; LN=131**

[RCL] [S] [↰] [=] [()] [RCL] [A] [×] [TAN] [RCL] [E] [>] [×] [RCL] [I] [×] [RCL] [O] [÷] [2] [+] [RCL] [W] [>] [×] [↰] [π]
[×] [RCL] [D] [×] [RCL] [O] [+] [()] [RCL] [B] [×] [TAN] [RCL] [F] [>] [×] [()] [RCL] [I] [×] [RCL] [O] [+] [RCL] [J] [×]
[RCL] [P] [÷] [2] [>] [+] [RCL] [X] [>] [×] [↰] [π] [×] [RCL] [D] [×] [RCL] [P] [+] [()] [RCL] [C] [×] [TAN] [RCL] [G] [>]
[×] [()] [RCL] [I] [×] [RCL] [O] [+] [RCL] [J] [×] [RCL] [P] [+] [RCL] [K] [×] [RCL] [Q] [÷] [2] [>] [+] [RCL] [Y] [>] [×]
[↰] [π] [×] [RCL] [D] [×] [RCL] [Q] [+] [()] [RCL] [V] [×] [TAN] [RCL] [H] [>] [×] [()] [RCL] [I] [×] [RCL] [O] [+] [RCL] [J]
[×] [RCL] [P] [+] [RCL] [K] [×] [RCL] [Q] [+] [RCL] [L] [×] [RCL] [R] [÷] [2] [>] [+] [RCL] [Z] [>] [×] [↰] [π] [×] [RCL]
[D] [×] [RCL] [R] [ENTER]

HP 33s Checksum; Length of Equation: **CK=9079; LN=131**

[RCL] [S] [↱] [=] [↱] [(] [RCL] [A] [×] [TAN] [RCL] [E] [↱] [)] [×] [RCL] [I] [×] [RCL] [O] [÷] [2] [+] [RCL] [W] [↱] [)]
[×] [↱] [π] [×] [RCL] [D] [×] [RCL] [O] [+] [↱] [(] [RCL] [B] [×] [TAN] [RCL] [F] [↱] [)] [×] [↱] [(] [RCL] [I] [×] [RCL]
[O] [+] [RCL] [J] [×] [RCL] [P] [÷] [2] [↱] [)] [+] [RCL] [X] [↱] [)] [×] [↱] [π] [×] [RCL] [D] [×] [RCL] [P] [+] [↱] [(]
[RCL] [C] [×] [TAN] [RCL] [G] [↱] [)] [×] [↱] [(] [RCL] [I] [×] [RCL] [O] [+] [RCL] [J] [×] [RCL] [P] [+] [RCL] [K] [×]
[RCL] [Q] [÷] [2] [↱] [)] [+] [RCL] [Y] [↱] [)] [×] [↱] [π] [×] [RCL] [D] [×] [RCL] [Q] [+] [↱] [(] [RCL] [V] [×] [TAN]
[RCL] [H] [↱] [)] [×] [↱] [(] [RCL] [I] [×] [RCL] [O] [+] [RCL] [J] [×] [RCL] [P] [+] [RCL] [K] [×] [RCL] [Q] [+] [RCL] [L]
[×] [RCL] [R] [÷] [2] [↱] [)] [+] [RCL] [Z] [↱] [)] [×] [↱] [π] [×] [RCL] [D] [×] [RCL] [R] [ENTER]

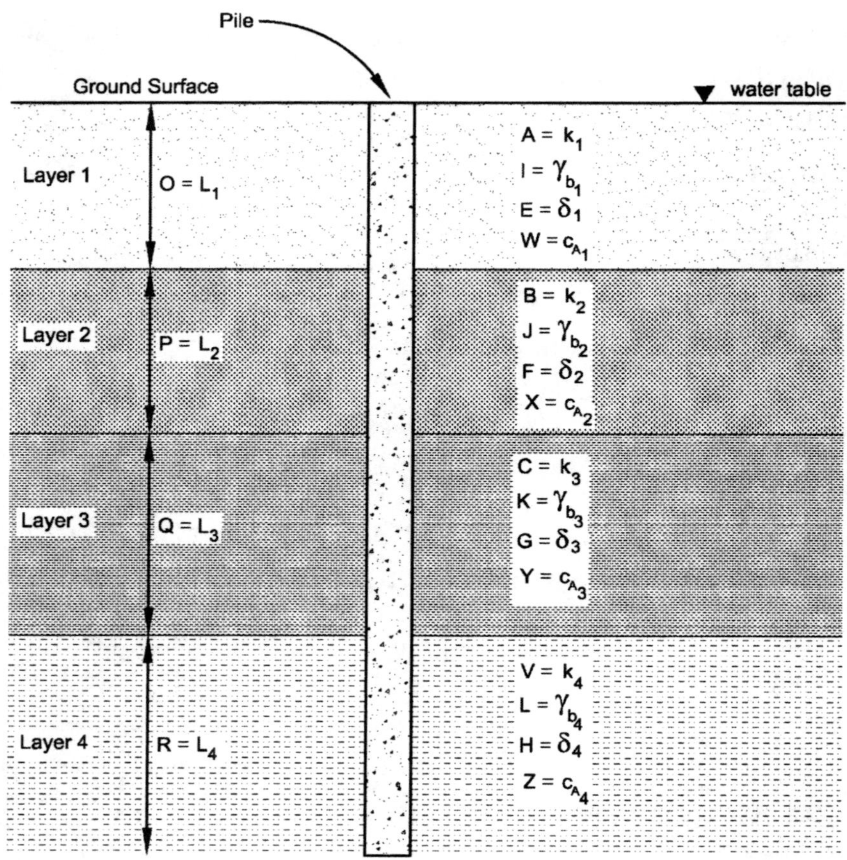

Figure 8-2 Pile on Sand with Clay with up to 4 Layers of Soil

Note: To determine the skin friction resistance of a square pile, multiply the diameter by 1.273.

≈≈≈≈≈≈≈≈≈≈

8.2 End-Bearing and Ultimate Capacities of Pile in Sand

8.2.1 Circular Pile Using Terzaghi Method with up to 4 Layers of Soil

$$Q_p = \left(\gamma_{b_1} L_1 + \gamma_{b_2} L_2 + \gamma_{b_3} L_3 + \gamma_{b_4} L_4\right)\frac{\pi}{4} D^2 N_q \qquad \text{Equation No. 87 (T)}$$

$$Q_{ult} = Q_s + Q_p \qquad \text{Equation No. 87 (U)}$$

The equations are entered as

87EBCIRC4LAYERS
T=(I×O+J×P+K×Q+L×R)×π÷4×D^2×N
U=S+T

Where:

T = end-bearing capacity Q_p (lb, kN)

I = buoyant unit weight of soil at layer 1 γ_{b_1} (lb/ft^3, kN/m^3). Use moist unit weight if not submerged.

O = thickness of layer 1 that is in contact with the pile L_1 (ft, m)

J = buoyant unit weight of soil at layer 2 γ_{b_2} (lb/ft^3, kN/m^3). Use moist unit weight if not submerged.

P = thickness of layer 2 that is in contact with the pile L_2 (ft, m)

K = buoyant unit weight of soil at layer 3 γ_{b_3} (lb/ft^3, kN/m^3). Use moist unit weight if not submerged.

Q = thickness of layer 3 that is in contact with the pile L_3 (ft, m)

L = buoyant unit weight of soil at layer 4 γ_{b_4} (lb/ft^3, kN/m^3). Use moist unit weight if not submerged.

R = thickness of layer 4 that is in contact with the pile L_4 (ft, m)

D = diameter of pile D (ft, m)

N = N_q at the tip of the pile

U = ultimate capacity of pile Q_{ult} (lb, kN)

S = skin friction resistance Q_s (lb, kN)

Keystrokes

T=(I×O+J×P+K×Q+L×R)×π÷4×D^2×N

HP 35s Checksum; Length of Equation: **CK=3BDA; LN=29**

[RCL] [T] [↰] [=] [()] [RCL] [I] [×] [RCL] [O] [+] [RCL] [J] [×] [RCL] [P] [+] [RCL] [K] [×] [RCL] [Q] [+] [RCL] [L] [×] [RCL] [R] [>] [×] [↰] [π] [÷] [4] [×] [RCL] [D] [y^x] [2] [×] [RCL] [N] [ENTER]

HP 33s Checksum; Length of Equation: **CK=3BDA; LN=29**

[RCL] [T] [↱] [=] [↱] [(] [RCL] [I] [×] [RCL] [O] [+] [RCL] [J] [×] [RCL] [P] [+] [RCL] [K] [×] [RCL] [Q] [+] [RCL] [L] [×] [RCL] [R] [↱] [)] [×] [↱] [π] [÷] [4] [×] [RCL] [D] [y^x] [2] [×] [RCL] [N] [ENTER]

U=S+T

HP 35s Checksum; Length of Equation: **CK=E4F9; LN=5**

[RCL] [U] [↰] [=] [RCL] [S] [+] [RCL] [T] [ENTER]

HP 33s Checksum; Length of Equation: **CK=E4F9; LN=5**

[RCL] [U] [↱] [=] [RCL] [S] [+] [RCL] [T] [ENTER]

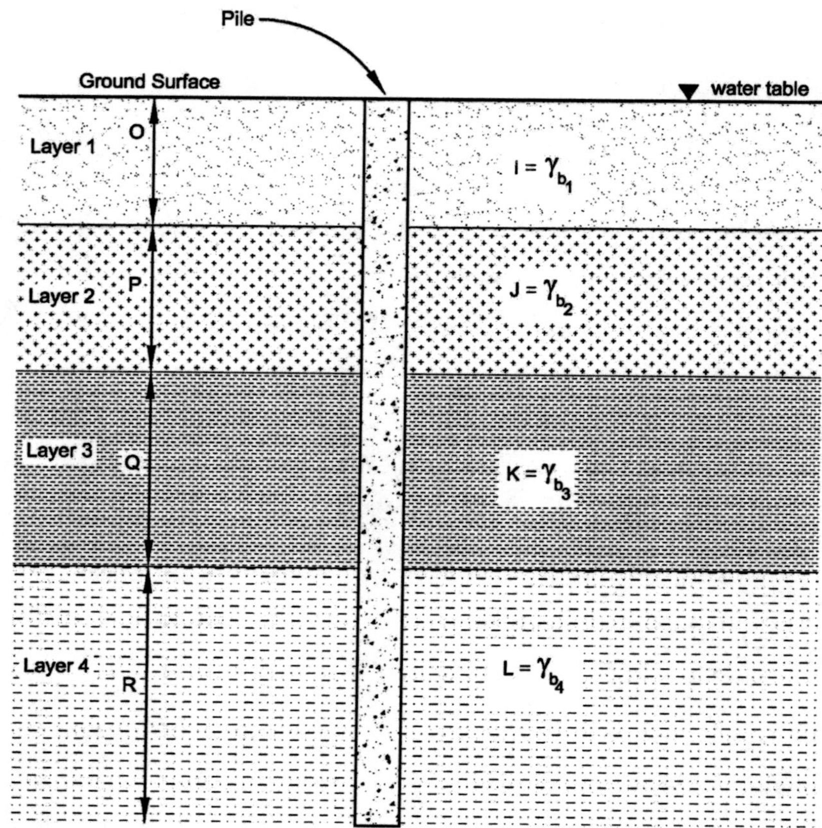

Figure 8-3 End-Bearing and Ultimate Capacities of Pile Using Terzaghi Method with up to 4 Layers of Soil

Note: To find the ultimate bearing capacity of a square pile, multiply the diameter by 1.273.

≈≈≈≈≈≈≈≈≈≈

8.3 Allowable Capacity of Pile in 1 Layer of Sand

8.3.1 Circular Pile

$$Q_{all} = \frac{\sigma \frac{\pi}{4} D^2 + f_s \pi D L}{FS}$$ Equation No. 88

The equation is entered as

88ALCAPSAND1LAYER
W=(V×π÷4×D^2+S×π×D×L)÷F

Where:

W = allowable capacity of pile Q_{all} (lb, kN)
V = end-bearing resistance σ (lb/ft^2, kN/m^2)
D = diameter of pile D (ft, m)
S = skin friction resistance f_s (lb/ft^2, kN/m^2)

L = length of pile L (ft, m)
F = factor of safety FS

Keystrokes

HP 35s Checksum; Length of Equation: **CK=D839; LN=23**

[RCL] [W] [↰] [=] [()] [RCL] [V] [×] [↰] [π] [÷] [4] [×] [RCL] [D] [yˣ] [2] [+] [RCL] [S] [×] [↰] [π] [×] [RCL] [D] [×] [RCL] [L] [>] [÷] [RCL] [F] [ENTER]

HP 33s Checksum; Length of Equation: **CK=D839; LN=23**

[RCL] [W] [↱] [=] [↱] [(] [RCL] [V] [×] [↱] [π] [÷] [4] [×] [RCL] [D] [yˣ] [2] [+] [RCL] [S] [×] [↱] [π] [×] [RCL] [D] [×] [RCL] [L] [↱] [)] [÷] [RCL] [F] [ENTER]

Notes: This equation shall be used to calculate the allowable capacity (lb, KN) of circular pile in 1 layer of sand, given skin friction and end-bearing resistances (lb/ft^2, kN/m^2), diameter of pile D (ft, m), length of pile L (ft, m), and factor of safety FS. For ultimate capacity of pile, the factor of safety is 1. If end-bearing is ignored, V is zero.

To calculate only the end-bearing capacity (lb, KN), do the following procedure:

Press ENTER, then enter the value of V (lb/ft^2, kN/m^2), press R/S, enter the diameter D (ft, m), press R/S, enter 0 for S, press R/S, enter 0 for L, press R/S, enter 1 for F, press R/S.

To determine only the skin friction capacity (lb, KN), do the following steps:

Press ENTER, then enter 0 for V (lb/ft^2, kN/m^2), press R/S, enter the diameter D (ft, m), press R/S, enter the value of S (lb/ft^2, kN/m^2), press R/S, enter the length of pile L (ft, m), press R/S, enter 1 for F, press R/S. For square pile, multiply the allowable capacity by 1.273.

≈≈≈≈≈≈≈≈≈≈

8.4 Skin Friction Resistance, End-Bearing and Ultimate Capacities of Pile in Clay Using α - Method

8.4.1 Circular Pile with up to 4 Layers of Clay

$$Q_s = (\alpha_1 c_1 L_1 + \alpha_2 c_2 L_2 + \alpha_3 c_3 L_3 + \alpha_4 c_4 L_4)\pi D \quad \text{Equation No. 89 (S)}$$

$$Q_p = 9c\frac{\pi}{4}D^2 \quad \text{Equation No. 89 (T)}$$

$$Q_{ult} = Q_s + Q_p \quad \text{Equation No. 89 (U)}$$

The equations are entered as

89STUALMETCP4LAYERS
S=(H×W×O+I×X×P+J×Y×Q+K×Z×R)×π×D
T=2.25×C×π×D^2
U=S+T

Where:

S = skin friction resistance Q_s (lb, kN)
H = adhesion factor of layer 1 α_1 (from published tables)
W = cohesion of clay at layer 1 c_1 (lb/ft^2, kN/m^2)
O = thickness of layer 1 that is in contact with the pile L_1 (ft, m)
I = adhesion factor of layer 2 α_2 (from published tables)
X = cohesion of clay at layer 2 c_2 (lb/ft^2, kN/m^2)
P = thickness of layer 2 that is in contact with the pile L_2 (ft, m)
J = adhesion factor of layer 3 α_3 (from published tables)
Y = cohesion of clay at layer 3 c_3 (lb/ft^2, kN/m^2)
Q = thickness of layer 3 that is in contact with the pile L_3 (ft, m)
K = adhesion factor of layer 4 α_4 (from published tables)
Z = cohesion of clay at layer 4 c_4 (lb/ft^2, kN/m^2)
R = thickness of layer 4 that is in contact with the pile L_4 (ft, m)
D = diameter of pile D (ft, m)
T = end-bearing capacity of pile Q_p (lb, kN)
C = cohesion of clay at the tip of the pile c (lb/ft^2, kN/m^2)
U = ultimate capacity of pile Q_{ult} (lb, kN)

Keystrokes

S=(H×W×O+I×X×P+J×Y×Q+K×Z×R)×π×D

HP 35s Checksum; Length of Equation: **CK=5A57; LN=31**

[RCL] [S] [↰] [=] [()] [RCL] [H] [×] [RCL] [W] [×] [RCL] [O] [+] [RCL] [I] [×] [RCL] [X] [×] [RCL] [P] [+] [RCL] [J] [×] [RCL] [Y] [×] [RCL] [Q] [+] [RCL] [K] [×] [RCL] [Z] [×] [RCL] [R] [>] [×] [↰] [π] [×] [RCL] [D] [ENTER]

HP 33s Checksum; Length of Equation: **CK=5A57; LN=31**

[RCL] [S] [↱] [=] [↱] [(] [RCL] [H] [×] [RCL] [W] [×] [RCL] [O] [+] [RCL] [I] [×] [RCL] [X] [×] [RCL] [P] [+] [RCL] [J] [×] [RCL] [Y] [×] [RCL] [Q] [+] [RCL] [K] [×] [RCL] [Z] [×] [RCL] [R] [↱] [)] [×] [↱] [π] [×] [RCL] [D] [ENTER]

T=2.25×C×π×D^2

HP 35s Checksum; Length of Equation: **CK=91D1; LN=14**

[RCL] [T] [↰] [=] [2] [·] [2] [5] [×] [RCL] [C] [×] [↰] [π] [×] [RCL] [D] [y^x] [2] [ENTER]

HP 33s Checksum; Length of Equation: **CK=91D1; LN=14**

[RCL] [T] [↱] [=] [2] [·] [2] [5] [×] [RCL] [C] [×] [↱] [π] [×] [RCL] [D] [y^x] [2] [ENTER]

U=S+T

HP 35s Checksum; Length of Equation: **CK=E4F9; LN=5**

RCL U ⬑ = RCL S + RCL T ENTER

HP 33s Checksum; Length of Equation: **CK=E4F9; LN=5**

RCL U ⮣ = RCL S + RCL T ENTER

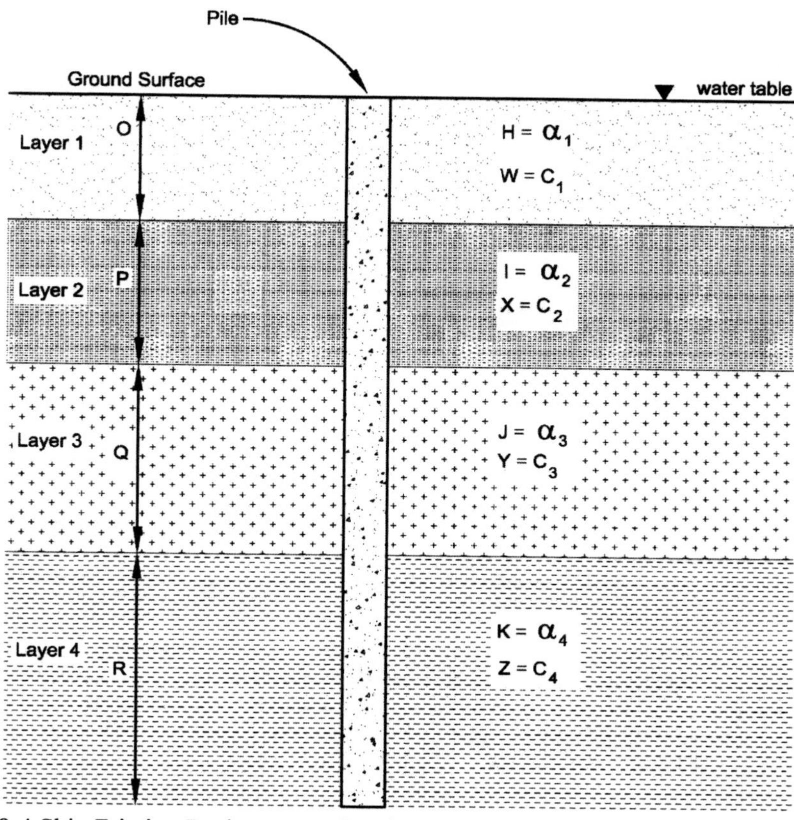

Figure 8-4 Skin Friction Resistance and End-Bearing Capacity of Pile Using α - Method

Notes: If the end-bearing is ignored, the cohesion c is zero. To find the ultimate capacity of a square pile, multiply the diameter by 1.273.

≈≈≈≈≈≈≈≈≈≈

8.5 Allowable Capacity of Pile in 1 Layer of Clay Using α - Method

8.5.1 Circular Pile

$$Q_{all} = \frac{9c\frac{\pi}{4}D^2 + \alpha VL\pi D}{FS}$$ Equation No. 90

The equation is entered as

90ALCAPAMCP1LAYER
W=(2.25×C×π×D^2+H×V×L×π×D)÷F

Where:

W = allowable capacity of pile Q_{all} (lb, kN)
C = cohesion of clay at the tip of pile for end-bearing resistance c (lb/ft^2, kN/m^2)
D = diameter of pile D (ft, m)
H = adhesion factor of clay α (from published table)
V = cohesion of clay for skin friction resistance V (lb/ft^2, kN/m^2)
L = length of pile L (ft, m)
F = factor of safety FS

Keystrokes

HP 35s Checksum; Length of Equation: **CK=E626; LN=28**

[RCL] [W] [↰] [=] [()] [2] [.] [2] [5] [×] [RCL] [C] [×] [↰] [π] [×] [RCL] [D] [y^x] [2] [+] [RCL] [H] [×] [RCL] [V] [×] [RCL] [L] [×] [↰] [π] [×] [RCL] [D] [>] [÷] [RCL] [F] [ENTER]

HP 33s Checksum; Length of Equation: **CK=E626; LN=28**

[RCL] [W] [↱] [=] [↱] [(] [2] [.] [2] [5] [×] [RCL] [C] [×] [↱] [π] [×] [RCL] [D] [y^x] [2] [+] [RCL] [H] [×] [RCL] [V] [×] [RCL] [L] [×] [↱] [π] [×] [RCL] [D] [↱] [)] [÷] [RCL] [F] [ENTER]

Notes: This equation shall be used to calculate the allowable capacity (lb, KN) of circular pile in 1 layer of clay using α -method given cohesion of clay (lb/ft^2, kN/m^2), diameter of pile D (ft, m), adhesion factor of clay α, length of pile L (ft, m), and factor of safety FS. For ultimate capacity of pile, the factor of safety is 1. If end-bearing resistance is ignored, C is zero.

To calculate only the end-bearing capacity (lb, KN), perform the following steps:

Press ENTER, then enter the value of C (lb/ft^2, kN/m^2), press R/S, enter the diameter D (ft, m), press R/S, enter 0 for adhesion factor of clay α, press R/S, enter 0 for L, press R/S, enter 1 for F, press R/S.

To determine only the skin friction capacity (lb, KN), execute the following procedure:

Press ENTER, then enter 0 for C (lb/ft^2, kN/m^2), press R/S, enter the diameter D (ft, m), press R/S, enter the adhesion factor of clay α, press R/S, enter the value of V (lb/ft^2, kN/m^2), press R/S, enter the length of pile L (ft, m), press R/S, enter 1 for F, press R/S.

To calculate the allowable capacity of a square pile, multiply the allowable capacity of circular pile by 1.273.

≈≈≈≈≈≈≈≈≈≈

8.6 Skin Friction Resistance, End-Bearing and Ultimate Capacities of Pile in Clay Using β- Method

8.6.1 Circular Pile with up to 4 Layers of Clay

$$Q_s = \frac{\gamma_{b_1} L_1^{\,2} \beta_1 \pi D}{2} + \left(\gamma_{b_1} L_1 + \gamma_{b_2} \frac{L_2}{2}\right)\beta_2 \pi D L_2 + \left(\gamma_{b_1} L_1 + \gamma_{b_2} L_2 + \gamma_{b_3} \frac{L_3}{2}\right)\beta_3 \pi D L_3$$

$$+\left(\gamma_{b_1} L_1 + \gamma_{b_2} L_2 + \gamma_{b_3} L_3 + \gamma_{b_4} \frac{L_4}{2}\right)\beta_4 \pi D L_4 \qquad \text{Equation No. 91 (S)}$$

$$Q_p = 9c\frac{\pi}{4}D^2 \qquad \text{Equation No. 91 (T)}$$

$$Q_{ult} = Q_s + Q_p \qquad \text{Equation No. 91 (U)}$$

The equations are entered as

91STUBMETCP4LAYERS
S=W×O^2×H×π×D÷2+(W×O+X×P÷2)×I×π×D×P+(W×O+X×P+Y×Q÷2)×J×π×D×Q+(W×O+X×P+Y×Q+Z×R÷2)×K×π×D×R
T=2.25×C×π×D^2
U=S+T

Where:

S = skin friction resistance Q_s (lb, kN)
W = buoyant unit weight of soil at layer 1 γ_{b_1} (lb/ft^3, kN/m^3). Use moist unit weight if not submerged.
O = thickness of layer 1 that is in contact with the pile L_1 (ft, m)
H = beta value of layer 1 β_1 (from published table)
D = diameter of pile D (ft, m)
X = buoyant unit weight of soil at layer 2 γ_{b_2} (lb/ft^3, kN/m^3). Use moist unit weight if not submerged.
P = thickness of layer 2 that is in contact with the pile L_2 (ft, m)
I = beta value of layer 2 β_2 (from published table)
Y = buoyant unit weight of soil at layer 3 γ_{b_3} (lb/ft^3, kN/m^3). Use moist unit weight if not submerged.
Q = thickness of layer 3 that is in contact with the pile L_3 (ft, m)
J = beta value of layer 3 β_3 (from published table)
Z = buoyant unit weight of soil at layer 4 γ_{b_4} (lb/ft^3, kN/m^3). Use moist unit weight if not submerged.
R = thickness of layer 4 that is in contact with the pile L_4 (ft, m)
K = beta value of layer 4 β_4 (from published table)
T = end-bearing capacity of pile Q_p (lb, kN)
C = cohesion of clay at the tip of the pile c (lb/ft^2, kN/m^2)
U = ultimate capacity of pile Q_{ult} (lb, kN)

Keystrokes

S=W×O^2×H×π×D÷2+(W×O+X×P÷2)×I×π×D×P+(W×O+X×P+Y×Q÷2)×J×π×D×Q+(W×O+X×P+Y×Q+Z ×R÷2)×K×π×D×R

HP 35s Checksum; Length of Equation: **CK=C763; LN=87**

[RCL] [S] [↰] [=] [RCL] [W] [×] [RCL] [O] [y^x] [2] [×] [RCL] [H] [×] [↰] [π] [×] [RCL] [D] [÷] [2] [+] [()] [RCL] [W] [×]
[RCL] [O] [+] [RCL] [X] [×] [RCL] [P] [÷] [2] [>] [×] [RCL] [I] [×] [↰] [π] [×] [RCL] [D] [×] [RCL] [P] [+] [()] [RCL] [W]
[×] [RCL] [O] [+] [RCL] [X] [×] [RCL] [P] [+] [RCL] [Y] [×] [RCL] [Q] [÷] [2] [>] [×] [RCL] [J] [×] [↰] [π] [×] [RCL] [D]
[×] [RCL] [Q] [+] [()] [RCL] [W] [×] [RCL] [O] [+] [RCL] [X] [×] [RCL] [P] [+] [RCL] [Y] [×] [RCL] [Q] [+] [RCL] [Z] [×]
[RCL] [R] [÷] [2] [>] [×] [RCL] [K] [×] [↰] [π] [×] [RCL] [D] [×] [RCL] [R] [ENTER]

HP 33s Checksum; Length of Equation: **CK=59B4; LN=87**

[RCL] [S] [↱] [=] [RCL] [W] [×] [RCL] [O] [y^x] [2] [×] [RCL] [H] [×] [↱] [π] [×] [RCL] [D] [÷] [2] [+] [↱] [(] [RCL] [W]
[×] [RCL] [O] [+] [RCL] [X] [×] [RCL] [P] [÷] [2] [↱] [)] [×] [RCL] [I] [×] [↱] [π] [×] [RCL] [D] [×] [RCL] [P] [+] [↱] [(]
[RCL] [W] [×] [RCL] [O] [+] [RCL] [X] [×] [RCL] [P] [+] [RCL] [Y] [×] [RCL] [Q] [÷] [2] [↱] [)] [×] [RCL] [J] [×] [↱] [π]
[×] [RCL] [D] [×] [RCL] [Q] [+] [↱] [(] [RCL] [W] [×] [RCL] [O] [+] [RCL] [X] [×] [RCL] [P] [+] [RCL] [Y] [×] [RCL] [Q] [+]
[RCL] [Z] [×] [RCL] [R] [÷] [2] [↱] [)] [×] [RCL] [K] [×] [↱] [π] [×] [RCL] [D] [×] [RCL] [R] [ENTER]

T=2.25×C×π×D^2

HP 35s Checksum; Length of Equation: **CK=91D1; LN=14**

[RCL] [T] [↰] [=] [2] [.] [2] [5] [×] [RCL] [C] [×] [↰] [π] [×] [RCL] [D] [y^x] [2] [ENTER]

HP 33s Checksum; Length of Equation: **CK=91D1; LN=14**

[RCL] [T] [↱] [=] [2] [.] [2] [5] [×] [RCL] [C] [×] [↱] [π] [×] [RCL] [D] [y^x] [2] [ENTER]

U=S+T

HP 35s Checksum; Length of Equation: **CK=E4F9; LN=5**

[RCL] [U] [↰] [=] [RCL] [S] [+] [RCL] [T] [ENTER]

HP 33s Checksum; Length of Equation: **CK=E4F9; LN=5**

[RCL] [U] [↱] [=] [RCL] [S] [+] [RCL] [T] [ENTER]

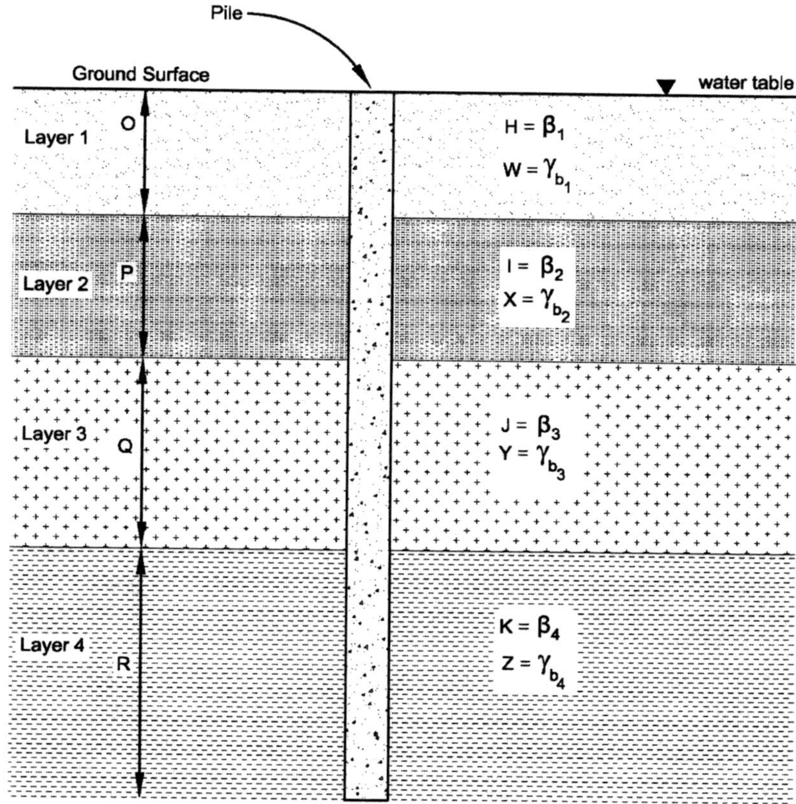

Figure 8-5 Skin Friction Resistance and End-Bearing Capacity of Pile Using β - Method

Note: To determine the skin friction resistance and end-bearing capacity of a square pile, multiply the diameter by 1.273.

≈≈≈≈≈≈≈≈≈≈

8.7 Allowable Capacity of Pile in 1 Layer of Clay Using β- Method

8.7.1 Circular Pile

$$Q_{all} = \frac{9c\frac{\pi}{4}D^2 + \frac{\gamma_b L^2 \beta \pi D}{2}}{FS}$$ Equation No. 92

The equation is entered as

92ALCAPBMCP1LAYER
W=(2.25×C×π×D^2+(X×L^2×H×π×D)÷2)÷F

Where:

W = allowable capacity of pile Q_{all} (lb, kN)
C = cohesion of clay at the tip of pile for end-bearing resistance c (lb/ft², kN/m²)
D = diameter of pile D (ft, m)
X = buoyant unit weight of clay γ_b (lb/ft³, kN/m³). Use moist unit weight if not submerged.

L = length of pile L (ft, m)
H = beta value of clay β
F = factor of safety FS

Keystrokes

HP 35s Checksum; Length of Equation: **CK=2047; LN=34**

[RCL] [W] [↰] [=] [()] [2] [.] [2] [5] [×] [RCL] [C] [×] [↰] [π] [×] [RCL] [D] [y^x] [2] [+] [()] [RCL] [X] [×] [RCL] [L] [y^x] [2] [×] [RCL] [H] [×] [↰] [π] [×] [RCL] [D] [>] [÷] [2] [>] [÷] [RCL] [F] [ENTER]

HP 33s Checksum; Length of Equation: **CK=2047; LN=34**

[RCL] [W] [↱] [=] [↱] [(] [2] [.] [2] [5] [×] [RCL] [C] [×] [↱] [π] [×] [RCL] [D] [y^x] [2] [+] [↱] [(] [RCL] [X] [×] [RCL] [L] [y^x] [2] [×] [RCL] [H] [×] [↱] [π] [×] [RCL] [D] [↱] [)] [÷] [2] [↱] [)] [÷] [RCL] [F] [ENTER]

Notes: This equation shall be used to calculate the allowable capacity (lb, KN) of circular pile in 1 layer of clay using β-method given cohesion of clay (lb/ft^2, kN/m^2), diameter of pile D (ft, m), buoyant unit weight of clay γ_b (lb/ft^3, kN/m^3), length of pile L (ft, m), beta β value of clay, and factor of safety FS. For ultimate capacity of pile, the factor of safety is 1. If end-bearing resistance is ignored, C (lb/ft^2, kN/m^2) is zero. This equation assumes that the water table is at the ground surface. If no water table, use the moist unit weight of clay.

To calculate only the end-bearing capacity (lb, KN), the following procedure must be implemented:

Press ENTER, then enter the value of C (lb/ft^2, kN/m^2), press R/S, enter the diameter D (ft, m), press R/S, enter 0 for X, press R/S, enter 0 for L, press R/S, enter 0 for beta β value of clay, press R/S, enter 1 for F, press R/S.

To determine only the skin friction capacity (lb, KN), the following steps must be performed:

Press ENTER, then enter 0 for C (lb/ft^2, kN/m^2), press R/S, enter the diameter D (ft, m), press R/S, enter the buoyant unit weight of clay γ_b (lb/ft^3, kN/m^3), press R/S, enter the length of pile L (ft, m), press R/S, enter the beta β value of clay, press R/S, enter 1 for F, press R/S.

For square pile, multiply the allowable capacity by 1.273.

≈≈≈≈≈≈≈≈≈≈

Problem 8.1

A concrete pile 12 in × 12 in is fully embedded in sand. Using critical depth of 15 × width of pile, the skin friction resistance is most nearly

(A) 100 kips
(B) 125 kips
(C) 150 kips
(D) 200 kips

Given:

Pile length	40 ft
Density of sand	110 lb/ft^3
Sand's friction angle	30°
Earth pressure coefficient	1.3
Soil-pile friction angle	24°

Solution

Calculate the skin friction resistance in sand. Use Equation No. 85, page 159. Press ENTER.

Display	Keys	Description
C?	15 R/S	Critical depth ratio
D?	1 R/S	Width of the pile (ft)
M?	110 R/S	Density of sand (lb/ft^3)
K?	1.3 R/S	Earth pressure coefficient
A?	24 R/S	Soil-pile friction angle
L?	40 R/S	Length of the pile (ft)
S = 97,508.7676	--	Skin friction resistance for circular pile (lb)
--	1.273 ×	Multiply the skin friction resistance by 1.273 for square pile
40.0000 124,128.6612	←	Skin friction resistance for square pile (lb)

The answer is (B).

Problem 8.2

A 35-foot-long, 14-inch-diameter steel pile is to be driven in the soil profile shown. Using the Mohr-Coulomb equation, what is most nearly the skin friction capacity of the pile? For clean steel, assume $c_A = 0.7c$.

(A) 70 kips
(B) 80 kips
(C) 92 kips
(D) 120 kips

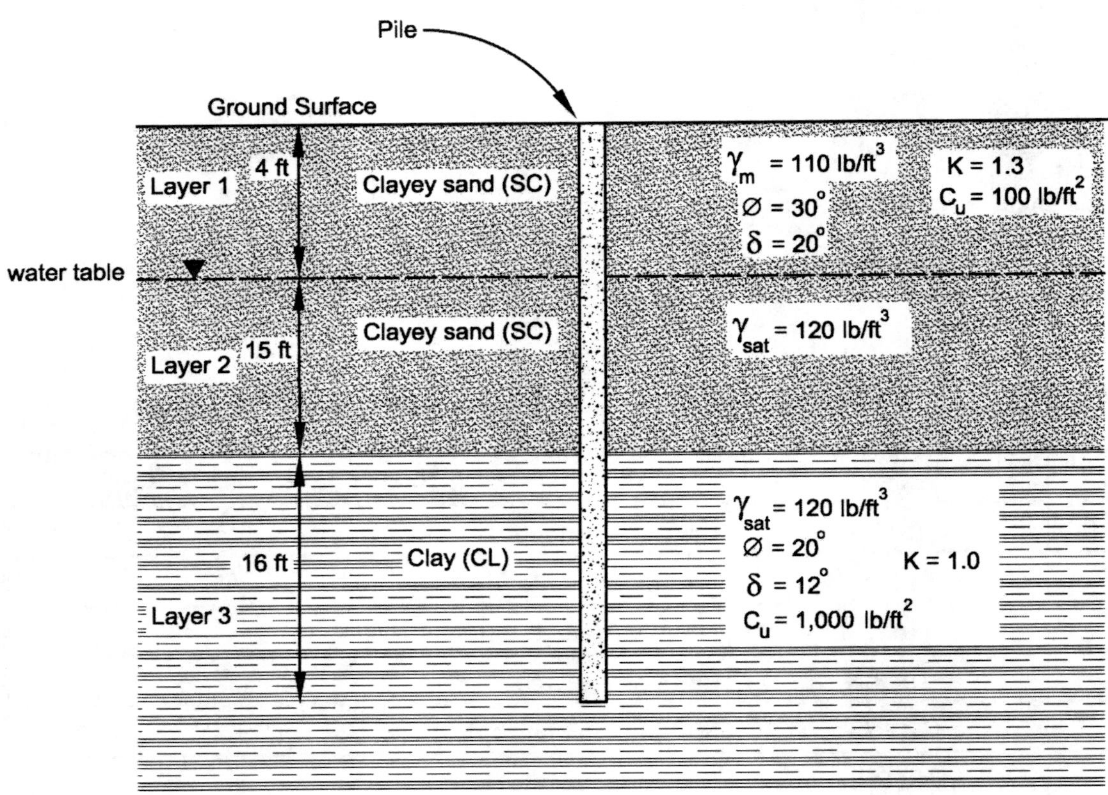

Solution

Compute the skin friction resistance. Use Equation No. 86, page 160. Press ENTER.

Display	Keys	Description
A?	1.3 R/S	Earth pressure coefficient of layer 1
E?	20 R/S	Soil-pile friction angle of layer 1
I?	110 R/S	Moist unit weight of soil at layer 1 (lb/ft³)
O?	4 R/S	Thickness of layer 1 that is in contact with the pile (ft)
W?	.7 ENTER 100 ×	c_A of layer 1 (0.7 × cohesion)
W? 70.0000	R/S	

Display	Keys	Description
D?	14 ENTER 12 ÷	Diameter of the pile (ft)
D? 1.1667	R/S	
B?	1.3 R/S	Earth pressure coefficient of layer 2
F?	20 R/S	Soil-pile friction angle of layer 2
J?	120 ENTER 62.4 –	Buoyant unit weight of soil at layer 2 (lb/ft^3)
J? 57.60000	R/S	
P?	15 R/S	Thickness of layer 2 that is in contact with the pile (ft)
X?	.7 ENTER 100 ×	c_A of layer 2 (0.7 × cohesion)
X? 70.0000	R/S	
C?	1 R/S	Earth pressure coefficient of layer 3
G?	12 R/S	Soil-pile friction angle of layer 3
K?	120 ENTER 62.4 –	Buoyant unit weight of soil at layer 3 (lb/ft^3)
K? 57.60000	R/S	
Q?	16 R/S	Thickness of layer 3 that is in contact with the pile (ft)
Y?	.7 ENTER 1000 ×	c_A of layer 3 (0.7 × cohesion)
Y? 700.0000	R/S	
V?	0 R/S	Earth pressure coefficient of layer 4
H?	0 R/S	Soil-pile friction angle of layer 4
L?	0 R/S	Buoyant unit weight of soil at layer 4 (lb/ft^3)
R?	0 R/S	Thickness of layer 4 that is in contact with the pile (ft)
Z?	0 R/S	c_A of layer 4 (0.7 × cohesion)
S = 92,132.8293	--	Skin friction resistance (lb)

Note: Although the upper 19 ft layer of clayey sand has the same properties, splitting them in 2 layers is necessary to separate the moist unit weight and the buoyant unit weight of soil.

The answer is (C).

Problem 8.3

A 14 in × 14 in precast concrete pile is fully embedded in the soil profile shown. The concrete unit weight is 150 lb/ft^3. Ignore the resistance of the organic sand layer but include the weight of the pile. Using Mohr-Coulomb equation for skin friction resistance, what is most nearly the allowable tensile capacity of the pile? Use a factor of safety of 3.

(A) 15 kips
(B) 28 kips
(C) 35 kips
(D) 40 kips

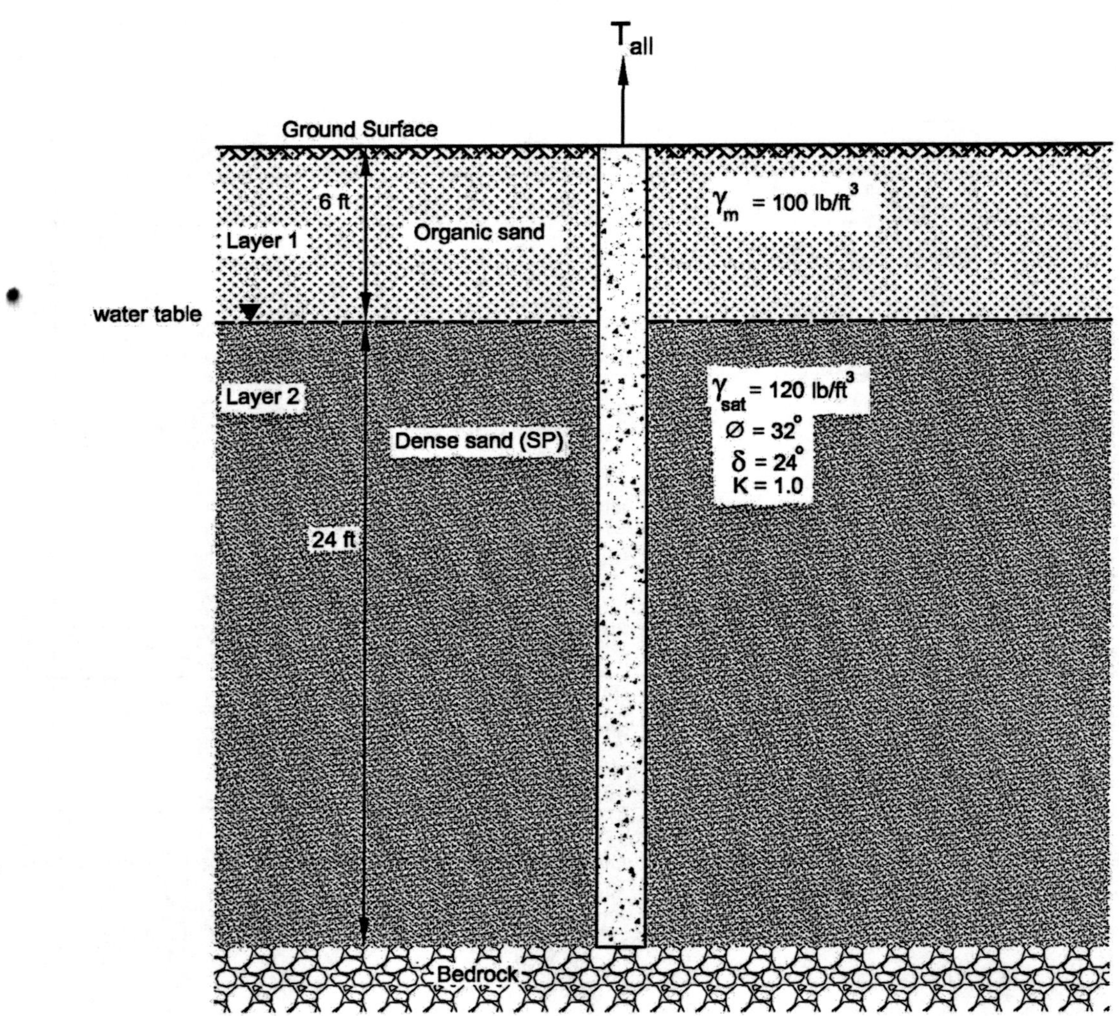

Solution

The following steps will calculate the allowable tensile capacity of the pile.

Step 1. Calculate the skin friction resistance. Use Equation No. 86, page 160. Press ENTER.

Display	Keys	Description
A?	0 R/S	Earth pressure coefficient of layer 1
E?	0 R/S	Soil-pile friction angle of layer 1
I?	100 R/S	Moist unit weight of soil at layer 1 (lb/ft³)
O?	6 R/S	Thickness of layer 1 that is in contact with the pile (ft)
W?	0 R/S	c_A of layer 1 (0.7 × cohesion)
D?	14 ENTER 12 ÷ 1.273 ×	Width of the pile (ft)
D? 1.4852	R/S	
B?	1 R/S	Earth pressure coefficient of layer 2
F?	24 R/S	Soil-pile friction angle of layer 2
J?	120 ENTER 62.4 –	Buoyant unit weight of soil at layer 2 (lb/ft³)
J? 57.6000	R/S	
P?	24 R/S	Thickness of layer 2 that is in contact with the pile (ft)
X?	0 R/S	c_A of layer 2 (0.7 × cohesion)
C?	0 R/S	Earth pressure coefficient of layer 3
G?	0 R/S	Soil-pile friction angle of layer 3
K?	0 R/S	Buoyant unit weight of soil at layer 3 (lb/ft³)
Q?	0 R/S	Thickness of layer 3 that is in contact with the pile (ft)
Y?	0 R/S	c_A of layer 3 (0.7 × cohesion)
V?	0 R/S	Earth pressure coefficient of layer 4
H?	0 R/S	Soil-pile friction angle of layer 4
L?	0 R/S	Buoyant unit weight of soil at layer 4 (lb/ft³)
R?	0 R/S	Thickness of layer 4 that is in contact with the pile (ft)
Z?	0 R/S	c_A of layer 4 (0.7 × cohesion)
Q = 64,374.3656	--	Skin friction resistance (lb)

Step 2. Determine the weight of the pile.

$$Pile_{weight} = 150\frac{lb}{ft^3} \times (1.1667\,ft)^2 \times 30\,ft$$

$$Pile_{weight} = 6{,}125.35\,lb$$

Step 3. Calculate the allowable pullout capacity. Divide the skin friction resistance (64,374.3656 lb) by the factor of safety (3) then add the weight of the pile (6,125.35 lb).

$$P_{all} = \frac{Q_s}{FS} + Pile_{weight}$$

$$P_{all} = \frac{64{,}374.3656lb}{3} + 6{,}125.35lb$$

$$P_{all} = 27{,}583.4719lb$$

Keys for calculating allowable pullout capacity using RPN:

After calculating the skin friction resistance (64,374.3656),

3 ÷ 150 ENTER 1.1667 [↱] [x^2] × 30 × + (HP 35s)
3 ÷ 150 ENTER 1.1667 [x^2] × 30 × + (HP 33s)

The answer is (B).

Problem 8.4

A precast concrete pile is 30 ft long and is fully embedded in the soil profile shown. The pile's cross section is 12 in × 12 in. What is most nearly the allowable loading capacity of the pile? Use a factor of safety of 4. Include the end-bearing resistance. Use Mohr-Coulomb equation in calculating the skin friction resistance.

(A) 45 kips
(B) 50 kips
(C) 55 kips
(D) 60 kips

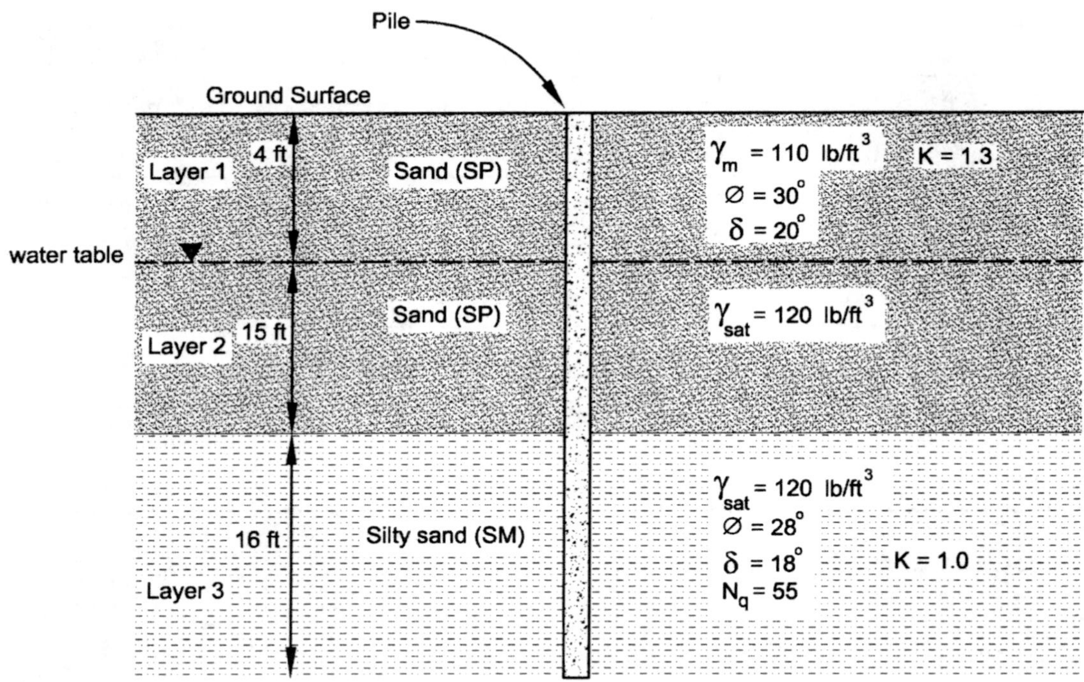

Solution

The allowable loading capacity of the pile can be determined from the following steps.

Step 1. Calculate the skin friction resistance. Use Equation No. 86, page 160. Press ENTER.

Display	Keys	Description
A?	1.3 R/S	Earth pressure coefficient of layer 1
E?	20 R/S	Soil-pile friction angle of layer 1
I?	110 R/S	Moist unit weight of soil at layer 1 (lb/ft^3)
O?	4 R/S	Thickness of layer 1 that is in contact with the pile (ft)
W?	0 R/S	c_A of layer 1 (0.7 × cohesion)
D?	1 ENTER 1.273 ×	Width of the pile (ft)
D? 1.2730	R/S	
B?	1.3 R/S	Earth pressure coefficient of layer 2
F?	20 R/S	Soil-pile friction angle of layer 2
J?	120 ENTER 62.4 –	Buoyant unit weight of soil at layer 2 (lb/ft^3)
J? 57.6000	R/S	
P?	15 R/S	Thickness of layer 2 that is in contact with the pile (ft)
X?	0 R/S	c_A of layer 2 (0.7 × cohesion)
C?	1 R/S	Earth pressure coefficient of layer 3
G?	18 R/S	Soil-pile friction angle of layer 3
K?	120 ENTER 62.4 –	Buoyant unit weight of soil at layer 3 (lb/ft^3)
K? 57.6000	R/S	
Q?	16 R/S	Thickness of layer 3 that is in contact with the pile (ft)
Y?	0 R/S	c_A of layer 3 (0.7 × cohesion)
V?	0 R/S	Earth pressure coefficient of layer 4
H?	0 R/S	Soil-pile friction angle of layer 4
L?	0 R/S	Buoyant unit weight of soil at layer 4 (lb/ft^3)
R?	0 R/S	Thickness of layer 4 that is in contact with the pile (ft)
Z?	0 R/S	c_A of layer 4 (0.7 × cohesion)
S = 63,108.2219	--	Skin friction resistance (lb)

Step 2. Determine the end-bearing capacity. Use Equation No. 87 (T), page 162. Press ENTER.

Display	Keys	Description
I? 110.0000	R/S	Moist unit weight of soil at layer 1 (lb/ft^3)
O? 4.0000	R/S	Thickness of layer 1 that is in contact with the pile (ft)
J? 57.6000	R/S	Buoyant unit weight of soil at layer 2 (lb/ft^3)
P? 15.0000	R/S	Thickness of layer 2 that is in contact with the pile (ft)
K? 57.6000	R/S	Buoyant unit weight of soil at layer 3 (lb/ft^3)
Q? 16.0000	R/S	Thickness of layer 3 that is in contact with the pile (ft)
L? 0.0000	R/S	Buoyant unit weight of soil at layer 4 (lb/ft^3)
R? 0.0000	R/S	Thickness of layer 4 that is in contact with the pile (ft)
D? 1.2730	R/S	Width of the pile (ft)
N?	55 R/S	N_q of soil at the tip of the pile
T = 155,796.0673	--	End-bearing capacity (lb)

Step 3. Compute the allowable pile capacity. Use Equation No. 87 (U), page 162. Press ENTER.

Display	Keys	Description
S? 63,108.2219	R/S	Skin friction resistance (lb)
T? 155,796.0673	R/S	End-bearing capacity (lb)
U = 218,904.2892	--	Ultimate pile capacity (lb)
--	4 ÷	Divide the ultimate pile capacity by the factor of safety of 4
155,796.0673 54,726.0723 ←		Allowable pile capacity (lb)

$$P_{all} = \frac{Q_s + Q_p}{FS}$$

$$P_{all} = \frac{63{,}108.2219 lb + 155{,}796.0673 lb}{4}$$

$$P_{all} = 54{,}726.0723 lb$$

The answer is (C).

Problem 8.5

What is most nearly the length L (ft) of the pile shown that can support an allowable design capacity of 200 kips? Include the end-bearing resistance of 20,000 lb/ft^2. The skin friction resistance is 2,000 lb/ft^2. Use a factor of safety of 2.

(A) 30 ft
(B) 40 ft
(C) 52 ft
(D) 63 ft

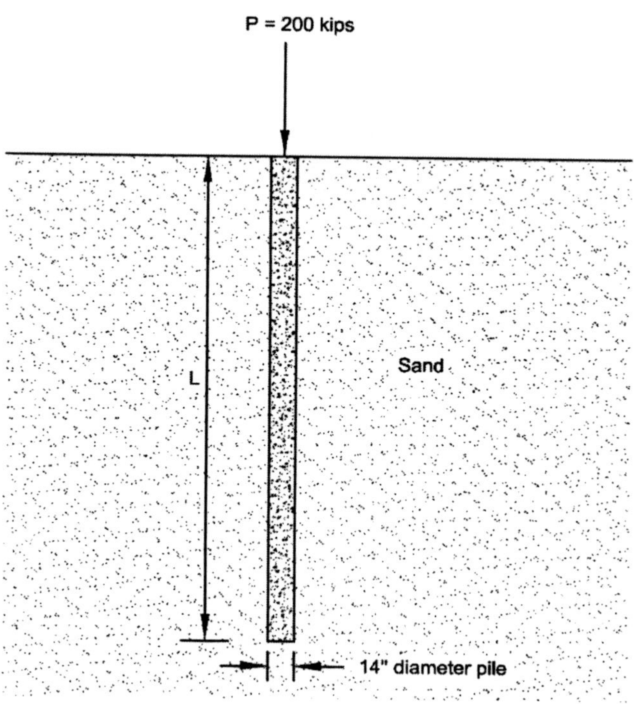

Solution

Solve the length of the pile. Use Equation No. 88, page 164. Press SOLVE L.

Display	Keys	Description
W?	200000 R/S	Allowable design capacity (lb)
V?	20000 R/S	End-bearing resistance (lb/ft^2)
D?	14 ENTER 12 ÷	Diameter of the pile (ft)
D? 1.1667	R/S	
S?	2000 R/S	Skin friction resistance (lb/ft^2)
F?	2 R/S	Factor of safety
L = 51.6507	--	Length of the pile (ft)

The answer is (C).

Problem 8.6

A 16-inch-diameter, 35-ft-long concrete pile is fully imbedded in the soil profile shown. What is most nearly the ultimate capacity Q_u of the pile? Use α - method in calculating the skin friction resistance.

(A) 95 kips
(B) 100 kips
(C) 107 kips
(D) 112 kips

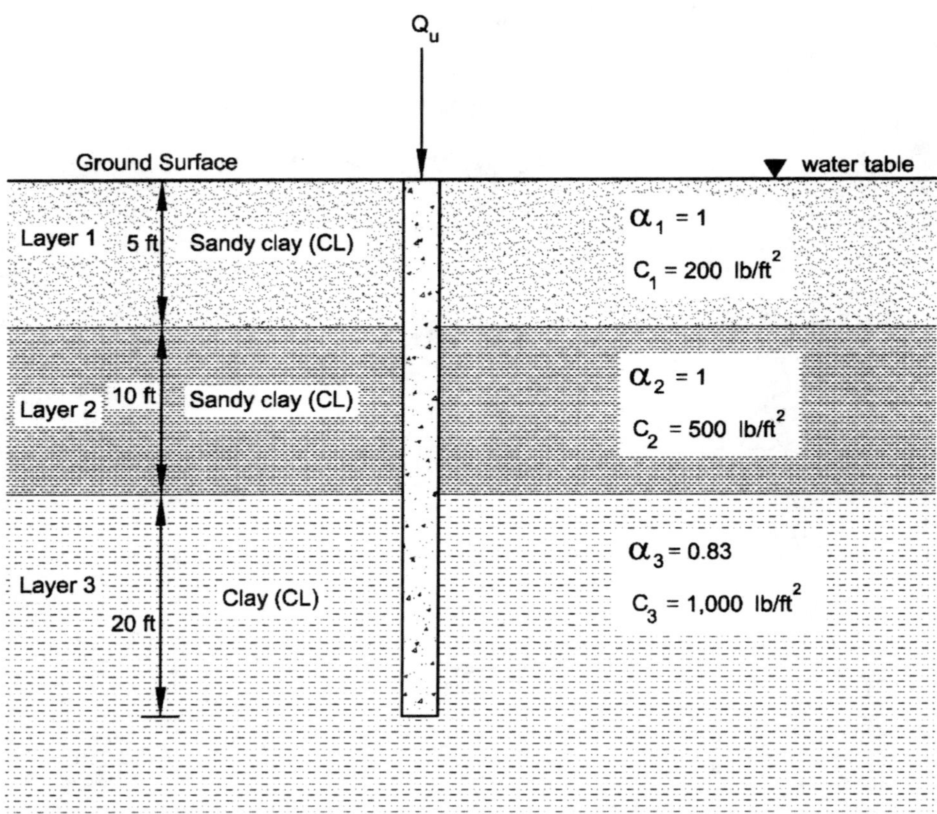

Solution

The following procedure can be used to find the ultimate capacity of the pile.

Step 1. Calculate the skin friction resistance using α - method. Use Equation No. 89 (S), page 165. Press ENTER.

Display	Keys	Description
H?	1 R/S	Adhesion factor of clay at layer 1
W?	200 R/S	Cohesion of clay at layer 1 (lb/ft^2)
O?	5 R/S	Thickness of layer 1 that is in contact with the pile (ft)
I?	1 R/S	Adhesion factor of clay at layer 2
X?	500 R/S	Cohesion of clay at layer 2 (lb/ft^2)
P?	10 R/S	Thickness of layer 2 that is in contact with the pile (ft)

Display	Keys	Description
J?	.83 R/S	Adhesion factor of clay at layer 3
Y?	1000 R/S	Cohesion of clay at layer 3 (lb/ft^2)
Q?	20 R/S	Thickness of layer 3 that is in contact with the pile (ft)
K?	0 R/S	Adhesion factor of clay at layer 4
Z?	0 R/S	Cohesion of clay at layer 4 (lb/ft^2)
R?	0 R/S	Thickness of layer 4 that is in contact with the pile (ft)
D?	16 ENTER 12 ÷	Diameter of the pile (ft)
D? 1.3333	R/S	
S = 94,666.6586	--	Skin friction resistance (lb)

Step 2. Determine the end-bearing capacity. Use Equation No. 89 (T), page 165. Press ENTER.

Display	Keys	Description
C?	1000 R/S	Cohesion of clay at the tip of the pile (lb/ft^2)
D? 1.3333	R/S	Diameter of the pile (ft)
T = 12,566.3706	--	End-bearing capacity (lb)

Step 3. Compute the ultimate capacity Q_u of the pile. Use Equation No. 89 (U), page 165. Press ENTER.

Display	Keys	Description
S? 94,666.6586	R/S	Skin friction resistance (lb)
T? 12,566.3706	R/S	End-bearing capacity (lb)
U = 107,233.0292	--	Ultimate capacity of the pile (lb)

The answer is (C).

Problem 8.7

What is most nearly the required length L (ft) of the pile shown that can support an allowable design capacity of 100 kips? Use a factor of safety of 2. Include the end-bearing resistance.

(A) 52 ft
(B) 55 ft
(C) 57 ft
(D) 60 ft

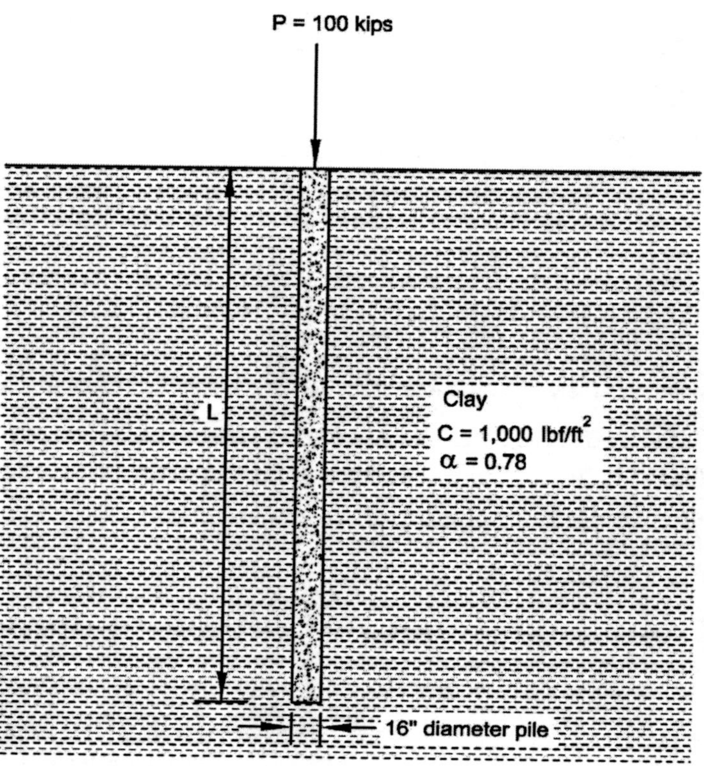

Solution

Solve the length of the pile using α - method. Use Equation No. 90, page 167. Press SOLVE L.

Display	Keys	Description
W?	100000 R/S	Allowable design capacity of the pile (lb)
C?	1000 R/S	Cohesion of clay at the tip of the pile (lb/ft^2)
D?	16 ENTER 12 ÷	Diameter of the pile (ft)
D? 1.3333	R/S	
H?	.78 R/S	Adhesion factor of clay
V?	1000 R/S	Cohesion of clay for skin friction resistance (lb/ft^2)
F?	2 R/S	Factor of safety
L = 57.3673	--	Length of the pile (ft)

The answer is (C).

PART II: WATER RESOURCES AND ENVIRONMENTAL

CHAPTER 9: FLOW MEASURING DEVICES

9.1 Pitot Tube

9.1.1 Solving Velocity of Water in the Pipe or Velocity Head

$$\gamma_w H + \gamma_w \frac{V^2}{2g} = 13.6\gamma_w H$$ Equation No. 93

The equation is entered as

93PITTUBSOLVH
W×H+W×V^2÷2÷G=13.6×W×H

Where:

W = unit weight of water γ_w (62.4 lb/ft^3, 9.81 kN/m^3)
H = velocity head or difference in height of Mercury reading H (ft, m)
V = velocity of water V (ft/sec, m/s)
G = gravitational acceleration g (32.2 ft/sec^2, 9.81 m/s^2)

Keystrokes

HP 35s Checksum: **CK=98E0; LN=22**

[RCL] [W] [×] [RCL] [H] [+] [RCL] [W] [×] [RCL] [V] [y^x] [2] [÷] [2] [÷] [RCL] [G] [↰] [=] [1] [3] [.] [6] [×] [RCL] [W] [×] [RCL] [H] [ENTER]

HP 33s Checksum: **CK=98E0; LN=22**

[RCL] [W] [×] [RCL] [H] [+] [RCL] [W] [×] [RCL] [V] [y^x] [2] [÷] [2] [÷] [RCL] [G] [↱] [=] [1] [3] [.] [6] [×] [RCL] [W] [×] [RCL] [H] [ENTER]

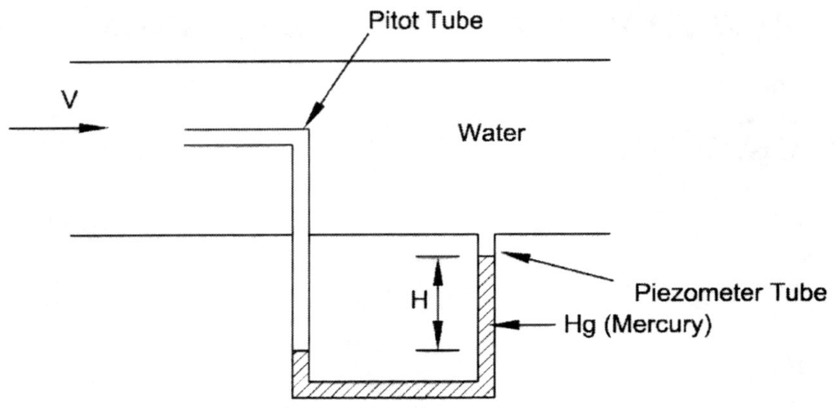

Figure 9-1 Pitot Tube with Manometer

≈≈≈≈≈≈≈≈≈≈

9.2 Venturi Meter

9.2.1 Solving Flow Rate or Velocity Head

$$Q = \frac{1}{\sqrt{1-\left(\frac{D_2}{D_1}\right)^4}} C_d \frac{\pi}{4} D_2^{\ 2} \sqrt{\frac{2g(13.6\gamma_w - \gamma_w)H}{\gamma_w}}$$ Equation No. 94

The equation is entered as

94VENTSOLVQH
Q=1÷(1–(E÷D)^4)^0.5×C×π÷4×E^2(2×G(13.6×W–W)×H÷W)^0.5

Where:

Q = flow rate Q (ft³/sec, m³/s)
E = diameter of throat D_2 (ft, m)
D = diameter of pipe D_1 (ft, m)
C = discharge coefficient C_d
G = gravitational acceleration g (32.2 ft/sec², 9.81 m/s²)
W = unit weight of water γ_w (62.4 lb/ft³, 9.81 kN/m³)
H = velocity head or difference in height of Mercury reading H (ft, m)

Keystrokes

HP 35s Checksum: **CK=9472; LN=52**

[RCL] [Q] [↰] [=] [1] [÷] [()] [1] [−] [()] [RCL] [E] [÷] [RCL] [D] [>] [y^x] [4] [>] [y^x] [.] [5] [×] [RCL] [C] [×] [↰] [π] [÷] [4] [×] [RCL] [E] [y^x] [2] [()] [2] [×] [RCL] [G] [()] [1] [3] [.] [6] [×] [RCL] [W] [−] [RCL] [W] [>] [×] [RCL] [H] [÷] [RCL] [W] [>] [y^x] [.] [5] [ENTER]

HP 33s Checksum: **CK=104E; LN=54**

[RCL] [Q] [↱] [=] [1] [÷] [↱] [(] [1] [−] [↱] [(] [RCL] [E] [÷] [RCL] [D] [↱] [)] [y^x] [4] [↱] [)] [y^x] [.] [5] [×] [RCL] [C] [×] [↱] [π] [÷] [4] [×] [RCL] [E] [y^x] [2] [×] [↱] [(] [2] [×] [RCL] [G] [×] [↱] [(] [1] [3] [.] [6] [×] [RCL] [W] [−] [RCL] [W] [↱] [)] [×] [RCL] [H] [÷] [RCL] [W] [↱] [)] [y^x] [.] [5] [ENTER]

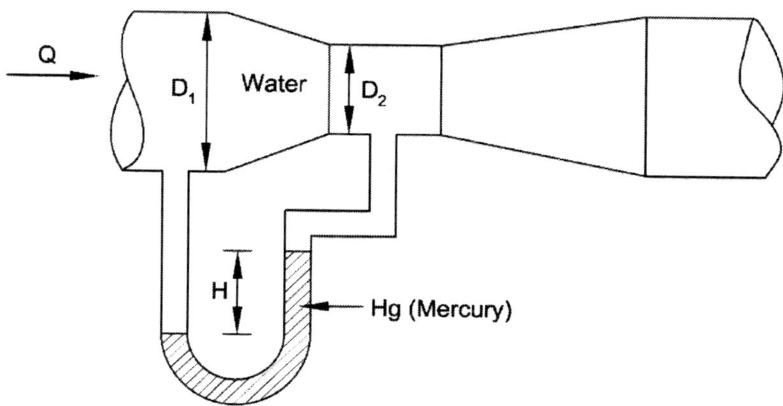

Figure 9-2 Venturi Meter with Manometer

≈≈≈≈≈≈≈≈≈≈

9.3 Orifice

9.3.1 Solving Flow Rate or Velocity Head

$$Q = C_f \frac{\pi}{4} D_o^{\ 2} \sqrt{\frac{2g(13.6\gamma_w - \gamma_w)H}{\gamma_w}}$$ Equation No. 95

The equation is entered as

95ORIFSOLVQH
Q=C×π÷4×D^2(2×G(13.6×W−W)×H÷W)^0.5

Where:

Q = flow rate Q (ft³/sec, m³/s)

C = flow coefficient C_f

D = diameter of orifice D_o (ft, m)

G = gravitational acceleration g (32.2 ft/sec², 9.81 m/s²)

W = unit weight of water γ_w (62.4 lb/ft³, 9.81 kN/m³)

H = velocity head or difference in height of Mercury reading H (ft, m)

Keystrokes

HP 35s Checksum: **CK=091D; LN=34**

[RCL] [Q] [↰] [=] [RCL] [C] [×] [↰] [π] [÷] [4] [×] [RCL] [D] [y^x] [2] [()] [2] [×] [RCL] [G] [()] [1] [3] [.] [6] [×] [RCL] [W] [−] [RCL] [W] [>] [×] [RCL] [H] [÷] [RCL] [W] [>] [y^x] [.] [5] [ENTER]

HP 33s Checksum: **CK=E3B0; LN=36**

[RCL] [Q] [↱] [=] [RCL] [C] [×] [↱] [π] [÷] [4] [×] [RCL] [D] [y^x] [2] [×] [↱] [(] [2] [×] [RCL] [G] [×] [↱] [(] [1] [3] [.] [6] [×] [RCL] [W] [−] [RCL] [W] [↱] [)] [×] [RCL] [H] [÷] [RCL] [W] [↱] [)] [y^x] [.] [5] [ENTER]

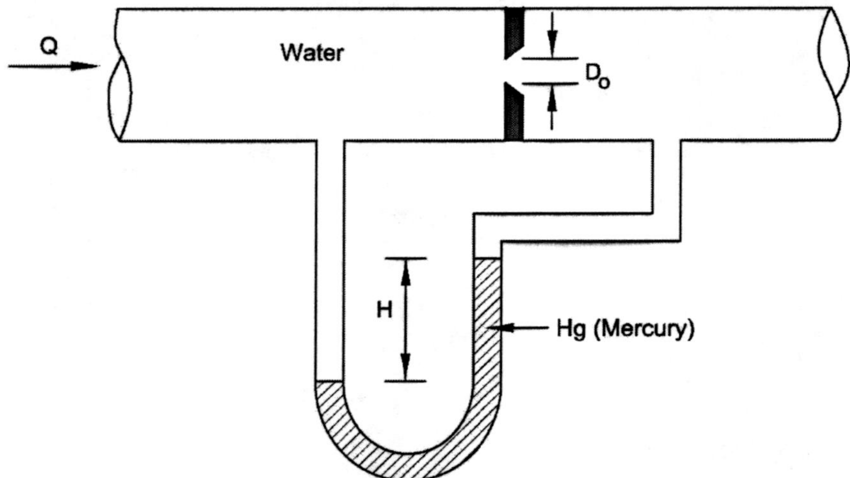

Figure 9-3 Orifice with Manometer

≈≈≈≈≈≈≈≈≈≈

Problem 9.1

Water flows through a pipe with an attached manometer as shown below. Mercury reading indicates a 6-inch difference in height as shown. The velocity of water flowing in the pipe is most nearly

(A) 12 ft/sec
(B) 20 ft/sec
(C) 25 ft/sec
(D) 28 ft/sec

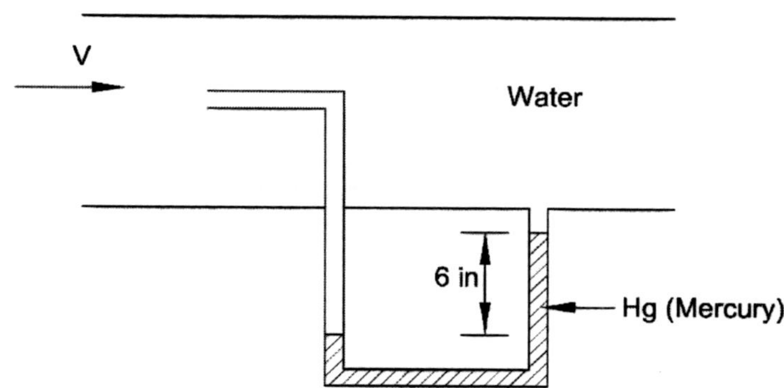

Solution

Solve the velocity of water flow. Use Equation No. 93, page 185. Press SOLVE V.

Display	Keys	Description
W?	62.4 R/S	Unit weight of water (lb/ft³)
H?	.5 R/S	Difference in height of Mercury (ft)
G?	32.2 R/S	Gravitational acceleration (ft/sec²)
V = 20.1425	--	Velocity of water flow (ft/sec)

The answer is (B).

Problem 9.2

Water flows through a venturi meter with an attached manometer. The discharge coefficient is 0.98. The flow rate of water is most nearly

(A) 13 ft^3/sec
(B) 20 ft^3/sec
(C) 25 ft^3/sec
(D) 28 ft^3/sec

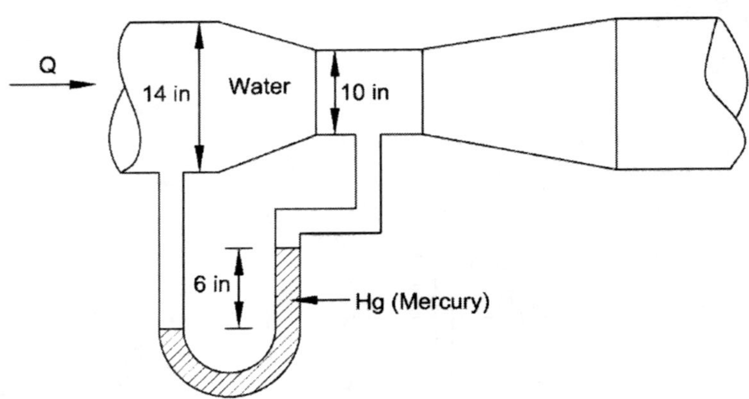

Solution

Calculate the flow rate of water. Use Equation No. 94, page 186. Press ENTER.

Display	Keys	Description
E?	10 ENTER 12 ÷	Diameter of the throat (ft)
E? 0.8333	R/S	
D?	14 ENTER 12 ÷	Diameter of the pipe (ft)
D? 1.1667	R/S	
C?	.98 R/S	Discharge coefficient
G?	32.2 R/S	Gravitational acceleration (ft/sec^2)
W?	62.4 R/S	Unit weight of water (lb/ft^3)
H?	.5 R/S	Difference in height of Mercury (ft)
Q = 12.5182	--	Flow rate of water (ft^3/sec)

The answer is (A).

CHAPTER 10: FLUID DYNAMICS

10.1 Reynolds Number

10.1.1 Reynolds Number Given Flow Rate

$$R_e = \frac{\left(\dfrac{Q}{\dfrac{\pi}{4}D^2}\right)D}{\upsilon}$$ Equation No. 96

The equation is entered as

96REYNO.GIVENQ
R=Q÷(π÷4×D^2)×D÷U

Where:

R = Reynolds number R_e
Q = flow rate Q (ft³/sec, m³/s)
D = diameter of pipe D (ft, m)
U = kinematic viscosity υ (ft²/s, m²/s)

Keystrokes

HP 35s Checksum; Length of Equation: **CK=A7EE; LN=17**

[RCL] [R] [←] [=] [RCL] [Q] [÷] [()] [←] [π] [÷] [4] [×] [RCL] [D] [yˣ] [2] [>] [×] [RCL] [D] [÷] [RCL] [U] [ENTER]

HP 33s Checksum; Length of Equation: **CK=A7EE; LN=17**

[RCL] [R] [→] [=] [RCL] [Q] [÷] [→] [(] [→] [π] [÷] [4] [×] [RCL] [D] [yˣ] [2] [→] [)] [×] [RCL] [D] [÷] [RCL] [U] [ENTER]

≈≈≈≈≈≈≈≈≈≈

10.2.1 Friction Factor Using Jain Equation Given Flow Rate

$$f = \frac{0.25}{\left(\log_{10}\left(\frac{\frac{\varepsilon}{D}}{3.7} + \frac{5.74}{\left(\frac{DV}{\upsilon}\right)^{0.9}}\right)\right)^2}$$ Equation No. 97

Velocity is

$$V = \frac{Q}{A} = \frac{Q}{\frac{\pi}{4}D^2}$$

The equation is entered as

97FFJAINGIVENQ
F=0.25÷LOG(((E÷D)÷3.7)+5.74÷((Q÷(π÷4×D^2))×D÷U)^0.9)^2

Where:

F = friction factor f
E = roughness of pipe material ε (ft, m)
D = diameter of pipe D (ft, m)
Q = flow rate Q (ft³/sec, m³/s)
U = kinematic viscosity υ (ft²/s, m²/s)

Keystrokes

HP 35s Checksum; Length of Equation: **CK=0C60; LN=54**

[RCL] [F] [↰] [=] [·] [2] [5] [÷] [↰] [LOG] [()] [()] [RCL] [E] [÷] [RCL] [D] [>] [÷] [3] [·] [7] [>] [+] [5] [·] [7] [4] [÷] [()] [()] [RCL] [Q] [÷] [()] [↰] [π] [÷] [4] [×] [RCL] [D] [yˣ] [2] [>] [>] [×] [RCL] [D] [÷] [RCL] [U] [>] [yˣ] [·] [9] [>] [yˣ] [2] [ENTER]

HP 33s Checksum; Length of Equation: **CK=0C60; LN=54**

[RCL] [F] [↱] [=] [·] [2] [5] [÷] [↰] [LOG] [↱] [(] [↱] [(] [RCL] [E] [÷] [RCL] [D] [↱] [)] [÷] [3] [·] [7] [↱] [)] [+] [5] [·] [7] [4] [÷] [↱] [(] [↱] [(] [RCL] [Q] [÷] [↱] [(] [↱] [π] [÷] [4] [×] [RCL] [D] [yˣ] [2] [↱] [)] [↱] [)] [×] [RCL] [D] [÷] [RCL] [U] [↱] [)] [yˣ] [·] [9] [↱] [)] [yˣ] [2] [ENTER]

≈≈≈≈≈≈≈≈≈≈

10.2.2 Friction Factor Using Jain Equation Given Velocity of Flow

$$f = \frac{0.25}{\left(\log_{10}\left(\frac{\frac{\varepsilon}{D}}{3.7} + \frac{5.74}{\left(\frac{DV}{\upsilon}\right)^{0.9}}\right)\right)^2}$$

Equation No. 98

The equation is entered as

98FFJAINGIVENV
F=0.25÷LOG(((E÷D)÷3.7)+5.74÷(D×V÷U)^0.9)^2

Where:

F = friction factor f
E = roughness of pipe material ε (ft, m)
D = diameter of pipe D (ft, m)
V = velocity of flow V (ft/sec, m/s)
U = kinematic viscosity υ (ft^2/s, m^2/s)

Keystrokes

HP 35s Checksum; Length of Equation: **CK=A757; LN=42**

[RCL] [F] [↰] [=] [·] [2] [5] [÷] [↰] [LOG] [()] [()] [RCL] [E] [÷] [RCL] [D] [>] [÷] [3] [·] [7] [>] [+] [5] [·] [7] [4] [÷] [()] [RCL] [D] [×] [RCL] [V] [÷] [RCL] [U] [>] [yˣ] [·] [9] [>] [yˣ] [2] [ENTER]

HP 33s Checksum; Length of Equation: **CK=A757; LN=42**

[RCL] [F] [↱] [=] [·] [2] [5] [÷] [↰] [LOG] [↱] [(] [↱] [(] [RCL] [E] [÷] [RCL] [D] [↱] [)] [÷] [3] [·] [7] [↱] [)] [+] [5] [·] [7] [4] [÷] [↱] [(] [RCL] [D] [×] [RCL] [V] [÷] [RCL] [U] [↱] [)] [yˣ] [·] [9] [↱] [)] [yˣ] [2] [ENTER]

≈≈≈≈≈≈≈≈≈≈

10.2.3 Friction Factor Using Jain Equation Given Roughness and Diameter of Pipe, and Reynolds Number

$$f = \frac{0.25}{\left(\log_{10}\left(\frac{\frac{\varepsilon}{D}}{3.7} + \frac{5.74}{R_e^{0.9}}\right)\right)^2}$$

Equation No. 99

The equation is entered as

99FFGIVENEDRE
F=0.25÷LOG(((E÷D)÷3.7)+5.74÷R^0.9)^2

Where:

F = friction factor f
E = roughness of pipe material ε (ft, m)
D = diameter of pipe D (ft, m)
R = Reynolds number R_e

Keystrokes

HP 35s Checksum; Length of Equation: **CK=267C; LN=36**

[RCL] [F] [↰] [=] [·] [2] [5] [÷] [↰] [LOG] [()] [()] [RCL] [E] [÷] [RCL] [D] [>] [÷] [3] [·] [7] [>] [+] [5] [·] [7] [4] [÷] [RCL] [R] [y^x] [·] [9] [>] [y^x] [2] [ENTER]

HP 33s Checksum; Length of Equation: **CK=267C; LN=36**

[RCL] [F] [↱] [=] [·] [2] [5] [÷] [↰] [LOG] [↱] [(] [↱] [(] [RCL] [E] [÷] [RCL] [D] [↱] [)] [÷] [3] [·] [7] [↱] [)] [+] [5] [·] [7] [4] [÷] [RCL] [R] [y^x] [·] [9] [↱] [)] [y^x] [2] [ENTER]

≈≈≈≈≈≈≈≈≈≈

10.3 Head Loss Due to Friction Using Darcy-Weisbach Method

10.3.1 Head Loss Given Flow Rate

$$H_L = \frac{fL\left(\dfrac{Q}{\dfrac{\pi}{4}D^2}\right)^2}{D2g}$$ Equation No. 100

The equation is entered as

100HLDARGIVENQ
J=F×L÷D(Q÷(π÷4×D^2))^2÷2÷G

Where:

J = head loss due to friction H_L (ft, m)
F = friction factor f
L = length of pipe L (ft, m)
D = diameter of pipe D (ft, m)
Q = flow rate Q (ft^3/sec, m^3/s)
G = gravitational acceleration g (32.2 ft/sec^2, 9.81 m/s^2)

Keystrokes

HP 35s Checksum; Length of Equation: **CK=D14C; LN=26**

[RCL] [J] [↰] [=] [RCL] [F] [×] [RCL] [L] [÷] [RCL] [D] [()] [RCL] [Q] [÷] [()] [↰] [π] [÷] [4] [×] [RCL] [D] [yˣ] [2] [>] [>]
[yˣ] [2] [÷] [2] [÷] [RCL] [G] [ENTER]

HP 33s Checksum; Length of Equation: **CK=6DD8; LN=27**

[RCL] [J] [↱] [=] [RCL] [F] [×] [RCL] [L] [÷] [RCL] [D] [×] [↱] [(] [RCL] [Q] [÷] [↱] [(] [↱] [π] [÷] [4] [×] [RCL] [D]
[yˣ] [2] [↱] [)] [↱] [)] [yˣ] [2] [÷] [2] [÷] [RCL] [G] [ENTER]

≈≈≈≈≈≈≈≈≈≈

10.3.2 Head Loss Given Velocity of Flow (Darcy-Weisbach)

$$H_L = \frac{fLV^2}{D2g}$$ Equation No. 101

The equation is entered as

101HLDARGIVENV
J=F×L÷D×V^2÷2÷G

Where:

J = head loss due to friction H_L (ft, m)
F = friction factor f
L = length of pipe L (ft, m)
D = diameter of pipe D (ft, m)
V = velocity of flow V (ft/sec, m/s)
G = gravitational acceleration g (32.2 ft/sec^2, 9.81 m/s^2)

Keystrokes

HP 35s Checksum; Length of Equation: **CK=61A5; LN=15**

[RCL] [J] [↰] [=] [RCL] [F] [×] [RCL] [L] [÷] [RCL] [D] [×] [RCL] [V] [yˣ] [2] [÷] [2] [÷] [RCL] [G] [ENTER]

HP 33s Checksum; Length of Equation: **CK=61A5; LN=15**

[RCL] [J] [↱] [=] [RCL] [F] [×] [RCL] [L] [÷] [RCL] [D] [×] [RCL] [V] [yˣ] [2] [÷] [2] [÷] [RCL] [G] [ENTER]

≈≈≈≈≈≈≈≈≈≈

10.4.1 Head Loss Given Flow Rate in Cubic Feet Per Second

$$H_L = \frac{3.022\left(\dfrac{Q}{\dfrac{\pi}{4}D^2}\right)^{1.85}_{ft/sec} L_{ft}}{C^{1.85} D_{ft}^{1.17}}$$ Equation No. 102

The equation is entered as

102HLHAZQCFS
J=3.022(Q÷(π÷4×D^2))^1.85×L÷C^1.85÷D^1.17

Where:

J = head loss due to friction H_L (ft)
Q = flow rate Q (ft³/sec)
D = diameter of pipe D (ft)
L = length of pipe L (ft)
C = roughness coefficient of pipe C

Keystrokes

HP 35s Checksum; Length of Equation: **CK=23BF; LN=41**

[RCL] [J] [↰] [=] [3] [.] [0] [2] [2] [()] [RCL] [Q] [÷] [()] [↰] [π] [÷] [4] [×] [RCL] [D] [y^x] [2] [>] [>] [y^x] [1] [.] [8] [5] [×] [RCL] [L] [÷] [RCL] [C] [y^x] [1] [.] [8] [5] [÷] [RCL] [D] [y^x] [1] [.] [1] [7] [ENTER]

HP 33s Checksum; Length of Equation: **CK=9A2E; LN=42**

[RCL] [J] [↱] [=] [3] [.] [0] [2] [2] [×] [↱] [(] [RCL] [Q] [÷] [↱] [(] [↱] [π] [÷] [4] [×] [RCL] [D] [y^x] [2] [↱] [)] [↱] [)] [y^x] [1] [.] [8] [5] [×] [RCL] [L] [÷] [RCL] [C] [y^x] [1] [.] [8] [5] [÷] [RCL] [D] [y^x] [1] [.] [1] [7] [ENTER]

≈≈≈≈≈≈≈≈≈≈

10.4.2 Head Loss Given Flow Rate in Gallons Per Minute

$$H_L = \frac{10.44 L_{ft} Q_{gpm}^{1.85}}{C^{1.85} D_{in}^{4.87}}$$ Equation No. 103

The equation is entered as

103HLHAZENQGPM
J=10.44×L×Q^1.85÷C^1.85÷D^4.87

Where:

J = head loss due to friction H_L (ft)
L = length of pipe L (ft)
Q = flow rate Q (gal/min)
C = roughness coefficient of pipe C
D = diameter of pipe D (in)

Keystrokes

HP 35s Checksum; Length of Equation: **CK=1FF7; LN=30**

[RCL] [J] [↰] [=] [1] [0] [·] [4] [4] [×] [RCL] [L] [×] [RCL] [Q] [y^x] [1] [·] [8] [5] [÷] [RCL] [C] [y^x] [1] [·] [8] [5] [÷] [RCL] [D] [y^x] [4] [·] [8] [7] [ENTER]

HP 33s Checksum; Length of Equation: **CK=1FF7; LN=30**

[RCL] [J] [↱] [=] [1] [0] [·] [4] [4] [×] [RCL] [L] [×] [RCL] [Q] [y^x] [1] [·] [8] [5] [÷] [RCL] [C] [y^x] [1] [·] [8] [5] [÷] [RCL] [D] [y^x] [4] [·] [8] [7] [ENTER]

≈≈≈≈≈≈≈≈≈≈

10.4.3 Head Loss Given Velocity of Flow (Hazen-Williams)

$$H_L = \frac{3.022 V_{ft/\sec}^{1.85} L_{ft}}{C^{1.85} D_{ft}^{1.17}}$$ Equation No. 104

The equation is entered as

104HLHAZENGIVV
J=3.022×V^1.85×L÷C^1.85÷D^1.17

Where:

J = head loss due to friction H_L (ft)
V = velocity of flow V (ft/sec)
L = length of pipe L (ft)
C = roughness coefficient of pipe C
D = diameter of pipe D (ft)

Keystrokes

HP 35s Checksum; Length of Equation: **CK=5C35; LN=30**

[RCL] [J] [↰] [=] [3] [.] [0] [2] [2] [×] [RCL] [V] [yx] [1] [.] [8] [5] [×] [RCL] [L] [÷] [RCL] [C] [yx] [1] [.] [8] [5] [÷] [RCL] [D] [yx] [1] [.] [1] [7] [ENTER]

HP 33s Checksum; Length of Equation: **CK=5C35; LN=30**

[RCL] [J] [↱] [=] [3] [.] [0] [2] [2] [×] [RCL] [V] [yx] [1] [.] [8] [5] [×] [RCL] [L] [÷] [RCL] [C] [yx] [1] [.] [8] [5] [÷] [RCL] [D] [yx] [1] [.] [1] [7] [ENTER]

≈≈≈≈≈≈≈≈≈≈

10.5 Head Loss Due to Fittings

10.5.1 Head Loss Given Velocity of Flow

$$H_F = \frac{NV^2}{2g}$$ Equation No. 105

The equation is entered as

105HLFITGIVENV
K=N×V^2÷2÷G

Where:

K = head loss due to fittings H_F (ft, m)
N = coefficient for fittings N
V = velocity of flow V (ft/sec, m/s)
G = gravitational acceleration g (32.2 ft/sec^2, 9.81 m/s^2)

Keystrokes

HP 35s Checksum; Length of Equation: **CK=06A3; LN=11**

[RCL] [K] [↰] [=] [RCL] [N] [×] [RCL] [V] [yx] [2] [÷] [2] [÷] [RCL] [G] [ENTER]

HP 33s Checksum; Length of Equation: **CK=06A3; LN=11**

[RCL] [K] [↱] [=] [RCL] [N] [×] [RCL] [V] [yx] [2] [÷] [2] [÷] [RCL] [G] [ENTER]

≈≈≈≈≈≈≈≈≈≈

10.5.2 Head Loss Given Flow Rate and Diameter of Pipe

$$H_F = \frac{N\left(\frac{Q}{\frac{\pi}{4}D^2}\right)^2}{2g} \qquad \text{Equation No. 106}$$

The equation is entered as

106HLFITGIVENQD
K=N(Q÷(π÷4×D^2))^2÷2÷G

Where:

K = head loss due to fittings H_F (ft, m)
N = coefficient for fittings N
Q = flow rate Q (ft^3/sec, m^3/s)
D = diameter of pipe D (ft, m)
G = gravitational acceleration g (32.2 ft/sec^2, 9.81 m/s^2)

Keystrokes

HP 35s Checksum; Length of Equation: **CK=65E1; LN=22**

[RCL] [K] [↰] [=] [RCL] [N] [()] [RCL] [Q] [÷] [()] [↰] [π] [÷] [4] [×] [RCL] [D] [y^x] [2] [>] [>] [y^x] [2] [÷] [2] [÷] [RCL] [G] [ENTER]

HP 33s Checksum; Length of Equation: **CK=2787; LN=23**

[RCL] [K] [↱] [=] [RCL] [N] [×] [↱] [(] [RCL] [Q] [÷] [↱] [(] [↱] [π] [÷] [4] [×] [RCL] [D] [y^x] [2] [↱] [)] [↱] [)] [y^x] [2] [÷] [2] [÷] [RCL] [G] [ENTER]

≈≈≈≈≈≈≈≈≈≈

10.6 Bernoulli Equation

10.6.1 Bernoulli Equation with Pump Head and 2 Different Pipe Sizes Given Flow Rate

$$\frac{P_1}{\gamma_w} + \frac{\left(\frac{Q}{\frac{\pi}{4}D^2}\right)^2}{2g} + H_1 + I = \frac{P_2}{\gamma_w} + \frac{\left(\frac{Q}{\frac{\pi}{4}O^2}\right)^2}{2g} + H_L + H_F + H_2 \qquad \text{Equation No. 107}$$

The equation is entered as

107BE1OR2DGIVQ
P÷W+(Q÷(π÷4×D^2))^2÷2÷G+H+I=S÷W+(Q÷(π÷4×O^2))^2÷2÷G+J+K+M

Where:

P = pressure at P_1 (lb/ft², kN/m²)
W = unit weight of water γ_w (62.4 lb/ft³, 9.81 kN/m³)
Q = flow rate Q (ft³/sec, m³/s)
D = diameter of pipe on energy source side D (ft, m)
G = gravitational acceleration g (32.2 ft/sec², 9.81 m/s²)
H = elevation at P_1 H_1 (ft, m)
I = pump head I (ft, m)
S = pressure at P_2 (lb/ft², kN/m²)
O = diameter of pipe on head loss side O (ft, m)
J = head loss due to friction H_L (ft, m)
K = head loss due to fittings H_F (ft, m)
M = elevation at P_2 H_2 (ft, m)

Keystrokes

HP 35s Checksum; Length of Equation: **CK=6C17; LN=57**

[RCL] [P] [÷] [RCL] [W] [+] [()] [RCL] [Q] [÷] [()] [↰] [π] [÷] [4] [×] [RCL] [D] [yˣ] [2] [>] [>] [yˣ] [2] [÷] [2] [÷] [RCL] [G] [+] [RCL] [H] [+] [RCL] [I] [↰] [=] [RCL] [S] [÷] [RCL] [W] [+] [()] [RCL] [Q] [÷] [()] [↰] [π] [÷] [4] [×] [RCL] [O] [yˣ] [2] [>] [>] [yˣ] [2] [÷] [2] [÷] [RCL] [G] [+] [RCL] [J] [+] [RCL] [K] [+] [RCL] [M] [ENTER]

HP 33s Checksum; Length of Equation: **CK=6C17; LN=57**

[RCL] [P] [÷] [RCL] [W] [+] [↱] [(] [RCL] [Q] [÷] [↱] [(] [↱] [π] [÷] [4] [×] [RCL] [D] [yˣ] [2] [↱] [)] [↱] [)] [yˣ] [2] [÷] [2] [÷] [RCL] [G] [+] [RCL] [H] [+] [RCL] [I] [↱] [=] [RCL] [S] [÷] [RCL] [W] [+] [↱] [(] [RCL] [Q] [÷] [↱] [(] [↱] [π] [÷] [4] [×] [RCL] [O] [yˣ] [2] [↱] [)] [↱] [)] [yˣ] [2] [÷] [2] [÷] [RCL] [G] [+] [RCL] [J] [+] [RCL] [K] [+] [RCL] [M] [ENTER]

≈≈≈≈≈≈≈≈≈≈

10.6.2 Bernoulli Equation Solving Velocity with Uniform Pipe Diameter

$$\frac{P_1}{\gamma_w}+\frac{V_1^2}{2g}+H_1+I=\frac{P_2}{\gamma_w}+\frac{V_2^2}{2g}+\frac{fLV^2}{D2g}+\frac{NV^2}{2g}+H_2$$ Equation No. 108

The equation is entered as

108BESOLVV1DIA
P÷W+V^2÷2÷G+H+I=S÷W+V^2÷2÷G+F×L÷D×V^2÷2÷G+N×V^2÷2÷G+M

Where:

P = pressure at P_1 (lb/ft², kN/m²)
W = unit weight of water γ_w (62.4 lb/ft³, 9.81 kN/m³)
V = velocity of flow V_1 , V_2, and V (ft/sec, m/s)
G = gravitational acceleration g (32.2 ft/sec², 9.81 m/s²)
H = elevation at P_1 H_1 (ft, m)
I = pump head I (ft, m)
S = pressure at P_2 (lb/ft², kN/m²)
F = friction factor f
L = length of pipe L (ft, m)
D = diameter of pipe D (ft, m)
N = coefficient for fittings N
M = elevation at P_2 H_2 (ft, m)

Keystrokes

HP 35s Checksum; Length of Equation: **CK=096C; LN=53**

[RCL] [P] [÷] [RCL] [W] [+] [RCL] [V] [yˣ] [2] [÷] [2] [÷] [RCL] [G] [+] [RCL] [H] [+] [RCL] [I] [↰] [=] [RCL] [S] [÷] [RCL] [W] [+] [RCL] [V] [yˣ] [2] [÷] [2] [÷] [RCL] [G] [+] [RCL] [F] [×] [RCL] [L] [÷] [RCL] [D] [×] [RCL] [V] [yˣ] [2] [÷] [2] [÷] [RCL] [G] [+] [RCL] [N] [×] [RCL] [V] [yˣ] [2] [÷] [2] [÷] [RCL] [G] [+] [RCL] [M] [ENTER]

HP 33s Checksum; Length of Equation: **CK=096C; LN=53**

[RCL] [P] [÷] [RCL] [W] [+] [RCL] [V] [yˣ] [2] [÷] [2] [÷] [RCL] [G] [+] [RCL] [H] [+] [RCL] [I] [↱] [=] [RCL] [S] [÷] [RCL] [W] [+] [RCL] [V] [yˣ] [2] [÷] [2] [÷] [RCL] [G] [+] [RCL] [F] [×] [RCL] [L] [÷] [RCL] [D] [×] [RCL] [V] [yˣ] [2] [÷] [2] [÷] [RCL] [G] [+] [RCL] [N] [×] [RCL] [V] [yˣ] [2] [÷] [2] [÷] [RCL] [G] [+] [RCL] [M] [ENTER]

Note: This equation shall be used if the head loss is calculated using Darcy-Weisbach equation.

≈≈≈≈≈≈≈≈≈≈

10.6.3 Bernoulli Equation with 2 Different Velocities

$$\frac{P_1}{\gamma_w} + \frac{V_1^2}{2g} + H_1 + I = \frac{P_2}{\gamma_w} + \frac{V_2^2}{2g} + H_L + H_F + H_2$$ Equation No. 109

The equation is entered as

109BESOLVV2DIA
P÷W+V^2÷2÷G+H+I=S÷W+U^2÷2÷G+J+K+M

Where:

P = pressure at P_1 (lb/ft², kN/m²)
W = unit weight of water γ_w (62.4 lb/ft³, 9.81 kN/m³)
V = velocity of flow V_1 (ft/sec, m/s)
G = gravitational acceleration g (32.2 ft/sec², 9.81 m/s²)
H = elevation at P_1 H_1 (ft, m)
I = pump head I (ft, m)
S = pressure at P_2 (lb/ft², kN/m²)
U = velocity of flow V_2 (ft/sec, m/s)
J = head loss due to friction H_L (ft, m)
K = head loss due to fittings H_F (ft, m)
M = elevation at P_2 H_2 (ft, m)

Keystrokes

HP 35s Checksum; Length of Equation: **CK=7A87; LN=33**

[RCL] [P] [÷] [RCL] [W] [+] [RCL] [V] [y^x] [2] [÷] [2] [÷] [RCL] [G] [+] [RCL] [H] [+] [RCL] [I] [↰] [=] [RCL] [S] [÷] [RCL] [W] [+] [RCL] [U] [y^x] [2] [÷] [2] [÷] [RCL] [G] [+] [RCL] [J] [+] [RCL] [K] [+] [RCL] [M] [ENTER]

HP 33s Checksum; Length of Equation: **CK=7A87; LN=33**

[RCL] [P] [÷] [RCL] [W] [+] [RCL] [V] [y^x] [2] [÷] [2] [÷] [RCL] [G] [+] [RCL] [H] [+] [RCL] [I] [↱] [=] [RCL] [S] [÷] [RCL] [W] [+] [RCL] [U] [y^x] [2] [÷] [2] [÷] [RCL] [G] [+] [RCL] [J] [+] [RCL] [K] [+] [RCL] [M] [ENTER]

≈≈≈≈≈≈≈≈≈≈

10.7 Pump Horsepower

10.7.1 Pump Horsepower for Head Loss

$$H_p = \frac{\gamma_w H_L Q}{550 \frac{\eta}{100}}$$ Equation No. 110

The equation is entered as

110PUMPHPHLOSS
T=W×J×Q÷550÷(E÷100)

Where:

T = pump horsepower H_P (hp)
W = unit weight of water γ_w (62.4 lb/ft³)
J = head loss due to friction H_L (ft)

Q = flow rate Q (ft³/sec)
E = efficiency of pump η (%)

Keystrokes

HP 35s Checksum; Length of Equation: **CK=76B9; LN=19**

[RCL] [T] [↰] [=] [RCL] [W] [×] [RCL] [J] [×] [RCL] [Q] [÷] [5] [5] [0] [÷] [()] [RCL] [E] [÷] [1] [0] [0] [ENTER]

HP 33s Checksum; Length of Equation: **CK=76B9; LN=19**

[RCL] [T] [↱] [=] [RCL] [W] [×] [RCL] [J] [×] [RCL] [Q] [÷] [5] [5] [0] [÷] [↱] [(] [RCL] [E] [÷] [1] [0] [0] [↱] [)] [ENTER]

≈≈≈≈≈≈≈≈≈≈

10.7.2 Pump Horsepower for Pump Head

$$H_p = \frac{\gamma_w IQ}{550\frac{\eta}{100}}$$ Equation No. 111

The equation is entered as

111PUMPHPPHEAD
T=W×I×Q÷550÷(E÷100)

Where:

T = pump horsepower H_p (hp)
W = unit weight of water γ_w (62.4 lb/ft³)
I = pump head I (ft)
Q = flow rate Q (ft³/sec)
E = efficiency of pump η (%)

Keystrokes

HP 35s Checksum; Length of Equation: **CK=959C; LN=19**

[RCL] [T] [↰] [=] [RCL] [W] [×] [RCL] [I] [×] [RCL] [Q] [÷] [5] [5] [0] [÷] [()] [RCL] [E] [÷] [1] [0] [0] [ENTER]

HP 33s Checksum; Length of Equation: **CK=959C; LN=19**

[RCL] [T] [↱] [=] [RCL] [W] [×] [RCL] [I] [×] [RCL] [Q] [÷] [5] [5] [0] [÷] [↱] [(] [RCL] [E] [÷] [1] [0] [0] [↱] [)] [ENTER]

≈≈≈≈≈≈≈≈≈≈

Problem 10.1

Water flows in a 10-inch-diameter commercial steel schedule 40 pipe 2,000 feet long at a flow rate of 1,200 gal/min. The water temperature is 70 °F. The Reynolds number, friction factor, and head loss are most nearly

	Reynolds Number	Friction Factor	Head Loss (ft)
(A)	1.8×10^5	0.012	10
(B)	2.2×10^5	0.014	12
(C)	3.9×10^5	0.016	15
(D)	4.5×10^5	0.02	20

Solution

a) Reynolds number

Calculate the Reynolds number with given flow rate Q. Use Equation No. 96, page 191. Press ENTER.

Display	Keys	Description
Q?	*	Flow rate of water (ft^3/sec)
Q? 2.6738	R/S	
D?	10 ENTER 12 ÷	Diameter of the pipe (ft)
D? 0.8333	R/S	
U?	1.059 E 5 +/− R/S	Kinematic viscosity of water at 70 °F (ft^2/s)
R = 385,765.8708	--	Reynolds number

* Keys for converting 1,200 gal/min to ft^3/sec using RPN:

1200 ENTER 7.48 ÷ 60 ÷

$$\frac{1{,}200\,gal}{\min} \times \frac{ft^3}{7.48\,gal} \times \frac{\min}{60\sec} = 2.6738\frac{ft^3}{\sec}$$

b) Friction factor

Determine the friction factor with given flow rate Q which was converted to ft^3/sec from previous calculation. Use Equation No. 97, page 192. Press ENTER.

Display	Keys	Description
E?	.0002 R/S	Specific roughness for steel (ft)
D? 0.8333	R/S	Diameter of the pipe (ft)

Display	Keys	Description
Q? 2.6738	R/S	Flow rate of water (ft^3/sec)
U? 1.0590 E ⁻5	R/S	Kinematic viscosity of water (ft^2/s)
F = 0.0162	--	Friction factor

c) Head loss

Compute the head loss with given flow rate Q which was converted to ft^3/sec. Use Equation No. 100, page 194. Press ENTER.

Display	Keys	Description
F? 0.0162	R/S	Friction factor
L?	2000 R/S	Length of the pipe (ft)
D? 0.8333	R/S	Diameter of the pipe (ft)
Q? 2.6738	R/S	Flow rate of water (ft^3/sec)
G?	32.2 R/S	Gravitational acceleration (ft/sec^2)
J = 14.5306	--	Head loss (ft)

The answer is (C).

Problem 10.2

Water flows in a 6-inch-diameter, 1,000-foot-long commercial steel schedule 40 pipe at a flow rate of 500 gal/min. The head loss due to friction using Hazen-Williams formula and C=110 is most nearly

(A) 12 ft
(B) 15 ft
(C) 21 ft
(D) 28 ft

Solution

Calculate the head loss using Hazen-Williams formula with given flow rate in gal/min, diameter of the pipe in inches, and length of the pipe in feet. Use Equation No. 103, page 196. Press ENTER.

Display	Keys	Description
L?	1000 R/S	Length of the pipe (ft)
Q?	500 R/S	Flow rate of water (gal/min)
C?	110 R/S	Hazen-Williams roughness coefficient of the pipe
D?	6 R/S	Diameter of the pipe (in)
J = 27.9011	--	Head loss (ft)

The answer is (D).

Problem 10.3

A 100-foot-long, 6-inch-diameter steel pipe discharges water from a large open reservoir. The water level of water in the reservoir is 75 feet above the outlet. Ignore minor losses and use friction factor of 0.02. The flow rate is most nearly

(A) 5 ft³/sec
(B) 7 ft³/sec
(C) 10 ft³/sec
(D) 13 ft³/sec

Solution

The flow rate can be calculated using the following procedure.

Step 1. Solve the velocity of flow using Darcy-Weisbach equation. Use Equation No. 101, page 195. Press SOLVE V.

Display	Keys	Description
J?	75 R/S	Head loss (ft)
F?	.02 R/S	Friction factor
L?	100 R/S	Length of the pipe (ft)
D?	.5 R/S	Diameter of the pipe (ft)
G?	32.2 R/S	Gravitational acceleration (ft/sec²)
V = 34.7491	--	Velocity of flow of water (ft/sec)

Step 2. Calculate the flow rate.

Display	Keys	Description
--	*	Flow rate calculation
34.7491 6.8230 ←		Flow rate (ft³/sec)

* Keys for calculating flow rate using RPN:

[↰] [π] 4 ÷ × .5 [↱] [x^2] × (HP 35s)
[↱] [π] 4 ÷ × .5 [x^2] × (HP 33s)

The answer is (B).

Problem 10.4

Water flows from points A to B at a flow rate of 1,000 gal/min. Neglect all friction losses. The pressure (psi) and velocity (ft/sec) at point B are most nearly

	Pressure at Point B (lb/in^2)	Velocity at Point B (ft/sec)
(A)	31	25
(B)	25	30
(C)	1,400	32
(D)	4,530	35

Point A
Elevation = 250 ft
D_1 = 6 in
P_1 = 100 psi
V_1 = 10 ft/sec

Point B
Elevation = 400 ft
D_2 = 4 in
P_2 = ?
V_2 = ?

Solution

The Bernoulli equation shall be used to solve this problem.

Step 1. Calculate the pressure P_2. Use Equation No. 107, page 199. This equation shall be used with 1 pipe size or 2 different pipe sizes. Press SOLVE S.

Display	Keys	Description
P?	*	Pressure at Point A (lb/ft^2), convert psi to lb/ft^2
P? 14,400.0000	R/S	
W?	62.4 R/S	Unit weight of water (lb/ft^3)
Q?	**	Flow rate of water (ft^3/sec)
Q? 2.2282	R/S	
D?	.5 R/S	Diameter of the pipe at Point A (ft)
G?	32.2 R/S	Gravitational acceleration (ft/sec^2)
H?	250 R/S	Elevation of Point A (ft)
I?	0 R/S	Pump head (ft)
O?	4 ENTER 12 ÷	Diameter of the pipe at Point B (ft)
O? 0.3333	R/S	
J?	0 R/S	Head loss due to friction (ft)

Display	Keys	Description
K?	0 R/S	Head loss due to fittings (ft)
M?	400 R/S	Elevation of Point B (ft)
S = 4,533.0449	--	Pressure at Point B (lb/ft²)
--	144 ÷	Divide the pressure at Point B by 144 to convert lb/ft² to lb/in²
4,533.0449 31.4798 ←		Pressure at Point B (lb/in²)

* Keys for converting 100 psi to psf using RPN:

100 ENTER 12 [↱] [x²] × (HP 35s)
100 ENTER 12 [x²] × (HP 33s)

$$100\frac{lb}{in^2}\times\frac{(12in)^2}{ft^2}=14{,}400\frac{lb}{ft^2}$$

** Keys for converting 1,000 gal/min to ft³/sec using RPN:

1000 ENTER 7.48 ÷ 60 ÷

$$1{,}000\frac{gal}{\text{min}}\times\frac{ft^3}{7.48gal}\times\frac{\text{min}}{60\text{sec}}=2.2282\frac{ft^3}{\text{sec}}$$

Step 2. Solve the velocity at Point B. Use Equation No. 109, page 201. Press SOLVE U.

Display	Keys	Description
P? 14,400.0000	R/S	Pressure at Point A (lb/ft²)
W? 62.4000	R/S	Unit weight of water (lb/ft³)
V?	10 R/S	Velocity of flow at Point A (ft/sec)
G? 32.2000	R/S	Gravitational acceleration (ft/sec²)
H? 250.0000	R/S	Elevation of point A (ft)
I? 0.0000	R/S	Pump head (ft)
S? 4,533.0949	R/S	Pressure at point B (lb/ft²)
J? 0.0000	R/S	Head loss due to friction (ft)
K? 0.0000	R/S	Head loss due to fittings (ft)
M? 400.0000	R/S	Elevation of point B (ft)
U = 24.9630	--	Velocity of flow at point B (ft/sec)

The answer is (A).

Problem 10.5

A 6-inch-diameter, 300-foot-long steel pipe conveys water from Reservoir 1 to Reservoir 2. Minor losses are insignificant. The flow rate is most nearly

(A) 3.5 ft^3/sec
(B) 7 ft^3/sec
(C) 15 ft^3/sec
(D) 18 ft^3/sec

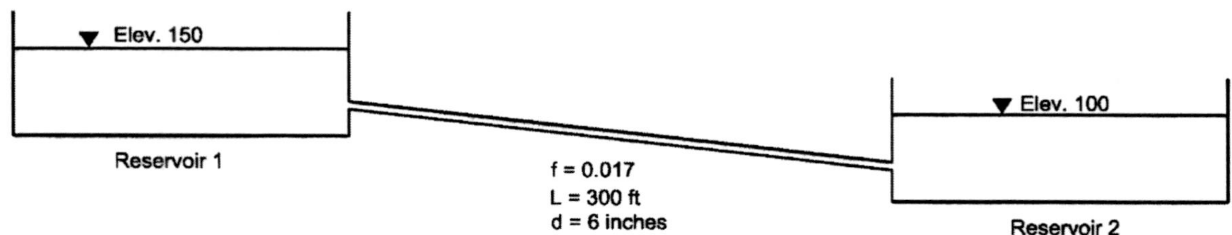

Solution

Solve the velocity of flow. Use Equation No. 101, page 195. Press SOLVE V.

Display	Keys	Description
J?	50 R/S	Head loss or difference of water surface elevations between 2 reservoirs (ft)
F?	.017 R/S	Friction factor
L?	300 R/S	Length of the pipe (ft)
D?	.5 R/S	Diameter of the pipe (ft)
G?	32.2 R/S	Gravitational acceleration (ft/sec²)
V = 17.7676	--	Velocity of flow (ft/sec)
--	*	Flow rate calculation
17.7676 3.4887 ←		Flow rate (ft³/sec)

* Keys for calculating flow rate using RPN:

[↰] [π] 4 ÷ × .5 [↱] [x²] × (HP 35s)
[↱] [π] 4 ÷ × .5 [x²] × (HP 33s)

$$Q = AV$$

$$= \frac{\pi}{4}(0.5\,ft)^2\left(17.7676\frac{ft}{\text{sec}}\right)$$

$$= 3.4887\frac{ft^3}{\text{sec}}$$

The answer is (A).

Problem 10.6

A pump is installed near Reservoir A to transport water to Reservoir B at a discharge rate of 5 ft^3/sec. The pump's efficiency is 85%. Ignoring minor losses, the horsepower required for the pump is most nearly

(A) 10 hp
(B) 12 hp
(C) 15 hp
(D) 17 hp

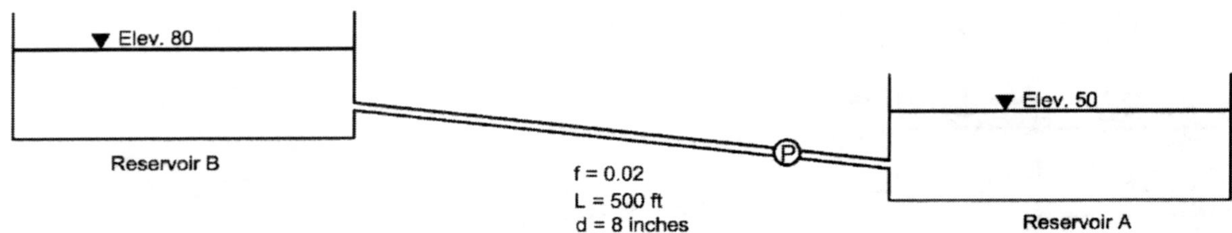

Solution

The calculation process for this exercise involves finding the head loss, pump head, and pump horsepower.

Step 1. Calculate the head loss with given discharge flow rate (ft^3/sec). Use Equation No. 100, page 194. Press ENTER.

Display	Keys	Description
F?	.02 R/S	Friction factor
L?	500 R/S	Length of the pipe (ft)
D?	8 ENTER 12 ÷	Diameter of the pipe (ft)
D? 0.6667	R/S	
Q?	5 R/S	Discharge flow rate (ft^3/sec)
G?	32.2 R/S	Gravitational acceleration (ft/sec^2)
J = 47.7893	--	Head loss (ft)

Step 2. Solve the pump head. Use Equation No. 107, page 199. Press SOLVE I.

Display	Keys	Description
P?	0 R/S	Atmospheric pressure at Reservoir B (lb/ft^2)
W?	62.4 R/S	Unit weight of water (lb/ft^3)
Q? 5.0000	R/S	Discharge flow rate (ft^3/sec)
D? 0.6667	R/S	Diameter of the pipe (ft)
G? 32.2000	R/S	Gravitational acceleration (ft/sec^2)
H?	80 R/S	Water surface elevation at Reservoir B (ft)
S?	0 R/S	Atmospheric pressure at Reservoir A (lb/ft^2)

Display	Keys	Description
O?	.6667 R/S	Diameter of the pipe (ft)
J? 47.7893	R/S	Head loss (ft)
K?	0 R/S	Head loss due to fittings (ft)
M?	50 R/S	Water surface elevation at Reservoir B (ft)
I = 17.7887	--	Pump head (ft)

Step 3. Determine the horsepower required for the pump. Use Equation No. 111, page 203. Press ENTER.

Display	Keys	Description
W? 62.4000	R/S	Unit weight of water (lb/ft^3)
I? 17.7887	R/S	Pump head (ft)
Q? 5.0000	R/S	Discharge flow rate (ft^3/sec)
E?	85 R/S	Efficiency of the pump (%)
T = 11.8718	--	Horsepower of the pump (hp)

The answer is (B).

Problem 10.7

Water flows in a 10-inch-diameter, 2,000-foot-long commercial steel schedule 40 pipe at a flow rate of 1,200 gal/min. The friction factor of the pipe is 0.016. What is most nearly the pump horsepower required if the pipe has 2 fully open gate valves and a fully open globe valve? The pump's efficiency is 80%. Use velocity head method.

(A) 5 hp
(B) 6 hp
(C) 7 hp
(D) 8 hp

Solution

The pump horsepower required can be determined using the following procedure.

Step 1. Calculate the head loss due to friction. Use Equation No. 100, page 194. Press ENTER.

Display	Keys	Description
F?	.016 R/S	Friction factor
L?	2000 R/S	Length of the pipe (ft)
D?	10 ENTER 12 ÷	Diameter of the pipe (ft)
D? 0.8333	R/S	
Q?	*	Flow rate of water (ft^3/sec)
Q? 2.6738	R/S	

Display	Keys	Description
G?	32.2 R/S	Gravitational acceleration (ft/sec^2)
J = 14.3300	--	Head loss due to friction (ft)

* Keys for converting 1,200 gal/min to ft^3/sec using RPN:

1200 ENTER 7.48 ÷ 60 ÷

$$1{,}200\frac{gal}{\text{min}}\times\frac{ft^3}{7.48gal}\times\frac{\text{min}}{60\,\text{sec}}=2.6738\frac{ft^3}{\text{sec}}$$

Step 2. Determine the head loss due to fittings.

Fitting Type	No. of fittings	×	Loss Coefficients	=	Velocity head coefficient
Fully open gate valve	2	×	0.19		0.38
				+	
Fully open globe valve	1	×	10		10.00
					10.38

Use Equation No. 106, page 199. Press ENTER.

Display	Keys	Description
N?	10.38 R/S	Velocity head coefficient due to fittings
Q? 2.6738	R/S	Flow rate of water (ft^3/sec)
D? 0.8333	R/S	Diameter of the pipe (ft)
G? 32.2000	R/S	Gravitational acceleration (ft/sec^2)
K = 3.8736	--	Head loss due to fittings (ft)

Step 3. Determine the total head loss due to friction and fittings. 14.3300 + 3.8736 = 18.2036 feet.

Step 4. Calculate the pump horsepower. Use Equation No. 110, page 202. Press ENTER.

Display	Keys	Description
W?	62.4 R/S	Unit weight of water (lb/ft^3)
J?	18.2036 R/S	Total head loss (ft)
Q? 2.6738	R/S	Flow rate (ft^3/sec)
E?	80 R/S	Efficiency of the pump (%)
T = 6.9027	--	Horsepower required (hp)

The answer is (C).

CHAPTER 11: OPEN CHANNEL FLOW AND ENVIRONMENTAL

11.1 Circular Channel

11.1.1 Million Gallons Per Day to Cubic Feet Per Second Conversion

$$Q = G\left(1\times10^{6}\,\frac{gal}{day}\right)\left(\frac{day}{86{,}400\sec}\right)\left(\frac{ft^{3}}{7.48\,gal}\right)$$ Equation No. 112

The equation is entered as

112MGDTOCFS
Q=G×1.547336106

Where:

Q = flow rate in ft³/sec Q
G = flow rate in million gallons per day G

Keystrokes

HP 35s Checksum; Length of Equation: **CK=C48F; LN=15**

[RCL] [Q] [↰] [=] [RCL] [G] [×] [1] [.] [5] [4] [7] [3] [3] [6] [1] [0] [6] [ENTER]

HP 33s Checksum; Length of Equation: **CK=C48F; LN=15**

[RCL] [Q] [↱] [=] [RCL] [G] [×] [1] [.] [5] [4] [7] [3] [3] [6] [1] [0] [6] [ENTER]

≈≈≈≈≈≈≈≈≈≈

11.1.2 Circular Channel Flowing Full Solving Flow Rate

$$Q = \frac{\pi}{4}D^{2}\frac{c}{n}\left(\frac{D}{4}\right)^{2/3}S^{1/2}$$ Equation No. 113

The equation is entered as

113CIRCLEFULLQ
Q=π÷4×D^2×C÷N(D÷4)^(2÷3)×S^0.5

Where:

Q = flow rate Q (ft³/sec, m³/s)
D = diameter of pipe D (ft, m)
C = 1.49 for English units, 1 for Metric units c
N = Manning roughness coefficient n
S = slope of energy line S (decimal)

Keystrokes

HP 35s Checksum; Length of Equation: **CK=DBDB; LN=30**

[RCL] [Q] [↰] [=] [↰] [π] [÷] [4] [×] [RCL] [D] [yˣ] [2] [×] [RCL] [C] [÷] [RCL] [N] [()] [RCL] [D] [÷] [4] [>] [yˣ] [()] [2] [÷] [3] [>] [×] [RCL] [S] [yˣ] [·] [5] [ENTER]

HP 33s Checksum; Length of Equation: **CK=797F; LN=31**

[RCL] [Q] [↱] [=] [↱] [π] [÷] [4] [×] [RCL] [D] [yˣ] [2] [×] [RCL] [C] [÷] [RCL] [N] [×] [↱] [(] [RCL] [D] [÷] [4] [↱] [)] [yˣ] [↱] [(] [2] [÷] [3] [↱] [)] [×] [RCL] [S] [yˣ] [·] [5] [ENTER]

≈≈≈≈≈≈≈≈≈≈

11.1.3 Circular Channel Flowing Full Solving Velocity of Flow

$$V = \frac{c}{n}\left(\frac{D}{4}\right)^{2/3} S^{1/2}$$ Equation No. 114

The equation is entered as

114CIRCLEFULLV
V=C÷N(D÷4)^(2÷3)×S^0.5

Where:

V = velocity of flow V (ft/sec, m/s)
C = 1.49 for English units, 1 for Metric units c
N = Manning roughness coefficient n
D = diameter of pipe D (ft, m)
S = slope of energy line S (decimal)

Keystrokes

HP 35s Checksum; Length of Equation: **CK=2C2A; LN=22**

[RCL] [V] [↰] [=] [RCL] [C] [÷] [RCL] [N] [()] [RCL] [D] [÷] [4] [>] [yˣ] [()] [2] [÷] [3] [>] [×] [RCL] [S] [yˣ] [·] [5] [ENTER]

HP 33s Checksum; Length of Equation: **CK=1787; LN=23**

[RCL] [V] [↱] [=] [RCL] [C] [÷] [RCL] [N] [×] [↱] [(] [RCL] [D] [÷] [4] [↱] [)] [yˣ] [↱] [(] [2] [÷] [3] [↱] [)] [×] [RCL] [S] [yˣ] [·] [5] [ENTER]

≈≈≈≈≈≈≈≈≈≈

11.1.4 Circular Channel Flowing Half-Full Solving Flow Rate

$$Q = 0.125\pi D^2 \frac{c}{n}\left(\frac{D}{4}\right)^{2/3} S^{1/2}$$ Equation No. 115

The equation is entered as

115CIRCLEHALFQ
Q=0.125×π×D^2×C÷N(D÷4)^(2÷3)×S^0.5

Where:

Q = flow rate Q (ft³/sec, m³/s)
D = diameter of pipe D (ft, m)
C = 1.49 for English units, 1 for Metric units c
N = Manning roughness coefficient n
S = slope of energy line S (decimal)

Keystrokes

HP 35s Checksum; Length of Equation: **CK=04DB; LN=34**

[RCL] [Q] [↰] [=] [.] [1] [2] [5] [×] [↰] [π] [×] [RCL] [D] [y^x] [2] [×] [RCL] [C] [÷] [RCL] [N] [()] [RCL] [D] [÷] [4] [>] [y^x] [()] [2] [÷] [3] [>] [×] [RCL] [S] [y^x] [.] [5] [ENTER]

HP 33s Checksum; Length of Equation: **CK=43ED; LN=35**

[RCL] [Q] [↱] [=] [.] [1] [2] [5] [×] [↱] [π] [×] [RCL] [D] [y^x] [2] [×] [RCL] [C] [÷] [RCL] [N] [×] [↱] [(] [RCL] [D] [÷] [4] [↱] [)] [y^x] [↱] [(] [2] [÷] [3] [↱] [)] [×] [RCL] [S] [y^x] [.] [5] [ENTER]

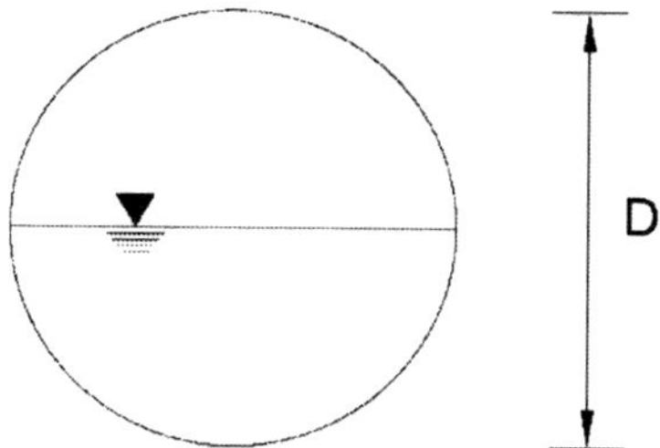

Figure 11-1 Circular Channel Flowing Half Full

≈≈≈≈≈≈≈≈≈≈

11.1.5 Circular Channel Flowing Half-Full Solving Velocity of Flow

$$V = \frac{c}{n}\left(\frac{D}{4}\right)^{2/3} S^{1/2}$$ Equation No. 116

The equation is entered as

116CIRCLEHALFV
V=C÷N(D÷4)^(2÷3)×S^0.5

Where:

V = velocity of flow V (ft/sec, m/s)
C = 1.49 for English units, 1 for Metric units c
N = Manning roughness coefficient n
D = diameter of pipe D (ft, m)
S = slope of energy line S (decimal)

Keystrokes

HP 35s Checksum; Length of Equation: **CK=2C2A; LN=22**

[RCL] [V] [↰] [=] [RCL] [C] [÷] [RCL] [N] [()] [RCL] [D] [÷] [4] [>] [yˣ] [()] [2] [÷] [3] [>] [×] [RCL] [S] [yˣ] [·] [5] [ENTER]

HP 33s Checksum; Length of Equation: **CK=1787; LN=23**

[RCL] [V] [↱] [=] [RCL] [C] [÷] [RCL] [N] [×] [↱] [(] [RCL] [D] [÷] [4] [↱] [)] [yˣ] [↱] [(] [2] [÷] [3] [↱] [)] [×] [RCL] [S] [yˣ] [·] [5] [ENTER]

Note: This equation is identical to Equation No. 114. I recommend placing this here for quick access.

≈≈≈≈≈≈≈≈≈≈

11.1.6 Circular Channel Flowing Half-Full Solving Froude Number

$$F_r = \frac{V}{\sqrt{g\frac{\pi D}{8}}}$$ Equation No. 117

The equation is entered as

117FRNO.CIRCHALF
F=V÷(G×π×D÷8)^0.5

Where:

F = Froude number F_r
V = velocity of flow V (ft/sec, m/s)
G = gravitational acceleration g (32.2 ft/sec^2, 9.81 m/s^2)
D = diameter of pipe D (ft, m)

Keystrokes

HP 35s Checksum; Length of Equation: **CK=BA11; LN=17**

[RCL] [F] [↰] [=] [RCL] [V] [÷] [()] [RCL] [G] [×] [↰] [π] [×] [RCL] [D] [÷] [8] [>] [y^x] [·] [5] [ENTER]

HP 33s Checksum; Length of Equation: **CK=BA11; LN=17**

[RCL] [F] [↱] [=] [RCL] [V] [÷] [↱] [(] [RCL] [G] [×] [↱] [π] [×] [RCL] [D] [÷] [8] [↱] [)] [y^x] [·] [5] [ENTER]

≈≈≈≈≈≈≈≈≈≈

11.1.7 Circular Channel Flowing Partially Full Solving Flow Rate

$$Q = \frac{c}{n} \frac{\left(\left(\frac{1}{2} \sin 2\theta + \pi \frac{\beta}{360^o} \right) \left(\frac{D}{2} \right)^2 \right)^{5/3}}{\left(\pi D \frac{\beta}{360^o} \right)^{2/3}} S^{1/2} \qquad \text{Equation No. 118}$$

in which $\theta = \cos^{-1}\left(\frac{H - \frac{D}{2}}{\frac{D}{2}} \right)$ and $\beta = 360^o - 2\theta$

The equation is entered as

118CIRPARFULLQ
Q=C÷N((0.5×SIN(ACOS((H−D÷2)÷(D÷2))×2)+π(360−ACOS((H−D÷2)÷(D÷2))×2)÷360)×(D÷2)^2)^(5÷3)÷(π×D(360−ACOS((H−D÷2)÷(D÷2))×2)÷360)^(2÷3)×S^0.5

Where:

Q = flow rate Q (ft³/sec, m³/s)
C = 1.49 for English units, 1 for Metric units c
N = Manning roughness coefficient n
H = depth of water H (ft, m)
D = diameter of pipe D (ft, m)
S = slope of energy line S (decimal)

Keystrokes

HP 35s Checksum; Length of Equation: **CK=1DE9; LN=135**

[RCL] [Q] [↰] [=] [RCL] [C] [÷] [RCL] [N] [()] [()] [·] [5] [×] [SIN] [↱] [ACOS] [()] [RCL] [H] [−] [RCL] [D] [÷] [2] [>] [÷] [()] [RCL] [D] [÷] [2] [>] [>] [×] [2] [>] [+] [↰] [π] [()] [3] [6] [0] [−] [↱] [ACOS] [()] [RCL] [H] [−] [RCL] [D] [÷] [2] [>] [÷] [()] [RCL] [D] [÷] [2] [>] [>] [×] [2] [>] [÷] [3] [6] [0] [>] [×] [()] [RCL] [D] [÷] [2] [>] [y^x] [2] [>] [y^x] [()] [5] [÷] [3] [>] [÷] [()] [↰] [π] [×] [RCL] [D] [()] [3] [6] [0] [−] [↱] [ACOS] [()] [RCL] [H] [−] [RCL] [D] [÷] [2] [>] [÷] [()] [RCL] [D] [÷] [2] [>] [>] [×] [2] [>] [÷] [3] [6] [0] [>] [y^x] [()] [2] [÷] [3] [>] [×] [RCL] [S] [y^x] [·] [5] [ENTER]

HP 33s Checksum; Length of Equation: **CK=70C2; LN=138**

RCL Q ↱ = RCL C ÷ RCL N × ↱ (↱ (· 5 × SIN ↰ ACOS ↱ (RCL H − RCL
D ÷ 2 ↱) ÷ ↱ (RCL D ÷ 2 ↱) ↱) × 2 ↱) + ↱ π × ↱ (3 6 0 −
↰ ACOS ↱ (RCL H − RCL D ÷ 2 ↱) ÷ ↱ (RCL D ÷ 2 ↱) ↱) × 2 ↱)
÷ 3 6 0 ↱) × ↱ (RCL D ÷ 2 ↱) y^x 2 ↱) y^x ↱ (5 ÷ 3 ↱) ÷ ↱ (
↱ π × RCL D × ↱ (3 6 0 − ↰ ACOS ↱ (RCL H − RCL D ÷ 2 ↱) ÷ ↱ (
RCL D ÷ 2 ↱) ↱) × 2 ↱) ÷ 3 6 0 ↱) y^x ↱ (2 ÷ 3 ↱) × RCL S
y^x · 5 ENTER

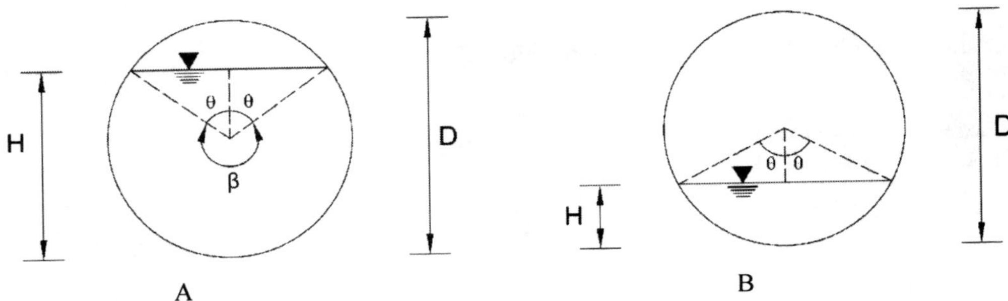

Figure 11-2 Circular Channel Flowing Partially Full

≈≈≈≈≈≈≈≈≈≈

11.1.8 Circular Channel Flowing Partially Full Solving Velocity of Flow

$$V = \frac{c}{n}\left(\frac{\left(\frac{1}{2}\sin 2\theta + \pi\frac{\beta}{360^o}\right)\left(\frac{D}{2}\right)^2}{\left(\pi D\frac{\beta}{360^o}\right)}\right)^{2/3} S^{1/2} \qquad \text{Equation No. 119}$$

in which $\theta = \cos^{-1}\left(\frac{H - \frac{D}{2}}{\frac{D}{2}}\right)$ and $\beta = 360^o - 2\theta$

The equation is entered as

119CIRPARFULLV
V=C÷N((0.5×SIN(ACOS((H−D÷2)÷(D÷2))×2)+π(360−ACOS((H−D÷2)÷(D÷2))×2)÷360)×(D÷2)^2÷(π×D(360−ACOS((H−D÷2)÷(D÷2))×2)÷360))^(2÷3)×S^0.5

Where:

V = velocity of flow V (ft/sec, m/s)
C = 1.49 for English units, 1 for Metric units c

N = Manning roughness coefficient n
H = depth of water H (ft, m)
D = diameter of pipe D (ft, m)
S = slope of energy line S (decimal)

Keystrokes

HP 35s Checksum; Length of Equation: **CK=3F12; LN=129**

[RCL] [V] [↰] [=] [RCL] [C] [÷] [RCL] [N] [()] [()] [·] [5] [×] [SIN] [↱] [ACOS] [()] [RCL] [H] [−] [RCL] [D] [÷] [2] [>] [÷]
[()] [RCL] [D] [÷] [2] [>] [>] [×] [2] [>] [+] [↰] [π] [()] [3] [6] [0] [−] [↱] [ACOS] [()] [RCL] [H] [−] [RCL] [D] [÷] [2] [>]
[÷] [()] [RCL] [D] [÷] [2] [>] [>] [×] [2] [>] [÷] [3] [6] [0] [>] [×] [()] [RCL] [D] [÷] [2] [>] [y^x] [2] [÷] [()] [↰] [π] [×]
[RCL] [D] [()] [3] [6] [0] [−] [↱] [ACOS] [()] [RCL] [H] [−] [RCL] [D] [÷] [2] [>] [÷] [()] [RCL] [D] [÷] [2] [>] [>] [×] [2]
[>] [÷] [3] [6] [0] [>] [>] [y^x] [()] [2] [÷] [3] [>] [×] [RCL] [S] [y^x] [·] [5] [ENTER]

HP 33s Checksum; Length of Equation: **CK=FA61; LN=132**

[RCL] [V] [↱] [=] [RCL] [C] [÷] [RCL] [N] [×] [↱] [(] [↱] [(] [·] [5] [×] [SIN] [↰] [ACOS] [↱] [(] [RCL] [H] [−] [RCL]
[D] [÷] [2] [↱] [)] [÷] [↱] [(] [RCL] [D] [÷] [2] [↱] [)] [↱] [)] [×] [2] [↱] [)] [+] [↱] [π] [×] [↱] [(] [3] [6] [0] [−]
[↰] [ACOS] [↱] [(] [RCL] [H] [−] [RCL] [D] [÷] [2] [↱] [)] [÷] [↱] [(] [RCL] [D] [÷] [2] [↱] [)] [↱] [)] [×] [2] [↱] [)]
[÷] [3] [6] [0] [↱] [)] [×] [(] [RCL] [D] [÷] [2] [↱] [)] [y^x] [2] [÷] [↱] [(] [↱] [π] [×] [RCL] [D] [×] [↱] [(] [3] [6] [0]
[−] [↰] [ACOS] [↱] [(] [RCL] [H] [−] [RCL] [D] [÷] [2] [↱] [)] [÷] [↱] [(] [RCL] [D] [÷] [2] [↱] [)] [↱] [)] [×] [2] [↱]
[)] [÷] [3] [6] [0] [↱] [)] [↱] [)] [y^x] [↱] [(] [2] [÷] [3] [↱] [)] [×] [RCL] [S] [y^x] [·] [5] [ENTER]

≈≈≈≈≈≈≈≈≈≈

11.1.9 Circular Channel Flowing Partially Full Solving Hydraulic Radius

$$R_H = \frac{\left(\frac{1}{2}\sin 2\theta + \pi\frac{\beta}{360^o}\right)\left(\frac{D}{2}\right)^2}{\pi D\frac{\beta}{360^o}}$$ Equation No. 120

in which $\theta = \cos^{-1}\left(\frac{H-\frac{D}{2}}{\frac{D}{2}}\right)$ and $\beta = 360^o - 2\theta$

The equation is entered as

120CIRPARFULHR
R=(0.5×SIN(ACOS((H−D÷2)÷(D÷2))×2)+π(360−ACOS((H−D÷2)÷(D÷2))×2)÷360)×(D÷2)^2÷(π×D(360−ACOS((H−D÷2)÷(D÷2))×2)÷360)

Where:

R = hydraulic radius R_H (ft, m)
H = depth of water H (ft, m)
D = diameter of pipe D (ft, m)

Keystrokes

HP 35s Checksum; Length of Equation: **CK=C829; LN=112**

[RCL] [R] [↰] [=] [()] [.] [5] [×] [SIN] [↱] [ACOS] [()] [RCL] [H] [−] [RCL] [D] [÷] [2] [>] [÷] [()] [RCL] [D] [÷] [2] [>] [>]
[×] [2] [>] [+] [↰] [π] [()] [3] [6] [0] [−] [↱] [ACOS] [()] [RCL] [H] [−] [RCL] [D] [÷] [2] [>] [÷] [()] [RCL] [D] [÷] [2] [>]
[>] [×] [2] [>] [÷] [3] [6] [0] [>] [×] [()] [RCL] [D] [÷] [2] [>] [yˣ] [2] [÷] [()] [↰] [π] [×] [RCL] [D] [()] [3] [6] [0] [−]
[↱] [ACOS] [()] [RCL] [H] [−] [RCL] [D] [÷] [2] [>] [÷] [()] [RCL] [D] [÷] [2] [>] [>] [×] [2] [>] [÷] [3] [6] [0] [ENTER]

HP 33s Checksum; Length of Equation: **CK=5FFC; LN=114**

[RCL] [R] [↱] [=] [↱] [(] [.] [5] [×] [SIN] [↰] [ACOS] [↱] [(] [RCL] [H] [−] [RCL] [D] [÷] [2] [↱] [)] [÷] [↱] [(] [RCL]
[D] [÷] [2] [↱] [)] [↱] [)] [×] [2] [↱] [)] [+] [↱] [π] [×] [↱] [(] [3] [6] [0] [−] [↰] [ACOS] [↱] [(] [RCL] [H] [−] [RCL]
[D] [÷] [2] [↱] [)] [÷] [↱] [(] [RCL] [D] [÷] [2] [↱] [)] [↱] [)] [×] [2] [↱] [)] [÷] [3] [6] [0] [↱] [)] [×] [(] [RCL]
[D] [÷] [2] [↱] [)] [yˣ] [2] [÷] [↱] [(] [↱] [π] [×] [RCL] [D] [×] [↱] [(] [3] [6] [0] [−] [↰] [ACOS] [↱] [(] [RCL] [H] [−]
[RCL] [D] [÷] [2] [↱] [)] [÷] [↱] [(] [RCL] [D] [÷] [2] [↱] [)] [↱] [)] [×] [2] [↱] [)] [÷] [3] [6] [0] [↱] [)] [ENTER]

≈≈≈≈≈≈≈≈≈≈

11.1.10 Circular Channel Flowing Partially Full Solving Wetted Perimeter

$$P = \pi D \frac{\beta}{360^o}$$ Equation No. 121

in which $\beta = 360^o - 2\theta$ and $\theta = \cos^{-1}\left(\frac{H - \frac{D}{2}}{\frac{D}{2}}\right)$

The equation is entered as

121CIRPARFULWP
P=π×D(360−ACOS((H−D÷2)÷(D÷2))×2)÷360

Where:

P = wetted perimeter P (ft, m)
H = depth of water H (ft, m)
D = diameter of pipe D (ft, m)

Keystrokes

HP 35s Checksum; Length of Equation: **CK=A0B2; LN=36**

[RCL] [P] [↰] [=] [↰] [π] [×] [RCL] [D] [()] [3] [6] [0] [−] [↱] [ACOS] [()] [RCL] [H] [−] [RCL] [D] [÷] [2] [>] [÷] [()]
[RCL] [D] [÷] [2] [>] [>] [×] [2] [>] [÷] [3] [6] [0] [ENTER]

HP 33s Checksum; Length of Equation: **CK=07EC; LN=37**

[RCL] [P] [↱] [=] [↱] [π] [×] [RCL] [D] [×] [↱] [(] [3] [6] [0] [−] [↰] [ACOS] [↱] [(] [RCL] [H] [−] [RCL] [D] [÷] [2]
[↱] [)] [÷] [↱] [(] [RCL] [D] [÷] [2] [↱] [)] [↱] [)] [×] [2] [↱] [)] [÷] [3] [6] [0] [ENTER]

≈≈≈≈≈≈≈≈≈≈

11.2 Rectangular Channel

11.2.1 Rectangular Channel Solving Flow Rate

$$Q = \frac{c}{n}\frac{(BD)^{5/3}}{(B+2D)^{2/3}}S^{1/2}$$ Equation No. 122

The equation is entered as

122RECTANGQ
Q=C÷N(B×D)^(5÷3)÷(B+2×D)^(2÷3)×S^0.5

Where:

Q = flow rate Q (ft³/sec, m³/s)
B = width of channel B (ft, m)
D = depth of water D (ft, m)
C = 1.49 for English units, 1 for Metric units c
N = Manning roughness coefficient n
S = slope of energy line S (decimal)

Keystrokes

HP 35s Checksum; Length of Equation: **CK=2112; LN=36**

[RCL] [Q] [↰] [=] [RCL] [C] [÷] [RCL] [N] [()] [RCL] [B] [×] [RCL] [D] [>] [yˣ] [()] [5] [÷] [3] [>] [÷] [()] [RCL] [B] [+] [2]
[×] [RCL] [D] [>] [yˣ] [()] [2] [÷] [3] [>] [×] [RCL] [S] [yˣ] [·] [5] [ENTER]

HP 33s Checksum; Length of Equation: **CK=FCCA; LN=37**

[RCL] [Q] [↱] [=] [RCL] [C] [÷] [RCL] [N] [×] [↱] [(] [RCL] [B] [×] [RCL] [D] [↱] [)] [yˣ] [↱] [(] [5] [÷] [3] [↱] [)] [÷]
[↱] [(] [RCL] [B] [+] [2] [×] [RCL] [D] [↱] [)] [yˣ] [↱] [(] [2] [÷] [3] [↱] [)] [×] [RCL] [S] [yˣ] [·] [5] [ENTER]

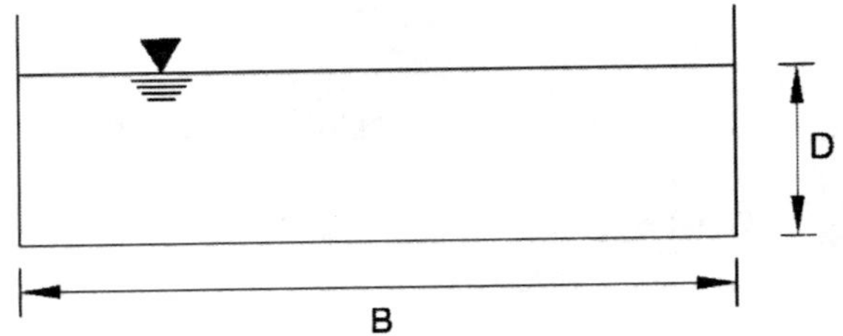

Figure 11-3 Rectangular Channel

≈≈≈≈≈≈≈≈≈≈

11.2.2 Rectangular Channel Solving Velocity of Flow

$$V = \frac{c}{n}\left(\frac{BD}{B+2D}\right)^{2/3} S^{1/2} \qquad \text{Equation No. 123}$$

The equation is entered as

123RECTANGV
V=C÷N(B×D÷(B+2×D))^(2÷3)×S^0.5

Where:

V = velocity of flow V (ft/sec, m/s)
C = 1.49 for English units, 1 for Metric units c
N = Manning roughness coefficient n
B = width of channel B (ft, m)
D = depth of water D (ft, m)
S = slope of energy line S (decimal)

Keystrokes

HP 35s Checksum; Length of Equation: **CK=6DC9; LN=30**

[RCL] [V] [↰] [=] [RCL] [C] [÷] [RCL] [N] [()] [RCL] [B] [×] [RCL] [D] [÷] [()] [RCL] [B] [+] [2] [×] [RCL] [D] [>] [>] [y^x] [()] [2] [÷] [3] [>] [×] [RCL] [S] [y^x] [·] [5] [ENTER]

HP 33s Checksum; Length of Equation: **CK=D2BF; LN=31**

[RCL] [V] [↱] [=] [RCL] [C] [÷] [RCL] [N] [×] [↱] [(] [RCL] [B] [×] [RCL] [D] [÷] [↱] [(] [RCL] [B] [+] [2] [×] [RCL] [D] [↱] [)] [↱] [)] [y^x] [↱] [(] [2] [÷] [3] [↱] [)] [×] [RCL] [S] [y^x] [·] [5] [ENTER]

≈≈≈≈≈≈≈≈≈≈

11.2.3 Rectangular Channel Solving Froude Number

$$F_r = \frac{V}{\sqrt{gD}} \qquad \text{Equation No. 124}$$

The equation is entered as

124RECTANGFRNO.
F=V÷(G×D)^0.5

Where:

F = Froude number F_r
V = velocity of flow V (ft/sec, m/s)
G = gravitational acceleration g (32.2 ft/sec^2, 9.81 m/s^2)
D = depth of water D (ft, m)

Keystrokes

HP 35s Checksum; Length of Equation: **CK=IB5C; LN=13**

[RCL] [F] [↰] [=] [RCL] [V] [÷] [()] [RCL] [G] [×] [RCL] [D] [>] [y^x] [·] [5] [ENTER]

HP 33s Checksum; Length of Equation: **CK=IB5C; LN=13**

[RCL] [F] [↱] [=] [RCL] [V] [÷] [↱] [(] [RCL] [G] [×] [RCL] [D] [↱] [)] [y^x] [·] [5] [ENTER]

≈≈≈≈≈≈≈≈≈≈

11.2.4 Rectangular Channel Solving Hydraulic Radius

$$R_H = \frac{BD}{B+2D}$$ Equation No. 125

The equation is entered as

125RECTANGHR
R=B×D÷(B+2×D)

Where:

R = hydraulic radius R_H (ft, m)
B = width of channel B (ft, m)
D = depth of water D (ft, m)

Keystrokes

HP 35s Checksum; Length of Equation: **CK=355F; LN=13**

[RCL] [R] [↰] [=] [RCL] [B] [×] [RCL] [D] [÷] [()] [RCL] [B] [+] [2] [×] [RCL] [D] [ENTER]

HP 33s Checksum; Length of Equation: **CK=355F; LN=13**

[RCL] [R] [↱] [=] [RCL] [B] [×] [RCL] [D] [÷] [↱] [(] [RCL] [B] [+] [2] [×] [RCL] [D] [↱] [)] [ENTER]

≈≈≈≈≈≈≈≈≈≈

11.2.5 Rectangular Channel Solving Critical Depth

$D_c^3 = \frac{Q^2}{gB^2}$ Equation No. 126

The equation is entered as

126RECCRITDEPTH
I=(Q^2÷G÷B^2)^(1÷3)

Where:

I = critical depth of water D_c (ft, m)
Q = flow rate Q (ft³/sec, m³/s)
G = gravitational acceleration g (32.2 ft/sec², 9.81 m/s²)
B = width of channel B (ft, m)

Keystrokes

HP 35s Checksum; Length of Equation: **CK=9F70; LN=19**

RCL I ⬑ = () RCL Q yˣ 2 ÷ RCL G ÷ RCL B yˣ 2 > yˣ () 1 ÷ 3 ENTER

HP 33s Checksum; Length of Equation: **CK=9F70; LN=19**

RCL I ⬏ = ⬏ (RCL Q yˣ 2 ÷ RCL G ÷ RCL B yˣ 2 ⬏) yˣ ⬏ (1 ÷ 3 ⬏) ENTER

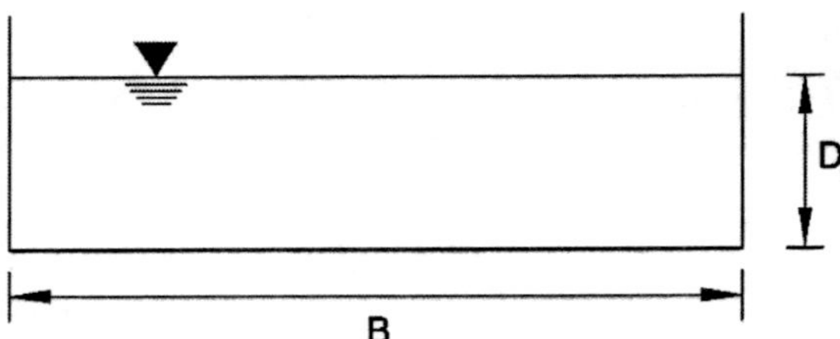

Figure 11-4 Critical Depth on Rectangular Channel

≈≈≈≈≈≈≈≈≈≈

11.2.6 Rectangular Channel Solving Critical Velocity

$V_c = \sqrt{gD_c}$ Equation No. 127

The equation is entered as

127RECTCRITVEL
J=(G×I)^0.5

Where:

J = critical velocity of flow V_c (ft/sec, m/s)
G = gravitational acceleration g (32.2 ft/sec^2, 9.81 m/s^2)
I = critical depth of water D_c (ft, m)

Keystrokes

HP 35s Checksum; Length of Equation: **CK=C478; LN=11**

[RCL] [J] [↰] [=] [()] [RCL] [G] [×] [RCL] [I] [>] [y^x] [•] [5] [ENTER]

HP 33s Checksum; Length of Equation: **CK=C478; LN=11**

[RCL] [J] [↱] [=] [↱] [(] [RCL] [G] [×] [RCL] [I] [↱] [)] [y^x] [•] [5] [ENTER]

≈≈≈≈≈≈≈≈≈≈

11.2.7 Rectangular Channel Solving Most Efficient Dimensions

$$Q = BD\frac{c}{n}\left(\frac{D}{2}\right)^{2/3} S^{1/2}$$ Equation No. 128

in which $D = \frac{B}{2}$ and $B = 2D$

The equation is entered as

128RECTMOSTEFF
Q=B×D×C÷N(D÷2)^(2÷3)×S^0.5

Where:

Q = design flow rate Q (ft^3/sec, m^3/s)
B = most efficient width of channel B (ft, m)
D = most efficient depth of channel D (ft, m)
C = 1.49 for English units, 1 for Metric units c
N = Manning roughness coefficient n
S = slope of energy line S (decimal)

Keystrokes

HP 35s Checksum; Length of Equation: **CK=30A2; LN=26**

[RCL] [Q] [↰] [=] [RCL] [B] [×] [RCL] [D] [×] [RCL] [C] [÷] [RCL] [N] [()] [RCL] [D] [÷] [2] [>] [y^x] [()] [2] [÷] [3] [>] [×]
[RCL] [S] [y^x] [•] [5] [ENTER]

HP 33s Checksum; Length of Equation: **CK=9136; LN=27**

RCL Q ↱ = RCL B × RCL D × RCL C ÷ RCL N × ↱ (RCL D ÷ 2 ↱) yˣ ↱ (2 ÷ 3 ↱) × RCL S yˣ · 5 ENTER

Note: To calculate the most efficient width, first calculate the most efficient depth of channel by using Equation No. 129 by pressing SOLVE D, then use Equation No. 128 by pressing SOLVE B.

≈≈≈≈≈≈≈≈≈≈

11.2.8 Rectangular Channel Most Efficient Solving D

$$Q = 2D^2 \frac{c}{n}\left(\frac{D}{2}\right)^{2/3} S^{1/2}$$ Equation No. 129

The equation is entered as

129RECMESOLVD
Q=2×D^2×C÷N(D÷2)^(2÷3)×S^0.5

Where:

Q = design flow rate Q (ft^3/sec, m^3/s)
D = most efficient depth of channel D (ft, m)
C = 1.49 for English units, 1 for Metric units c
N = Manning roughness coefficient n
S = slope of energy line S (decimal)

Keystrokes

HP 35s Checksum; Length of Equation: **CK=4A8F; LN=28**

RCL Q ↰ = 2 × RCL D yˣ 2 × RCL C ÷ RCL N () RCL D ÷ 2 > yˣ () 2 ÷ 3 > × RCL S yˣ · 5 ENTER

HP 33s Checksum; Length of Equation: **CK=63EB; LN=29**

RCL Q ↱ = 2 × RCL D yˣ 2 × RCL C ÷ RCL N × ↱ (RCL D ÷ 2 ↱) yˣ ↱ (2 ÷ 3 ↱) × RCL S yˣ · 5 ENTER

≈≈≈≈≈≈≈≈≈≈

11.3 Hydraulic Jump in Rectangular Channel

11.3.1 Hydraulic Jump Solving D_1 Given V_2 and D_2

$$d_1 = -\frac{1}{2}d_2 + \sqrt{\frac{2v_2^2 d_2}{g} + \frac{d_2^2}{4}}$$ Equation No. 130

The equation is entered as

130HJSOLVD1
D=−0.5×E+(2×U^2×E÷G+E^2÷4)^0.5

Where:

D = depth of water before the jump d_1 (ft, m)
E = depth of water after the jump d_2 (ft, m)
U = velocity of flow after the jump v_2 (ft/sec, m/s)
G = gravitational acceleration g (32.2 ft/sec², 9.81 m/s²)

Keystrokes

HP 35s — Checksum; Length of Equation: **CK=68AA; LN=30**

[RCL] [D] [↰] [=] [+/−] [·] [5] [×] [RCL] [E] [+] [()] [2] [×] [RCL] [U] [yˣ] [2] [×] [RCL] [E] [÷] [RCL] [G] [+] [RCL] [E] [yˣ] [2] [÷] [4] [>] [yˣ] [·] [5] [ENTER]

HP 33s — Checksum; Length of Equation: **CK=3197; LN=30**

[RCL] [D] [↱] [=] [+/−] [·] [5] [×] [RCL] [E] [+] [↱] [(] [2] [×] [RCL] [U] [yˣ] [2] [×] [RCL] [E] [÷] [RCL] [G] [+] [RCL] [E] [yˣ] [2] [÷] [4] [↱] [)] [yˣ] [·] [5] [ENTER]

≈≈≈≈≈≈≈≈≈≈

11.3.2 Hydraulic Jump Solving D_2 Given V_1

$$d_2 = -\frac{1}{2}d_1 + \sqrt{\frac{2v_1^2 d_1}{g} + \frac{d_1^2}{4}}$$ Equation No. 131

The equation is entered as

131HJSOLVD2
E=−0.5×D+(2×V^2×D÷G+D^2÷4)^0.5

Where:

E = depth of water after the jump d_2 (ft, m)
D = depth of water before the jump d_1 (ft, m)
V = velocity of flow before the jump v_1 (ft/sec, m/s)
G = gravitational acceleration g (32.2 ft/sec², 9.81 m/s²)

Keystrokes

HP 35s — Checksum; Length of Equation: **CK=10E8; LN=30**

[RCL] [E] [↰] [=] [+/−] [·] [5] [×] [RCL] [D] [+] [()] [2] [×] [RCL] [V] [yˣ] [2] [×] [RCL] [D] [÷] [RCL] [G] [+] [RCL] [D] [yˣ] [2] [÷] [4] [>] [yˣ] [·] [5] [ENTER]

HP 33s Checksum; Length of Equation: **CK=49D5; LN=30**

[RCL] [E] [↱] [=] [+/−] [·] [5] [×] [RCL] [D] [+] [↱] [(] [2] [×] [RCL] [V] [yˣ] [2] [×] [RCL] [D] [÷] [RCL] [G] [+] [RCL] [D] [yˣ] [2] [÷] [4] [↱] [)] [yˣ] [·] [5] [ENTER]

≈≈≈≈≈≈≈≈≈≈

11.3.3 Froude Number after the Jump

$$F_r = \frac{V}{\sqrt{gD}}$$ Equation No. 132

The equation is entered as

132FRN0.AFTJUMP
F=U÷(G×E)^0.5

Where:

F = Froude number after the jump
U = velocity of flow after the jump V_2 (ft/sec, m/s)
G = gravitational acceleration g (32.2 ft/sec², 9.81 m/s²)
E = depth of water after the jump d_2 (ft, m)

Keystrokes

HP 35s Checksum; Length of Equation: **CK=2606; LN=13**

[RCL] [F] [↰] [=] [RCL] [U] [÷] [()] [RCL] [G] [×] [RCL] [E] [>] [yˣ] [·] [5] [ENTER]

HP 33s Checksum; Length of Equation: **CK=2606; LN=13**

[RCL] [F] [↱] [=] [RCL] [U] [÷] [↱] [(] [RCL] [G] [×] [RCL] [E] [↱] [)] [yˣ] [·] [5] [ENTER]

≈≈≈≈≈≈≈≈≈≈

11.3.4 Head Loss in the Jump

$$H_L = \frac{(d_2 - d_1)^3}{4d_1d_2}$$ Equation No. 133

The equation is entered as

133HEADLOSJUMP
H=(E−D)^3÷4÷D÷E

Where:

H = head loss H_L (ft, m)
E = depth of water after the jump d_2 (ft, m)
D = depth of water before the jump d_1 (ft, m)

Keystrokes

HP 35s Checksum; Length of Equation: **CK=6FC6; LN=15**

[RCL] [H] [↰] [=] [()] [RCL] [E] [−] [RCL] [D] [>] [y^x] [3] [÷] [4] [÷] [RCL] [D] [÷] [RCL] [E] [ENTER]

HP 33s Checksum; Length of Equation: **CK=6FC6; LN=15**

[RCL] [H] [↱] [=] [↱] [(] [RCL] [E] [−] [RCL] [D] [↱] [)] [y^x] [3] [÷] [4] [÷] [RCL] [D] [÷] [RCL] [E] [ENTER]

≈≈≈≈≈≈≈≈≈≈

11.3.5 Total Power Dissipated

$$P = \frac{Q\gamma_w H_L}{550}$$ Equation No. 134

The equation is entered as

134HORSEPOWER
P=Q×W×H÷550

Where:

P = horse power P (hp)
Q = discharge flow rate Q (ft^3/sec)
W = unit weight of water γ_w (62.4 lb/ft^3)
H = head loss H_L (ft)

Keystrokes

HP 35s Checksum; Length of Equation: **CK=5777; LN=11**

[RCL] [P] [↰] [=] [RCL] [Q] [×] [RCL] [W] [×] [RCL] [H] [÷] [5] [5] [0] [ENTER]

HP 33s Checksum; Length of Equation: **CK=5777; LN=11**

[RCL] [P] [↱] [=] [RCL] [Q] [×] [RCL] [W] [×] [RCL] [H] [÷] [5] [5] [0] [ENTER]

≈≈≈≈≈≈≈≈≈≈

11.4 Symmetrical Trapezoidal Channel

11.4.1 Trapezoidal Channel Solving Flow Rate Given Side Slope Horizontal:Vertical

$$Q = \frac{c}{n} \frac{((B + XD)D)^{5/3}}{\left(B + \left(2\sqrt{X^2 + 1}\right)D\right)^{2/3}} S^{1/2}$$ Equation No. 135

The equation is entered as

135TRAPQX1
Q=C÷N((B+X×D)×D)^(5÷3)÷(B+2(X^2+1)^0.5×D)^(2÷3)×S^0.5

Where:

Q = flow rate Q (ft³/sec, m³/s)
C = 1.49 for English units, 1 for Metric units c
N = Manning roughness coefficient n
B = width of channel B (ft, m)
X = side slope horizontal X
D = depth of water D (ft, m)
S = slope of energy line S (decimal)

Keystrokes

HP 35s Checksum; Length of Equation: **CK=3C3F; LN=53**

[RCL] [Q] [↰] [=] [RCL] [C] [÷] [RCL] [N] [()] [()] [RCL] [B] [+] [RCL] [X] [×] [RCL] [D] [>] [×] [RCL] [D] [>] [yˣ] [()] [5] [÷] [3] [>] [÷] [()] [RCL] [B] [+] [2] [()] [RCL] [X] [yˣ] [2] [+] [1] [>] [yˣ] [·] [5] [×] [RCL] [D] [>] [yˣ] [()] [2] [÷] [3] [>] [×] [RCL] [S] [yˣ] [·] [5] [ENTER]

HP 33s Checksum; Length of Equation: **CK=DF5B; LN=55**

[RCL] [Q] [↱] [=] [RCL] [C] [÷] [RCL] [N] [×] [↱] [(] [↱] [(] [RCL] [B] [+] [RCL] [X] [×] [RCL] [D] [↱] [)] [×] [RCL] [D] [↱] [)] [yˣ] [↱] [(] [5] [÷] [3] [↱] [)] [÷] [↱] [(] [RCL] [B] [+] [2] [×] [↱] [(] [RCL] [X] [yˣ] [2] [+] [1] [↱] [)] [yˣ] [·] [5] [×] [RCL] [D] [↱] [)] [yˣ] [↱] [(] [2] [÷] [3] [↱] [)] [×] [RCL] [S] [yˣ] [·] [5] [ENTER]

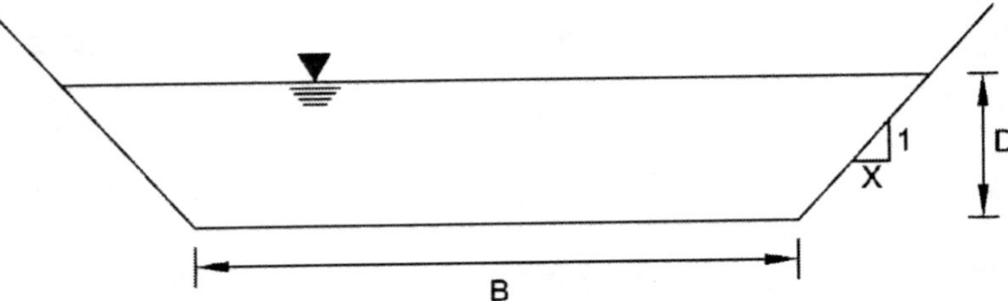

Figure 11-5 Trapezoidal Channel Given Side Slope Horizontal:Vertical

Note: Side slope horizontal is X divided by side slope vertical if side slope vertical is greater or less than 1.

≈≈≈≈≈≈≈≈≈≈

11.4.2 Trapezoidal Channel Solving Velocity of Flow Given Side Slope Horizontal:Vertical

$$V = \frac{c}{n}\left(\frac{(B + XD)D}{B + \left(2\sqrt{X^2 + 1}\right)D}\right)^{2/3} S^{1/2}$$ Equation No. 136

The equation is entered as

136TRAPVX1
V=C÷N((B+X×D)×D÷(B+2(X^2+1)^0.5×D))^(2÷3)×S^0.5

Where:

V = velocity of flow V (ft/sec, m/s)
C = 1.49 for English units, 1 for Metric units c
N = Manning roughness coefficient n
B = base width of channel B (ft, m)
X = side slope horizontal X
D = depth of water D (ft, m)
S = slope of energy line S (decimal)

Keystrokes

HP 35s Checksum; Length of Equation: **CK=7238; LN=47**

[RCL] [V] [↰] [=] [RCL] [C] [÷] [RCL] [N] [()] [()] [RCL] [B] [+] [RCL] [X] [×] [RCL] [D] [>] [×] [RCL] [D] [÷] [()] [RCL] [B] [+] [2] [()] [RCL] [X] [yˣ] [2] [+] [1] [>] [yˣ] [·] [5] [×] [RCL] [D] [>] [>] [yˣ] [()] [2] [÷] [3] [>] [×] [RCL] [S] [yˣ] [·] [5] [ENTER]

HP 33s Checksum; Length of Equation: **CK=FDFC; LN=49**

[RCL] [V] [↱] [=] [RCL] [C] [÷] [RCL] [N] [×] [↱] [(] [↱] [(] [RCL] [B] [+] [RCL] [X] [×] [RCL] [D] [↱] [)] [×] [RCL] [D] [÷] [↱] [(] [RCL] [B] [+] [2] [×] [↱] [(] [RCL] [X] [yˣ] [2] [+] [1] [↱] [)] [yˣ] [·] [5] [×] [RCL] [D] [↱] [)] [↱] [)] [yˣ] [↱] [(] [2] [÷] [3] [↱] [)] [×] [RCL] [S] [yˣ] [·] [5] [ENTER]

≈≈≈≈≈≈≈≈≈≈

11.4.3 Trapezoidal Channel Solving Froude Number Given Side Slope Horizontal:Vertical

$$F_r = \frac{V}{\sqrt{g\left(\frac{(B + XD)D}{B + 2XD}\right)}}$$ Equation No. 137

The equation is entered as

137TRAPFRNO.X1
F=V÷(G(B+X×D)×D÷(B+2×X×D))^0.5

Where:

F = Froude number F_r
V = velocity of flow V (ft/sec, m/s)
G = gravitational acceleration g (32.2 ft/sec², 9.81 m/s²)
B = base width of channel B (ft, m)
X = side slope horizontal X
D = depth of water D (ft, m)

Keystrokes

HP 35s Checksum; Length of Equation: **CK=3AF7; LN=30**

[RCL] [F] [↰] [=] [RCL] [V] [÷] [()] [RCL] [G] [()] [RCL] [B] [+] [RCL] [X] [×] [RCL] [D] [>] [×] [RCL] [D] [÷] [()] [RCL] [B] [+] [2] [×] [RCL] [X] [×] [RCL] [D] [>] [>] [y^x] [·] [5] [ENTER]

HP 33s Checksum; Length of Equation: **CK=7CBE; LN=31**

[RCL] [F] [↱] [=] [RCL] [V] [÷] [↱] [(] [RCL] [G] [×] [↱] [(] [RCL] [B] [+] [RCL] [X] [×] [RCL] [D] [↱] [)] [×] [RCL] [D] [÷] [↱] [(] [RCL] [B] [+] [2] [×] [RCL] [X] [×] [RCL] [D] [↱] [)] [↱] [)] [y^x] [·] [5] [ENTER]

≈≈≈≈≈≈≈≈≈≈

11.4.4 Trapezoidal Channel Solving Critical Depth Given Side Slope Horizontal:Vertical

$$\frac{Q^2}{g} = \frac{((B + XD_c)D_c)^3}{B + 2XD_c} \quad \text{Equation No. 138}$$

The equation is entered as

138TRAPCRIDEX1
Q^2÷G=((B+X×I)×I)^3÷(B+2×X×I)

Where:

Q = flow rate Q (ft³/sec, m³/s)
G = gravitational acceleration g (32.2 ft/sec², 9.81 m/s²)
B = base width of channel B (ft, m)
X = side slope horizontal X
I = critical depth of water D_c (ft, m)

Keystrokes

HP 35s Checksum; Length of Equation: **CK=AEEC; LN=29**

[RCL] [Q] [y^x] [2] [÷] [RCL] [G] [↰] [=] [()] [()] [RCL] [B] [+] [RCL] [X] [×] [RCL] [I] [>] [×] [RCL] [I] [>] [y^x] [3] [÷] [()] [RCL] [B] [+] [2] [×] [RCL] [X] [×] [RCL] [I] [ENTER]

HP 33s Checksum; Length of Equation: **CK=AEEC; LN=29**

RCL Q y^x 2 ÷ RCL G ↱ = ↱ (↱ (RCL B + RCL X × RCL I ↱) × RCL I ↱) y^x 3 ÷ ↱ (RCL B + 2 × RCL X × RCL I ↱) ENTER

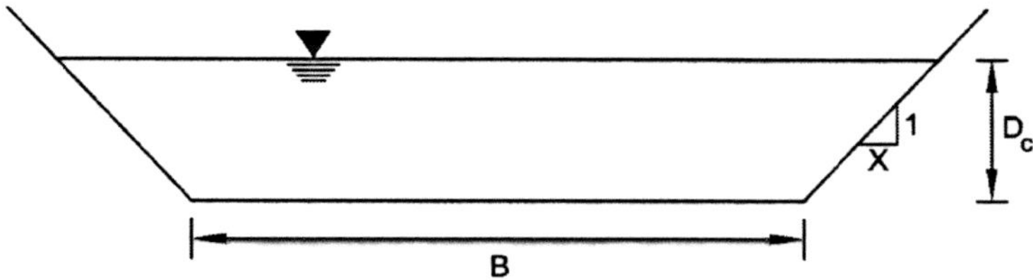

Figure 11-6 Critical Depth on Trapezoidal Channel Given Side Slope Horizontal:Vertical

≈≈≈≈≈≈≈≈≈≈

11.4.5 Trapezoidal Channel Solving Critical Velocity

$V_c = \sqrt{gD_c}$ Equation No. 139

The equation is entered as

139TRAPCRITVEL
J=(G×I)^0.5

Where:

J = critical velocity of flow V_c (ft/sec, m/s)
G = gravitational acceleration g (32.2 ft/sec², 9.81 m/s²)
I = critical depth of water D_c (ft, m)

Keystrokes

HP 35s Checksum; Length of Equation: **CK=C478; LN=11**

RCL J ↰ = () RCL G × RCL I > y^x · 5 ENTER

HP 33s Checksum; Length of Equation: **CK=C478; LN=11**

RCL J ↱ = ↱ (RCL G × RCL I ↱) y^x · 5 ENTER

≈≈≈≈≈≈≈≈≈≈

11.4.6 Trapezoidal Channel Solving Hydraulic Radius Given Side Slope Horizontal:Vertical

$R = \dfrac{(B+XD)D}{B+2\left(\left(\sqrt{X^2+1}\right)D\right)}$ Equation No. 140

The equation is entered as

140TRAPHRX1
R=(B+X×D)×D÷(B+2(X^2+1)^0.5×D)

Where:

R = hydraulic radius R (ft, m)
B = base width of channel B (ft, m)
X = side slope horizontal X
D = depth of water D (ft, m)

Keystrokes

HP 35s Checksum; Length of Equation: **CK=C9EE; LN=30**

[RCL] [R] [↰] [=] [()] [RCL] [B] [+] [RCL] [X] [×] [RCL] [D] [>] [×] [RCL] [D] [÷] [()] [RCL] [B] [+] [2] [()] [RCL] [X] [y^x] [2] [+] [1] [>] [y^x] [·] [5] [×] [RCL] [D] [ENTER]

HP 33s Checksum; Length of Equation: **CK=72B1; LN=31**

[RCL] [R] [↱] [=] [↱] [(] [RCL] [B] [+] [RCL] [X] [×] [RCL] [D] [↱] [)] [×] [RCL] [D] [÷] [↱] [(] [RCL] [B] [+] [2] [×] [↱] [(] [RCL] [X] [y^x] [2] [+] [1] [↱] [)] [y^x] [·] [5] [×] [RCL] [D] [↱] [)] [ENTER]

≈≈≈≈≈≈≈≈≈≈

11.4.7 Trapezoidal Channel Solving Wetted Perimeter Given Side Slope Horizontal:Vertical

$P = B + 2\left(\sqrt{X^2 + 1}\right)D$ Equation No. 141

The equation is entered as

141TRAPWPX1
P=B+2(X^2+1)^0.5×D

Where:

P = wetted perimeter P (ft, m)
B = base width of channel B (ft, m)
X = side slope horizontal X
D = depth of water D (ft, m)

Keystrokes

HP 35s Checksum; Length of Equation: **CK=F48F; LN=18**

[RCL] [P] [↰] [=] [RCL] [B] [+] [2] [()] [RCL] [X] [y^x] [2] [+] [1] [>] [y^x] [·] [5] [×] [RCL] [D] [ENTER]

HP 33s Checksum; Length of Equation: **CK=ED4E; LN=19**

[RCL] [P] [↱] [=] [RCL] [B] [+] [2] [×] [↱] [(] [RCL] [X] [y^x] [2] [+] [1] [↱] [)] [y^x] [·] [5] [×] [RCL] [D] [ENTER]

11.4.8 Trapezoidal Channel Solving Flow Rate Given Side Angle

$$Q=\frac{c}{n}\frac{\left(\left(B+\frac{D}{\tan\theta}\right)D\right)^{5/3}}{\left(B+2\frac{D}{\sin\theta}\right)^{2/3}}S^{1/2} \qquad \text{Equation No. 142}$$

The equation is entered as

142TRAPQANGLE
Q=C÷N((B+D÷TAN(A))×D)^(5÷3)÷(B+2×D÷SIN(A))^(2÷3)×S^0.5

Where:

Q = flow rate Q (ft³/sec, m³/s)
C = 1.49 for English units, 1 for Metric units c
N = Manning roughness coefficient n
B = base width of channel B (ft, m)
D = depth of water D (ft, m)
A = side angle θ
S = slope of energy line S (decimal)

Keystrokes

HP 35s Checksum; Length of Equation: **CK=978B; LN=54**

[RCL] [Q] [◄] [=] [RCL] [C] [÷] [RCL] [N] [()] [()] [RCL] [B] [+] [RCL] [D] [÷] [TAN] [RCL] [A] [>] [>] [×] [RCL] [D] [>] [y^x] [()] [5] [÷] [3] [>] [÷] [()] [RCL] [B] [+] [2] [×] [RCL] [D] [÷] [SIN] [RCL] [A] [>] [>] [y^x] [()] [2] [÷] [3] [>] [×] [RCL] [S] [y^x] [·] [5] [ENTER]

HP 33s Checksum; Length of Equation: **CK=9910; LN=55**

[RCL] [Q] [►] [=] [RCL] [C] [÷] [RCL] [N] [×] [►] [(] [►] [(] [RCL] [B] [+] [RCL] [D] [÷] [TAN] [RCL] [A] [►] [)] [►] [)] [×] [RCL] [D] [►] [)] [y^x] [►] [(] [5] [÷] [3] [►] [)] [÷] [►] [(] [RCL] [B] [+] [2] [×] [RCL] [D] [÷] [SIN] [RCL] [A] [►] [)] [►] [)] [y^x] [►] [(] [2] [÷] [3] [►] [)] [×] [RCL] [S] [y^x] [·] [5] [ENTER]

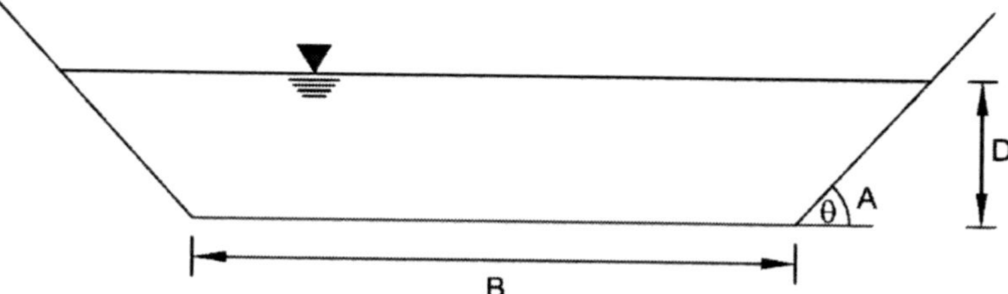

Figure 11-7 Trapezoidal Channel Given Side Angle

Note: For "V" channel, B is zero.

≈≈≈≈≈≈≈≈≈≈

11.4.9 Trapezoidal Channel Solving Velocity of Flow Given Side Angle

$$V = \frac{c}{n}\left(\frac{\left(B+\frac{D}{\tan\theta}\right)D}{B+2\frac{D}{\sin\theta}}\right)^{2/3} S^{1/2} \qquad \text{Equation No. 143}$$

The equation is entered as

143TRAPVANGLE
V=C÷N((B+D÷TAN(A))×D÷(B+2×D÷SIN(A)))^(2÷3)×S^0.5

Where:

V = velocity of flow V (ft/sec, m/s)
C = 1.49 for English units, 1 for Metric units c
N = Manning roughness coefficient n
B = base width of channel B (ft, m)
D = depth of water D (ft, m)
A = side angle θ
S = slope of energy line S (decimal)

Keystrokes

HP 35s Checksum; Length of Equation: **CK=EF26; LN=48**

[RCL] [V] [↰] [=] [RCL] [C] [÷] [RCL] [N] [()] [()] [RCL] [B] [+] [RCL] [D] [÷] [TAN] [RCL] [A] [>] [>] [×] [RCL] [D] [÷] [()] [RCL] [B] [+] [2] [×] [RCL] [D] [÷] [SIN] [RCL] [A] [>] [>] [>] [yˣ] [()] [2] [÷] [3] [>] [×] [RCL] [S] [yˣ] [.] [5] [ENTER]

HP 33s Checksum; Length of Equation: **CK=36E8; LN=49**

[RCL] [V] [↱] [=] [RCL] [C] [÷] [RCL] [N] [×] [↱] [(] [↱] [(] [RCL] [B] [+] [RCL] [D] [÷] [TAN] [RCL] [A] [↱] [)] [↱] [)] [×] [RCL] [D] [÷] [↱] [(] [RCL] [B] [+] [2] [×] [RCL] [D] [÷] [SIN] [RCL] [A] [↱] [)] [↱] [)] [↱] [)] [yˣ] [↱] [(] [2] [÷] [3] [↱] [)] [×] [RCL] [S] [yˣ] [.] [5] [ENTER]

≈≈≈≈≈≈≈≈≈≈

11.4.10 Trapezoidal Channel Solving Froude Number Given Side Angle

$$F_r = \frac{V}{\sqrt{g\left(\frac{\left(B+\frac{D}{\tan\theta}\right)D}{B+2\frac{D}{\tan\theta}}\right)}} \qquad \text{Equation No. 144}$$

The equation is entered as

144TRAPFRNO.ANGLE
F=V÷(G(B+D÷TAN(A))×D÷(B+2×D÷TAN(A)))^0.5

Where:

F = Froude number F_r
V = velocity of flow V (ft/sec, m/s)
G = gravitational acceleration g (32.2 ft/sec², 9.81 m/s²)
B = base width of channel B (ft, m)
D = depth of water D (ft, m)
A = side angle θ

Keystrokes

HP 35s Checksum; Length of Equation: **CK=38FC; LN=40**

[RCL] [F] [↰] [=] [RCL] [V] [÷] [()] [RCL] [G] [()] [RCL] [B] [+] [RCL] [D] [÷] [TAN] [RCL] [A] [>] [>] [×] [RCL] [D] [÷] [()]
[RCL] [B] [+] [2] [×] [RCL] [D] [÷] [TAN] [RCL] [A] [>] [>] [>] [yˣ] [·] [5] [ENTER]

HP 33s Checksum; Length of Equation: **CK=A45C; LN=41**

[RCL] [F] [↱] [=] [RCL] [V] [÷] [↱] [(] [RCL] [G] [×] [↱] [(] [RCL] [B] [+] [RCL] [D] [÷] [TAN] [RCL] [A] [↱] [)] [↱] [)]
[×] [RCL] [D] [÷] [↱] [(] [RCL] [B] [+] [2] [×] [RCL] [D] [÷] [TAN] [RCL] [A] [↱] [)] [↱] [)] [↱] [)] [yˣ] [·] [5] [ENTER]

≈≈≈≈≈≈≈≈≈≈

11.4.11 Trapezoidal Channel Solving Critical Depth Given Side Angle

$$\frac{Q^2}{g} = \frac{\left(\left(B + \frac{D_c}{\tan\theta}\right)D_c\right)^3}{B + 2\frac{D_c}{\tan\theta}} \qquad \text{Equation No. 145}$$

The equation is entered as

145TRAPCRIDEANGLE
Q^2÷G=((B+I÷TAN(A))×I)^3÷(B+2×I÷TAN(A))

Where:

Q = flow rate Q (ft³/sec, m³/s)
G = gravitational acceleration g (32.2 ft/sec², 9.81 m/s²)
B = base width of channel B (ft, m)
I = critical depth of water D_c (ft, m)
A = side angle θ

Keystrokes

HP 35s Checksum; Length of Equation: **CK=8A26; LN=39**

[RCL] [Q] [y^x] [2] [÷] [RCL] [G] [↰] [=] [()] [()] [RCL] [B] [+] [RCL] [I] [÷] [TAN] [RCL] [A] [>] [>] [×] [RCL] [I] [>] [y^x] [3] [÷] [()] [RCL] [B] [+] [2] [×] [RCL] [I] [÷] [TAN] [RCL] [A] [ENTER]

HP 33s Checksum; Length of Equation: **CK=8A26; LN=39**

[RCL] [Q] [y^x] [2] [÷] [RCL] [G] [↱] [=] [↱] [(] [↱] [(] [RCL] [B] [+] [RCL] [I] [÷] [TAN] [RCL] [A] [↱] [)] [↱] [)] [×] [RCL] [I] [↱] [)] [y^x] [3] [÷] [↱] [(] [RCL] [B] [+] [2] [×] [RCL] [I] [÷] [TAN] [RCL] [A] [↱] [)] [↱] [)] [ENTER]

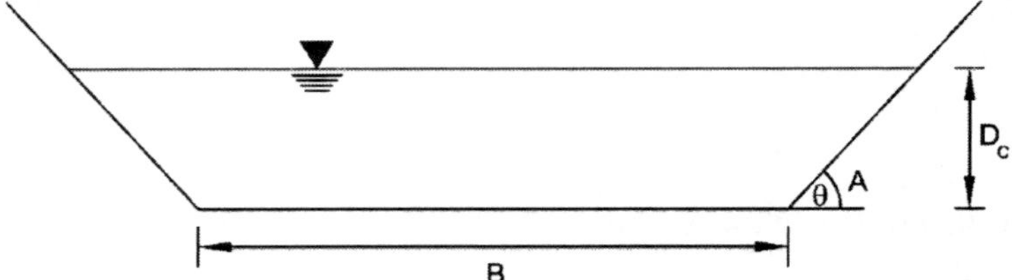

Figure 11-8 Critical Depth on Trapezoidal Channel Given Side Angle

≈≈≈≈≈≈≈≈≈≈

11.4.12 Trapezoidal Channel Solving Hydraulic Radius Given Side Angle

$$R = \frac{\left(B + \dfrac{D}{\tan\theta}\right)D}{B + 2\dfrac{D}{\sin\theta}}$$ Equation No. 146

The equation is entered as

146TRAPHRANGLE
R=(B+D÷TAN(A))×D÷(B+2×D÷SIN(A))

Where:

R = hydraulic radius R (ft, m)
B = base width of channel B (ft, m)
D = depth of water D (ft, m)
A = side angle θ

Keystrokes

HP 35s Checksum; Length of Equation: **CK=B0DB; LN=31**

[RCL] [R] [↰] [=] [()] [RCL] [B] [+] [RCL] [D] [÷] [TAN] [RCL] [A] [>] [>] [×] [RCL] [D] [÷] [()] [RCL] [B] [+] [2] [×] [RCL] [D] [÷] [SIN] [RCL] [A] [ENTER]

HP 33s Checksum; Length of Equation: **CK=B0DB; LN=31**

[RCL] [R] [↱] [=] [↱] [(] [RCL] [B] [+] [RCL] [D] [÷] [TAN] [RCL] [A] [↱] [)] [↱] [)] [×] [RCL] [D] [÷] [↱] [(] [RCL] [B] [+] [2] [×] [RCL] [D] [÷] [SIN] [RCL] [A] [↱] [)] [↱] [)] [ENTER]

≈≈≈≈≈≈≈≈≈≈

11.4.13 Trapezoidal Channel Solving Wetted Perimeter Given Side Angle

$$P = B + 2\frac{D}{\sin\theta}$$ Equation No. 147

The equation is entered as

147TRAPWPANGLE
P=B+2×D÷SIN(A)

Where:

P = wetted perimeter P (ft, m)
B = base width of channel B (ft, m)
D = depth of water D (ft, m)
A = side angle θ

Keystrokes

HP 35s Checksum; Length of Equation: **CK=B932; LN=14**

[RCL] [P] [↰] [=] [RCL] [B] [+] [2] [×] [RCL] [D] [÷] [SIN] [RCL] [A] [ENTER]

HP 33s Checksum; Length of Equation: **CK=B932; LN=14**

[RCL] [P] [↱] [=] [RCL] [B] [+] [2] [×] [RCL] [D] [÷] [SIN] [RCL] [A] [↱] [)] [ENTER]

≈≈≈≈≈≈≈≈≈≈

11.4.14 Trapezoidal Channel Solving Most Efficient Dimensions

$$Q = \left(\left(B + \frac{D}{\tan 60^o}\right)D\right)\frac{c}{n}\left(\frac{D}{2}\right)^{2/3} S^{1/2}$$ Equation No. 148

The equation is entered as

148TRAPMOSTEFF
Q=(B+D÷TAN(60))×D×C÷N(D÷2)^(2÷3)×S^0.5

Where:

Q = design flow rate Q (ft³/sec, m³/s)
B = most efficient base width of channel B (ft, m)
D = most efficient depth of channel D (ft, m)
C = 1.49 for English units, 1 for Metric units c
N = Manning roughness coefficient n
S = slope of energy line S (decimal)

Keystrokes

HP 35s Checksum; Length of Equation: **CK=FEE3; LN=38**

[RCL] [Q] [↰] [=] [()] [RCL] [B] [+] [RCL] [D] [÷] [TAN] [6] [0] [>] [>] [×] [RCL] [D] [×] [RCL] [C] [÷] [RCL] [N] [()] [RCL] [D] [÷] [2] [>] [yˣ] [()] [2] [÷] [3] [>] [×] [RCL] [S] [yˣ] [·] [5] [ENTER]

HP 33s Checksum; Length of Equation: **CK=E8B4; LN=39**

[RCL] [Q] [↱] [=] [↱] [(] [RCL] [B] [+] [RCL] [D] [÷] [TAN] [6] [0] [↱] [)] [↱] [)] [×] [RCL] [D] [×] [RCL] [C] [÷] [RCL] [N] [×] [↱] [(] [RCL] [D] [÷] [2] [↱] [)] [yˣ] [↱] [(] [2] [÷] [3] [↱] [)] [×] [RCL] [S] [yˣ] [·] [5] [ENTER]

≈≈≈≈≈≈≈≈≈≈

11.5 Aquifers

11.5.1 Confined Aquifer

$$Q = \frac{2\pi Kb(y_1 - y_2)}{\ln\left(\frac{r_1}{r_2}\right)} \qquad \text{Equation No. 149}$$

The equation is entered as

149CONFAQUIFER
Q=2×π×K×B(Y−Z)÷LN(R÷S)

Where:

Q = discharge flow rate Q (ft³/sec)
K = hydraulic conductivity K (ft/sec)
B = thickness of aquifer b (ft)
Y = piezometric head at radial distance R y_1 (ft)
Z = piezometric head at radial distance S y_2 (ft)
R = radial distance R from center of pumping well to center of well 1 r_1 (ft)
S = radial distance S from center of pumping well to center of well 2 r_2 (ft)

Keystrokes

HP 35s | Checksum; Length of Equation: **CK=8995; LN=22**

[RCL] [Q] [↰] [=] [2] [×] [↰] [π] [×] [RCL] [K] [×] [RCL] [B] [()] [RCL] [Y] [−] [RCL] [Z] [>] [÷] [↱] [LN] [RCL] [R] [÷] [RCL] [S] [ENTER]

HP 33s | Checksum; Length of Equation: **CK=FC97; LN=23**

[RCL] [Q] [↱] [=] [2] [×] [↱] [π] [×] [RCL] [K] [×] [RCL] [B] [×] [↱] [(] [RCL] [Y] [−] [RCL] [Z] [↱] [)] [÷] [LN] [RCL] [R] [÷] [RCL] [S] [↱] [)] [ENTER]

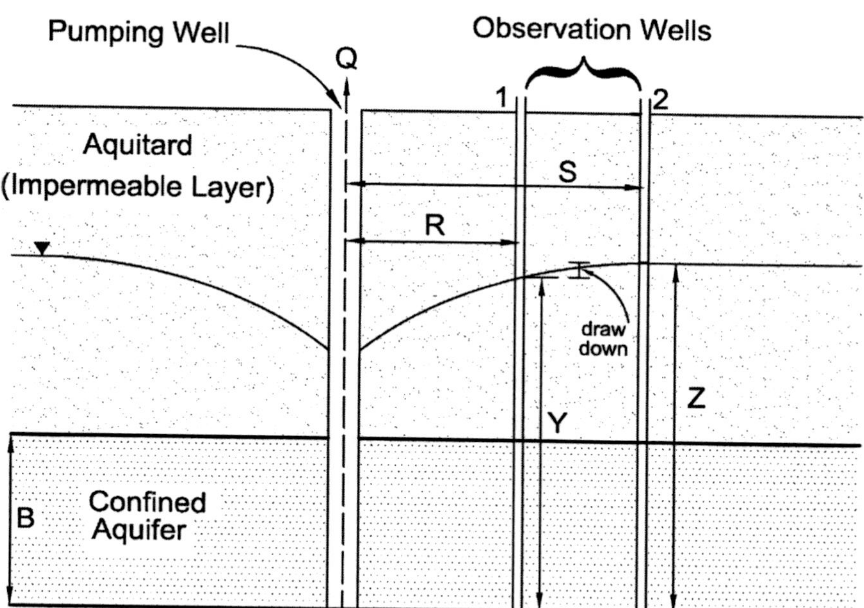

Figure 11-9 Confined Aquifer

≈≈≈≈≈≈≈≈≈≈

11.5.2 Unconfined Aquifer

$$Q = \frac{\pi K\left(y_1^2 - y_2^2\right)}{\ln\left(\dfrac{r_1}{r_2}\right)}$$ Equation No. 150

The equation is entered as

150UNCONAQUIFER
Q=π×K(Y^2−Z^2)÷LN(R÷S)

Where:

Q = discharge flow rate Q (ft³/sec)
K = hydraulic conductivity K (ft/sec)
Y = piezometric head at radial distance R y_1 (ft)
Z = piezometric head at radial distance S y_2 (ft)
R = radial distance R from center of pumping well to center of well 1 r_1 (ft)
S = radial distance S from center of pumping well to center of well 2 r_2 (ft)

Keystrokes

HP 35s Checksum; Length of Equation: **CK=D295; LN=22**

[RCL] [Q] [⬑] [=] [⬑] [π] [×] [RCL] [K] [( )] [RCL] [Y] [yˣ] [2] [−] [RCL] [Z] [yˣ] [2] [>] [÷] [⬏] [LN] [RCL] [R] [÷] [RCL] [S] [ENTER]

HP 33s Checksum; Length of Equation: **CK=2239; LN=23**

[RCL] [Q] [⬏] [=] [⬏] [π] [×] [RCL] [K] [×] [⬏] [(] [RCL] [Y] [yˣ] [2] [−] [RCL] [Z] [yˣ] [2] [⬏] [)] [÷] [LN] [RCL] [R] [÷] [RCL] [S] [⬏] [)] [ENTER]

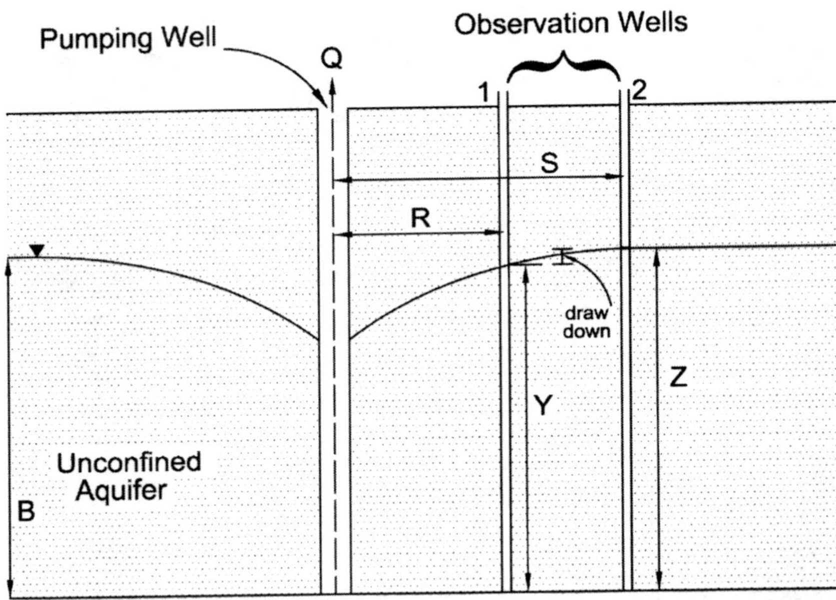

Figure 11-10 Unconfined Aquifer

≈≈≈≈≈≈≈≈≈≈

11.6.1 Chemical Feed Rate

$$R_f = \frac{DQ8.34}{P}$$ Equation No. 151

The equation is entered as

151CHEMFEEDRATE
R=D×Q×8.34÷P

Where:

R = feed rate in lbm/day of active chemical R_f
D = dose of chemical required D (mg/L)
Q = flow rate Q (million gallons per day)
P = potency P (decimal)

Keystrokes

HP 35s Checksum; Length of Equation: **CK=E0B4; LN=12**

[RCL] [R] [↰] [=] [RCL] [D] [×] [RCL] [Q] [×] [8] [.] [3] [4] [÷] [RCL] [P] [ENTER]

HP 33s Checksum; Length of Equation: **CK=E0B4; LN=12**

[RCL] [R] [↱] [=] [RCL] [D] [×] [RCL] [Q] [×] [8] [.] [3] [4] [÷] [RCL] [P] [ENTER]

≈≈≈≈≈≈≈≈≈≈

11.6.2 Rapid Mixing

$$G = \sqrt{\frac{P}{\mu V}}$$ Equation No. 152

The equation is entered as

152RAPIDMIXING
P=G^2×U×V

Where:

P = power requirement P (ft-lb/s)
G = velocity gradient G (s^{-1})
U = dynamic viscosity μ (lb-s/ft^2)
V = volume of tank V (ft^3)

Keystrokes

HP 35s Checksum; Length of Equation: **CK=A2CA; LN=9**

[RCL] [P] [↰] [=] [RCL] [G] [y^x] [2] [×] [RCL] [U] [×] [RCL] [V] [ENTER]

HP 33s Checksum; Length of Equation: **CK=A2CA; LN=9**

[RCL] [P] [↱] [=] [RCL] [G] [y^x] [2] [×] [RCL] [U] [×] [RCL] [V] [ENTER]

Note: To calculate the power requirement in hp, divide the ft-lb/s by 550.

≈≈≈≈≈≈≈≈≈≈

11.6.3 Overflow Rate

$$O = \frac{Q}{A_s}$$ Equation No. 153

The equation is entered as

153OVERFLOWRATE
O=Q÷A

Where:

O = overflow rate O (gal/day/ft^2)
Q = flow rate Q (gal/day)
A = basin surface area A_s (ft^2)

Keystrokes

HP 35s Checksum; Length of Equation: **CK=784C; LN=5**

[RCL] [O] [↰] [=] [RCL] [Q] [÷] [RCL] [A] [ENTER]

HP 33s Checksum; Length of Equation: **CK=784C; LN=5**

[RCL] [O] [↱] [=] [RCL] [Q] [÷] [RCL] [A] [ENTER]

≈≈≈≈≈≈≈≈≈≈

11.6.4 Detention Time

$$T = \frac{V}{Q}$$ Equation No. 154

The equation is entered as

154DETENTIME
T=V÷Q

Where:

T = detention time T (hours)
V = basin volume V (ft^3)
Q = flow rate Q (ft^3/hour)

Keystrokes

HP 35s Checksum; Length of Equation: **CK=0748; LN=5**

[RCL] [T] [↰] [=] [RCL] [V] [÷] [RCL] [Q] [ENTER]

HP 33s Checksum; Length of Equation: **CK=0748; LN=5**

[RCL] [T] [↱] [=] [RCL] [V] [÷] [RCL] [Q] [ENTER]

≈≈≈≈≈≈≈≈≈≈

11.6.5 Weir Loading Rate

$$W = \frac{Q}{L}$$ Equation No. 155

The equation is entered as

155WEIRLOADRATE
W=Q÷L

Where:

W = weir loading rate W (gal/day/ft)
Q = flow rate Q (gal/day)
L = weir length L (ft)

Keystrokes

HP 35s Checksum; Length of Equation: **CK=AF96; LN=5**

[RCL] [W] [↰] [=] [RCL] [Q] [÷] [RCL] [L] [ENTER]

HP 33s Checksum; Length of Equation: **CK=AF96; LN=5**

[RCL] [W] [↱] [=] [RCL] [Q] [÷] [RCL] [L] [ENTER]

≈≈≈≈≈≈≈≈≈≈

Sample Problems

Problem 11.1

A 16-inch-diameter storm sewer (n = 0.012) is flowing full at a slope of 0.1%. The flow rate and velocity are most nearly

	Flow Rate (ft^3/sec)	Velocity of Flow (ft/sec)
(A)	3	2
(B)	6	4
(C)	8	6
(D)	26	19

Solution

Step 1. Calculate the flow rate. Use Equation No. 113, page 213. Press ENTER.

Display	Keys	Description
D?	16 ENTER 12 ÷	Diameter of the pipe (ft)
D? 1.3333	R/S	
C?	1.49 R/S	Constant for English units
N?	.012 R/S	Manning roughness coefficient of the pipe
S?	.001 R/S	Slope of energy line (decimal)
Q = 2.6357	--	Flow rate (ft^3/sec)

Step 2. Compute the velocity of flow. Use Equation No. 114, page 214. Press ENTER. Press R/S every time you are prompted. You'll get V = 1.8877 (ft/sec).

The answer is (A).

Problem 11.2

A 4-foot-diameter smooth concrete sewer pipe is flowing half-full at a slope of 0.02. The flow rate, velocity of flow, and Froude number are most nearly

	Flow Rate (ft^3/sec)	Velocity of Flow (ft/sec)	Froude Number
(A)	30	12	1.0
(B)	45	14	1.5
(C)	50	16	2
(D)	110	18	2.5

Solution

a) Flow rate

Calculate the flow rate. Use Equation No. 115, page 215. Press ENTER.

Display	Keys	Description
D?	4 R/S	Diameter of the pipe (ft)
C?	1.49 R/S	Constant for English units
N?	.012 R/S	Manning roughness coefficient of the pipe
S?	.02 R/S	Slope of energy line (decimal)
Q = 110.3316	--	Flow rate (ft^3/sec)

b) Velocity of flow

Compute the velocity of flow. Use Equation No. 116, page 215. Press ENTER. Press R/S every time you are prompted. You'll get V = 17.5598 (ft/sec).

c) Froude number

Calculate the Froude number. Use Equation No. 117, page 216. Press ENTER.

Display	Keys	Description
V? 17.5598	R/S	Velocity of flow (ft/sec)
G?	32.2 R/S	Gravitational acceleration (ft/sec^2)
D? 4.0000	R/S	Diameter of the pipe (ft)
F = 2.4691	--	Froude number

The answer is (D).

Problem 11.3

A 4-foot-diameter finished concrete pipe is laid at a slope of 0.2%. The depth of water is 3 feet. The flow rate and velocity of flow are most nearly

	Flow Rate (ft^3/sec)	Velocity of Flow (ft/sec)
(A)	40	4
(B)	50	5
(C)	65	6
(D)	635	63

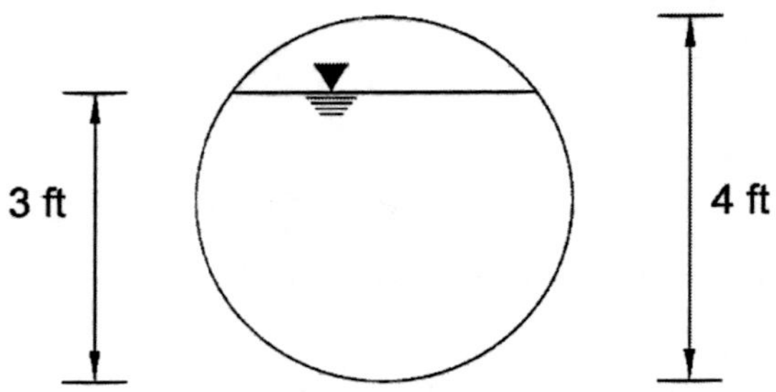

Solution

The flow rate and velocity of flow can be calculated using the Manning equation.

Step 1. Calculate the flow rate. Use Equation No. 118, page 217. Press ENTER.

Display	Keys	Description
C?	1.49 R/S	Constant for English units
N?	.012 R/S	Manning roughness coefficient of the pipe
H?	3 R/S	Depth of water (ft)
D?	4 R/S	Diameter of the pipe (ft)
S?	.002 R/S	Slope of energy line (decimal)
Q = 63.6307	--	Flow rate (ft^3/sec)

Step 2. Compute the velocity of flow. Use Equation No. 119, page 218. Press ENTER. Press R/S every time you are prompted. You'll get V = 6.2941 (ft/sec).

The answer is (C).

Problem 11.4

Water is flowing at a rate of 5 ft^3/sec in a 3-foot-diameter sanitary sewer line (n = 0.012) at a slope of 0.002, n varies with depth. The flow is uniform and steady. The depth of flow in inches is most nearly

(A) 5.6 in
(B) 11.2 in
(C) 15 in
(D) 18 in

Solution

The depth of flow can be obtained using the following procedure.

Step 1. Calculate the Q_{full}. Use Equation No. 113, page 213. Press ENTER.

Display	Keys	Description
D?	3 R/S	Diameter of the pipe (ft)
C?	1.49 R/S	Constant for English units
N?	.012 R/S	Manning roughness coefficient of the pipe

Display	Keys	Description
S?	.002 R/S	Slope of energy line (decimal)
Q = 32.4011	--	Flow rate flowing full (ft^3/sec)

Step 2. Determine the Q/Q_{full}.

Display	Keys	Description
--	5 x↔y ÷	Q/Q_{full} calculation
0.0020 0.1543 ←	←	 Q/Q_{full}

$$\frac{Q}{Q_{full}} = \frac{5\frac{ft^3}{\sec}}{32.4011\frac{ft^3}{\sec}} = 0.1543$$

Step 3. From the Circular Channels Ratios (varying n) using relation d/D = Q/Q_{full}. Determine the value of d/D by interpolation. The Interpolation Equation in this book can be used. Press ENTER, then enter 0.3 for A, enter 0.1543 for E, enter 0.14 for D, enter 0.26 for F, enter 0.4 for B. The interpolation value is (I = 0.3119).

d/D = 0.3119

d = D × 0.3119

d = 36 in × 0.3119

d = 11.2284 in

The answer is (B).

Problem 11.5

A rectangular open channel is to be constructed with finished concrete on a slope of 0.03 and is 8 feet wide. The depth of water is 2 feet. The flow rate, velocity of flow, hydraulic radius, and critical depth are most nearly

	Flow Rate (ft^3/sec)	Velocity of Flow (ft/sec)	Hydraulic Radius (ft)	Critical Depth (ft)
(A)	200	20	1.1	3
(B)	300	25	1.2	4
(C)	400	26	1.3	4.5
(D)	450	30	1.5	5

Solution

a) Flow rate

Calculate the flow rate. Use Equation No. 122, page 221. Press ENTER.

Display	Keys	Description
C?	1.49 R/S	Constant for English units
N?	.012 R/S	Manning roughness coefficient of the channel
B?	8 R/S	Width of the channel (ft)
D?	2 R/S	Depth of water (ft)
S?	.03 R/S	Slope of energy line (decimal)
Q = 416.8484	--	Flow rate (ft^3/sec)

b) Velocity of flow

Compute the velocity of flow. Use Equation No. 123, page 222. Press ENTER. Press R/S every time you are prompted. You'll get V = 26.0530 (ft/sec).

c) Hydraulic radius

Determine the hydraulic radius. Use Equation No. 125, page 223. Press ENTER. Press R/S every time you are prompted. You'll get R = 1.3333 (ft).

d) Critical depth

Calculate the critical depth. Use Equation No. 126, page 224. Press ENTER.

Display	Keys	Description
Q? 416.8484	R/S	Flow rate (ft^3/sec)
G?	32.2 R/S	Gravitational acceleration (ft/sec^2)
B? 8.0000	R/S	Width of the channel (ft)
I = 4.3850	--	Critical depth (ft)

The answer is (C).

Problem 11.6

A rectangular open channel is being designed to carry a flow rate of 300 ft^3/sec. The Manning's coefficient n is 0.012 and the slope is 0.003. The most efficient dimensions are most nearly

	Depth (ft)	Width (ft)
(A)	2.2	6.5
(B)	3.8	7.6
(C)	4.5	8.5
(D)	5.0	9.0

Solution

The most efficient dimensions can be determined using the following steps.

Step 1. Solve the most efficient depth. Use Equation No. 129, page 226. Press SOLVE D.

Display	Keys	Description
Q?	300 R/S	Designed flow rate (ft^3/sec)
C?	1.49 R/S	Constant for English units
N?	.012 R/S	Manning roughness coefficient of the channel
S?	.003 R/S	Slope of energy line (decimal)
D = 3.7938	--	Most efficient depth (ft)

Step 2. Calculate the most efficient width. Use Equation No. 128, page 225. Press SOLVE B. Press R/S every time you are prompted. You'll get B = 7.5877 (ft).

The answer is (B).

Problem 11.7

In a 5-foot-wide rectangular channel, the water depth is 2 feet flowing at a discharge rate of 200 ft^3/sec. The water will experience a hydraulic jump. The depth of water after the jump, Froude number before and after the jump, and horsepower lost in the jump are most nearly

	Depth of Water After the Jump (ft)	Froude Number Before the Jump	Froude Number After the Jump	Horsepower Lost in the Jump (hp)
(A)	6	2.5	0.5	32
(B)	10	3	1	35
(C)	12	3.5	1.5	40
(D)	14	4	2	42

Solution

a) Depth of water after the jump

Calculate the depth of water after the jump. Use Equation No. 131, page 227. Press ENTER.

Display	Keys	Description
D?	2 R/S	Depth of water before the jump (ft)
V?	200 ENTER 10 ÷	Velocity of flow before the jump (ft/sec)
V? 20.0000	R/S	
G?	32.2 R/S	Gravitational acceleration (ft/sec^2)
E = 6.1197	--	Depth of water after the jump (ft)

Calculation of velocity of flow before the jump:

$$Q = AV$$

$$V = \frac{200 \frac{ft^3}{\sec}}{5\,ft \times 2\,ft}$$

$$V = 20 \frac{ft}{\sec}$$

b) Froude number before and after the jump

Step 1. Calculate the Froude number before the jump. Use Equation No. 124, page 222. Press ENTER. Press R/S every time you are prompted. You'll get F = 2.4922.

Step 2. Solve the velocity of flow after the jump. Use Equation No. 130, page 226. Press SOLVE U. Press R/S every time you are prompted. You'll get U = 6.5363 (ft/sec) for the velocity of flow after the jump.

Step 3. Calculate the Froude number after the jump. Use Equation No. 132, page 228. Press ENTER. Press R/S every time you are prompted. You'll get F = 0.4656.

c) Horsepower

Step 1. Calculate the head loss. Use Equation No. 133, page 228. Press ENTER. Press R/S every time you are prompted. You'll get H = 1.4281 (ft) for the head loss.

Step 2. Compute the horsepower lost in the jump. Use Equation No. 134, page 229. Press ENTER.

Display	Keys	Description
Q?	200 R/S	Flow rate of water (ft^3/sec)
W?	62.4 R/S	Unit weight of water (lb/ft^3)
H? 1.4281	R/S	Head loss (ft)
P = 32.4053	--	Horse power lost in the jump (hp)

The answer is (A).

Problem 11.8

A trapezoidal open channel shown has a Manning roughness coefficient of 0.012 and is laid at a slope of 0.3%. The flow rate, velocity of flow, hydraulic radius, critical depth, and Froude number are most nearly

	Flow Rate (ft^3/sec)	Velocity of Flow (ft/sec)	Hydraulic Radius (ft)	Critical Depth (ft)	Froude Number
(A)	255	7	1	2.5	1.8
(B)	300	8	1.5	3	1
(C)	405	11	2	3.5	1.3
(D)	530	12	2.5	4	1.5

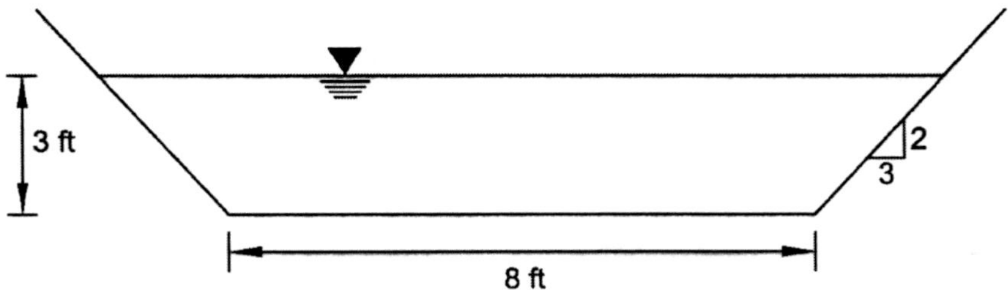

Solution

a) Flow rate

Calculate the flow rate. Use Equation No. 135, page 230. Press ENTER.

Display	Keys	Description
C?	1.49 R/S	Constant for English units
N?	.012 R/S	Manning roughness coefficient of the channel
B?	8 R/S	Base width of the channel (ft)
X?	3 ENTER 2 ÷	Side slope horizontal
X? 1.5000	R/S	
D?	3 R/S	Depth of water (ft)
S?	.003 R/S	Slope of energy line (decimal)
Q = 403.8836	--	Flow rate (ft^3/sec)

b) Velocity of flow

Determine the velocity of flow. Use Equation No. 136, page 231. Press ENTER. Press R/S every time you are prompted. You'll get V = 10.7702 (ft/sec).

c) Hydraulic radius

Calculate the hydraulic radius. Use Equation No. 140, page 233. Press ENTER. Press R/S every time you are prompted. You'll get R = 1.9929 (ft).

d) Critical depth

Solve the critical depth. Use Equation No. 138, page 232. Press SOLVE I.

Display	Keys	Description
Q? 403.8836	R/S	Flow rate (ft^3/sec)
G?	32.2 R/S	Gravitational acceleration (ft/sec^2)
B? 8.0000	R/S	Base width of the channel (ft)
X? 1.5000	R/S	Side slope horizontal
I = 3.4403	--	Critical depth (ft)

e) Froude number

Calculate the Froude number. Use Equation No. 137, page 231. Press ENTER. Press R/S every time you are prompted. You'll get F = 1.2779.

The answer is (C).

Problem 11.9

What is most nearly the depth of water flowing on a trapezoidal open channel shown? The flow rate is 200 ft^3/sec, the Manning roughness coefficient is 0.012 and the slope is 0.002.

(A) 1.5 ft
(B) 2 ft
(C) 2.5 ft
(D) 3 ft

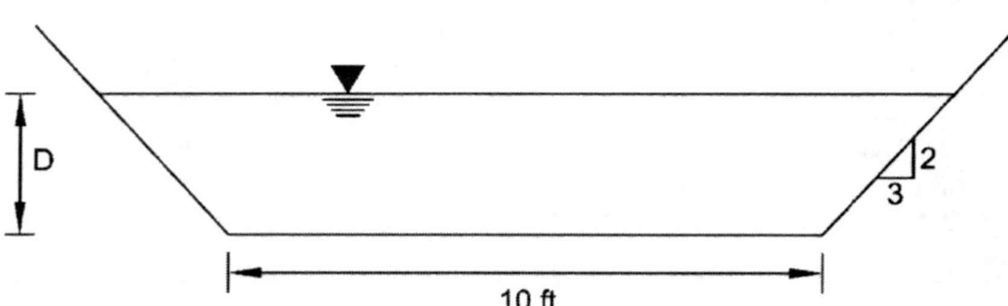

Solution

Solve the depth of water. Use Equation No. 135, page 230. Press SOLVE D.

Display	Keys	Description
Q?	200 R/S	Flow rate (ft^3/sec)
C?	1.49 R/S	Constant for English units
N?	.012 R/S	Manning roughness coefficient of the channel
B?	10 R/S	Base width of the channel (ft)
X?	3 ENTER 2 ÷	Side slope horizontal
X? 1.5000	R/S	
S?	.002 R/S	Slope of energy line (decimal)
D = 2.0582	--	Depth of water (ft)

The answer is (B).

Problem 11.10

What is most nearly the discharge rate of the confined aquifer shown below in gal/min? The hydraulic conductivity of the aquifer is 5 ft/day.

(A) 60 gal/min
(B) 95 gal/min
(C) 100 gal/min
(D) 110 gal/min

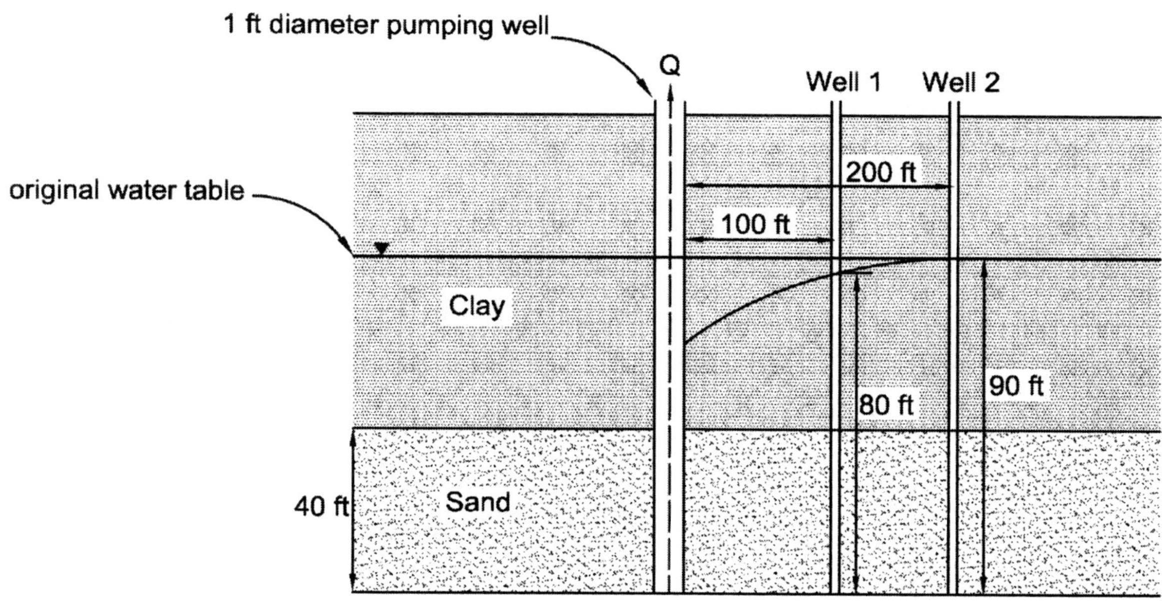

Solution

Calculate the discharge rate of the aquifer. Use Equation No. 149, page 240. Press ENTER.

Display	Keys	Description
K?	5 ENTER 86400 ÷	Hydraulic conductivity of the aquifer (ft/sec)
K? 0.0001	R/S	
B?	40 R/S	Thickness of the aquifer (ft)
Y?	80 R/S	Piezometric head at radial distance R (ft)
Z?	90 R/S	Piezometric head at radial distance S (ft)
R?	100.5 R/S	Radial distance from center of pumping well to well 1 (ft)
S?	200.5 R/S	Radial distance from center of pumping well to well 2 (ft)
Q = 0.2106	--	Discharge of aquifer (ft³/sec)
--	60 × 7.48 ×	Conversion of ft³/sec to gal/min
200.5000 94.5120 ←		Discharge of aquifer (gal/min)

Conversion for hydraulic conductivity from 5 ft/day to ft/sec:

$$\frac{5\,ft}{day}\times\frac{day}{86{,}400\,\text{sec}}=0.0001\frac{ft}{\text{sec}}$$

Conversion for 0.2106 ft³/sec to gal/min:

$$0.2106\frac{ft^3}{\text{sec}}\times\frac{60\,\text{sec}}{\text{min}}\times\frac{7.48\,gal}{ft^3}=94.5120\frac{gal}{\text{min}}$$

The answer is (B).

Problem 11.11

What is most nearly the discharge rate of the unconfined aquifer shown below in gal/min if the aquifer has reached steady-state? The hydraulic conductivity of the aquifer is 10 ft/day.

(A) 60 gal/min
(B) 95 gal/min
(C) 100 gal/min
(D) 200 gal/min

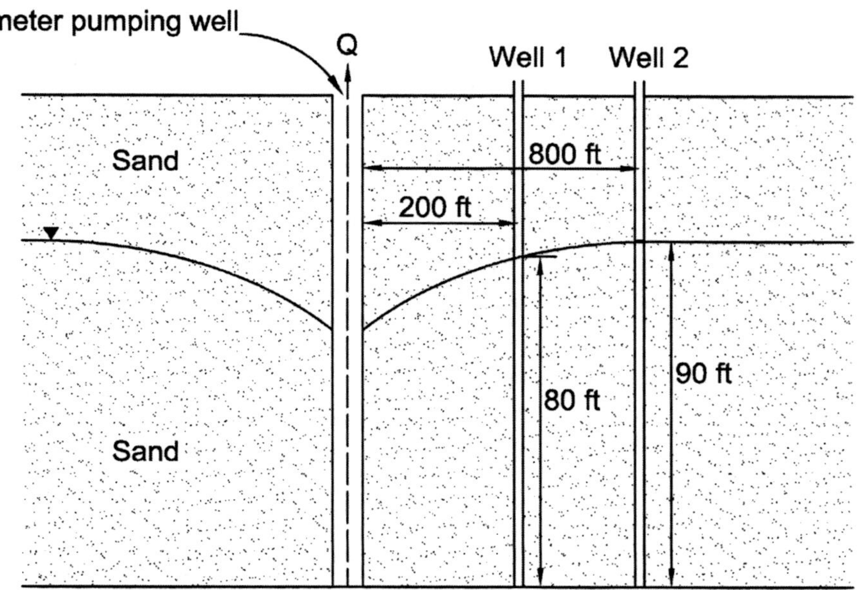

Solution

Calculate the discharge rate of the aquifer. Use Equation No. 150, page 241. Press ENTER.

Display	Keys	Description
K?	10 ENTER 86400 ÷	Hydraulic conductivity of the aquifer (ft/sec)
K? 0.0001	R/S	
Y?	80 R/S	Piezometric head at radial distance R (ft)
Z?	90 R/S	Piezometric head at radial distance S (ft)
R?	200.5 R/S	Radial distance from center of pumping well to well 1 (ft)
S?	800.5 R/S	Radial distance from center of pumping well to well 2 (ft)
Q = 0.2232	--	Discharge of aquifer in (ft³/sec)
--	60 × 7.48 ×	Conversion of ft³/sec to gal/min
800.5000 100.1934 ←	←	Discharge of aquifer (gal/min)

Conversion for hydraulic conductivity from 10 ft/day to ft/sec:

$$\frac{10\,ft}{day} \times \frac{day}{86{,}400\,\text{sec}} = 0.0001\frac{ft}{\text{sec}}$$

Conversion for 0.2232 ft³/sec to gal/min:

$$0.2232\frac{ft^3}{\text{sec}} \times \frac{60\,\text{sec}}{\text{min}} \times \frac{7.48\,gal}{ft^3} = 100.1934\frac{gal}{\text{min}}$$

The answer is (C).

Problem 11.12

A water treatment plant uses lime during softening at a dosage of 250 mg/L. The required mass of lime to soften 5 MGD of water each day is most nearly

(A) 5,000 lb/day
(B) 10,500 lb/day
(C) 12,000 lb/day
(D) 15,000 lb/day

Solution

Calculate the feed rate. Use Equation No. 151, page 243. Press ENTER.

Display	Keys	Description
D?	250 R/S	Dose of lime required (mg/L)
Q?	5 R/S	Flow rate (million gallons per day)
P?	1 R/S	Potency (decimal)
R = 10,425.0000	--	Feed rate (lb/day)

The answer is (B).

Problem 11.13

A water treatment plant with a capacity of 7 MGD has rapid mixing facilities to mix water and chemicals. The velocity gradient is 1,000 s^{-1} and hydraulic detention time is 15 seconds. The dynamic viscosity is 2.050 x 10^{-5}. The power required for mixing in horsepower is most nearly

(A) 2 hp
(B) 4 hp
(C) 6 hp
(D) 8 hp

Solution

Compute the power requirement. Use Equation No. 152, page 243. Press ENTER.

Display	Keys	Description
G?	1000 R/S	Velocity gradient (s^{-1})
U?	2.05 E 5 +/− R/S	Dynamic viscosity (lb-s/ft^2)
V?	*	Volume of the tank (ft^3)
V? 162.4703	R/S	
P = 3,330.6410	--	Power requirement (ft-lb/s)
--	550 ÷	Divide the power requirement by 550 to convert ft-lb/s to hp

Display	Keys	Description
162.4703		
6.0557 ←	←	Power requirement (hp)

* Keys for calculating volume of tank using RPN:

7 E 6 ENTER 86400 ÷ 7.48 ÷ 15 ×

$$Vol_{tank} = 7\times10^6 \frac{gal}{day}\times\frac{day}{86{,}400\sec}\times\frac{ft^3}{7.48gal}\times 15\sec$$

$$Vol_{tank} = 162.4703\,ft^3$$

The answer is (C).

Problem 11.14

A water treatment plant has two primary clarifiers to treat a design flow rate of 3 MGD. Each clarifier is 40 feet in diameter, 10 feet in depth, and has 250 feet weir length. The detention time, overflow rate, and weir loading rate of each clarifier are most nearly

	Detention Time (hr)	Overflow Rate (ft^3/ft^2-hr)	Weir Loading Rate (ft^3/ft-hr)
(A)	1.0	5.5	25
(B)	1.5	6.5	33.5
(C)	2.0	12	35
(D)	2.5	15	40

Solution

a) Detention time

Determine the detention time. Use Equation No. 154, page 244. Press ENTER.

Display	Keys	Description
V?	*	Volume of each clarifier (ft^3)
V? 12,566.3706	R/S	
Q?	**	Flow rate of each clarifier (ft^3/hr)
Q? 8,355.6150	R/S	
T = 1.5039	--	Detention time (hr)

* Keys for calculating volume of each clarifier using RPN:

[shift-left] [π] 4 ÷ 40 [shift-right] [x^2] × 10 × (HP 35s)
[shift-right] [π] 4 ÷ 40 [x^2] × 10 × (HP 33s)

$$V = \frac{\pi}{4}(40\,ft)^2(10\,ft)$$
$$V = 12{,}566.3706\,ft^3$$

** Keys for calculating flow rate of each clarifier using RPN:

1.5 E 6 ENTER 24 ÷ 7.48 ÷

$$Q = 1.5 \times 10^6 \frac{gal}{day} \times \frac{day}{24hr} \times \frac{ft^3}{7.48gal}$$
$$Q = 8{,}355.6150 \frac{ft^3}{hr}$$

b) Overflow rate

Calculate the overflow rate. Use Equation No. 153, page 244. Press ENTER.

Display	Keys	Description
Q? 8,355.6150	R/S	Flow rate of each clarifier (ft^3/hr)
A?	*	Surface area of each clarifier (ft^2)
A? 1,256.6371	R/S	
O = 6.6492	--	Overflow rate (ft^3/ft^2-hr)

* Keys for calculating surface area of each clarifier using RPN:

[shift-left] [π] 4 ÷ 40 [shift-right] [x^2] × (HP 35s)
[shift-right] [π] 4 ÷ 40 [x^2] × (HP 33s)

$$A_s = \frac{\pi}{4}(40\,ft)^2$$
$$A_s = 1{,}256.6371\,ft^2$$

c) Weir loading rate

Calculate the weir loading rate. Use Equation No. 155, page 245. Press ENTER.

Display	Keys	Description
Q? 8,355.6150	R/S	Flow rate of each clarifier (ft^3/hr)
L?	250 R/S	Weir length of clarifier (ft)
W = 33.4225	--	Weir loading rate of each clarifier (ft^3/ft-hr)

The answer is (B).

PART III: TRANSPORTATION

CHAPTER 12: VEHICLE DYNAMICS (ENGLISH UNITS)

12.1 Miles Per Hour to Feet Per Second Conversion

$$v = M \times \frac{5280}{3600}$$ Equation No. 156

The equation is entered as

156MPHTOFPS
V=M×5280÷3600

Where:

V = velocity of car v (ft/sec)
M = velocity of car M (mi/hr)

Keystrokes

HP 35s Checksum; Length of Equation: **CK=0E72; LN=13**

[RCL] [V] [↰] [=] [RCL] [M] [×] [5] [2] [8] [0] [÷] [3] [6] [0] [0] [ENTER]

HP 33s Checksum; Length of Equation: **CK=0E72; LN=13**

[RCL] [V] [↱] [=] [RCL] [M] [×] [5] [2] [8] [0] [÷] [3] [6] [0] [0] [ENTER]

≈≈≈≈≈≈≈≈≈≈

12.2 Stopping Distance

12.2.1 Distance Before Braking

$A = tv$ Equation No. 157

The equation is entered as

157DISTB4BRAKE
A=T×V

Where:

A = distance before brakes are applied A (ft)
T = braking reaction time t (sec)
V = velocity of car v (ft/sec)

Keystrokes

HP 35s Checksum; Length of Equation: **CK=6B91; LN=5**

[RCL] [A] [↰] [=] [RCL] [T] [×] [RCL] [V] [ENTER]

HP 33s Checksum; Length of Equation: **CK=6B91; LN=5**

[RCL] [A] [↱] [=] [RCL] [T] [×] [RCL] [V] [ENTER]

≈≈≈≈≈≈≈≈≈≈

12.2.2 Distance during the Braking Maneuver

$$B = \frac{v^2}{64.4(f+G)}$$ Equation No. 158

The equation is entered as

158DISTDURBRAKE
B=V^2÷64.4÷(F+G÷100)

Where:

B = distance during the braking maneuver B (ft)
V = velocity of car v (ft/sec)
F = coefficient of friction between the tire and pavement f (decimal)
G = grade of pavement G (%)

Keystrokes

HP 35s Checksum; Length of Equation: **CK=38C8; LN=20**

[RCL] [B] [↰] [=] [RCL] [V] [y^x] [2] [÷] [6] [4] [•] [4] [÷] [()] [RCL] [F] [+] [RCL] [G] [÷] [1] [0] [0] [ENTER]

HP 33s Checksum; Length of Equation: **CK=38C8; LN=20**

[RCL] [B] [↱] [=] [RCL] [V] [y^x] [2] [÷] [6] [4] [•] [4] [÷] [↱] [(] [RCL] [F] [+] [RCL] [G] [÷] [1] [0] [0] [↱] [)]
[ENTER]

≈≈≈≈≈≈≈≈≈≈

Note: The grade of pavement is (+) if the car skids uphill, (−) if the car skids downhill, and (0) if the pavement is level.

12.2.3 Total Stopping Distance

$S = A + B$ Equation No. 159

The equation is entered as

159TOTALSTOPDIST
S=A+B

Where:

S = total stopping distance S (ft)
A = distance before brakes are applied A (ft)
B = distance during the braking maneuver B (ft)

Keystrokes

HP 35s Checksum; Length of Equation: **CK=7688; LN=5**

[RCL] [S] [↰] [=] [RCL] [A] [+] [RCL] [B] [ENTER]

HP 33s Checksum; Length of Equation: **CK=7688; LN=5**

[RCL] [S] [↱] [=] [RCL] [A] [+] [RCL] [B] [ENTER]

≈≈≈≈≈≈≈≈≈≈

12.3 Stopping Sight Distance

12.3.1 Stopping Sight Distance Given Deceleration

$$S = 1.47tv + \frac{v^2}{30\left(\frac{a}{32.2} + G\right)}$$ Equation No. 160

The equation is entered as

160SSDGIVDECVG
S=1.47×T×V+V^2÷30÷(A÷32.2+G÷100)

Where:

S = stopping sight distance S (ft)
T = braking reaction time t (sec)
V = design speed v (mi/hr)
A = deceleration rate a (ft/sec^2)
G = grade of pavement G (%)

Keystrokes

HP 35s Checksum; Length of Equation: **CK=878C; LN=32**

[RCL] [S] [shift] [=] [1] [.] [4] [7] [×] [RCL] [T] [×] [RCL] [V] [+] [RCL] [V] [y^x] [2] [÷] [3] [0] [÷] [()] [RCL] [A] [÷] [3] [2] [.] [2] [+] [RCL] [G] [÷] [1] [0] [0] [ENTER]

HP 33s Checksum; Length of Equation: **CK=878C; LN=32**

[RCL] [S] [shift] [=] [1] [.] [4] [7] [×] [RCL] [T] [×] [RCL] [V] [+] [RCL] [V] [y^x] [2] [÷] [3] [0] [÷] [shift] [(] [RCL] [A] [÷] [3] [2] [.] [2] [+] [RCL] [G] [÷] [1] [0] [0] [shift] [)] [ENTER]

≈≈≈≈≈≈≈≈≈≈

12.3.2 Stopping Sight Distance Given Coefficient of Friction

$$S = 1.47tv + \frac{v^2}{30(f + G)}$$ Equation No. 161

The equation is entered as

161SSDGIVCOFVG
S=1.47×T×V+V^2÷30÷(F+G÷100)

Where:

S = stopping sight distance S (ft)
T = braking reaction time t (sec)
V = design speed v (mi/hr)
F = coefficient of friction between the tire and pavement f (decimal)
G = grade of pavement G (%)

Keystrokes

HP 35s Checksum; Length of Equation: **CK=51C4; LN=27**

[RCL] [S] [shift] [=] [1] [.] [4] [7] [×] [RCL] [T] [×] [RCL] [V] [+] [RCL] [V] [y^x] [2] [÷] [3] [0] [÷] [()] [RCL] [F] [+] [RCL] [G] [÷] [1] [0] [0] [ENTER]

HP 33s Checksum; Length of Equation: **CK=51C4; LN=27**

[RCL] [S] [shift] [=] [1] [.] [4] [7] [×] [RCL] [T] [×] [RCL] [V] [+] [RCL] [V] [y^x] [2] [÷] [3] [0] [÷] [shift] [(] [RCL] [F] [+] [RCL] [G] [÷] [1] [0] [0] [shift] [)] [ENTER]

≈≈≈≈≈≈≈≈≈≈

Problem 12.1

A section of a freeway has the following design criteria:

Design speed:	75 mi/hr
Coefficient of friction:	0.3
Driver reaction time:	2.5 seconds
Driver eye height:	3.5 ft
Object height:	0.5 ft
Grade:	0%

The total stopping sight distance is most nearly

(A) 275 ft
(B) 625 ft
(C) 900 ft
(D) 1,000 ft

Solution:

a) Distance traveled by the vehicle during the perception and reaction of the driver before stopping.

Step 1. Convert the design speed from (mi/hr) to (ft/sec). Use Equation No. 156, page 263. Press ENTER.

Display	Keys	Description
C?	75 R/S	Design speed (mi/hr)
V = 110.0000	--	Design speed (ft/sec)

Step 2. Calculate the distance traveled by the vehicle during the perception and reaction of the driver before stopping. Use Equation No. 157, page 263. Press ENTER.

Display	Keys	Description
T?	2.5 R/S	Driver reaction time (seconds)
V? 110.0000	R/S	Design speed (ft/sec)
A = 275.0000	--	Distance traveled by the vehicle during the perception and reaction of the driver before stopping (ft).

b) Distance traveled by the vehicle while decelerating to a stop.

Calculate the distance traveled by the vehicle while decelerating to a stop. Use Equation No. 158, page 264. Press ENTER.

Display	Keys	Description
V? 110.0000	R/S	Design speed (ft/sec)
F?	.3 R/S	Coefficient of friction between the tire and pavement
G?	0 R/S	Grade of pavement (%)
B = 626.2940	--	Distance traveled by the vehicle while decelerating (ft)

c) Total stopping distance (ft).

Compute the total stopping distance. Use Equation No. 159, page 265. Press ENTER. Press R/S every time you are prompted.

Display	Keys	Description
A? 275.0000	R/S	Distance traveled by the vehicle during the perception and reaction of the driver before stopping (ft)
B? 626.2940	R/S	Distance traveled by the vehicle while decelerating (ft)
S = 901.2940	--	Total stopping distance (ft)

The answer is (C).

Problem 12.2

A car is traveling at a speed of 60 mi/hr on a highway with a grade of 1% downhill when suddenly debris appeared on the car's path. The driver's reaction time is 2.5 seconds and the deceleration rate is 12.2 ft/sec^2. What is most nearly the stopping sight distance required to avoid hitting the debris?

(A) 400 ft
(B) 500 ft
(C) 550 ft
(D) 600 ft

Solution

Calculate the stopping sight distance. Use Equation No. 160, page 265 given deceleration. Press ENTER.

Display	Keys	Description
T?	2.5 R/S	Driver reaction time (sec)
V?	60 R/S	Speed of car (mi/hr)
A?	12.2 R/S	Deceleration rate (ft/sec^2)
G?	1 +/− R/S	Grade of pavement (%)
S = 545.8073	--	Stopping sight distance (ft)

The answer is (C).

Notes: The grade of pavement is negative (–) because the car is traveling downhill. The +/– key is located at the right side of ENTER key for HP 35s and above the 8 key for HP 33s.

Problem 12.3

A car is traveling at a speed of 60 mi/hr on a highway with a grade of 1% downhill when suddenly debris appeared on the car's path. The coefficient of friction between the tires and the pavement is 0.35. The driver's reaction time is 2.5 seconds. What is most nearly the stopping sight distance required to avoid hitting the debris?

(A) 450 ft
(B) 500 ft
(C) 550 ft
(D) 575 ft

Solution

Step 1. Calculate the stopping sight distance. Use Equation No. 161, page 266 given coefficient of friction. Press ENTER.

Display	Keys	Description
T?	2.5 R/S	Driver reaction time (seconds)
V?	60 R/S	Speed of the car (mi/hr)
F?	.35 R/S	Coefficient of friction between the tire and pavement
G?	1 +/– R/S	Grade of pavement (%)
S = 573.4412	--	Stopping sight distance (ft)

The answer is (D).

CHAPTER 13: HORIZONTAL CURVE (ENGLISH UNITS)

13.1 Radius of Curve

13.1.1 Radius of Curve Given Long Chord and Intersection Angle

$$R = \frac{C}{2\sin\left(\frac{I}{2}\right)}$$ Equation No. 162

The equation is entered as

162RADIUSGIVCI
R=C÷2÷SIN(I÷2)

Where:

R = radius of curve R (ft)
C = long chord C (ft) (PC to PT)
I = intersection angle I (deg)

Keystrokes

HP 35s Checksum; Length of Equation: **CK=9758; LN=14**

[RCL] [R] [↰] [=] [RCL] [C] [÷] [2] [÷] [SIN] [RCL] [I] [÷] [2] [ENTER]

HP 33s Checksum; Length of Equation: **CK=9758; LN=14**

[RCL] [R] [↱] [=] [RCL] [C] [÷] [2] [÷] [SIN] [RCL] [I] [÷] [2] [↱] [)] [ENTER]

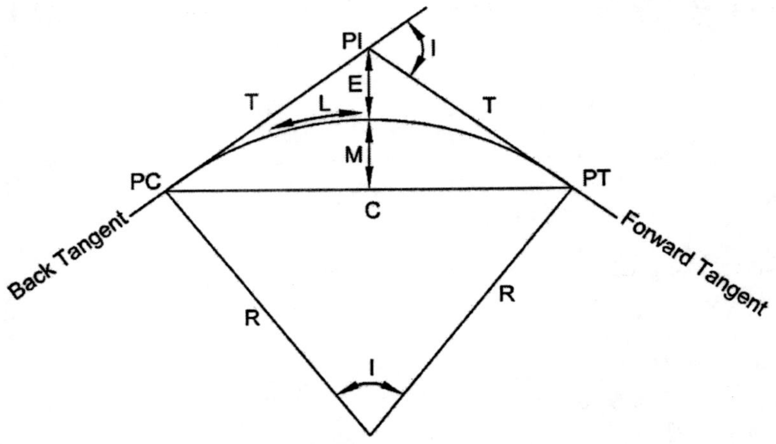

Figure 13-1 Horizontal Curve

≈≈≈≈≈≈≈≈≈≈

13.1.2 Radius of Curve Given Degree of Curve

$R = \dfrac{5729.58}{D}$ Equation No. 163

The equation is entered as

163RADIUSGIVD
R=5729.58÷D

Where:

R = radius of curve R (ft)
D = degree of curve D (deg)

Keystrokes

HP 35s Checksum; Length of Equation: **CK=D3AC; LN=11**

[RCL] [R] [↰] [=] [5] [7] [2] [9] [.] [5] [8] [÷] [RCL] [D] [ENTER]

HP 33s Checksum; Length of Equation: **CK=D3AC; LN=11**

[RCL] [R] [↱] [=] [5] [7] [2] [9] [.] [5] [8] [÷] [RCL] [D] [ENTER]

≈≈≈≈≈≈≈≈≈≈

13.2 Tangent of Curve

13.2.1 Tangent of Curve Given Radius and Intersection Angle

$$T = R\tan\left(\frac{I}{2}\right)$$ Equation No. 164

The equation is entered as

164TANGIVRI
T=R×TAN(I÷2)

Where:

T = tangent of curve T (ft)
R = radius of curve R (ft)
I = intersection angle I (deg)

Keystrokes

HP 35s Checksum; Length of Equation: **CK=7443; LN=12**

[RCL] [T] [↰] [=] [RCL] [R] [×] [TAN] [RCL] [I] [÷] [2] [ENTER]

HP 33s Checksum; Length of Equation: **CK=7443; LN=12**

[RCL] [T] [↱] [=] [RCL] [R] [×] [TAN] [RCL] [I] [÷] [2] [↱] [)] [ENTER]

≈≈≈≈≈≈≈≈≈≈

13.2.2 Tangent of Curve Given Long Chord and Intersection Angle

$$T = \frac{C}{2\cos\left(\frac{I}{2}\right)}$$ Equation No. 165

The equation is entered as

165TANGIVCI
T=C÷2÷COS(I÷2)

Where:

T = tangent of curve T (ft)
C = long chord C (ft) (PC to PT)
I = intersection angle I (deg)

Keystrokes

HP 35s Checksum; Length of Equation: **CK=5469; LN=14**

[RCL] [T] [↰] [=] [RCL] [C] [÷] [2] [÷] [COS] [RCL] [I] [÷] [2] [ENTER]

HP 33s Checksum; Length of Equation: **CK=5469; LN=14**

[RCL] [T] [↱] [=] [RCL] [C] [÷] [2] [÷] [COS] [RCL] [I] [÷] [2] [↱] [)] [ENTER]

≈≈≈≈≈≈≈≈≈≈

13.3 Length of Curve

13.3.1 Length of Curve Given Radius and Intersection Angle

$$L = \frac{\pi RI}{180}$$ Equation No. 166

The equation is entered as

166LOFCURVGIVRI
L=π×R×I÷180

Where:

L = length of curve L (ft)
R = radius of curve R (ft)
I = intersection angle I (deg)

Keystrokes

HP 35s Checksum; Length of Equation: **CK=61F4; LN=11**

[RCL] [L] [↰] [=] [↰] [π] [×] [RCL] [R] [×] [RCL] [I] [÷] [1] [8] [0] [ENTER]

HP 33s Checksum; Length of Equation: **CK=61F4; LN=11**

[RCL] [L] [↱] [=] [↱] [π] [×] [RCL] [R] [×] [RCL] [I] [÷] [1] [8] [0] [ENTER]

≈≈≈≈≈≈≈≈≈≈

13.3.2 Length of Curve Given Intersection Angle and Degree of Curve

$$L = \frac{I}{D} \times 100$$ Equation No. 167

The equation is entered as

167LOFCURVGIVID
L=I÷D×100

Where:

L = length of curve L (ft)
I = intersection angle I (deg)
D = degree of curve D (deg)

Keystrokes

HP 35s Checksum; Length of Equation: **CK=F4BC; LN=9**

[RCL] [L] [↰] [=] [RCL] [I] [÷] [RCL] [D] [×] [1] [0] [0] [ENTER]

HP 33s Checksum; Length of Equation: **CK=F4BC; LN=9**

[RCL] [L] [↱] [=] [RCL] [I] [÷] [RCL] [D] [×] [1] [0] [0] [ENTER]

≈≈≈≈≈≈≈≈≈≈

13.4 Middle Ordinate

13.4.1 Middle Ordinate Given Radius of Curve and Intersection Angle

$$\frac{R-M}{R}=\cos\left(\frac{I}{2}\right)$$ Equation No. 168

The equation is entered as

168MIDORDRI
(R−M)÷R=COS(I÷2)

Where:

R = radius of curve R (ft)
M = middle ordinate of curve M (ft)
I = intersection angle I (deg)

Keystrokes

HP 35s Checksum; Length of Equation: **CK=B036; LN=16**

[()] [RCL] [R] [−] [RCL] [M] [>] [÷] [RCL] [R] [↰] [=] [COS] [RCL] [I] [÷] [2] [ENTER]

HP 33s Checksum; Length of Equation: **CK=B036; LN=16**

[↱] [(] [RCL] [R] [−] [RCL] [M] [↱] [)] [÷] [RCL] [R] [↱] [=] [COS] [RCL] [I] [÷] [2] [↱] [)] [ENTER]

Note: Press SOLVE M to solve for the middle ordinate of curve.

≈≈≈≈≈≈≈≈≈≈

13.5 External Distance

13.5.1 External Distance with Radius of Curve and Intersection Angle

$$E = R\left[\frac{1}{\cos\left(\frac{I}{2}\right)} - 1\right]$$ Equation No. 169

The equation is entered as

169EXTDISTRI
E=R(1÷COS(I÷2)−1)

Where:

E = external distance of curve E (ft)
R = radius of curve R (ft)
I = intersection angle I (deg)

Keystrokes

HP 35s Checksum; Length of Equation: **CK=0F4F; LN=17**

[RCL] [E] [↰] [=] [RCL] [R] [()] [1] [÷] [COS] [RCL] [I] [÷] [2] [>] [−] [1] [ENTER]

HP 33s Checksum; Length of Equation: **CK=AAE6; LN=18**

[RCL] [E] [↱] [=] [RCL] [R] [×] [↱] [(] [1] [÷] [COS] [RCL] [I] [÷] [2] [↱] [)] [−] [1] [↱] [)] [ENTER]

≈≈≈≈≈≈≈≈≈≈

Sample Problem

Problem 13.1

A horizontal curve with a 2,000-foot radius is shown below. The station of the point of intersection (PI) is 35+00. The tangent distance, degree of curve, length of curve, external distance, and length of middle ordinate are most nearly

	Tangent Distance (ft)	Degree of Curve (deg)	Length of Curve (ft)	External Distance (ft)	Length of Middle Ordinate (ft)
(A)	1,700	2	2,000	800	575
(B)	1,800	2	2,500	700	450
(C)	1,900	2.5	3,000	750	500
(D)	2,000	3	3,100	800	575

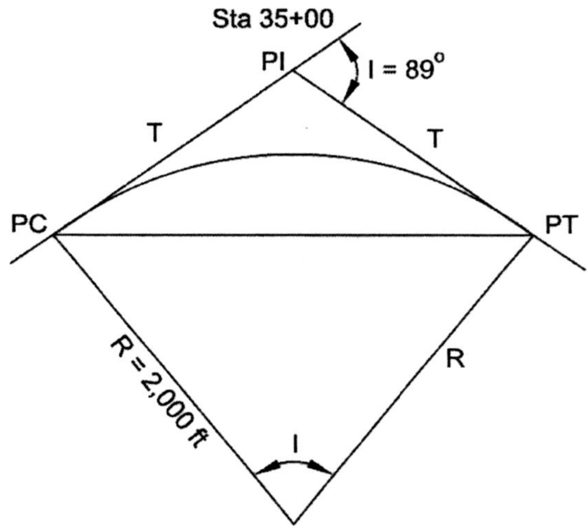

Solution

a) Tangent distance

Calculate the tangent distance. Use Equation No. 164, page 273. Press ENTER.

Display	Keys	Description
R?	2000 R/S	Radius of horizontal curve (ft)
I?	89 R/S	Intersection angle
T = 1,965.3945	--	Tangent distance (ft)

Note: If the intersection angle is 89° 28' 30'', press 89.2830 [↰] 8 for HP 35s, 89.2830 [↰] 5 for HP 33s.

b) Degree of curve.

Solve the degree of curve. Use Equation No. 163, page 272. Press SOLVE D.

Display	Keys	Description
R? 2,000.0000	R/S	Radius of horizontal curve (ft)
D = 2.8648	--	Degree of curve (deg)

c) Length of curve

Calculate the length of curve. Use Equation No. 166, page 274. Press ENTER. Press R/S every time you are prompted. You'll get L = 3,106.6861 (ft).

d) External distance

Compute the external distance. Use Equation No. 169, page 276. Press ENTER. Press R/S every time you are prompted. You'll get E = 804.0641 (ft).

e) Length of middle ordinate

Solve the middle ordinate of curve. Use Equation No. 168, page 275. Press SOLVE M. Press R/S every time you are prompted. You'll get M = 573.4991 (ft).

The answer is (D).

CHAPTER 14: EQUAL-TANGENT VERTICAL CURVES (ENGLISH UNITS)

14.1 Crest Curve

14.1.1 Stopping Sight Distance Less Than Length of Curve (S < L)

$$L = \frac{(G_1 - G_2)S^2}{2158}$$ Equation No. 170

The equation is entered as

170SSDCRESTSLTL
L=(G−H)×S^2÷2158

Where:

L = length of curve L (ft)
G = grade of G_1 (%) +
H = grade of G_2 (%) −
S = stopping sight distance according to design speed S (ft)

Keystrokes

HP 35s Checksum; Length of Equation: **CK=4BDE; LN=16**

[RCL] [L] [↰] [=] [()] [RCL] [G] [−] [RCL] [H] [>] [×] [RCL] [S] [y^x] [2] [÷] [2] [1] [5] [8] [ENTER]

HP 33s Checksum; Length of Equation: **CK=4BDE; LN=16**

[RCL] [L] [↱] [=] [↱] [(] [RCL] [G] [−] [RCL] [H] [↱] [)] [×] [RCL] [S] [y^x] [2] [÷] [2] [1] [5] [8] [ENTER]

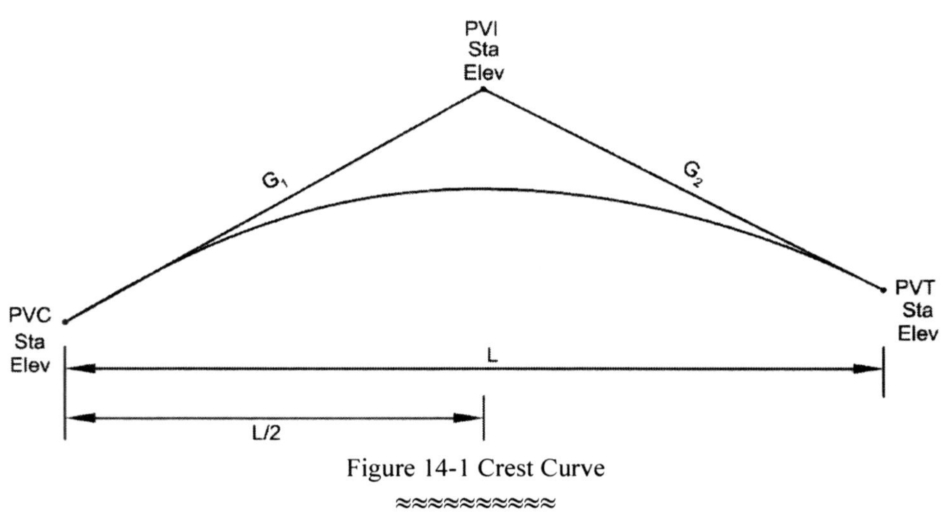

Figure 14-1 Crest Curve

≈≈≈≈≈≈≈≈≈≈

14.1.2 Stopping Sight Distance Greater Than Length of Curve (S > L)

$$L = 2S - \frac{2158}{G_1 - G_2}$$ Equation No. 171

The equation is entered as

171SSDCRESTSGTL
L=2×S−2158÷(G−H)

Where:

L = length of curve L (ft)
S = stopping sight distance according to design speed S (ft)
G = grade of G_1 (%) +
H = grade of G_2 (%) −

Keystrokes

HP 35s Checksum; Length of Equation: **CK=D960; LN=16**

[RCL] [L] [↰] [=] [2] [×] [RCL] [S] [−] [2] [1] [5] [8] [÷] [()] [RCL] [G] [−] [RCL] [H] [ENTER]

HP 33s Checksum; Length of Equation: **CK=D960; LN=16**

[RCL] [L] [↱] [=] [2] [×] [RCL] [S] [−] [2] [1] [5] [8] [÷] [↱] [(] [RCL] [G] [−] [RCL] [H] [↱] [)] [ENTER]

≈≈≈≈≈≈≈≈≈≈

14.1.3 Passing Sight Distance Less Than Length of Curve (S < L)

$$L = \frac{(G_1 - G_2)S^2}{2800}$$ Equation No. 172

The equation is entered as

172PSDSLTL
L=(G−H)×S^2÷2800

Where:

L = length of curve L (ft)
G = grade of G_1 (%) +
H = grade of G_2 (%) −
S = passing sight distance S (ft)

Keystrokes

HP 35s Checksum; Length of Equation: **CK=ABB2; LN=16**

[RCL] [L] [↰] [=] [()] [RCL] [G] [−] [RCL] [H] [>] [×] [RCL] [S] [y^x] [2] [÷] [2] [8] [0] [0] [ENTER]

HP 33s Checksum; Length of Equation: **CK=ABB2; LN=16**

[RCL] [L] [↱] [=] [↱] [(] [RCL] [G] [−] [RCL] [H] [↱] [)] [×] [RCL] [S] [y^x] [2] [÷] [2] [8] [0] [0] [ENTER]

≈≈≈≈≈≈≈≈≈≈

14.1.4 Passing Sight Distance Greater Than Length of Curve (S > L)

$$L = 2S - \frac{2800}{G_1 - G_2}$$ Equation No. 173

The equation is entered as

173PSDSGTL
L=2×S−2800÷(G−H)

Where:

L = length of curve L (ft)
S = passing sight distance according to design speed S (ft)
G = grade of G_1 (%) +
H = grade of G_2 (%) −

Keystrokes

HP 35s Checksum; Length of Equation: **CK=C0AF; LN=16**

[RCL] [L] [↰] [=] [2] [×] [RCL] [S] [−] [2] [8] [0] [0] [÷] [()] [RCL] [G] [−] [RCL] [H] [ENTER]

HP 33s Checksum; Length of Equation: **CK=C0AF; LN=16**

[RCL] [L] [↱] [=] [2] [×] [RCL] [S] [−] [2] [8] [0] [0] [÷] [↱] [(] [RCL] [G] [−] [RCL] [H] [↱] [)] [ENTER]

≈≈≈≈≈≈≈≈≈≈

14.2 Sag Curve

14.2.1 Stopping Sight Distance Less Than Length of Curve (S < L)

$$L = \frac{(G_2 - G_1)S^2}{400 + 3.5S}$$ Equation No. 174

The equation is entered as

174SSDSAGSLTL
L=(H−G)×S^2÷(400+3.5×S)

Where:

L = length of curve L (ft)
H = grade of G_2 (%) +
G = grade of G_1 (%) −
S = stopping sight distance according to design speed S (ft)

Keystrokes

HP 35s Checksum; Length of Equation: **CK=5230; LN=23**

[RCL] [L] [↰] [=] [()] [RCL] [H] [−] [RCL] [G] [>] [×] [RCL] [S] [y^x] [2] [÷] [()] [4] [0] [0] [+] [3] [·] [5] [×] [RCL] [S] [ENTER]

HP 33s Checksum; Length of Equation: **CK=5230; LN=23**

[RCL] [L] [↱] [=] [↱] [(] [RCL] [H] [−] [RCL] [G] [↱] [)] [×] [RCL] [S] [y^x] [2] [÷] [↱] [(] [4] [0] [0] [+] [3] [·] [5] [×] [RCL] [S] [↱] [)] [ENTER]

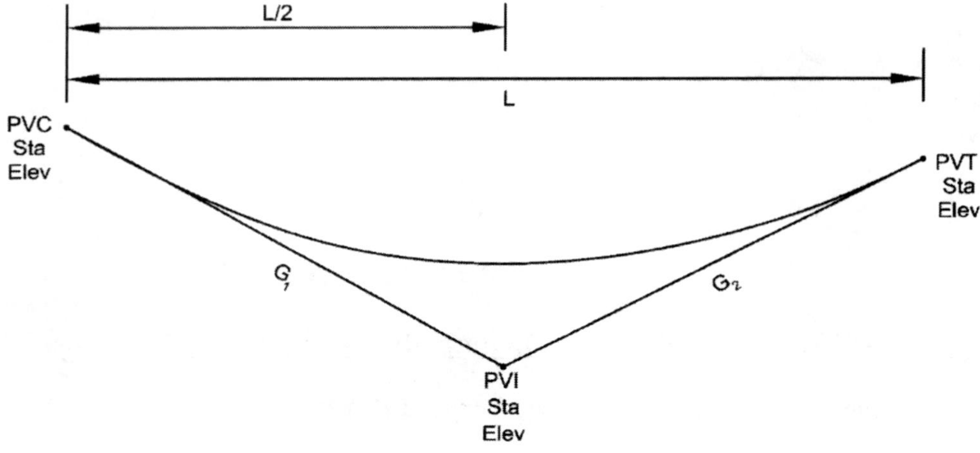

Figure 14-2 Sag Curve

≈≈≈≈≈≈≈≈≈≈

14.2.2 Stopping Sight Distance Greater Than Length of Curve (S > L)

$$L = 2S - \frac{400 + 3.5S}{G_2 - G_1} \qquad \text{Equation No. 175}$$

The equation is entered as

175SSDSAGSGTL
L=2×S−(400+3.5×S)÷(H−G)

Where:

L = length of curve L (ft)
S = stopping sight distance according to design speed S (ft)
H = grade of G_2 (%) +
G = grade of G_1 (%) −

Keystrokes

HP 35s Checksum; Length of Equation: **CK=FF42; LN=23**

[RCL] [L] [↰] [=] [2] [×] [RCL] [S] [−] [()] [4] [0] [0] [+] [3] [·] [5] [×] [RCL] [S] [>] [÷] [()] [RCL] [H] [−] [RCL] [G]
[ENTER]

HP 33s Checksum; Length of Equation: **CK=FF42; LN=23**

[RCL] [L] [↱] [=] [2] [×] [RCL] [S] [−] [↱] [(] [4] [0] [0] [+] [3] [·] [5] [×] [RCL] [S] [↱] [)] [÷] [↱] [(] [RCL] [H]
[−] [RCL] [G] [↱] [)] [ENTER]

≈≈≈≈≈≈≈≈≈≈

14.3 Curve Elevation

14.3.1 Curve Elevation Given Elevation of Point of Vertical Curve (PVC)

$$C = PVC_{elev} + G_1X + \left(\frac{G_2 - G_1}{200L}\right)X^2 \qquad \text{Equation No. 176}$$

The equation is entered as

176CEGIVELPVC
C=Y+G÷100×X+(H−G)÷200÷L×X^2

Where:

C = curve elevation at point on crest or sag curve C (ft)
Y = Point of Vertical Curve (PVC) elevation PVC_{elev} (ft)
G = grade of G_1 (%) + or −
X = distance from PVC to point or from PVC to highest or lowest point of curve X (ft)
H = grade of G_2 (%) − or +
L = length of curve L (ft)

Keystrokes

HP 35s Checksum; Length of Equation: **CK=5B26; LN=27**

[RCL] [C] [↰] [=] [RCL] [Y] [+] [RCL] [G] [÷] [1] [0] [0] [×] [RCL] [X] [+] [()] [RCL] [H] [−] [RCL] [G] [>] [÷] [2] [0] [0] [÷] [RCL] [L] [×] [RCL] [X] [y^x] [2] [ENTER]

HP 33s Checksum; Length of Equation: **CK=5B26; LN=27**

[RCL] [C] [↱] [=] [RCL] [Y] [+] [RCL] [G] [÷] [1] [0] [0] [×] [RCL] [X] [+] [↱] [(] [RCL] [H] [−] [RCL] [G] [↱] [)] [÷] [2] [0] [0] [÷] [RCL] [L] [×] [RCL] [X] [y^x] [2] [ENTER]

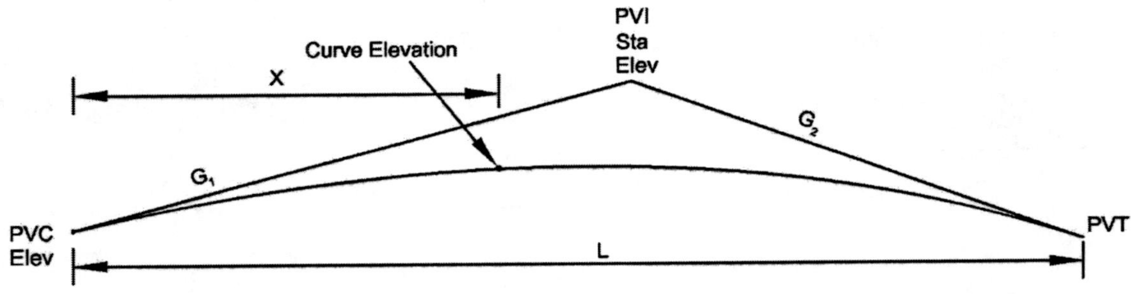

Figure 14-3 Vertical Curve Elevation

≈≈≈≈≈≈≈≈≈≈

14.3.2 Curve Elevation Given Elevation of Point of Vertical Intersection (PVI) and Length of Curve

$$C = PVI_{elev} - \frac{G_1}{200}L + \frac{G_1}{100}X + \left(\frac{G_2 - G_1}{200L}\right)X^2$$ Equation No. 177

The equation is entered as

177CEGIVELPVI
C=E−G÷200×L+G÷100×X+(H−G)÷200÷L×X^2

Where:

C = curve elevation at point on crest or sag curve C (ft)
E = PVI elevation PVI_{elev} (ft)
G = grade of G_1 (%) + or −
L = length of curve L (ft)
X = distance from PVC to point or from PVC to highest or lowest point of curve X (ft)
H = grade of G_2 (%) – or +

Keystrokes

HP 35s Checksum; Length of Equation: **CK=5B78; LN=35**

[RCL] [C] [↰] [=] [RCL] [E] [−] [RCL] [G] [÷] [2] [0] [0] [×] [RCL] [L] [+] [RCL] [G] [÷] [1] [0] [0] [×] [RCL] [X] [+] [()] [RCL] [H] [−] [RCL] [G] [>] [÷] [2] [0] [0] [÷] [RCL] [L] [×] [RCL] [X] [y^x] [2] [ENTER]

HP 33s Checksum; Length of Equation: **CK=5B78; LN=35**

[RCL] [C] [↱] [=] [RCL] [E] [−] [RCL] [G] [÷] [2] [0] [0] [×] [RCL] [L] [+] [RCL] [G] [÷] [1] [0] [0] [×] [RCL] [X] [+] [↱] [(] [RCL] [H] [−] [RCL] [G] [↱] [)] [÷] [2] [0] [0] [÷] [RCL] [L] [×] [RCL] [X] [y^x] [2] [ENTER]

Notes: The elevation of the highest point on the curve can be calculated by first finding the X using Equation No. 179, page 286. Then, use Equation No. 177 with given PVI elevation and length of curve. The elevation of the lowest point on the curve can be obtained by first calculating the X using Equation No. 181, page 288. Then, use Equation No. 177 with given PVI elevation and length of curve. Sometimes the length of the curve is not given but the stations of PVI and PVT are given; the length of the curve can be determined by subtracting the station of PVC from the station of PVT.

≈≈≈≈≈≈≈≈≈≈

14.3.3 Curve Elevation for Clearance Given Elevation of Point of Vertical Intersection (PVI), Station of Structure, and Length of Curve

$$C = PVI_{elev} - \frac{G_1}{200}L + \frac{G_1}{100}\left[S - \left(I - \frac{L}{2}\right)\right] + \left(\frac{G_2 - G_1}{200L}\right)\left[S - \left(I - \frac{L}{2}\right)\right]^2$$ Equation No. 178

The equation is entered as

178CEVERTCLEAR
C=E−G÷200×L+G÷100(S−(I−L÷2))+(H−G)÷200÷L(S−(I−L÷2))^2

Where:

C = curve elevation at point on crest or sag curve C (ft)
E = PVI elevation PVI_{elev} (ft)
G = grade of G_1 (%) + or −
L = length of curve L (ft)
S = station of structure vertical to the curve for vertical clearance S (ft)
I = station of PVI I (ft)
H = grade of G_2 (%) – or +

Keystrokes

HP 35s Checksum; Length of Equation: **CK=A6EF; LN=53**

RCL C ↰ = RCL E − RCL G ÷ 2 0 0 × RCL L + RCL G ÷ 1 0 0 () RCL S − () RCL I − RCL L ÷ 2 > > + () RCL H − RCL G > ÷ 2 0 0 ÷ RCL L () RCL S − () RCL I − RCL L ÷ 2 > > yˣ 2 ENTER

HP 33s Checksum; Length of Equation: **CK=F645; LN=55**

RCL C ↱ = RCL E − RCL G ÷ 2 0 0 × RCL L + RCL G ÷ 1 0 0 × ↱ (RCL S − ↱ (RCL I − RCL L ÷ 2 ↱) ↱) + ↱ (RCL H − RCL G ↱) ÷ 2 0 0 ÷ RCL L × ↱ (RCL S − ↱ (RCL I − RCL L ÷ 2 ↱) ↱) yˣ 2 ENTER

Notes: This equation can be used to calculate the curve elevation with given station and elevation of PVI, station of PVC, elevation and station of structure (e.g., bridge). You can then calculate the vertical clearance between the curve and the structure.

≈≈≈≈≈≈≈≈≈≈

14.4 Crest Curve Solving Station of Highest Point

14.4.1 Solving Distance from Point of Vertical Curve (PVC) to Highest Point

$$X = \frac{G_1 L}{G_1 - G_2}$$ Equation No. 179

The equation is entered as

179CRESDISTXHP
X=G×L÷(G−H)

Where:

X = distance from PVC to highest point X (ft)
G = grade of G_1 (%) +
L = length of curve L (ft)
H = grade of G_2 (%) −

Keystrokes

HP 35s Checksum; Length of Equation: **CK=D405; LN=11**

RCL X ↰ = RCL G × RCL L ÷ () RCL G − RCL H ENTER

HP 33s Checksum; Length of Equation: **CK=D405; LN=11**

RCL X ↱ = RCL G × RCL L ÷ ↱ (RCL G − RCL H ↱) ENTER

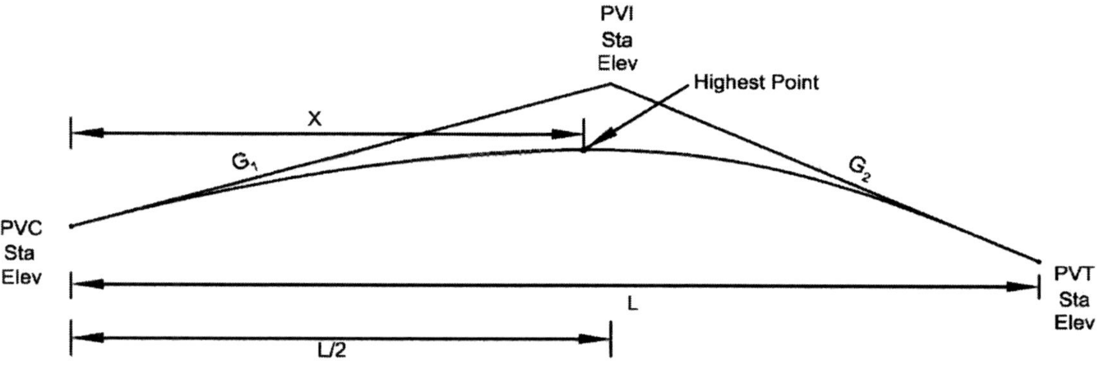

Figure 14-4 Crest Curve with Highest Point

≈≈≈≈≈≈≈≈≈≈

14.4.2 Station of Highest Point Given Station of Point of Vertical Intersection (PVI) and Length of Curve

$$S = I - \frac{L}{2} + \frac{G_1 L}{G_1 - G_2}$$ Equation No. 180

The equation is entered as

180STAHPGIVIL
S=I−L÷2+G×L÷(G−H)

Where:

S = station of highest point S
I = station of PVI I
L = length of curve L (ft)
G = grade of G_1 (%) +
H = grade of G_2 (%) −

Keystrokes

HP 35s Checksum; Length of Equation: **CK=7AD3; LN=17**

[RCL] [S] [↰] [=] [RCL] [I] [−] [RCL] [L] [÷] [2] [+] [RCL] [G] [×] [RCL] [L] [÷] [()] [RCL] [G] [−] [RCL] [H] [ENTER]

HP 33s Checksum; Length of Equation: **CK=7AD3; LN=17**

[RCL] [S] [↱] [=] [RCL] [I] [−] [RCL] [L] [÷] [2] [+] [RCL] [G] [×] [RCL] [L] [÷] [↱] [(] [RCL] [G] [−] [RCL] [H] [↱] [)] [ENTER]

≈≈≈≈≈≈≈≈≈≈

14.5.1 Solving Distance from Point of Vertical Curve (PVC) to Lowest Point

$$X = \frac{-G_1 L}{G_2 - G_1}$$ Equation No. 181

The equation is entered as

181SAGDISTXLP
X=−G×L÷(H−G)

Where:

X = distance from PVC to lowest point X (ft)
G = grade of G_1 (%) −
L = length of curve L (ft)
H = grade of G_2 (%) +

Keystrokes

HP 35s Checksum; Length of Equation: **CK=E9DE; LN=12**

[RCL] [X] [⮌] [=] [+/−] [RCL] [G] [×] [RCL] [L] [÷] [()] [RCL] [H] [−] [RCL] [G] [ENTER]

HP 33s Checksum; Length of Equation: **CK=125A; LN=12**

[RCL] [X] [⮎] [=] [+/−] [RCL] [G] [×] [RCL] [L] [÷] [⮎] [(] [RCL] [H] [−] [RCL] [G] [⮎] [)] [ENTER]

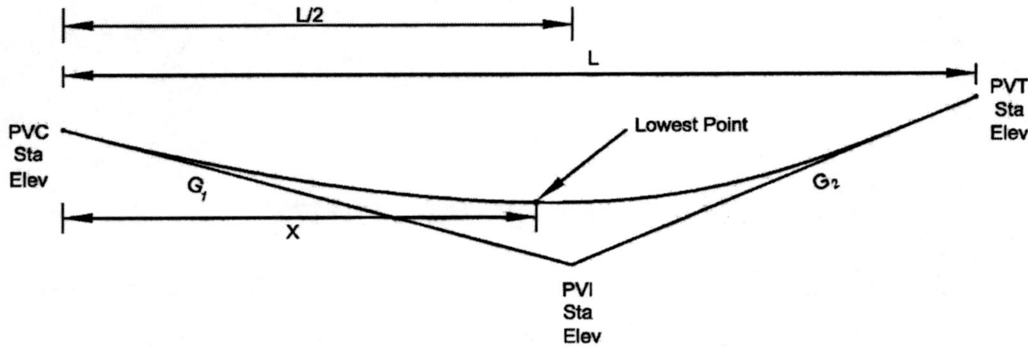

Figure 14-5 Sag Curve with Lowest Point

≈≈≈≈≈≈≈≈≈≈

14.5.2 Station of Lowest Point Given Station of Point of Vertical Intersection (PVI) and Length of Curve

$$S = I - \frac{L}{2} - \frac{G_1 L}{G_2 - G_1}$$ Equation No. 182

The equation is entered as

182STALPTGIVIL
S=I−L÷2−(G×L÷(H−G))

Where:

S = station of lowest point S
I = station of PVI I
L = length of curve L (ft)
G = grade of G_1 (%) −
H = grade of G_2 (%) +

Keystrokes

HP 35s Checksum; Length of Equation: **CK=CAC2; LN=19**

[RCL] [S] [↰] [=] [RCL] [I] [−] [RCL] [L] [÷] [2] [−] [()] [RCL] [G] [×] [RCL] [L] [÷] [()] [RCL] [H] [−] [RCL] [G] [ENTER]

HP 33s Checksum; Length of Equation: **CK=CAC2; LN=19**

[RCL] [S] [↱] [=] [RCL] [I] [−] [RCL] [L] [÷] [2] [−] [↱] [(] [RCL] [G] [×] [RCL] [L] [÷] [↱] [(] [RCL] [H] [−] [RCL] [G] [↱] [)] [↱] [)] [ENTER]

≈≈≈≈≈≈≈≈≈≈

Problem 14.1

A freeway has a 60 mi/hr design speed. The vertical alignment of the freeway is shown. What is most nearly the stopping sight distance assuming the height of driver's eye is 3.5 feet above the roadway and object's height is 2 feet?

(A) 555 ft (C) 715 ft
(B) 655 ft (D) 815 ft

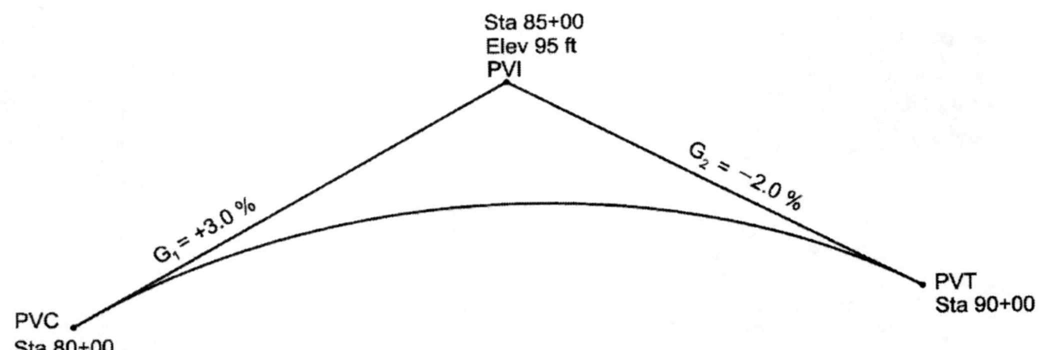

Solution

Solve the stopping sight distance. Assume S (stopping sight distance) < L (length of curve). Use Equation No. 170, page 279. Press SOLVE S.

Display	Keys	Description
L?	9000 ENTER 8000 −	Length of the curve (ft)
L? 1000.0000	R/S	
G?	3 R/S	Grade of G_1 (%)
H?	2 +/− R/S	Grade of G_2 (%)
S = 656.9627	--	Stopping sight distance (ft)

Assuming S > L, use Equation No. 171. S is equal to 715.8000 which is less than the length of curve. Therefore, this is incorrect answer. The assumption S < L with Equation No. 170 is correct. Therefore, the stopping sight distance is 656.9627 ft.

The answer is (B).

Note: The +/− key is located at the right side of ENTER key for HP 35s and above the 8 key for HP 33s.

Problem 14.2

The required length of a vertical curve with an uphill grade of 2% followed by a downhill grade of −3% for a highway with a 70 mi/hr design speed is most nearly

(A) 950 ft (C) 1,030 ft
(B) 1,000 ft (D) 1,235 ft

Solution

Calculate the required length of curve. Assume S (stopping sight distance) < L (length of curve). Use Equation No. 170, page 279. Press ENTER.

Display	Keys	Description
G?	2 R/S	Grade of G_1 (%)
H?	3 +/− R/S	Grade of G_2 (%)
S?	730 R/S	Stopping sight distance based on designed speed from published table (ft)
L = 1,234.7081	--	Required length of the curve (ft)

Assuming S > L, use Equation No. 171. S is equal to 1,028.4000 which is less than the required length of curve. Therefore, this is incorrect answer. The assumption S < L with Equation No. 170 is correct. Therefore, the required length of curve is 1,234.7081ft.

The answer is (D).

Problem 14.3

The vertical alignment of a highway is shown below. The stopping sight distance is most nearly

(A) 600 ft (C) 800 ft
(B) 700 ft (D) 900 ft

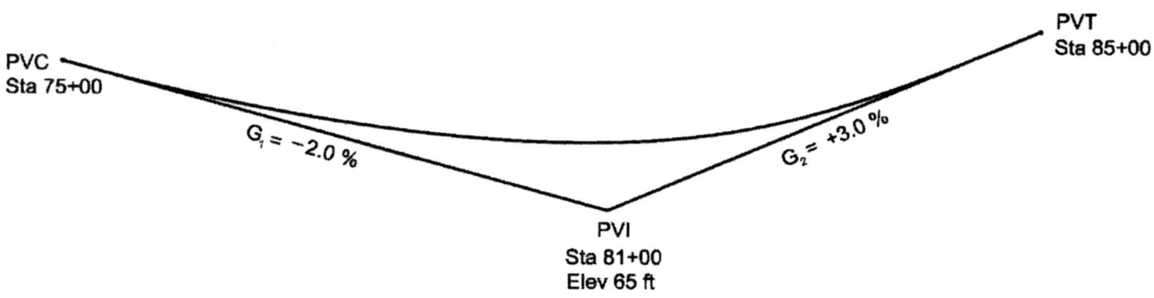

Solution

Solve the stopping sight distance. Assume S (stopping sight distance) < L (length of curve). Use Equation No. 174, page 281. Press SOLVE S.

Display	Keys	Description
L?	8500 ENTER 7500 –	Length of the curve (ft)
L? 1000.0000	R/S	
H?	3 R/S	Grade of G_2 (%)
G?	2 +/– R/S	Grade of G_1 (%)
S = 800.0000	--	Stopping sight distance (ft)

Assuming S > L, use Equation No. 175. S is equal to 830.7692 which is less than the length of curve. Therefore, this is incorrect answer. The assumption S < L with Equation No. 174 is correct. Therefore, the stopping sight distance is 800 ft.

The answer is (C).

Problem 14.4

A freeway has a 70 mi/hr design speed. The vertical alignment of the freeway is shown. The maximum required length of the vertical curve is most nearly

(A) 922 ft
(B) 992 ft
(C) 1,000 ft
(D) 1,010 ft

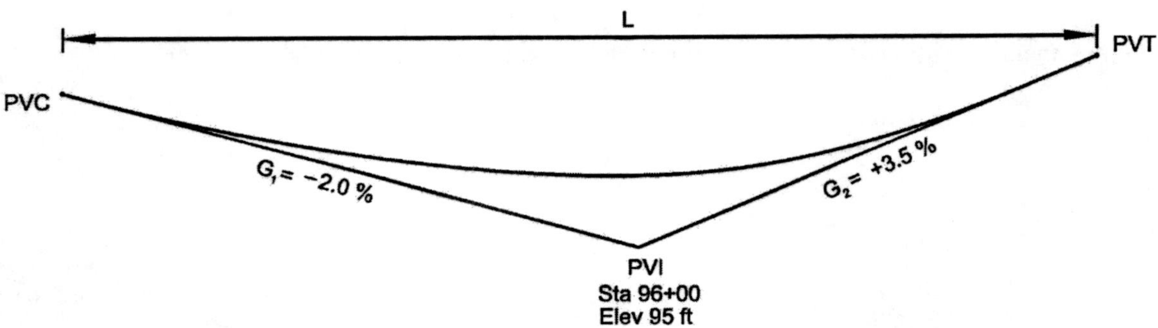

Solution

Calculate the maximum required length of vertical curve. Assume S (stopping sight distance) < L (length of curve). Use Equation No. 174, page 281. Press ENTER.

Display	Keys	Description
H?	3.5 R/S	Grade of G_2 (%)
G?	2 +/– R/S	Grade of G_1 (%)
S?	730 R/S	Stopping sight distance based on designed speed from published table (ft)
L = 991.8613	--	Maximum length of curve (ft)

Assuming S > L, use Equation No. 175. L is equal to 922.7273 which is greater than the stopping sight distance. Therefore, this is incorrect answer. The assumption S < L with Equation No. 174 is correct. Therefore, the maximum required length of curve is 991.8613 ft.

The answer is (B).

Problem 14.5

A 1,000-foot crest vertical curve with equal legs has a G_1 grade of 3% and a G_2 grade of −3% as shown. The Point of Vertical Intersection is located at Sta. 95+00 and elevation 155 feet. The elevations at Stations 93+00, 96+00, and 98+00 are most nearly

	Elevation at Sta 93+00 (ft)	Elevation at Sta 96+00 (ft)	Elevation at Sta 98+00 (ft)
(A)	146	147	145
(B)	149	150	145
(C)	150	152	146
(D)	150	147	146

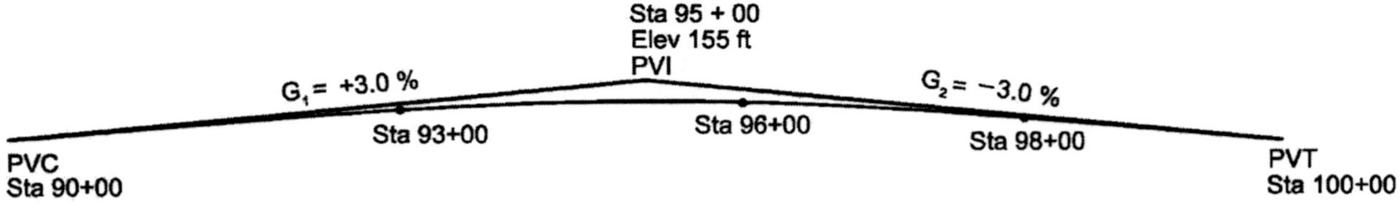

Solution

Option 1

Step 1. Calculate the elevation at Sta 93+00. Use Equation No. 176, page 283. Press ENTER.

Display	Keys	Description
Y?	155 ENTER 500 ENTER .03 × –	Elevation at PVC (ft)
Y? 140.0000	R/S	
G?	3 R/S	Grade of G_1 (%)
X?	300 R/S	Distance from PVC to Station 93+00 (ft)
H?	3 +/– R/S	Grade of G_2 (%)
L?	1000 R/S	Length of the curve (ft)
C = 146.3000	--	Elevation at Station 93+00 (ft)

Step 2. Compute the elevation at Station 96+00. Use Equation No. 176, page 283. Press ENTER.

Display	Keys	Description
Y? 140.0000	R/S	Elevation at PVC (ft)
G? 3.0000	R/S	Grade of G_1 (%)
X?	600 R/S	Distance from PVC to Station 93+00 (ft)
H? −3.0000	R/S	Grade of G_2 (%)
L? 1,000.0000	R/S	Length of the curve (ft)
C = 147.2000	--	Elevation at Station 96+00 (ft)

Step 3. Determine the elevation at Station 98+00. Use Equation No. 176, page 283. Press ENTER.

Display	Keys	Description
Y? 140.0000	R/S	Elevation at PVC (ft)
G? 3.0000	R/S	Grade of G_1 (%)
X?	800 R/S	Distance from PVC to Station 93+00 (ft)
H? −3.0000	R/S	Grade of G_2 (%)
L? 1,000.0000	R/S	Length of the curve (ft)
C = 144.8000	--	Elevation at Station 98+00 (ft)

Option 2

Step 1. Calculate the elevation at Sta 93+00. The station and elevation of PVI are given; Use Equation No. 178, page 285. Press ENTER.

Display	Keys	Description
E?	155 R/S	Elevation at PVI (ft)
G?	3 R/S	Grade of G_1 (%)
L?	1000 R/S	Length of the curve (ft)
S?	9300 R/S	Station of point on the curve (ft)
I?	9500 R/S	Station of PVI
H?	3 +/− R/S	Grade of G_2 (%)
C = 146.3000	--	Elevation at Station 93+00 (ft)

Step 2. Compute the elevation at Station 96+00. Use Equation No. 178, page 285. Press ENTER.

Display	Keys	Description
E? 155.0000	R/S	Elevation at PVI (ft)
G? 3.0000	R/S	Grade of G_1 (%)
L? 1,000.0000	R/S	Length of the curve (ft)
S?	9600 R/S	Station of point on the curve (ft)
I? 9,500.0000	R/S	Station of PVI
H? −3.0000	R/S	Grade of G_2 (%)
C = 147.2000	--	Elevation at Station 96+00 (ft)

Step 3. Calculate the elevation at Station 98+00. Use Equation No. 178, page 285. Press ENTER.

Display	Keys	Description
E? 155.0000	R/S	Elevation at PVI (ft)
G? 3.0000	R/S	Grade of G_1 (%)
L? 1,000.0000	R/S	Length of the curve (ft)
S?	9800 R/S	Station of point on the curve (ft)
I? 9,500.0000	R/S	Station of PVI
H? −3.0000	R/S	Grade of G_2 (%)
C = 144.8000	--	Elevation at Station 98+00 (ft)

The answer is (A).

Problem 14.6

The length of vertical curve shown is most nearly

(A) 467 ft
(B) 500 ft
(C) 1,000 ft
(D) 1,400 ft

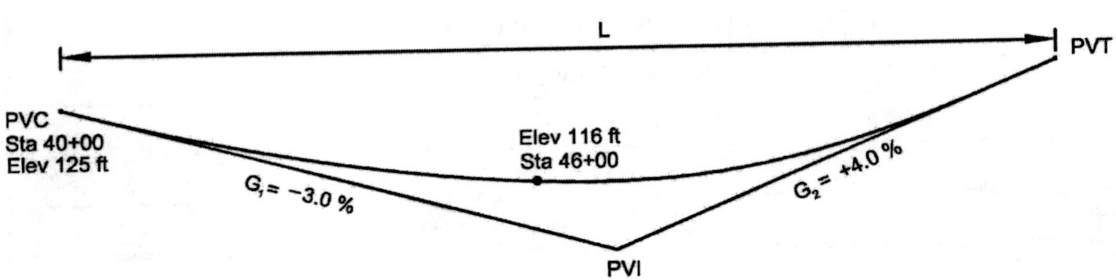

Solution

Solve the length of curve. Use Equation No. 176, page 283. Press SOLVE L.

Display	Keys	Description
C?	116 R/S	Elevation at Station 46+00 (ft)
Y?	125 R/S	Elevation at PVC (ft)
G?	3 +/− R/S	Grade of G_1 (%)
X?	4600 ENTER 4000 −	Distance from PVC to Station 46+00 (ft)
X? 600.0000	R/S	
H?	4 R/S	Grade of G_2 (%)
L = 1,400.0000	--	Length of the curve (ft)

The answer is (D).

Problem 14.7

A sag vertical curve is shown below. The stationing of Point A at elevation 82 feet is most nearly

(A) 17+00 (C) 18+00
(B) 17+85 (D) 18+10

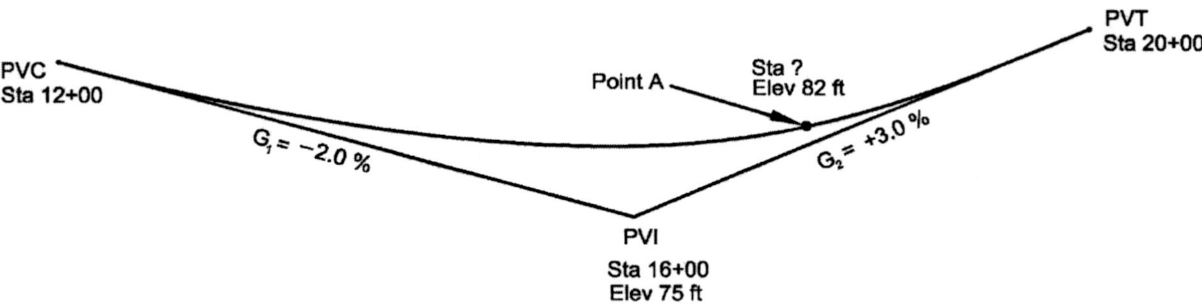

Solution

Option 1

Step 1. Solve the horizontal distance from PVC to Point A. Use Equation No. 176, page 283. Press SOLVE X.

Display	Keys	Description
C?	82 R/S	Elevation at Point A (ft)
Y?	75 ENTER .02 ENTER 400 × +	Elevation at PVC (ft)
Y? 83.0000	R/S	
G?	2 +/− R/S	Grade of G_1 (%)
H?	3 R/S	Grade of G_2 (%)
L?	800 R/S	Length of the curve (ft)
X = 585.3300	--	Horizontal distance from PVC to Point A (ft)

Step 2. Calculate the Stationing of Point A.

Display	Keys	Description
--	1200 +	Add the Station of PVC to calculate the station of Point A
585.3300 1,785.3300 ←	←	Station of Point A (17+85.33)

Option 2

Step 1. The elevation of PVI is given. Solve the horizontal distance from PVC to Point A. Use Equation No. 177, page 284. Press SOLVE X.

Display	Keys	Description
C?	82 R/S	Elevation at Point A (ft)
E?	75 R/S	Elevation at PVI (ft)
G?	2 +/− R/S	Grade of G_1 (%)
L?	800 R/S	Length of the curve (ft)
H?	3 R/S	Grade of G_2 (%)
X = 585.3300	--	Horizontal distance from PVC to Point A (ft)

Step 2. Calculate the Stationing of Point A.

Display	Keys	Description
--	1200 +	Add the Station of PVC to calculate the station of Point A
585.3300 1,785.3300 ←	←	Station Point A (17+85.33)

The answer is (B).

Problem 14.8

A vertical curve has a G_1 grade of 2% and a G_2 grade of −1.5% intersecting at Station 500+00 and elevation 73 feet. The length of the vertical curve is 800 feet. The elevation and station of the highest point on the curve are most nearly

	Elevation of Highest Point (ft)	Station of Highest Point
(A)	70	500+57
(B)	72	500+65
(C)	74	500+70
(D)	76	500+85

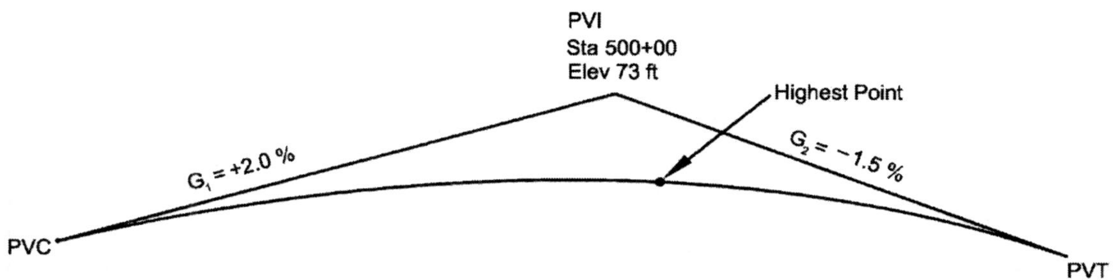

Solution

Option 1

Step 1. Calculate the horizontal distance from PVC to the highest point. Use Equation No. 179, page 286. Press ENTER.

Display	Keys	Description
G?	2 R/S	Grade of G_1 (%)
L?	800 R/S	Length of the curve (ft)
H?	1.5 +/− R/S	Grade of G_2 (%)
X = 457.1429	--	Horizontal distance from PVC to the highest point (ft)

Step 2. Compute the elevation of the highest point on the curve. Use Equation No. 176, page 283. Press ENTER.

Display	Keys	Description
Y?	73 ENTER .02 ENTER 400 × −	Elevation at PVC (ft)
Y? 65.0000	R/S	
G? 2.0000	R/S	Grade of G_1 (%)
X? 457.1429	R/S	Horizontal distance from PVC to highest point (ft)
H? −1.5000	R/S	Grade of G_2 (%)
L? 800.0000	R/S	Length of the curve (ft)
C = 69.5714	--	Elevation of the highest point on the curve (ft)

Step 3. Calculate the station of the highest point on the curve. Use Equation No. 180, page 287. Press ENTER.

Display	Keys	Description
I?	50000 R/S	Station of PVI (ft)
L? 800.0000	R/S	Length of the curve (ft)
G? 2.0000	R/S	Grade of G_1 (%)
H? −1.5000	R/S	Grade of G_2 (%)
S = 50,057.1429	--	Station of the highest point on the curve (Sta 500+57.1429)

Option 2

Step 1. Calculate the horizontal distance from PVC to the highest point. Use Equation No. 179, page 286. Press ENTER

Display	Keys	Description
G?	2 R/S	Grade of G_1 (%)
L?	800 R/S	Length of the curve (ft)
H?	1.5 +/− R/S	Grade of G_2 (%)
X = 457.1429	--	Horizontal distance from PVC to the highest point (ft)

Step 2. The elevation of PVI is given. Compute the elevation of the highest point on the curve. Use Equation No. 177, page 284. Press ENTER.

Display	Keys	Description
E?	73 R/S	Elevation at PVI (ft)
G? 2.0000	R/S	Grade of G_1 (%)
L? 800.0000	R/S	Length of the curve (ft)
X? 457.1429	R/S	Horizontal distance from PVC to highest point (ft)
H? −1.5000	R/S	Grade of G_2 (%)
C = 69.5714	--	Elevation of the highest point on the curve (ft)

Step 3. Calculate the station of the highest point on the curve. Use Equation No. 180, page 287. Press ENTER.

Display	Keys	Description
I?	50000 R/S	Station of PVI (ft)
L? 800.0000	R/S	Length of the curve (ft)
G? 2.0000	R/S	Grade of G_1 (%)
H? −1.5000	R/S	Grade of G_2 (%)

Display	Keys	Description
S = 50,057.1429	--	Station of the highest point on the curve (Sta 500+57.1429)

The answer is (A).

Problem 14.9

The length of a vertical sag curve shown is 900 ft. The elevation and station of lowest point on the curve are most nearly

	Elevation of Lowest Point (ft)	Station of Lowest Point
(A)	110	70+57
(B)	115	76+50
(C)	120	77+00
(D)	127	78+80

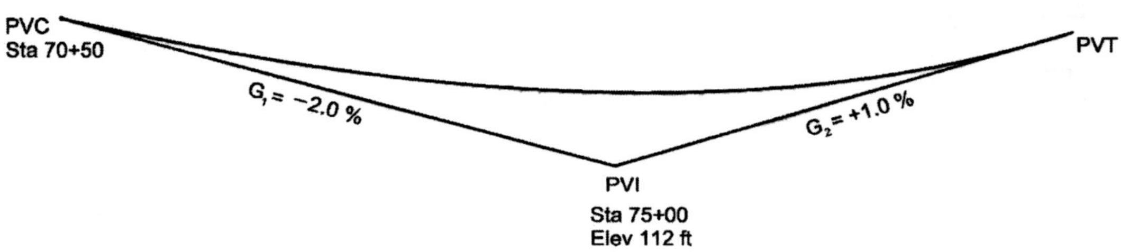

Solution

Option 1

Step 1. Calculate the distance from PVC to the lowest point of curve. Use Equation No. 181, page 288. Press ENTER.

Display	Keys	Description
G?	2 +/− R/S	Grade of G_1 (%)
L?	900 R/S	Length of the curve (ft)
H?	1 R/S	Grade of G_2 (%)
X = 600.0000	--	Distance from PVC to the lowest point (ft)

Step 2. Determine the elevation of lowest point using the Vertical Curve Elevation equation. Use Equation No. 176, page 283. Press ENTER.

Display	Keys	Description
Y?	112 ENTER .02 ENTER 450 × +	Elevation at PVC (ft)
Y? 121.0000	R/S	
G? −2.0000	R/S	Grade of G_1 (%)
X? 600.0000	R/S	Distance from PVC to the lowest point (ft)
H? 1.0000	R/S	Grade of G_2 (%)
L? 900.0000	R/S	Length of the curve (ft)
C = 115.0000	--	Elevation of lowest point on the curve (ft)

Step 3. Calculate the station of lowest point. Use Equation No. 182, page 289. Press ENTER.

Display	Keys	Description
I?	7500 R/S	Station of PVI (ft)
L? 900.0000	R/S	Length of the curve (ft)
G? −2.0000	R/S	Grade of G_1 (%)
H? 1.0000	R/S	Grade of G_2 (%)
S = 7,650.0000	--	Station of lowest point on the curve (Sta 76+50)

Option 2

Step 1. Calculate the distance from PVC to the lowest point of curve. Use Equation No. 181, page 288. Press ENTER.

Display	Keys	Description
G?	2 +/− R/S	Grade of G_1 (%)
L?	900 R/S	Length of the curve (ft)
H?	1 R/S	Grade of G_2 (%)
X = 600.0000	--	Distance from PVC to the lowest point (ft)

Step 2. The elevation of PVI is given. Compute the elevation of lowest point. Use Equation No. 177, page 284. Press ENTER.

Display	Keys	Description
E?	112 R/S	Elevation at PVI (ft)
G? −2.0000	R/S	Grade of G_1 (%)

Display	Keys	Description
L? 900.0000	R/S	Length of the curve (ft)
X? 600.0000	R/S	Distance from PVC to highest point (ft)
H? 1.0000	R/S	Grade of G_2 (%)
C = 115.0000	--	Elevation of lowest point on the curve (ft)

Step 3. Calculate the station of lowest point. Use Equation No. 182, page 289. Press ENTER.

Display	Keys	Description
I?	7500 R/S	Station of PVI (ft)
L? 900.0000	R/S	Length of the curve (ft)
G? −2.0000	R/S	Grade of G_1 (%)
H? 1.0000	R/S	Grade of G_2 (%)
S = 7,650.0000	--	Station of lowest point on the curve (Sta 76+50)

The answer is (B).

Problem 14.10

The vertical clearance between the sag curve and Point A is most nearly

(A) 18 ft
(B) 22 ft
(C) 26 ft
(D) 30 ft

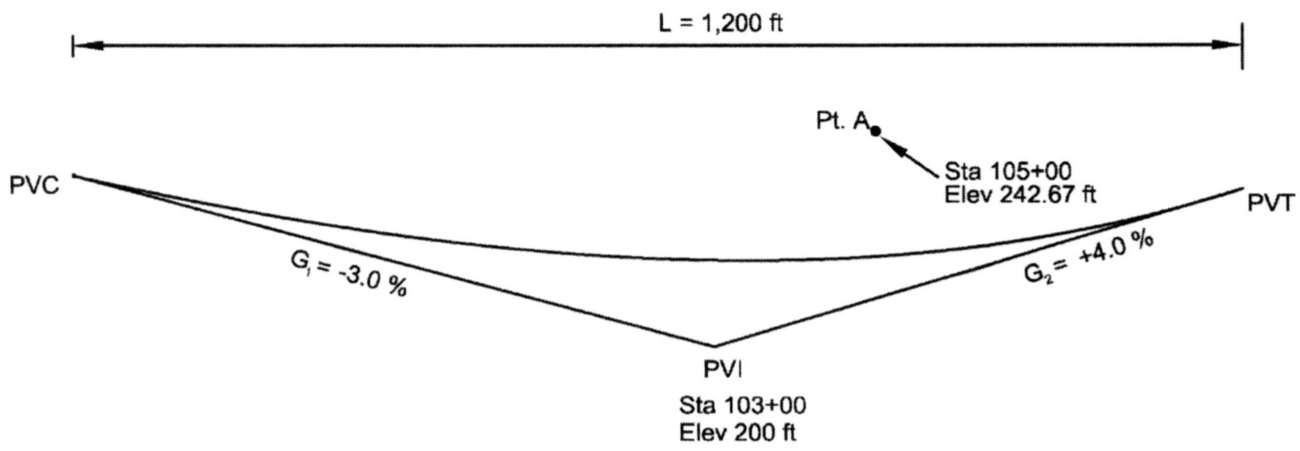

Solution

Option 1

Step 1. Calculate the curve elevation at Station 105+00. Use Equation No. 176, page 283. Press ENTER.

Display	Keys	Description
Y?	200 ENTER .03 ENTER 600 × +	Elevation at PVC (ft)
Y? 218.0000	R/S	
G?	3 +/– R/S	Grade of G_1 (%)
X?	10500 ENTER 10300 – 600 +	Horizontal distance from PVC to Station 105+00 (ft)
X? 800.0000	R/S	
H?	4 R/S	Grade of G_2 (%)
L?	1200 R/S	Length of the curve (ft)
C = 212.6667	--	Curve elevation at Station 105+00 (ft)

Step 2. Compute the vertical clearance.

Display	Keys	Description
--	242.67 [x↔y] –	Vertical clearance calculation
1,200.0000 30.00333 ←		Vertical clearance between Point A and the curve (ft)

Option 2

Step 1. Calculate the curve elevation at Station 105+00 where the vertical clearance between Point A and the curve is needed. The elevation and station of PVI are given; use Equation No. 178, page 285. Press ENTER.

Display	Keys	Description
E?	200 R/S	Elevation at PVI (ft)
G?	3 +/– R/S	Grade of G_1 (%)
L?	1200 R/S	Length of the curve (ft)
S?	10500 R/S	Station of Point A (ft)
I?	10300 R/S	Station of PVI (ft)
H?	4 R/S	Grade of G_2 (%)
C = 212.6667	--	Curve elevation at Station 105+00 (ft)

Step 2. Compute the vertical clearance.

Display	Keys	Description
--	242.67 [X↔Y] –	Vertical clearance calculation
1,200.0000 30.00333 ←		Vertical clearance between Point A and the curve (ft)

The answer is (D).

CHAPTER 15: PAVEMENT DESIGN

15.1 Flexible Pavement Design (AASHTO Method)

$$\log_{10} W_{18} = Z_R S_O + 9.36\log_{10}(SN_R + 1) - 0.20 + \frac{\log_{10}\left(\frac{\Delta PSI}{4.2 - 1.5}\right)}{0.40 + \frac{10.94}{(SN_R + 1)^{5.19}}} + 2.32\log_{10}(M_R) - 8.07$$

Equation No. 183

The equation is entered as

183FLEXPAVEMENT
LOG(W)=Z×O+9.36×LOG(N+1)−0.2+LOG(I÷2.7)÷(0.4+(10.94÷(N+1)^5.19))
+2.32×LOG(M)−8.07

Where:

W = 18-kip equivalent single-axle load W_{18}
Z = standard normal deviation Z_R
O = standard deviation S_O
N = structural number SN_R
I = change in serviceability ΔPSI (initial serviceability – terminal serviceability)
M = resilient modulus M_R (lb/in^2)

Keystrokes

HP 35s Checksum; Length of Equation: **CK=FB20; LN=81**

[↰] [LOG] [RCL] [W] [>] [↰] [=] [RCL] [Z] [×] [RCL] [O] [+] [9] [·] [3] [6] [×] [↰] [LOG] [RCL] [N] [+] [1] [>] [−] [·] [2]
[+] [↰] [LOG] [RCL] [I] [÷] [2] [·] [7] [>] [÷] [()] [·] [4] [+] [()] [1] [0] [·] [9] [4] [÷] [()] [RCL] [N] [+] [1] [>] [y^x] [5]
[·] [1] [9] [>] [>] [+] [2] [·] [3] [2] [×] [↰] [LOG] [RCL] [M] [>] [−] [8] [·] [0] [7] [ENTER]

HP 33s Checksum; Length of Equation: **CK=A310; LN=81**

[↰] [LOG] [RCL] [W] [↱] [)] [↱] [=] [RCL] [Z] [×] [RCL] [O] [+] [9] [·] [3] [6] [×] [↰] [LOG] [RCL] [N] [+] [1] [↱] [)] [−]
[·] [2] [+] [↰] [LOG] [RCL] [I] [÷] [2] [·] [7] [↱] [)] [÷] [↱] [(] [·] [4] [+] [↱] [(] [1] [0] [·] [9] [4] [÷] [↱] [(]
[RCL] [N] [+] [1] [↱] [)] [y^x] [5] [·] [1] [9] [↱] [)] [↱] [)] [+] [2] [·] [3] [2] [×] [↰] [LOG] [RCL] [M] [↱] [)] [−] [8]
[·] [0] [7] [ENTER]

Note: This equation can be used to calculate the structural number.

≈≈≈≈≈≈≈≈≈≈

$$\log_{10} W_{18} = Z_R S_O + 7.35\log_{10}(D+1) - 0.06 + \frac{\log_{10}\left(\frac{\Delta PSI}{4.5-1.5}\right)}{1+\frac{1.624\times10^{7}}{(D+1)^{8.46}}} + (4.22-0.32P_t)\log_{10}\left(\frac{S_c' C_d \left(D^{0.75}-1.132\right)}{215.63J\left[D^{0.75}-\frac{18.42}{\left(\frac{E_c}{k}\right)^{0.25}}\right]}\right)$$

Equation No. 184

The equation is entered as

184RIGIDPAVEMENT
LOG(W)=Z×O+7.35×LOG(D+1)−0.06+LOG(I÷3)÷(1+1.624×10^7÷(D+1)^8.46)+(4.22−0.32×P)×LOG(S×C(D^0.75−1.132)÷215.63÷J÷(D^0.75−(18.42÷(E÷K)^0.25)))

Where:

W = 18-kip equivalent single-axle load W_{18}
Z = standard normal deviation Z_R
O = standard deviation S_O
D = depth of concrete required D (in)
I = change in serviceability ΔPSI (initial serviceability – terminal serviceability)
P = terminal serviceability P_t
S = concrete modulus of rupture S_c' (lb/in^2)
C = drainage coefficient C_d
J = load transfer coefficient J
E = concrete's modulus of elasticity E_c (lb/in^2)
K = modulus of subgrade reaction k (lb/in^3)

Keystrokes

HP 35s Checksum; Length of Equation: **CK=162C; LN=135**

[↰] [LOG] [RCL] [W] [>] [↰] [=] [RCL] [Z] [×] [RCL] [O] [+] [7] [·] [3] [5] [×] [↰] [LOG] [RCL] [D] [+] [1] [>] [−] [·] [0]
[6] [+] [↰] [LOG] [RCL] [I] [÷] [3] [>] [÷] [()] [1] [+] [1] [·] [6] [2] [4] [E] [7] [÷] [()] [RCL] [D] [+] [1] [>] [yˣ] [8] [·]
[4] [6] [>] [+] [()] [4] [·] [2] [2] [−] [·] [3] [2] [×] [RCL] [P] [>] [×] [↰] [LOG] [RCL] [S] [×] [RCL] [C] [()] [RCL] [D] [yˣ]
[·] [7] [5] [−] [1] [·] [1] [3] [2] [>] [÷] [2] [1] [5] [·] [6] [3] [÷] [RCL] [J] [÷] [()] [RCL] [D] [yˣ] [·] [7] [5] [−] [()] [1]
[8] [·] [4] [2] [÷] [()] [RCL] [E] [÷] [RCL] [K] [>] [yˣ] [·] [2] [5] [ENTER]

HP 33s Checksum; Length of Equation: **CK=8124; LN=136**

[↰] [LOG] [RCL] [W] [↱] [)] [↱] [=] [RCL] [Z] [×] [RCL] [O] [+] [7] [·] [3] [5] [×] [↰] [LOG] [RCL] [D] [+] [1] [↱] [)] [−]
[·] [0] [6] [+] [↰] [LOG] [RCL] [I] [÷] [3] [↱] [)] [÷] [↱] [(] [1] [+] [1] [·] [6] [2] [4] [E] [7] [÷] [↱] [(] [RCL] [D] [+]
[1] [↱] [)] [y^x] [8] [·] [4] [6] [↱] [)] [+] [↱] [(] [4] [·] [2] [2] [−] [·] [3] [2] [×] [RCL] [P] [↱] [)] [×] [↰] [LOG]
[RCL] [S] [×] [RCL] [C] [×] [↱] [(] [RCL] [D] [y^x] [·] [7] [5] [−] [1] [·] [1] [3] [2] [↱] [)] [÷] [2] [1] [5] [·] [6] [3] [÷]
[RCL] [J] [÷] [↱] [(] [RCL] [D] [y^x] [·] [7] [5] [−] [↱] [(] [1] [8] [·] [4] [2] [÷] [↱] [(] [RCL] [E] [÷] [RCL] [K] [↱] [)]
[y^x] [·] [2] [5] [↱] [)] [↱] [)] [↱] [)] [ENTER]

Notes: The [E] after 1.624 is the exponent key. This equation can be used to calculate the depth of concrete required.

≈≈≈≈≈≈≈≈≈≈

Problem 15.1

Using the AASHTO design equation for flexible pavement, the structural number (SN) required for the pavement using the given design variables is most nearly

(A) 2.5
(B) 3.5
(C) 4.1
(D) 4.7

Design variables:

18-kip equivalent single-axle load (ESAL) = 5×10^6
Reliability = 90%
$Z_R = -1.282$ (Standard normal deviation based on reliability taken from published table)
Standard deviation (S_o) = 0.45
Resilient modulus (M_R) = 7,500 lb/in^2
Initial serviceability (P_I) = 4.2
Terminal serviceability (P_T) = 2.5

Solution

Solve for the structural number. Use Equation No. 183, page 307. Press SOLVE N.

Display	Keys	Description
W?	5 E 6 R/S	18-kip equivalent single-axle load (ESAL)
Z?	1.282 +/− R/S	Standard normal deviation
O?	.45 R/S	Standard deviation
I?	1.7 R/S	Change in serviceability
M?	7500 R/S	Resilient modulus of soil (lb/in^2)
N = 4.6739	--	Structural number

The answer is (D).

Problem 15.2

Using the AASHTO design equation for rigid pavement, the required depth of concrete using the given design variables is most nearly

(A) 7 in
(B) 8 in
(C) 9 in
(D) 10 in

Design variables:

18-kip equivalent single-axle load (ESAL) = 5×10^6
Reliability = 95%
$Z_R = -1.645$ (Standard Normal deviation based on Reliability taken from published table)
Standard deviation (S_o) = 0.45
Initial serviceability (P_I) = 4.2
Terminal serviceability (P_T) = 2.5
Concrete modulus of rupture (S_c) = 600 lb/in^2
Drainage coefficient (C_d) = 1
Load transfer coefficient (J) = 3.2
Concrete's modulus of elasticity (E_c) = 5×10^6 lb/in^2
Modulus of subgrade reaction (K) = 250 lb/in^3

Solution

Find the required thickness of concrete. Use Equation No. 184, page 308. Press SOLVE D.

Display	Keys	Description
W?	5 E 6 R/S	18-kip equivalent single-axle load (ESAL)
Z?	1.645 +/– R/S	Standard normal deviation
O?	.35 R/S	Standard deviation
I?	1.7 R/S	Change in serviceability
P?	2.5 R/S	Terminal serviceability
S?	600 R/S	Concrete modulus of rupture (lb/in^2)
C?	1 R/S	Drainage coefficient
J?	3.2 R/S	Load transfer coefficient
E?	5 E 6 R/S	Concrete's modulus of elasticity (lb/in^2)
K?	250 R/S	Modulus of subgrade reaction (lb/in^3)
D = 9.9413	--	Depth of concrete required (in)

The answer is (D).

PART IV: STRUCTURAL

CHAPTER 16: BEAMS (ENGLISH UNITS)

The units in this chapter are **kips** for the load P, **ft** for the length of beam L, **kips/ft** for the uniform load of beam W, **ft-kips** for the maximum moment M_{max}, **in** for the dimensions, location of neutral axis, and maximum deflection of beam δ, **in⁴** for the moment of inertia I, and **ksi** for maximum tensile stress, compressive stress, and modulus of elasticity of beam.

16.1 Maximum Moment of Beam

16.1.1 Simply Supported Beam with Load in the Middle

$$M_{max} = \frac{PL}{4}$$ Equation No. 185

The equation is entered as

185MMSSBLOADMID
M=P×L÷4

Where:

M = maximum moment M_{max} (ft-kips)
P = load P (kips)
L = length of beam L (ft)

Keystrokes

HP 35s Checksum; Length of Equation: **CK=45F9; LN=7**

[RCL] [M] [↰] [=] [RCL] [P] [×] [RCL] [L] [÷] [4] [ENTER]

HP 33s Checksum; Length of Equation: **CK=45F9; LN=7**

[RCL] [M] [↱] [=] [RCL] [P] [×] [RCL] [L] [÷] [4] [ENTER]

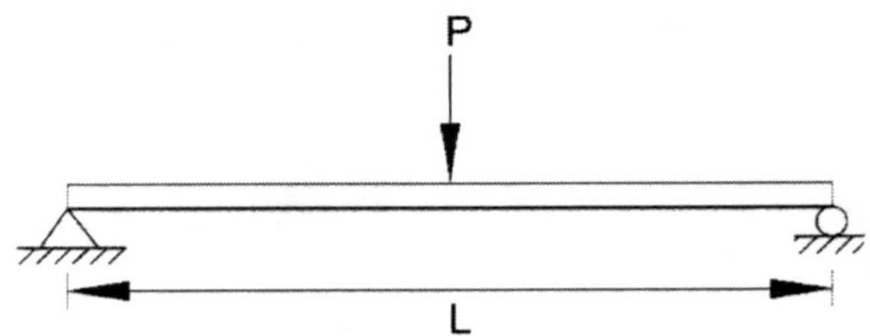

Figure 16-1 Simply Supported Beam with Load in the Middle

≈≈≈≈≈≈≈≈≈≈

16.1.2 Simply Supported Beam with Uniform Load

$$M_{\max} = \frac{WL^2}{8}$$ Equation No. 186

The equation is entered as

186MMSSBUNIFLOAD
M=W×L^2÷8

Where:

M = maximum moment $M_{\max}$ (ft-kips)
W = uniform load W (kips/ft)
L = length of beam L (ft)

Keystrokes

HP 35s Checksum; Length of Equation: **CK=C4F4; LN=9**

[RCL] [M] [↰] [=] [RCL] [W] [×] [RCL] [L] [y^x] [2] [÷] [8] [ENTER]

HP 33s Checksum; Length of Equation: **CK=C4F4; LN=9**

[RCL] [M] [↱] [=] [RCL] [W] [×] [RCL] [L] [y^x] [2] [÷] [8] [ENTER]

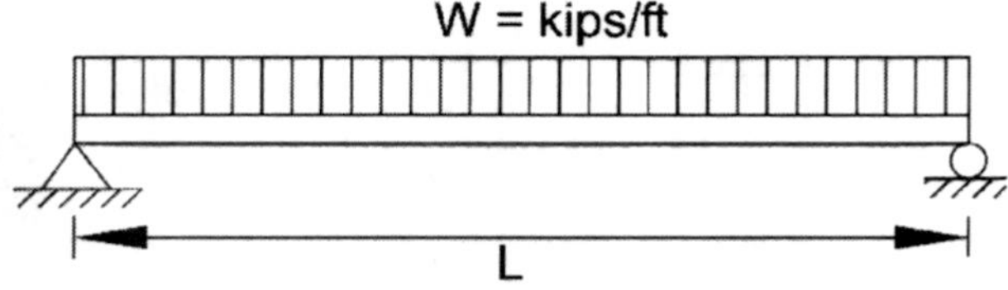

Figure 16-2 Simply Supported Beam with Uniform Load

≈≈≈≈≈≈≈≈≈≈

16.1.3 Cantilever Beam with Load at the Tip

$M_{max} = PL$ Equation No. 187

The equation is entered as

187MMCBEAMLOADTIP
M=P×L

Where:

M = maximum moment M_{max} (ft-kips)
P = load P (kips)
L = length of beam L (ft)

Keystrokes

HP 35s Checksum; Length of Equation: **CK=8F01; LN=5**

RCL M ↰ = RCL P × RCL L ENTER

HP 33s Checksum; Length of Equation: **CK=8F01; LN=5**

RCL M ↱ = RCL P × RCL L ENTER

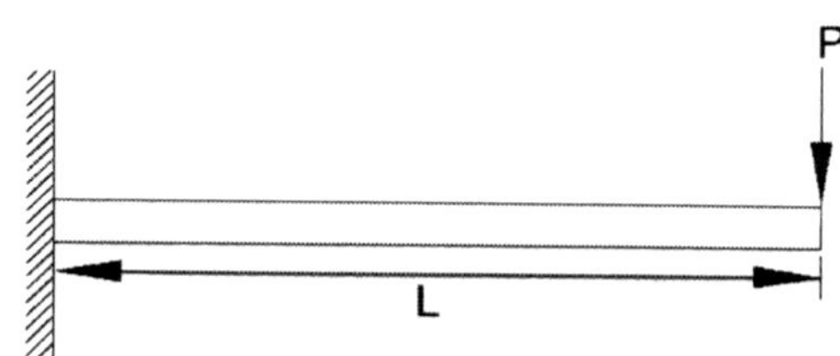

Figure 16-3 Cantilever Beam with Load at the Tip

≈≈≈≈≈≈≈≈≈≈

16.1.4 Cantilever Beam with Uniform Load

$$M_{max} = \frac{WL^2}{2}$$ Equation No. 188

The equation is entered as

188MMCBUNIFLOAD
M=W×L^2÷2

Where:

M = maximum moment M_{max} (ft-kips)
W = uniform load W (kips/ft)
L = length of beam L (ft)

Keystrokes

HP 35s Checksum; Length of Equation: **CK=65BE; LN=9**

[RCL] [M] [↰] [=] [RCL] [W] [×] [RCL] [L] [yˣ] [2] [÷] [2] [ENTER]

HP 33s Checksum; Length of Equation: **CK=65BE; LN=9**

[RCL] [M] [↱] [=] [RCL] [W] [×] [RCL] [L] [yˣ] [2] [÷] [2] [ENTER]

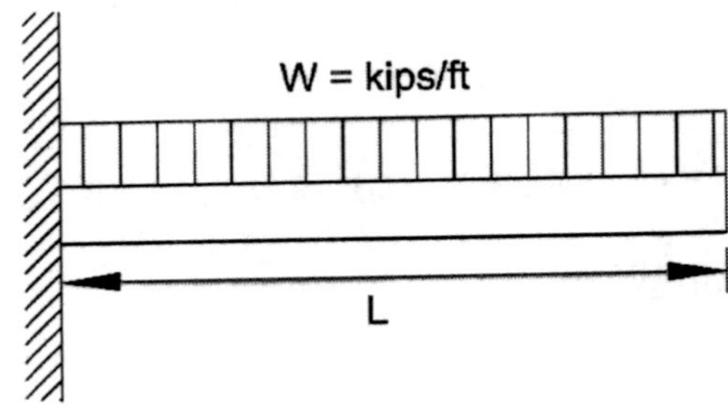

Figure 16-4 Cantilever Beam with Uniform Load

≈≈≈≈≈≈≈≈≈≈

16.2 Moment of Inertia

16.2.1 Moment of Inertia for Rectangular Beam

$I = \frac{BA^3}{12}$ Equation No. 189

The equation is entered as

189MOIRECTBEAM
I=B×A^3÷12

Where:

I = moment of inertia I (in^4)
B = width of beam B (in)
A = depth of beam A (in)

Keystrokes

HP 35s Checksum; Length of Equation: **CK=2189; LN=10**

RCL I ↰ = RCL B × RCL A y^x 3 ÷ 1 2 ENTER

HP 33s Checksum; Length of Equation: **CK=2189; LN=10**

RCL I ↱ = RCL B × RCL A y^x 3 ÷ 1 2 ENTER

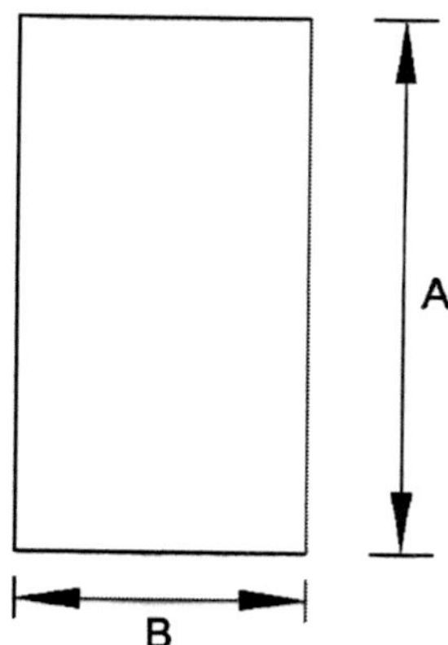

Figure 16-5 Rectangular Beam

≈≈≈≈≈≈≈≈≈≈

16.2.2 Moment of Inertia for I-Beam, T-Beam, and Inverted T-Beam on X Axis

$$I = \frac{BA^3}{3} + \frac{CH^3}{12} + HC\left(\frac{H}{2} + A\right)^2 + \frac{GF^3}{12} + GF\left(\frac{F}{2} + H + A\right)^2 \quad \text{Equation No. 190}$$

The equation is entered as

190MOIXAXIS
I=B×A^3÷3+C×H^3÷12+H×C(H÷2+A)^2+G×F^3÷12+G×F(F÷2+H+A)^2

Where:

I = moment of inertia for I-beam, T-beam, and inverted T-beam on X axis I (in^4)
B = width of lower flange B (in)
A = thickness of lower flange A (in)
C = thickness of web C (in)
H = height of web H (in)
G = width of upper flange G (in)
F = thickness of upper flange F (in)

Keystrokes

HP 35s Checksum; Length of Equation: **CK=AA0C; LN=55**

RCL I ↰ = RCL B × RCL A y^x 3 ÷ 3 + RCL C × RCL H y^x 3 ÷ 1 2 + RCL H × RCL C () RCL H ÷ 2 + RCL A > y^x 2 + RCL G × RCL F y^x 3 ÷ 1 2 + RCL G × RCL F () RCL F ÷ 2 + RCL H + RCL A > y^x 2 ENTER

HP 33s Checksum; Length of Equation: **CK=B98C; LN=57**

RCL I ↱ = RCL B × RCL A y^x 3 ÷ 3 + RCL C × RCL H y^x 3 ÷ 1 2 + RCL H × RCL C × ↱ (RCL H ÷ 2 + RCL A ↱) y^x 2 + RCL G × RCL F y^x 3 ÷ 1 2 + RCL G × RCL F × ↱ (RCL F ÷ 2 + RCL H + RCL A ↱) y^x 2 ENTER

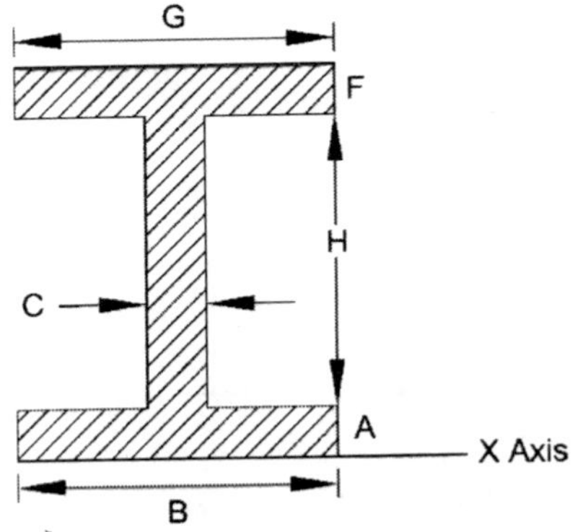

Figure 16-6 I-beam with Moment of Inertia on X Axis

Notes: For T-beam, A and B are zero. For inverted T-beam, G and F are zero.

≈≈≈≈≈≈≈≈≈≈

16.2.3 Moment of Inertia for I-Beam, T-Beam, and Inverted T-Beam on Neutral Axis Using Parallel Axis Theorem

$$\bar{y} = \frac{AB\left(\frac{A}{2}\right) + CH\left(A + \frac{H}{2}\right) + GF\left(A + H + \frac{F}{2}\right)}{AB + CH + GF}$$ Equation No. 191 (Y)

$$I = \frac{BA^3}{12} + BA\left(\bar{y} - \frac{A}{2}\right)^2 + \frac{CH^3}{12} + CH\left(\bar{y} - \left(A + \frac{H}{2}\right)\right)^2 + \frac{GF^3}{12} + GF\left(\bar{y} - \left(A + H + \frac{F}{2}\right)\right)^2$$

Equation No. 191 (I)

The equations are entered as

191MOIPARAXIS
Y=(0.5×A^2×B+C×H(A+H÷2)+G×F(A+H+F÷2))÷(A×B+C×H+G×F)
I=B×A^3÷12+B×A(Y−A÷2)^2+C×H^3÷12+C×H(Y−(A+H÷2))^2+G×F^3÷12
+G×F(Y−(A+H+F÷2))^2

Where:

Y = distance from the bottom of beam to neutral axis $\bar{y}$ (in)
A = thickness of lower flange A (in)
B = width of lower flange B (in)
C = thickness of web C (in)
H = height of web H (in)
G = width of upper flange G (in)
F = thickness of upper flange F (in)
I = moment of inertia for I-beam, T-beam, and inverted T-beam on neutral axis I (in^4)

Keystrokes

Y=(0.5×A^2×B+C×H(A+H÷2)+G×F(A+H+F÷2))÷(A×B+C×H+G×F)

HP 35s　　　　Checksum; Length of Equation: **CK=153B; LN=51**

[RCL] [Y] [↰] [=] [()] [.] [5] [×] [RCL] [A] [y^x] [2] [×] [RCL] [B] [+] [RCL] [C] [×] [RCL] [H] [()] [RCL] [A] [+] [RCL] [H]
[÷] [2] [>] [+] [RCL] [G] [×] [RCL] [F] [()] [RCL] [A] [+] [RCL] [H] [+] [RCL] [F] [÷] [2] [>] [>] [÷] [()] [RCL] [A] [×]
[RCL] [B] [+] [RCL] [C] [×] [RCL] [H] [+] [RCL] [G] [×] [RCL] [F] [ENTER]

HP 33s　　　　Checksum; Length of Equation: **CK=DDB8; LN=53**

[RCL] [Y] [↱] [=] [↱] [(] [.] [5] [×] [RCL] [A] [y^x] [2] [×] [RCL] [B] [+] [RCL] [C] [×] [RCL] [H] [×] [↱] [(] [RCL] [A]
[+] [RCL] [H] [÷] [2] [↱] [)] [+] [RCL] [G] [×] [RCL] [F] [×] [↱] [(] [RCL] [A] [+] [RCL] [H] [+] [RCL] [F] [÷] [2] [↱] [)]
[↱] [)] [÷] [↱] [(] [RCL] [A] [×] [RCL] [B] [+] [RCL] [C] [×] [RCL] [H] [+] [RCL] [G] [×] [RCL] [F] [↱] [)] [ENTER]

**I=B×A^3÷12+B×A(Y−A÷2)^2+C×H^3÷12+C×H(Y−(A+H÷2))^2+G×F^3÷12
+G×F(Y−(A+H+F÷2))^2**

HP 35s　　　　Checksum; Length of Equation: **CK=3F2A; LN=77**

[RCL] [I] [↰] [=] [RCL] [B] [×] [RCL] [A] [y^x] [3] [÷] [1] [2] [+] [RCL] [B] [×] [RCL] [A] [()] [RCL] [Y] [−] [RCL] [A] [÷]
[2] [>] [y^x] [2] [+] [RCL] [C] [×] [RCL] [H] [y^x] [3] [÷] [1] [2] [+] [RCL] [C] [×] [RCL] [H] [()] [RCL] [Y] [−] [()] [RCL] [A]
[+] [RCL] [H] [÷] [2] [>] [>] [y^x] [2] [+] [RCL] [G] [×] [RCL] [F] [y^x] [3] [÷] [1] [2] [+] [RCL] [G] [×] [RCL] [F] [()] [RCL]
[Y] [−] [()] [RCL] [A] [+] [RCL] [H] [+] [RCL] [F] [÷] [2] [>] [>] [y^x] [2] [ENTER]

HP 33s　　　　Checksum; Length of Equation: **CK=E549; LN=80**

[RCL] [I] [↱] [=] [RCL] [B] [×] [RCL] [A] [y^x] [3] [÷] [1] [2] [+] [RCL] [B] [×] [RCL] [A] [×] [↱] [(] [RCL] [Y] [−] [RCL]
[A] [÷] [2] [↱] [)] [y^x] [2] [+] [RCL] [C] [×] [RCL] [H] [y^x] [3] [÷] [1] [2] [+] [RCL] [C] [×] [RCL] [H] [×] [↱] [(] [RCL]
[Y] [−] [↱] [(] [RCL] [A] [+] [RCL] [H] [÷] [2] [↱] [)] [↱] [)] [y^x] [2] [+] [RCL] [G] [×] [RCL] [F] [y^x] [3] [÷] [1] [2] [+]
[RCL] [G] [×] [RCL] [F] [×] [↱] [(] [RCL] [Y] [−] [↱] [(] [RCL] [A] [+] [RCL] [H] [+] [RCL] [F] [÷] [2] [↱] [)] [↱] [)]
[y^x] [2] [ENTER]

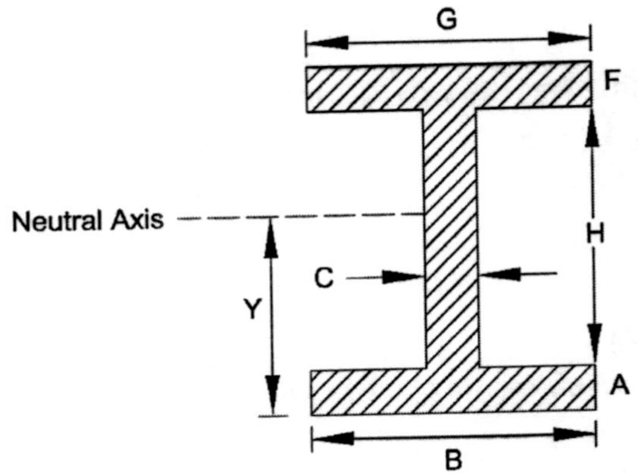

Figure 16-7 I-beam with Moment of Inertia on Neutral Axis

≈≈≈≈≈≈≈≈≈≈

16.2.4 Moment of Inertia for Symmetrical I-Beam on Neutral Axis

$$I = \frac{B(2A+H)^3}{12} - \frac{(B-C)H^3}{12}$$ Equation No. 192

The equation is entered as

192MOISYMBEAM
I=B(2×A+H)^3÷12−(B−C)×H^3÷12

Where:

I = moment of inertia for symmetrical I-beam on neutral axis I (in^4)
B = width of lower and upper flanges B (in)
A = thickness of lower and upper flanges A (in)
H = height of web H (in)
C = thickness of web C (in)

Keystrokes

HP 35s Checksum; Length of Equation: **CK=D7DD; LN=28**

[RCL] [I] [↰] [=] [RCL] [B] [()] [2] [×] [RCL] [A] [+] [RCL] [H] [>] [yx] [3] [÷] [1] [2] [−] [()] [RCL] [B] [−] [RCL] [C] [>] [×] [RCL] [H] [yx] [3] [÷] [1] [2] [ENTER]

HP 33s Checksum; Length of Equation: **CK=06D2; LN=29**

[RCL] [I] [↱] [=] [RCL] [B] [×] [↱] [(] [2] [×] [RCL] [A] [+] [RCL] [H] [↱] [)] [yx] [3] [÷] [1] [2] [−] [↱] [(] [RCL] [B] [−] [RCL] [C] [↱] [)] [×] [RCL] [H] [yx] [3] [÷] [1] [2] [ENTER]

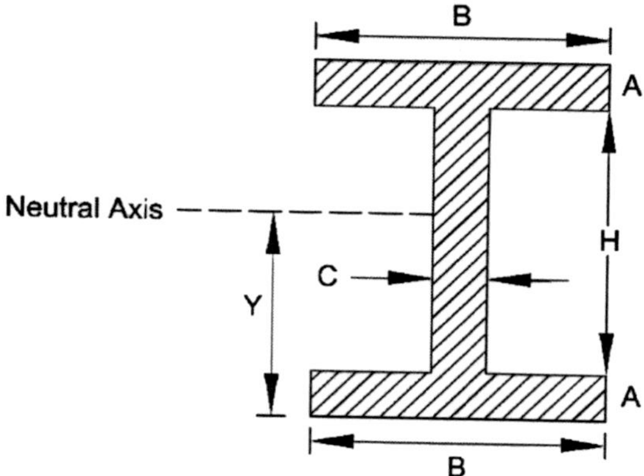

Figure 16-8 Symmetrical I-beam with Moment of Inertia on Neutral Axis

Note: Y is half of total depth.

≈≈≈≈≈≈≈≈≈≈

16.3 Maximum Bending Stresses for Simply Supported and Cantilever Beams

16.3.1 Maximum Tensile Bending Stress for Simply Supported Beam

$$\sigma_t = \frac{M_{\max}\bar{y}}{I}$$ Equation No. 193

The equation is entered as

193MTBSTRE4SSB
S=M×12×Y÷I

Where:

S = maximum tensile bending stress σ_t (ksi)
M = maximum moment $M_{\max}$ (ft-kips)
Y = distance from the bottom of beam to neutral axis $\bar{y}$ (in)
I = moment of inertia I (in^4)

Keystrokes

HP 35s Checksum; Length of Equation: **CK=B5D6; LN=10**

[RCL] [S] [↰] [=] [RCL] [M] [×] [1] [2] [×] [RCL] [Y] [÷] [RCL] [I] [ENTER]

HP 33s Checksum; Length of Equation: **CK=B5D6; LN=10**

[RCL] [S] [↱] [=] [RCL] [M] [×] [1] [2] [×] [RCL] [Y] [÷] [RCL] [I] [ENTER]

≈≈≈≈≈≈≈≈≈≈

16.3.2 Maximum Compressive Bending Stress for Simply Supported Beam

$$\sigma_c = \frac{M_{\max}(A + H + F - \bar{y})}{I}$$ Equation No. 194

The equation is entered as

194MCBSTRE4SSB
S=M×12(A+H+F−Y)÷I

Where:

S = maximum compressive bending stress σ_c (ksi)
M = maximum moment $M_{\max}$ (ft-kips)
A = thickness of lower flange A (in)
H = height of web H (in)
F = thickness of upper flange F (in)
Y = distance from the bottom of beam to neutral axis $\bar{y}$ (in)
I = moment of inertia I (in^4)

Keystrokes

HP 35s Checksum; Length of Equation: **CK=690A; LN=17**

[RCL] [S] [↰] [=] [RCL] [M] [×] [1] [2] [()] [RCL] [A] [+] [RCL] [H] [+] [RCL] [F] [−] [RCL] [Y] [>] [÷] [RCL] [I] [ENTER]

HP 33s Checksum; Length of Equation: **CK=B4AC; LN=18**

[RCL] [S] [↱] [=] [RCL] [M] [×] [1] [2] [×] [↱] [(] [RCL] [A] [+] [RCL] [H] [+] [RCL] [F] [−] [RCL] [Y] [↱] [)] [÷] [RCL] [I] [ENTER]

Notes: For rectangular beam, A and F are zero. For T-beam, A is zero. For inverted T-beam, F is zero.

≈≈≈≈≈≈≈≈≈≈

16.3.3 Maximum Tensile Bending Stress for Cantilever Beam

$$\sigma_t = \frac{M_{\max}(A + H + F - \bar{y})}{I}$$ Equation No. 195

The equation is entered as

195MTBSTRES4CB
S=M×12(A+H+F−Y)÷I

Where:

S = maximum tensile bending stress σ_t (ksi)
M = maximum moment M_{max} (ft-kips)
A = thickness of lower flange A (in)
H = height of web H (in)
F = thickness of upper flange F (in)
Y = distance from the bottom of beam to neutral axis $\bar{y}$ (in)
I = moment of inertia I (in^4)

Keystrokes

HP 35s Checksum; Length of Equation: **CK=690A; LN=17**

[RCL] [S] [↰] [=] [RCL] [M] [×] [1] [2] [()] [RCL] [A] [+] [RCL] [H] [+] [RCL] [F] [−] [RCL] [Y] [>] [÷] [RCL] [I] [ENTER]

HP 33s Checksum; Length of Equation: **CK=B4AC; LN=18**

[RCL] [S] [↱] [=] [RCL] [M] [×] [1] [2] [×] [↱] [(] [RCL] [A] [+] [RCL] [H] [+] [RCL] [F] [−] [RCL] [Y] [↱] [)] [÷] [RCL] [I] [ENTER]

Notes: For rectangular beam, A and F are zero. For T-beam, A is zero. For inverted T-beam, F is zero.

≈≈≈≈≈≈≈≈≈≈

16.3.4 Maximum Compressive Bending Stress for Cantilever Beam

$$\sigma_c = \frac{M_{max}\bar{y}}{I}$$ Equation No. 196

The equation is entered as

196MCBSTRES4CB
S=M×12×Y÷I

Where:

S = maximum compressive bending stress σ_c (ksi)
M = maximum moment M_{max} (ft-kips)
Y = distance from the bottom of beam to neutral axis $\bar{y}$ (in)
I = moment of inertia I (in^4)

Keystrokes

HP 35s Checksum; Length of Equation: **CK=B5D6; LN=10**

[RCL] [S] [↰] [=] [RCL] [M] [×] [1] [2] [×] [RCL] [Y] [÷] [RCL] [I] [ENTER]

HP 33s Checksum; Length of Equation: **CK=B5D6; LN=10**

[RCL] [S] [↱] [=] [RCL] [M] [×] [1] [2] [×] [RCL] [Y] [÷] [RCL] [I] [ENTER]

≈≈≈≈≈≈≈≈≈≈

16.4 Deflection of Simply Supported and Cantilever Beams

16.4.1 Simply Supported Beam with Load in the Middle

$$\delta = \frac{36PL^3}{EI}$$ Equation No. 197

The equation is entered as

197DEFSSBLOADMID
D=36×P×L^3÷E÷I

Where:

D = deflection of simply supported beam with load in the middle δ (in)
P = load P (kips)
L = length of beam L (ft)
E = modulus of elasticity E (ksi)
I = moment of inertia I (in^4)

Keystrokes

HP 35s Checksum; Length of Equation: **CK=8129; LN=14**

[RCL] [D] [↰] [=] [3] [6] [×] [RCL] [P] [×] [RCL] [L] [y^x] [3] [÷] [RCL] [E] [÷] [RCL] [I] [ENTER]

HP 33s Checksum; Length of Equation: **CK=8129; LN=14**

[RCL] [D] [↱] [=] [3] [6] [×] [RCL] [P] [×] [RCL] [L] [y^x] [3] [÷] [RCL] [E] [÷] [RCL] [I] [ENTER]

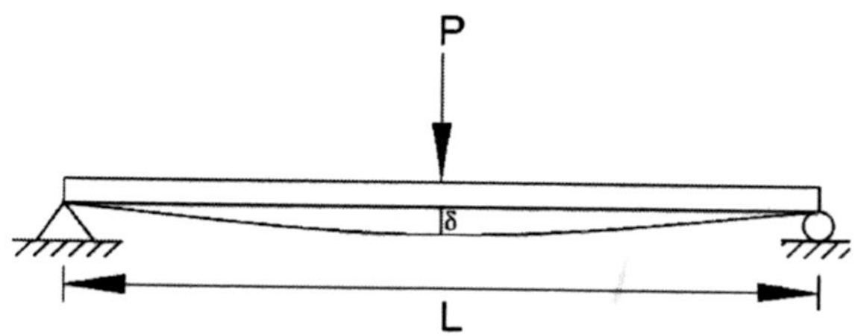

Figure 16-9 Deflection of Simply Supported Beam with Load in the Middle

≈≈≈≈≈≈≈≈≈≈

16.4.2 Simply Supported Beam with Uniform Load

$$\delta = \frac{22.5WL^4}{EI}$$ Equation No. 198

The equation is entered as

198DEFSSBUNIFLOAD
D=22.5×W×L^4÷E÷I

Where:

D = deflection of simply supported beam with uniform load δ (in)
W = uniform load W (kips/ft)
L = length of beam L (ft)
E = modulus of elasticity E (ksi)
I = moment of inertia I (in^4)

Keystrokes

HP 35s Checksum; Length of Equation: **CK=7A28; LN=16**

[RCL] [D] [↰] [=] [2] [2] [·] [5] [×] [RCL] [W] [×] [RCL] [L] [y^x] [4] [÷] [RCL] [E] [÷] [RCL] [I] [ENTER]

HP 33s Checksum; Length of Equation: **CK=7A28; LN=16**

[RCL] [D] [↱] [=] [2] [2] [·] [5] [×] [RCL] [W] [×] [RCL] [L] [y^x] [4] [÷] [RCL] [E] [÷] [RCL] [I] [ENTER]

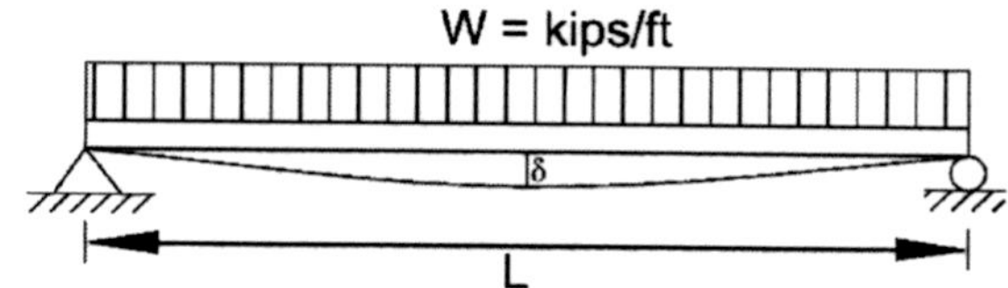

Figure 16-10 Deflection of Simply Supported Beam with Uniform Load

≈≈≈≈≈≈≈≈≈≈

16.4.3 Cantilever Beam with Load at the Tip

$$\delta = \frac{576PL^3}{EI}$$ Equation No. 199

The equation is entered as

199DEFCBLOADPTIP
D=576×P×L^3÷E÷I

Where:

D = deflection of cantilever beam with load at the tip δ (in)
P = load P (kips)
L = length of beam L (ft)
E = modulus of elasticity E (ksi), for steel = 29,000
I = moment of inertia I (in^4)

Keystrokes

HP 35s Checksum; Length of Equation: **CK=D691; LN=15**

RCL D ↰ = 5 7 6 × RCL P × RCL L yˣ 3 ÷ RCL E ÷ RCL I ENTER

HP 33s Checksum; Length of Equation: **CK=D691; LN=15**

RCL D ↱ = 5 7 6 × RCL P × RCL L yˣ 3 ÷ RCL E ÷ RCL I ENTER

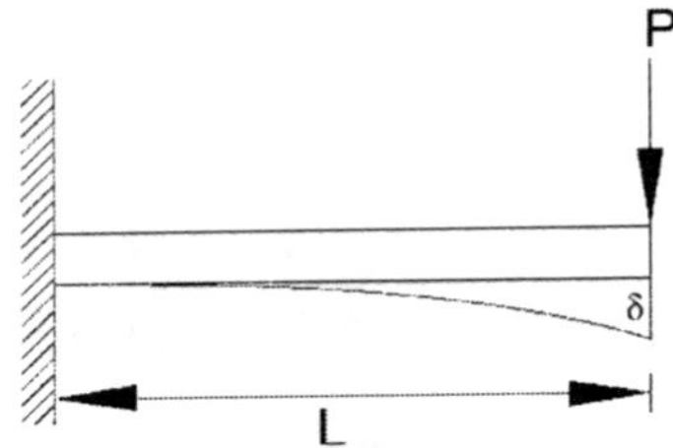

Figure 16-11 Deflection of Cantilever Beam with Load at the Tip

≈≈≈≈≈≈≈≈≈≈

16.4.4 Cantilever Beam with Uniform Load

$$\delta = \frac{216WL^4}{EI}$$ Equation No. 200

The equation is entered as

200DEFCBUNIFLOAD
D=216×W×L^4÷E÷I

Where:

D = deflection of cantilever beam with uniform load δ (in)
W = uniform load W (kips/ft)
L = length of beam L (ft)
E = modulus of elasticity E (ksi)
I = moment of inertia I (in^4)

Keystrokes

HP 35s Checksum; Length of Equation: **CK=C1D8; LN=15**

[RCL] [D] [↰] [=] [2] [1] [6] [×] [RCL] [W] [×] [RCL] [L] [y^x] [4] [÷] [RCL] [E] [÷] [RCL] [I] [ENTER]

HP 33s Checksum; Length of Equation: **CK=C1D8; LN=15**

[RCL] [D] [↱] [=] [2] [1] [6] [×] [RCL] [W] [×] [RCL] [L] [y^x] [4] [÷] [RCL] [E] [÷] [RCL] [I] [ENTER]

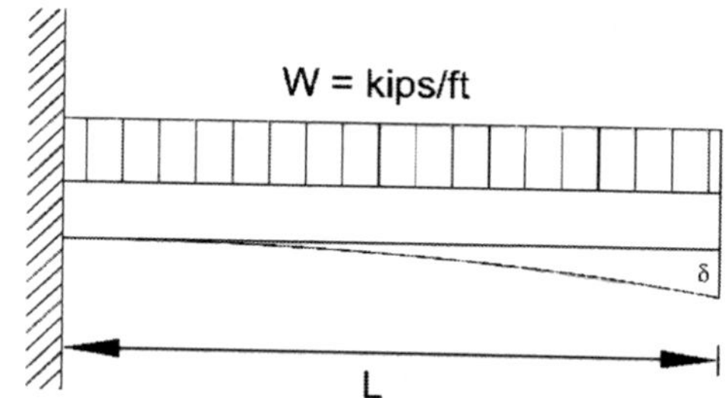

Figure 16-12 Deflection of Cantilever Beam with Uniform Load

≈≈≈≈≈≈≈≈≈≈

Problem 16.1

The moment of inertia about the neutral axis for the T-beam shown is most nearly

(A) 36 in^4 (C) 236 in^4
(B) 136 in^4 (D) 736 in^4

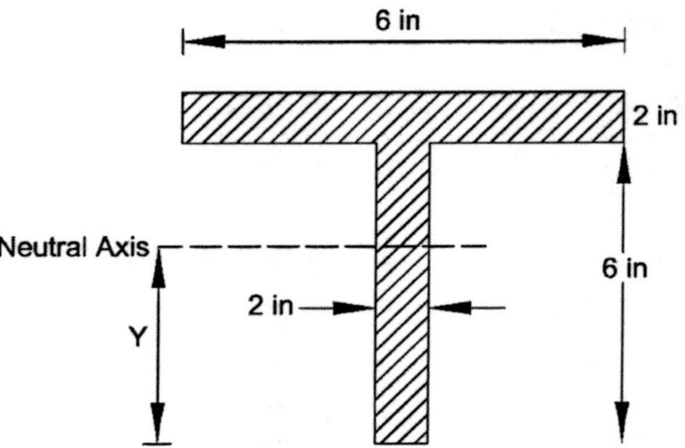

Solution

This procedure covers the determination of the moment of inertia about the neutral axis.

Step 1. Calculate the location of neutral axis from the base of the beam. Use Equation No. 191 (Y), page 318. Press ENTER.

Display	Keys	Description
A?	0 R/S	Thickness of the lower flange (in)
B?	0 R/S	Width of the lower flange (in)
C?	2 R/S	Thickness of the web (in)
H?	6 R/S	Height of the web (in)
G?	6 R/S	Width of the upper flange (in)
F?	2 R/S	Thickness of the upper flange (in)
Y = 5.0000	--	Location of neutral axis from the bottom of the beam (in)

Step 2. Calculate the moment of inertia. Use Equation No. 191 (I), page 318. Press ENTER. Press R/S every time you are prompted. You'll get I = 136.0000 (in^4).

The answer is (B).

Notes: For inverted T-beam, G and F are zero. For T-beam, A and B are zero.

Problem 16.2

The moment of inertia about the neutral axis for the symmetrical I-beam shown is most nearly

(A) 533 in^4
(B) 693 in^4
(C) 783 in^4
(D) 2,133 in^4

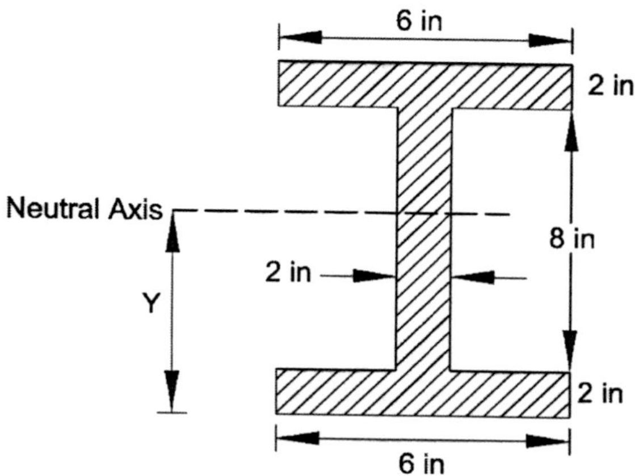

Solution

Calculate the moment of inertia about the neutral axis. Use Equation No. 192, page 320. Press ENTER.

Display	Keys	Description
B?	6 R/S	Width of lower and upper flanges (in)
A?	2 R/S	Thickness of lower and upper flanges (in)
H?	8 R/S	Height of the web (in)
C?	2 R/S	Thickness of the web (in)
I = 693.3333	--	Moment of inertia about the neutral axis (in^4)

The answer is (B).

Problem 16.3

A 10-ft-long, simply supported T-beam is carrying a uniform load of 4 kips/ft. The maximum tensile bending stress and maximum compressive bending stress are most nearly

	Maximum Tensile Bending Stress (ksi)	Maximum Compressive Bending Stress (ksi)
(A)	19	10
(B)	29	17
(C)	32	18
(D)	35	22

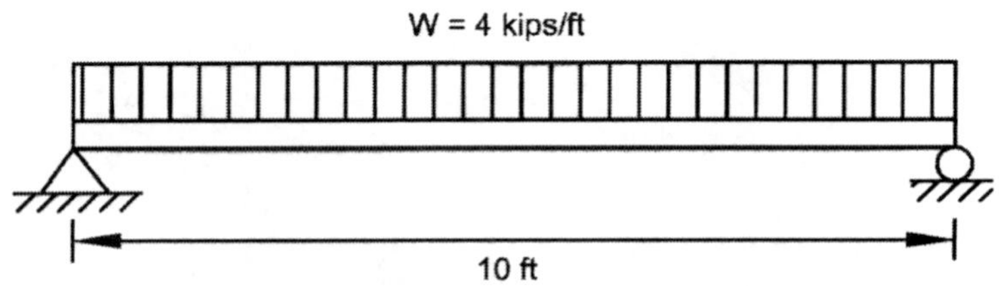

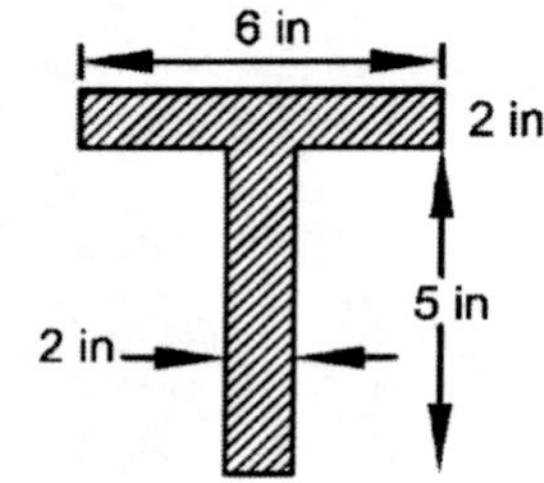

Solution

This practice can be used to determine the maximum tensile bending stress and maximum compressive bending stress of T-beam with uniform load.

Step 1. Calculate the maximum moment for simply supported beam with uniform distributed load. Use Equation No. 186, page 314. Press ENTER.

Display	Keys	Description
W?	4 R/S	Uniform distributed load on the beam (kips/ft)
L?	10 R/S	Length of the beam (ft)
M = 50.0000	--	Maximum moment (ft-kips)

Step 2. Compute the location of neutral axis from the base of the beam. Use Equation No. 191 (Y), page 318. Press ENTER.

Display	Keys	Description
A?	0 R/S	Thickness of the lower flange (in)
B?	0 R/S	Width of the lower flange (in)
C?	2 R/S	Thickness of the web (in)
H?	5 R/S	Height of the web (in)
G?	6 R/S	Width of the upper flange (in)
F?	2 R/S	Thickness of the upper flange (in)

Display	Keys	Description
Y = 4.4091	--	Location of neutral axis from bottom of the beam (in)

Step 3. Determine the moment of inertia. Use Equation No. 191 (I), page 318. Press ENTER. Press R/S every time you are prompted. You'll get I = 91.6515 (in^4).

Step 4. Calculate the maximum tensile bending stress for simply supported beam. Use Equation No. 193, page 321. Press ENTER. Press R/S every time you are prompted. You'll get S = 28.8643 (ksi).

Step 5. Calculate the maximum compressive bending stress for simply supported beam. Use Equation No. 194, page 322. Press ENTER. Press R/S every time you are prompted. You'll get S = 16.9615 (ksi).

The answer is (B).

Problem 16.4

A simply supported beam is carrying 10 kips load in the middle. The modulus of elasticity of the beam is 29,000 ksi. The maximum deflection in the beam is most nearly

(A) 0.1 in
(B) 0.2 in
(C) 0.3 in
(D) 1 in

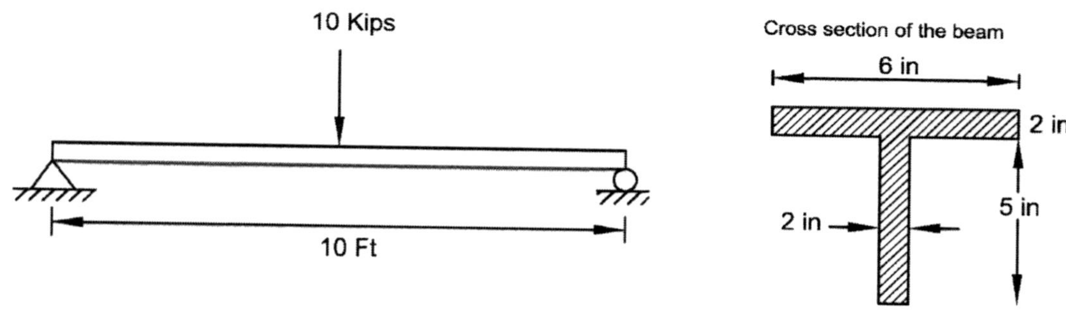

Solution

This procedure is intended to be used in calculating the maximum deflection in the beam.

Step 1. Calculate the location of neutral axis from the base of the beam. Use Equation No. 191 (Y), page 318. Press ENTER.

Display	Keys	Description
A?	0 R/S	Thickness of the lower flange (in)
B?	0 R/S	Width of the lower flange (in)
C?	2 R/S	Thickness of the web (in)
H?	5 R/S	Height of the web (in)
G?	6 R/S	Width of the upper flange (in)

Display	Keys	Description
F?	2 R/S	Thickness of the upper flange (in)
Y = 4.4091	--	Location of neutral axis from the base (in)

Step 2. Calculate the moment of inertia of the beam. Use Equation No. 191 (I), page 318. Press ENTER. Press R/S every time you are prompted. You'll get I = 91.6515 (in^4).

Step 3. Calculate the deflection of simply supported beam with load in the middle. Use Equation No. 197, page 324. Press ENTER.

Display	Keys	Description
P?	10 R/S	Load on the beam (kips)
L?	10 R/S	Length of the beam (ft)
E?	29000 R/S	Modulus of elasticity of the beam (ksi)
I? 91.6515	R/S	Moment of inertia of the beam (in^4)
D = 0.1354	--	Maximum deflection of the beam (in)

The answer is (A).

CPSIA information can be obtained at www.ICGtesting.com
Printed in the USA
LVOW09s0024230416

484887LV00016BA/277/P

9 781483 9515